ALSO BY H. LINCOLN FOSTER

Rock Gardening: A Guide to Growing Alpines and Other Wildflowers in the American Garden

ALSO BY LAURA LOUISE FOSTER

Keer-loo: The True Story of a Young Wood Duck

ILLUSTRATED BY LAURA LOUISE FOSTER

Rock Gardening: A Guide to Growing Alpines and Other Wildflowers in the American Garden

A Field Guide to Ferns & Their Related Families: Northeastern and Central North America, by Boughton Cobb

The Opinionated Gardener: Random Offshoots from an Alpine Garden, by Geoffrey Charlesworth

CUTTINGS

from a

ROCK GARDEN

The woodland garden, showing the Phlox Bank (foreground) and an understory that is part of the Fosters' famed azalea and rhododendron collection.

CUTTINGS

from a

ROCK GARDEN

Plant Portraits and Other Essays

H. LINCOLN FOSTER

and

LAURA LOUISE FOSTER

With drawings by Laura Louise Foster

Edited by Norman Singer

ATLANTIC MONTHLY PRESS

"Glossary" is from *Rock Gardening* by H. Lincoln Foster. Copyright © 1968 by H. Lincoln Foster. Reprinted by permission of Timber Press, Inc., Portland.

Grateful acknowledgment is made to the American Rock Garden Society *Bulletin* and the *Connecticut Plantsman,* in which portions of this book originally appeared.

Published simultaneously in Canada
Printed in the United States of America

Library of Congress Cataloging-in-Publication Data
Foster, H. Lincoln.
Cuttings from a rock garden: plant portraits and other essays/
H. Lincoln Foster, Laura Louise Foster: with illustrations by Laura
Louise Foster.
ISBN: 0-87113-376-8
1. Gardening. 2. Rock gardens. I. Foster, Laura Louise.
II. Title.
SB455.3.F67 1990 635—dc20 89-48846

Design by Julie Duquet

The Atlantic Monthly Press
19 Union Square West
New York, NY 10003

First printing

CONTENTS

———

FOREWORD
Norman Singer
vii

INTRODUCTION
Panayoti Kelaidis
xi

PART I
MILLSTREAM The Story of a Rock Garden
Laura Louise Foster
I

PART II
PLANT PORTRAITS
H. Lincoln and Laura Louise Foster
115

PART III
ESSAYS Reflections on the Gardening Art
H. Lincoln and Laura Louise Foster
345

———

Summer Is Dying 347
Gentian 348
The Gardener's Patience 349

Ruminations on the Origins of Horticulture 352

Green 357

Ten Best Plants 361

Variation 371

Plant Names 379

Some Problems and Pleasures of Drawing Plants 383

Seed Collecting and Seed Cleaning 389

Seed Sowing 394

Seed-Sowing Media 401

Light Boxes 402

Bog Hopping 405

Conservation 409

Mus Musculus 413

The Changing Year 415

And So to Bed 418

Winter 421

GLOSSARY

424

INDEX OF PLANT NAMES

439

FOREWORD

H. Lincoln Foster   *Laura Louise Foster*
1906–1989   1918–1988

Although they were, on occasion, referred to as "the Royal Family of American Rock Gardening," H. Lincoln and Laura Louise Foster were more affectionately known to thousands simply as "Linc and Timmy." Not long after Timmy died in the winter of 1988, Linc found an unfinished manuscript by her in which she described the early history and development of "Millstream," their famous garden in northwestern Connecticut. Linc showed the manuscript to me and to several other friends, and the consensus was that it wasn't publishable in its original form, but that there was much in the manuscript of great general interest. And the writing itself was truly superb.

For some time there had been suggestions that Linc compile his own writings, most of these from issues of the *Bulletin* of the American Rock Garden Society. A book combining portions of Timmy's manuscript with a selection of Linc's pieces certainly would be fitting given their lifelong collaboration at Millstream. To this collection would be added some of Timmy's essays written for the *Bulletin* during her tenure as its editor. Included in the book, of course, would be as many of Timmy's exquisite drawings as could be found, particularly those that had never before been published.

Out of these promising pieces has come this Foster collection. *Cuttings from a Rock Garden* provides us not only a fascinating picture of two outstanding gardeners, but affords useful and evocative insights we can all use in our own gardens.

Linc knew that I had had some modest editing experience in overseeing publication of Geoffrey Charlesworth's book *The Opinionated Gardener*. And I had worked with Timmy on her illustrations for that book, so Linc asked me to assist with this new collection and to be his "literary agent." By this time, the end of the summer of 1988, Linc knew that he was terminally ill. The doctor told him he could count on Thanksgiving and Christmas, but the doctor wouldn't promise "crocuses in spring." Linc's energies soon left him, and by midwinter he said he felt he was "melting away." My concern was to keep him involved in the project and yet not tax his dwindling energy. He was prepared to say "yes" or "no," but he wanted to leave to me all editing and associated aspects of bringing the book to publication. This was flattering, but above all it meant that I had frequent valuable opportunities to be with Linc, whom I had always referred to as our horticultural "guru." Linc died in April 1989, the week before the first draft of the final manuscript went to the typist.

We have kept editing to a minimum except in Timmy's unfinished manuscript. Certain chapters of it, although fascinating, seemed either too parochial or too didactic (Linc's word) to be suitable, and Linc and I agreed that they should be dropped. In the remaining material reprinted here, minor changes were made for grammatical clarification. We tried not to duplicate material in Linc's classic book *Rock Gardening,* though many of the plants described at length in this collection had been given perhaps a one- or two-line mention in *Rock Gardening.* I have also tried to excise repetitions of descriptions or anecdotes which appeared in articles originally published in the *Bulletin* perhaps many years apart. In the overview articles on American woodland plants and phloxes there will be references to plants described more fully elsewhere in the book.

Most of these plant portraits and essays first appeared in the American Rock Garden Society *Bulletin,* to which we are grateful for permission to reprint. Others came from the short-lived *Connecticut Plantsman,* newsletter of the Connecticut ARGS chapter. The two above-mentioned articles on woodland plants and phloxes originally appeared in *Alpines of America,* the report of the 1976 First Interim International Rock Garden Plant Conference. The section on the culture of saxifrages appeared in "Porophyllum Saxifrages" by Horny, Weber and Byam-Grounds, published in England by Byam-Grounds Publications. We are grateful for permission to reprint it. We are especially grateful for permission granted by Timber Press, Portland, Oregon, to reprint the illustrated glossary from *Rock Gardening;* it will add much to our enjoyment and understanding.

In selecting articles for inclusion I was originally guided by Linc, but the final compilation is my own responsibility. I believe this Foster collection contains all of Linc and Timmy's important writings with duplications eliminated.

We were most fortunate, thanks to her family, to have access to Timmy's portfolio so that many of her wonderful pen-and-ink and pencil drawings, never before seen, could be printed. The total compilation of plant portraits, gardening advice, philosophical musings, even poetry, allows us to enter the lives of two of America's most important gardeners.

Throughout the book, the initials L.L.F. (Laura Louise Foster) and H.L.F. (H. Lincoln Foster) found at the end of essays identify the author. I am indebted to Dianne Rugh, who generously volunteered to prepare the index, and to John Barstow, editor at Atlantic Monthly Press, for guidance and for working patiently with me toward publication.

The Fosters are buried alongside each other in a tiny cemetery remote from town but only fifty yards from Millstream, in Falls

Village, Connecticut. On the face of Timmy's tombstone, which includes a relief of a fern, is the legend "She Made a Garden." Linc's stone has a dodecatheon—emblem of the American Rock Garden Society—and the legend "They Shared a Garden."

It is characteristic of Lincoln Foster that he asked that all of his royalties from the sale of this book should be given to the American Rock Garden Society.

NORMAN SINGER
Sandisfield, Massachusetts
August 1989

INTRODUCTION

——

Those who came to know the Fosters (and how many, many did) will never have trouble conjuring up an image of them. Linc with his springing gait, Homeric profile; Timmy, with such aristocratic diction and gentle yet inquisitive glances that somehow reminded me of those tiny, delicate birds that nevertheless fly across oceans. Most of us came to know the Fosters by reading Linc's landmark *Rock Gardening,* or by their occasional writings in various horticultural publications, or else by hearing Linc talk at a meeting. One speaks of seeing someone's slide talk: in Linc's case the deep, gravelly but mellifluous voice and lucid blend of emotion and intellect when he lectured resonated long afterwards, as after an evening at the symphony. Linc was a horticultural synaesthete whose very words blossomed, transplanting concepts as easily as seedlings from one realm of sensibility to another. Linc loved words as well as plants: if only Linc and Timmy had recorded their thoughts as carefully on tape as they did on paper! The music of their voices would add a rich patina to their words.

In this book, various essays and articles the Fosters issued in a number of publications are gathered together, revealing the tremendous range of their curiosity and experience. As in *Rock Gardening,* their writing manages to be detailed and encyclopaedic, and yet to carry the conversational tone of good bedside reading. Encyclopaedic, perhaps, but unlike so many recent books on horticulture, their writing is emphatically not a pastiche of other books and hearsay. Even Farrer's *English Rock Garden* is based in part on herbarium specimens and conjecture. The Fosters made it a point to discuss only plants they knew from their own experience. Their descriptions are drawn from life, episodes in a love affair all gardeners seem to have with a succession of genera and plants. Their writing may seem spontaneous, but it is the fruit of years of love and intimate study of nature. I turn to their articles and to *Rock Gardening* again and again to find that they have tested many of the same avenues, and have valuable information to share. It strikes me as I return to their writings how simply and directly they speak to our curiosity and needs.

Of course, much transpired in the Fosters' horticultural life after their classic manual was published in 1968: a long series of more detailed researches found their way to print in a number of different publications over the next decades. These occasional writings are more casual, less concise than *Rock Gardening*. There is a wealth of personal and professional experience distilled in them that is of enduring value to American horticulture. These writings, gathered together in this book, are a portrait gallery of the best American rock garden and woodland plants. Now that gardening with natives is becoming fashionable, we will find many occasions to refer to the record and see what these pioneers in growing plants naturally have to report from their experience. This book will be an indelible monument to the Fosters' life work, and to a grand garden called Millstream.

Gardens are the most mercurial of art forms: they are at the whim of weather and seasons, light and shadow and an inconceivable number of variables that make gallery art seem like painting by numbers. Millstream evolved dramatically from a steep mountainside buried in brush to a more and more sophisticated palette of wildflowers from all corners of the temperate world, to mass plantings of the best forms and best-adapted taxa—and finally, slowly, it's reverting to nature once again. Like all gardens,

Millstream was a gorgeous laboratory where the Fosters grew an astonishing assortment of plants. It was a canvas of heroic proportions where they painted a grand picture that was somehow homey and magnificent all at once. I don't think another private garden, or even a botanic garden has ever existed in the western hemisphere that could begin to compare with Millstream for sheer drama, seasonal display of color, or the reference value of its collections.

Within a few years of its beginning, Millstream became a Mecca for rock gardeners from all over the world. After all, here was a magnificent setting where two energetic, charismatic, and resourceful individuals were busily forging a novel, natural American horticulture. It was featured repeatedly in national publications, in the bulletins of the many alpine-garden societies, and on television. An army of garden clubs and botanic-garden tours began to show up at the Fosters' door, along with an ever-expanding flood of homeowners who wanted to study, take notes, and return some of Millstream's magic to their own gardens. We must have brought more bother than pleasure, and how many of us took away plants?

And yet, the Fosters put up with it, for they placed a high premium on participation and involvement in the horticultural community. They were as active in rhododendron circles as they were with rock gardeners, and rarely missed nearby meetings of either group. Linc's long tenure as president of the American Rock Garden Society marks the crucial phase when that society evolved from a coterie of East Coast connoisseurs to being a truly national society with a broad base of support. Linc is credited for this important shift. When Timmy assumed the editorship of the national bulletin of the same society in 1977, the Foster collaboration produced a nine-year golden age for the *Bulletin* of ARGS, which reached new heights of excellence.

As they developed Millstream, the Fosters were delightfully out of step with the slick, suburban tone of the last half of the twentieth century. Armies of homeowners elsewhere were busily acquiring household appliances and expensive gadgets, while Linc and Timmy practiced the simple life, drew, gardened, and studied nature. They explored little-known corners of the Eastern hills and forests: observing, gathering horticultural grist for Millstream and their writings. Western civilization has a tendency to stress accomplishment at the expense of fulfillment, and there is no question that the Fosters accomplished great things in the course of their lives. I think it is significant, however, that they were revered among gardeners not just for their accomplishments and their knowledge but for their sensibility and wisdom. Who hasn't been struck by their fresh interaction with one another and the world, by their receptivity and voracious curiosity about everything? How rare to find two artists, writers, and lecturers who made such a point of listening.

Observation is a keynote throughout the Fosters' work: the ability to observe plants in nature and imitate their precise microclimate in a subtle niche within Millstream, where a mere sprig in time would spread to fill an entire vale with a single clone of *Phlox stolonifera* such as 'Daybreak' or 'Home Fires'—the same power of observation that selected the proud series of Millstream phloxes, which prove their mettle in more and more gardens. While most gardeners are delighted to merely recognize, or possess a single plant of *Rodgersia,* say, the Fosters found just the right spot where each species would prosper and naturalize in their woods. One would have to go to Japan or China to find stands of *Rodgersia* as extensive as those at Millstream. Not even the summits of alpine peaks in full glory inspire the awe Millstream did in visitors in late May when the ground story of the forest was a pastel tapestry of flowers, with hundreds of azaleas and flowering trees dizzily blooming overhead. Even the dullest visitor could hardly help but notice one dazzling vista opening up after another, climbing higher and higher up the steep slope, and gazing down toward the stream and Millpond in the echoing, flowery distance.

The Fosters' powers of observation extended far beyond rock garden plants and gardening: Linc was a literary scholar who produced a scholarly edition of *Moby Dick* and had a deep interest in popular as well as literary culture. Linc and Timmy both were world travelers who were interested in all manner of human and natural phenomena. Timmy's artwork reveals powers of observation commensurate with Linc's horticultural scholarship. For gardeners, the intricate, ramifying root systems she depicts are sheer poetry: the mesh of roots is, after all, the most permanent portion of a plant. Leaves and flowers come and go, but roots not only anchor a plant in place, they derive moisture and nutrients to sustain its growth. Consider the spring ephemerals that grew so luxuriantly at Millstream: these emerge from their roots for only a few weeks in spring. Their tubers and roots make up the whole plant for the remaining bulk of the year. If you consider all the plants that passed through the Fosters' loving hands through the decades, and all the roots that were delicately tucked into the fragrant forest duff there, is it any wonder Timmy took such pains with the portions of plants invisible to nongardeners?

For many, many years, Timmy's role at Millstream was undervalued even by their closest friends: she was partly to blame herself for the situation, since she constantly stressed her role as the weeder and nothing more. Her years as editor of the American Rock Garden Society *Bulletin* revealed more and more the extent of her own knowledge: in her last decades she began to write and even speak publicly more often about gardening and her point of view. Gardening may seem a solitary task, but

gardeners tend to come in pairs. Sometimes a neighbor down the
street or in the next town, sometimes a favorite horticulture
writer is the stand-in companion, but how much more easy it is
to learn from concrete experience of a close associate! And when
your double lives in the same house, a *Doppelgänger* to compare
yourself to, to learn from, you are doubly blest. Is there any
doubt that Timmy was equal to Linc in artistic sensibility and
critical faculties? The secret of Millstream was the rich interaction
of the intellect and senses of these two artists who collaborated,
and complemented one another's talents. Millstream attains immortality in Timmy's tender biography of that garden. Would
that all gardens could be so preserved.

Let's not forget that the plants, the companionship, the garden
are what matter. How lucky that we can travel so effortlessly
through Millstream on command. Here is the house, so decep-
tively simple, perched above the road. You can hear Linc's thun-
derous voice from a distance, and Timmy is buried up to her
shoulders in the meadow like a meadow nymph, a sprite. Cheerful greetings are exchanged, a quick glance at the intricate alpines
around the patio, and off we plunge through the meadow, across
the bridge, onto the steep, dewy mountainside as mysterious and
infinite as Mount Olympus. Welcome, reader, to Millstream and
the Fosters.

PANAYOTI KELAIDIS
Curator, Rock Alpine Garden
Denver Botanic Gardens

I

MILLSTREAM

The Story of a Rock Garden

Dodecatheon amethystinum   A variable species with wide distribution.

I

What is the why of a garden? Most gardens have been created primarily as a setting—a pleasant adjunct to a home, a bit of landscape tamed and tidied and made bright with color.

For some people this is the only reason for a garden. Those who are sufficiently affluent will buy such a landscape, custom-designed and planted, and hire someone to keep it trim and flowering, much as they would purchase ornaments and pictures for their rooms, or display on their sideboards maid-polished silver. Others, though they may wish the amenity of a garden, are either unable or unwilling to go to such expense. They may, perhaps, have it professionally designed but will usually plant it themselves and will plan hopefully to tend it personally a few hours each week with or without the part-time help of what frequently turns out to be an unknowledgeable, unwilling high-school boy.

Many such garden owners even believe they will learn to love gardening; indeed, a few will discover in themselves an affinity for horticulture. But most will find it a discouraging chore. True, in the first warm days of spring they may get an atavistic pleasure in poking about in the moist, richly scented soil and discovering uncurling, upthrusting stems among the soggy debris of winter. They will revel then in spading up a bed and sprinkling it with the contents of brightly colored seed packets, or in tucking nursery-bought plants into the newly turned earth. They will greet each sprout, each new leaf with the pride of creation and cheerfully pull up the tiniest weeds.

But soon this initial enthusiasm dwindles. A day slips by, then a week, without so much as a glance at those plants, which do not seem to be growing as fast as they did at first. Other interests impinge, and suddenly that bed—neat and clean only yesterday—is filled with weeds. Conscience-stricken, the gardener pulls and scratches to release his plants, only to find that next week it has all to be done again. Gradually, as the sun presses with greater heat, even this minimal attention is begrudged. Summer weekends are all too short. Guests arrive. The children must be ferried to the beach. The tennis court, the golf course, a shaded terrace are all more appealing than weeding and wrestling with hoses. Besides, summer is a time for friendship—and gardening is a solitary chore.

And so the dream garden becomes increasingly unkempt: weeds shoot up, the plants do not flower as well as the catalogues indicated, they develop blights, are chewed by bugs; some even vanish completely. It is all very discouraging. After a few heroic but sporadic attempts at cleaning up the mess have been made, the beds are sometimes resodded for the sake of tidiness and simple upkeep; as frequently they are allowed to go completely wild, a permanent reminder of unattained hope.

There are, it must be conceded, many gardens planned, planted, and cared for primarily as settings for a house which are neither professionally tended nor allowed to become unsightly weed patches. For just as a conscientious housewife will spend time and effort—though usually grudgingly—on the bedmaking, tidying, dusting, and vacuum cleaning essential to maintaining the inside of an attractive home, so will she or her husband weed and trim the plantings which enhance the outside.

A desired landscape is not, however, the only why of a garden. Many are created by those for whom gardening itself is a joy, where the decorative aspect is a result rather than the intent. We

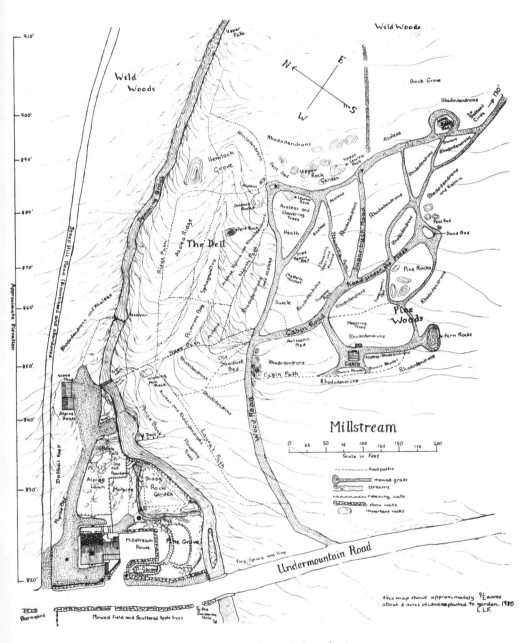

Millstream

0	25	50	75	100	125	150	175	200	

Scale in Feet

- - - - - - - footpaths

mowed grass

streams

retaining walls

stone walls

important rocks

this map shows approximately 9½ acres
about 6 acres of which are planted to garden. 1980
L.F.

Millstream House and gardens

are definitely in this category. Our lives would be diminished without a garden in which to work.

Those who visit our garden at Millstream almost always want to know how long we have lived here and the age of the garden itself. The first part of the question is easily answered. We moved into Millstream House in December of 1949—bag, baggage, four children, and a dog. There is, however, no quick answer to the second part of the query. There were, when we first arrived, a few overgrown remains of plantings: we began cutting brush and pulling weeds before we actually moved into the house: we started clearing the area which eventually became the Shady Rock Garden that first winter. Over the years this original nucleus has sent out tentacles and colonies of growth, sometimes at considerable distance from the main body. Sections have been destroyed, renewed, built, and rebuilt. The garden has changed and is still changing and growing, aging and being reborn so that like an amoeba it has no age but is ageless, as old as its first beginnings, as young as tomorrow.

In addition to wanting to know the age of the garden, many people ask if we chose this place because it fitted a preconceived landscape we wished to create. The answer is "no." The house and property belonged to my Aunt Do, and she moved out so we could move in.

Living with a rock garden rather quickly leads to the question of whether you own the rock garden or it owns you, though perhaps the relationship is more of a symbiosis than a question of ownership. Certainly the rock garden is dependent on the gardener for its existence, but the rock gardener very soon discovers he is almost equally dependent on rock gardening.

Let me point out, however, that though a person can rather easily become infected with rock garden fever, this does not necessarily mean he will come down with its most virulent form, plantsmanship. Despite continual exposure for over thirty years, I have avoided the latter affliction.

The chances of my becoming even a rock gardener were highly unlikely. I was brought up on a sand dune on the southeastern tip of Long Island, New York, within spitting distance of the Atlantic Ocean. My personal experience with rock gardens was not only practically nil, it was decidedly negative. Those few I had seen in the front yards of the houses on that end of Long Island were of two kinds. The most common was a moderately steep, short bank alongside the road or driveway, pocked with rounded stones (frequently painted) and planted with thin, weedy grass, glowing magenta moss pink, a few half-dead bearded iris, cerise portulaca, and occasionally some clumps of marigolds and a sprinkling of spindly snapdragons. In the other, more ambitious, type of rock garden the stones were piled in the center of the lawn. The plantings were similar to those in the bank type, but were usually enlivened by a pedestaled, cast-concrete bird bath and sometimes a gnome or two or a squatting painted plaster boy holding a fishpole.

It was with this background in rock gardening that I heard my newly acquired fiancé enthusiastically announce that the property onto which we were about to move would make an ideal site for a rock garden. I was appalled to say the least, but as a bride-to-be, I tried to conceal my dismay by saying I had rather hoped to plant ferns and wildflowers under the trees. Linc undoubtedly sensed my feelings, for he quickly told me that wildflowers were perfectly suitable in a rock garden. When I suggested in a small voice that I had heard rock gardens were a great deal of work, he pooh-poohed the idea, and waving away the tangle of brush, grape vine, nettles, and scouring rush that occupied the prospective rock garden, said, "You'll see. Once we get rid of this stuff and get it planted, it will practically take care of itself." Limited as my experience with gardening was, I was a bit doubtful; no garden I knew of took care of itself, but I felt it was hardly the moment to say so.

Little did I know what I was getting into. I soon discovered that in marrying Linc I was not only marrying a rock garden, but the American Rock Garden Society. Shortly before our wedding Linc off-handedly mentioned that he had recently taken over the job of handling the society's seed exchange, and he hoped I wouldn't mind helping him.

It may seem to you that I was extremely dumb not to realize I was marrying a confirmed rock gardener prior to taking the fateful step. I knew, of course, of his interest in plants. He talked of very little else, but in those days it was mostly of rhododendrons and azaleas. He was at that time working for Great Mountain Forest in Norfolk, Connecticut, where among other things, he was growing tree seedlings for the experimental plantations. His main enthusiasm, however, was for the work he was doing hybridizing rhododendrons. This was the primary topic of conversation on our first date. As my side of Canaan Mountain, in an extension of the valley of the Housatonic River, was underlain by limestone, I expressed surprise that he could grow these plants in limy soil. I was rather pleased to be able to come up with this remark so glibly. It happened that it was about the extent of my knowledge on the subject.

Linc explained, "Only the valleys are limy. Canaan Mountain is schist, and Norfolk has acid soil. The problem is that most rhododendrons, except a few iron-clads, aren't hardy in this climate, and most of these are magenta in color. What I'm trying to do is hybridize tender ones with the hardy ones so as to create hardy strains with greater variation in growth habit and flower color." He was off and running, and as the unfamiliar terms rained upon my head, all I could do was nod and try to look intelligent and occasionally interject "Uh-huh" and "How excit-ing!" at what I hoped were appropriate moments.

I guess I passed muster, as Linc continued to date me, and in the spring he invited me over to see his plants. I was enthralled by the azaleas and rhododendrons. Some were deliciously scented and of charming pastel shades. Rather as an afterthought he showed me two small rock gardens he had built for his employer, Ted Childs. These were a vast improvement over those I had seen on Long Island: no painted plaster dwarfs, and some of the flowers were truly lovely, small of stature and brilliant with blossoms. But the gardens had been neglected and were fairly full of the weedy grasses that I associated with rock gardens. I was not overly impressed.

Linc courted me that spring and summer with plants for the tiny garden I had started behind my house and won over my two boys by taking them, along with his own two children Becky and Ben, on excursions and picnics during which we collected frogs, snakes, and salamanders as well as wildflowers. It took me several months to decide I wanted to embark on matrimony again, but I finally succumbed and announced to my family that I was planning to marry Linc.

Aunt Do, my only local relative, who had been partially responsible for introducing me to Linc, was delighted, perhaps because she was only too glad to foist on someone else the responsibility of keeping an eye on a headstrong niece with two small sons. She did have a cautionary comment, however, "Are you sure you want to spend the rest of your life with a dour New Englander?"

"Linc was born in New Jersey," I countered, "and I don't think he's all that dour."

Her next question was more to the point, "And where are you going to live?"

Millstream House from Under Mountain Road.

She already knew that Linc was leaving his job with Great Mountain Forest and planning to go back into teaching, and that the house he was living in in Norfolk went with his job and would therefore not be available to us. She also knew that the little house I was renting from her would be much too small for a family of six. This had presented us with a quandary at first, as rental houses in the area were about as common as igloos in Hawaii, but I was glad to be able to tell her that Linc's boss had offered to rent us an old vacant farm house he owned on top of Canaan Mountain.

Aunt Do was horrified. "You're a city child. You can't possibly live up there on that dirt road with no one around but rattlesnakes. How'll you get down in winter and spring to get the children to school and do the marketing? The school bus won't go up there. Neither can the snow plow half the time. And in spring that road turns into a pig wallow. You'd better live here on a hardtop road, and I'll move into the Saltbox. It will suit me much better than rattling around in this big house, and I'd like a change of scenery." My protests were feeble. It was like being handed the keys of Heaven. And so it was decided. We were to live at Millstream.

That fall there was a piecemeal shuttling of goods and chattels from one house to another. Aunt Do's Jeep did yeoman service transferring sofas, chairs, bureaus, book cases, even the refrigerator, the box spring of my four-poster bed, and the grandmother clock.

Aunt Do's barnyard, pastures, and enormous vegetable garden across the road from the house were immaculate, but she couldn't be bothered with landscaping and posies. There was a small lawn around the front of the house that was kept mowed, but on the slope behind the house the soil was so thin that it couldn't support anything but a sparse cover of weedy grass. To prevent tree seedlings from getting a hold, the grass was scythed once or twice a year by Aunt Do's hired man, George Opley, a gaunt, taciturn New Englander. The foundation planting consisted of privet, lilac, and native barberry. The lilacs were planted on the north side of the house where in deep shade and overhung by maple trees they struggled to survive but never succeeded in blooming. The privet, on the other hand, throve only too well against the south-facing front wall and reached halfway up the front window despite being cut back periodically by Mr. Opley. Another privet hedge ran along the top of the stone retaining wall that

raised the narrow strip of front lawn above the road. The barber-
ries Aunt Do had had dug from the pasture and planted at the
corners of the house had succeeded in climbing high enough to
look in the second-story windows.

In addition to the four big maples that overhung the northwestern end of the house and a crumbling apple tree off the north
corner, two huge elms, planted when the kitchen wing had been
added in the mid-1850s, flanked the path leading up to the kitchen
door. They were healthy specimens when we moved in. Their
fluted boles towered above the roof, and their arching limbs were
haunted by flying squirrels who sailed down to do gymnastics on
the porch clothesline. A few years later the elms succumbed to
Dutch elm disease and had to be taken down, first one and then,
ten years later, the other. We counted the growth rings: 100 in
the stump of the first to be cut, 110 in the second.

Though the remains of the sawmill, which had stood behind
the house beside the brook, had long since been carted away, its
square stone foundation jutting out into the brook still stood
firm, as did the wings of the dam that had held back the water
of the millpond. Also in good repair was the massive eight-foot-
high retaining wall that supported the weedy slope of land extending from the mill to the back of the house. Aunt Do had
crowned this wall also with a row of privet, a shrub to which
she seemed overly attached.

When I asked her, "Why privet?" she retorted that she didn't
particularly like it, but when you stuck it in the ground it grew
without fuss into something you could see without waiting fifty
years.

You could certainly see the privet hedge on top of the wall.
It had grown to mammoth proportions. Its roots threatened the
stability of the wall, and its unkempt top leaned out in every
direction in a broken tangle of heavy branches. With Aunt Do's

permission, even before she moved out of the house and we moved in, one of our very first efforts at landscaping was to cut this hedge down to stubs. The following year we grubbed it out.

We are most fortunate in our situation in that our house sits on the Waloosac Formation just below its contact with the acidic schist of Canaan Mountain. Therefore, the soil of the lower garden, which surrounds the house, is somewhat alkaline. It is here we grow plants from the European Alps, the Middle East, Greece, Italy, Spain, and those sections of our own country where the soils are basically limy. The upper reaches of the garden, on the other hand, are underlain with predominantly acidic rock, and it is here that we grow our azaleas, rhododendrons, and those others which prefer an acid soil.

This in itself permits us to grow a wider variety of plants than would be possible in many gardens. We do lack one type of soil: we have practically no clay, or very little, in the sections we garden. On the whole our soils are very light, drain rapidly, and are not well suited to those plants which require a fairly rich and heavy soil. Most of the meadow plants do not do well for us, and we are not successful with lilies and some of the other bulbous plants, though our difficulties with these may be due to rodents, which can tunnel easily through our friable earth to reach and devour the succulent bulbs no matter how deeply we plant them. Lilies thrive in the old vegetable garden below the road where the soil contains a greater proportion of clay and the mice are not as rampant, but we regret our inability to grow them in the garden proper where they would look splendid among the azaleas and the dwarf rhododendrons and give us mid- and late-season summer bloom.

This is a minor complaint, however, when we can grow so many other lovely things, for, in addition to the variation in the acidity of our soils, there is a great variation in the amount of

Millstream House in winter, viewed from the alpine lawn.

moisture available in different parts of the garden. There are well-drained knobs and slopes to suit those plants from the more arid sections of the world. There are also moist areas, underwatered by the ceaseless seep of ground water from the high, flat top of Canaan Mountain, and such situations provide us with that condition so often described in gardening books as "moist but well drained," a condition difficult to achieve in most gardens without the use of complicated underground watering systems. This natural drainage down the slope of the mountain permits us to grow many of the high-alpine plants which require a continual flow of moving water around their roots but abhor stagnant moisture. We have, however, a few low pockets partway up the slope above Deming Brook where ground water collects and keeps the soil fairly wet throughout the year. One of the wettest of these we have excavated and filled with peat to make a miniature bog. In this supersaturated muck we have been able to grow some of the plants which thrive under these conditions: pitcher plant *(Sarracenia purpurea)*, arrowhead *(Sagittaria)*, wild calla *(Calla palustris)*, and buckbean *(Menyanthes trifoliata)*. We have not succeeded in growing here the bog orchids, however, as these apparently require more sterile conditions than we can provide, but the opulent showy lady's slipper *(Cypripedium reginae)* has persisted on the bank just above the bog.

These advantages of soil and moisture are not our only blessings. Our situation also permits us to grow many plants that would not ordinarily survive the winter climate of this area. Temperatures in northwestern Connecticut frequently linger below zero degrees Fahrenheit for weeks at a time and upon occasion plunge to over thirty below. When such low temperatures are combined with wind, the chill factor reaches arctic proportions, but we are protected to a great extent from the worst of the northerly winds by the bulwark of Canaan Moun-

tain. Though a south-facing slope has some disadvantages during
the scorching days of summer, it is also warmed in winter by the
low-traveling sun, which from October to April may shine upon
a northern slope only a few hours a day or not at all. The soil
remains open longer in the fall, thaws earlier in the spring, and
never becomes as deeply frozen as it does on north-facing flanks
of the mountain.

Our position partway up this south-facing slope is of further
benefit: because cold air is heavier than warm and flows downhill
to collect in low pockets, it is in valleys that temperatures drop
the lowest, frosts come early in fall, and spring frosts strike late
to blight unfurling buds. We can thus grow in our garden plants
which are not winter-hardy in the valley below our house. We
have even bloomed some rhododendrons whose flower buds are
blasted in the relatively milder climate around Hartford.

So we must give credit where credit is due, and tactless visitors
who attribute the beauty of our garden to its setting are in the
main quite right, though they probably do not recognize the true
values inherent in that setting.

It is indeed infuriating, to be told—as we frequently are—by
visitors to our garden that, of course, we have a perfect setting.
Aunt Do once remarked to such a guest, "You should have seen
it when it was left to God and me." Our visitors are right,
however. We do have a lovely landscape. And though it is now
hard to remember how it looked when we first came, when it
was blurred by trees and brush and clogged with weed growth,
the bones were there—the potential. The garden has inevitably
been shaped and bounded by the land on which it lies as well as
by us who live within it.

The property in its entirety is long and narrow, a somewhat
wedge-shaped slice of fields and woodland sliding down the
southwest slope of Canaan Mountain, which thrusts up to a

height of 1,962 feet in the northwestern corner of Connecticut. The wide upper end of our land is lost among the forest trees of the mountain; the fields and meadows of its chisel tip rest against the brook in the valley below the house. Across this brook rises the 1,260-foot-high hummock of Cobble Hill. Blocking the upper eastern end of the valley that lies between Cobble Hill and Canaan Mountain, "Our Valley," as we call it, is diked by a deep deposit of glacial gravel. Thus the gathered waters that flow off the southern slope of Canaan Mountain must weave westerly.

About halfway down the valley's five-mile length a quartzy buttress of Canaan Mountain juts toward Cobble Hill like a partially closed gate so that the upper eastern end is in effect an enclosed oval bowl encompassed by heaped hills. This section, above which our house is situated, was once called "Friendly Valley" by Odell Shepard, a Trinity College professor who has written several books about the Nutmeg State. And it does have a welcoming warmth and remote peace as it stretches in the summer sun between the enfolding heights of Canaan Mountain on the north and the rounded ridges of Cobble Hill that curve along its southerly border.

This end of the valley lies about 650 feet above sea level and is wide for the size of the brook that curls down its length. This stream was originally known as Peck Brook and is so designated on old maps and deeds, though on the modern geodetic survey map it has been renamed Wangum Lake Brook, an epithet derived from one of its sources, Wangum Lake, on top of Canaan Mountain. It has several other tributaries, however, among them Deming Brook, the millstream that waters our garden and gives our home its name, Millstream House.

Under Mountain Road winds the length of the valley, from Route 7 to Route 63, rising and falling as it curves and curls along the shoulder of Canaan Mountain. It slices across our land.

Our house stands just above this road, its front windows looking across it, down the long slope to the valley floor and beyond to the forested rise of the Cobble. This lower section of the property is farmed by a neighbor. Pasture, field, and hay meadow stretch across its narrow length, divided from each other by tumbled stone walls reinforced with post and wire fences, the smooth expanse of grass and furrow lined and broken by tall old trees under which the cattle stand in summer.

Across the road from the house, a little to the west and down the slope—where they do not block the view—are the barn and old apple orchard. Here we made nursery beds and built cold frames for the plants we needed for our own garden and those we made for others. On this open, south-facing slope the sun lovers can bask, and yet there is shade beneath the apple trees for those who need it.

Also below Under Mountain Road, but to the east, a small dam briefly obstructs the flow of Deming Brook as it plunges down past our house and under the road to join Wangum Lake Brook. Though our children swam from May to October in the pool thus formed, and our grandchildren swim in it now from frost to frost, Linc and I only venture into its frigid waters during the dog days of August. Here too, below the road, we had a large vegetable garden for many years when the children were home. This was later used as a small nursery for trees and shrubs. Our main garden, however, is on the slope that rises behind the house.

The view from our back windows and terrace is of the mountain and the forest. From here we look up the rockbound, leaping course of Deming Brook as it stumbles and spills from among the trees. This brook is not only an important feature of the garden, it is our main water supply. Its flow is piped underground to the house by gravity from a small reservoir in the bed of the stream where, above the house and in the center of our outlook, a rough dam of wedged boulders backed by cement creates a deep pool and a fall of white water. Only deer, chipmunks, raccoons, wildcats, and foxes live on the mountain above us, and the water is clear and pure, and icy cold even in midsummer.

The brook rises just behind Bradford Peak, Canaan Mountain's highest point. Here, from the heights above, the drainage collects in a small, swampy basin from which it drips and trickles over mossy ledges through a deeply forested glen where the air is always cool and still under the high leaves, and ferns grow tall as a man. As the brook flows downward, more water seeps from the surrounding knolls to reinforce the stream. It widens and deepens, purling over the rocks and sliding in dark, glinting pools around the ancient roots of hemlocks until it reaches the very brink of the mountain plateau. Here, blocked by a stony lip of hard rock, it pauses yet again and spreads into a wide boggy swamp, thick with alder, where it gathers its waters before plunging in a series of falls down the steep escarpment that forms the south face of Canaan Mountain.

During the dry summer months, when the trees are sucking up the surface moisture, Deming Brook becomes only a series of pools with long expanses of dry, bouldery stream bed between. Then, during the day, the water in our reservoir sinks, leaking out as fast as it trickles in, and we must use it carefully. At night, however, when the trees are not transpiring as rapidly, the water level usually rises a little. Only twice since we have lived at Millstream—and then only for a short period—has the brook gotten so low that we could not use the water. During years of normal rainfall the stream never dries up enough to cause us any anxiety; one good day of rain will swell it to a rushing watercourse, and it responds to even brief thunder showers. But during the long drought of 1961–66, the worst in the history of the

Northeast, we came perilously close to having the reservoir go bone-dry. So, as an emergency supply, we hooked into our water system the formerly unused well located on the bank of the stream a little way above the house.

This drilled well, though only about thirty feet deep, is a good one and should, we hope, tide us over future droughty years. But the water from it is hard and tasteless compared to the water of the stream, and because it has such a small head, this well can be quickly pumped dry if too many faucets are turned on at once. We therefore cannot use it for watering the garden, even that part directly around the house.

We have never been able to use the household water system for watering the gardens up in the woods, as these are above the brook. For a number of years we resorted to a portable gasoline pump that crouched at the edge of the stream during the summer. With a horrid hysterical clatter this pump forced water through a plastic hose that snaked upward to our plantings high on the slope above. But during the six-year drought the reservoir became so low we did not dare use any water other than that needed for the house, and we discovered that our plants survived. They looked dreadful, it must be admitted: most were limp and desiccated, and the lower leaves of the rhododendrons turned yellow and fell off. But they survived, so we no longer water during dry spells, though we occasionally carry water by hand to newly planted plants. Fortunately the brook usually flows to some extent most of the year; singing through our days and nights all spring, summer, and fall, though its voice may sink to a whisper in July and August. Only in freezing weather is its song silenced beneath a sheath of ice. We are accustomed to its sound, but guests, hearing its rushing soliloquy after dark, frequently mistake it for a heavy downpour of rain.

In spring thaws or when the rains of late summer and autumn

drench the land, the brook can swell to a cataract thirty feet across that seethes against the banks and sometimes overleaps them. Then the voice of the stream deepens to a throaty roar as it surges down the mountain, at times developing that low, grumbling undernote of threatening flood, the grind of boulders moving in its bed. When the brook is in spate, its thunder becomes a continuous cannonading; the earth vibrates to the concussion of the uptorn rocks as they roll from ledge to ledge, dragged by the relentless water.

Although Deming Brook has carved our landscape and is the focal point of our view of the garden as seen from the house and, indeed, has been a primary force in the shaping of that garden, it is not the sole element that has determined its form and texture; the underlying rock has played a major role. Its very presence so close beneath the surface, thrusting at times through the thin flesh of soil or lying about in broken shards of every shape and dimension, has inevitably influenced the contours of our plantings. Though in a minor way we have meddled with this bony structure, it is only in detail that we have been able to rearrange it; fundamentally our gardening has been directed by this insistent skeletal armature. Indeed, this rocky substrate has not only determined the shaping of our landscape, it has specified to a large extent the very kinds of plants we grow and their placement. Ours is no garden for lush perennial borders and bedded annuals; the soil is too thin and not rich enough to support the tall, luxuriant plants whose ancestors grew in rich meadows and river bottoms.

The geological history of any area is a major factor in the creation of its soil and thus influences the plants that grow there. Our land has been folded and worn, uplifted, tilted, scoured by glaciers and buried under accumulations of ice age material. Its geology is extraordinarily intricate and sufficiently confused so that unraveling its history is difficult even for trained geologists.

The main brook's otherwise rather straight course down into the valley had been deflected quite sharply to the southeast by the dam foundation and by an outcropping of fairly high limestone ledges that thrust out into the stream just below it. These ledges had over the years caught enough debris—huge chunks of rock torn from the bed of the stream, tree limbs, soil, and generations of leaves washed down from the mountain during periods of high water—to form an island sizable enough to support a grove of six or seven mature trees and considerable bushy undergrowth. The upstream tip of this half-moon-shaped island lay about ten feet out from below the mill foundation, its curved side toward the retaining wall, its straight side scoured by the brook. Its upper end had been joined to the mill foundation by a short rough drystone wall that fairly effectively prevented the stream from running down the slot between the island and the high retaining wall. It did allow water to seep between the rocks of this dam and, when the stream was in spate, slop over the top. At one time the tail-of-the-race (the spent water that turned the overshot mill wheel) must have run down through this slot to rejoin the brook just below the house.

The tail-of-the-race was a dank spot shaded by a gigantic double-trunked sycamore that had rooted itself on the floor of this miniature ravine. This slot was also cluttered by a dozen or so grossly overgrown *Taxus cuspidata* which Aunt Do had planted at the foot of the retaining wall and around the periphery of the graveled parking area that she had had put in front of the underground wagon shed (now garage) under the kitchen wing. It was in the tail-of-the-race and on the island that Linc planned to build a rock garden.

The tail-of-the-race could be reached by mounting two narrow stone steps leading up from the parking area. The main access was down a wide flight of beautifully proportioned steps descending through the high retaining wall from the end of the brick patio just behind the house. The patio and steps had been built by a young sculptor and his wife who had owned the house briefly for a year or two prior to its purchase by my aunt.

Unfortunately both these entrances to the tail-of-the-race were completely blocked by the stout, reaching branches of the enormous yews planted many years before as innocent youngsters. Aunt Do had purchased these from an itinerant salesman who had stopped by the house one day with a truckload of them. She was very proud of their subsequent flourishing growth; however, she did give us permission to trim them back so as to make it possible to get into the tail-of-the-race.

This "trimming" had to be done with a saw and powerful loppers, as most of the limbs of the taxus were two to three inches through, and yew is very hard wood. I was horrified by the appearance of the gaunt stubs that were left and dreaded Aunt Do's reaction when she saw the result of our trimming, but she took it in stride, and Linc assured us both that in no time adventitious buds would sprout along the naked branches and cover them completely with new growth. I was doubtful, but he was quite right, and for the next twenty years I had to prune them yearly to keep them within their allotted bounds. It was not until a few years after Aunt Do's death that we finally removed most of the yews entirely.

In the evenings and on inclement weekends, when Linc was not reading books or writing papers for his courses at Trinity College or preparing the speeches he gave in the Connecticut House of Representatives in Hartford, we would clean, package, file, and list the seeds contributed to the ARGS seed exchange and send them out to those requesting them. Though the number of species contributed back in 1950 was paltry (348) compared to the riches available today, it seemed a tremendous number to me. We kept them all in two large, mouse-proof bureau drawers in the un-heated study–guest room in the attic. I cannot now remember how many members wrote in for seeds at three cents per packet, but fifty-seven donors sent in seed. It was the first time that they had been requested to send in all their seed by a specific deadline so that a single complete list could be published and sent out shortly thereafter. Previously, members had sent in seed as they collected it, and every issue of the *Bulletin* listed what seed had been received since the last issue under the name of the donor. With the advent of the single list, Linc instituted the system of numbering each donor and placing the donor number after each species listed. This may be appreciated by our members, but it has been an infernal nuisance to subsequent seed exchanges.

In those days the generic and specific name on each package of seed sent out by the exchange chairman was handwritten on the packet, and as I wrote each name over and over and over again, Linc would tell me how to pronounce it, and he would describe the plant. When he didn't know, and sometimes when he did, we would look it up in Farrer's *English Rock Garden,* and he would read aloud the glowing or condemnatory terms in Farrer's rotund and vivid prose. It was a great way to learn about rock gardening plants and certainly relieved the tedium of writ-ing *Anthoxanthum odoratus* or *Penstemon confertus* var. *caeruleo-purpureus* on packet after packet.

Our most immediate problem, once we had moved in, was to clear a few places where Linc could put the plants he wanted to bring over from his former home in Norfolk, on the northern slope of Canaan Mountain. These were mainly rhododendrons and azaleas, many of them his own hybrids, but there were also a number of rock garden plants, including some of his hybrid

Phlox subulata. Prior to our marriage, when Linc had worked for several years for Mr. Childs, the owner of Great Mountain Forest, trees, from seed to lumber, had mainly occupied his time, but he had also done considerable hybridizing of hardy rhododendrons and azaleas and had had two fairly large rock gardens. He was anxious to bring some of this stock over the mountain where he could keep a close eye on it, though he planned to go back to teaching once we were married.

Teaching had been Linc's original profession, and he had taught for nearly twenty years in private schools, eventually becoming co-headmaster of a small college-preparatory school for boys in Norfolk. It was not until this school closed during World War II that he had turned his avocation of horticulture into a vocation. Switching back to teaching was, therefore, not a major shift in his life, but because he wanted to take this opportunity to try public school teaching, his decision did create some problems; for despite his many years of experience in private schools it was necessary that he have courses in education in order to receive a certificate permitting him to teach in Connecticut's public school system. So for the first year of our marriage he became a student once more, commuting almost daily to Trinity College in Hartford. This fitted into his schedule fairly well, as he was serving the last year of his term as Norfolk's representative in the State Assembly and had to spend considerable time in Hartford anyway. It did mean, however, that he had very little time for gardening, particularly as our weekends were largely preempted by excursions with the children: hikes, climbs, picnics, even spelunking, equipped with dim flashlights and balls of grocery string, in the underground passages of the nearby Twin Lakes Caves. Also, there was the fascinating but time-consuming seed exchange.

My gardening experience, until I was pitch-forked into horticulture by my marriage to Linc, was limited to planting radish seeds and tomato plants and to the creation and care of a small perennial border at my former home on Long Island, where I had lived until moving to Falls Village shortly after the war. The flat landscape and sandy loam of central and eastern Long Island, where the only rocks are polished glacial boulders, had given me no background for Linc's special interest, rock gardening. My knowledge on the subject was abysmal. There was, however, a plethora of rocks at Millstream, and Linc assured me that wild-flowers, which I did want to grow, would thrive in such a site. He asserted that all true rock garden plants are wildflowers some-where in the world, that they combined quite contentedly with our native flora, and that it would be foolishly parochial to grow only those wildflowers that grew in the northeastern United States. To clinch his argument he pointed out that we had very few sites suited to a mixed border of annuals and perennials, most of which are meadow plants requiring sun and rich soil.

My lack of gardening experience made it difficult to refute his reasoning, but my capitulation was not complete; privately I planned to restore the D-Garden (Aunt Do's garden parallel to the road) for perennials and, eventually, to plant an herbaceous border along the top of the high retaining wall in lieu of the hideous privet. It seemed only logical, however, to prepare areas suitable for the shrubs, rock garden plants, and native woodland-ers which were then available.

So we went to work, confining our first operations to the tail-of-the-race and the rocky peninsula. While we were about it we also trimmed up the snarl of dead branches on the lower trunks of the pines between the parking area and the brook. Linc hoped to use this area for some of the rhododendrons and azaleas he wanted to bring over from Norfolk. Though the soil around the house was underlain by limestone and, therefore, not really suitable for these ericaceous shrubs, he thought that possibly the gravelly fill under the pines had been sufficiently acidified by the fall of pine needles to accommodate these plants at least temporarily. Trimming up the pines also made it possible to walk beneath them, thus opening a third way into the tail-of-the-race from the D-Garden.

In addition to these three entries into the area we wanted to make it possible to go down into it from the top of the mill foundation. A flight of wooden steps seemed the simplest solution, so Linc burrowed through the pile of scrap lumber stored in the shed of the barn and, as luck would have it, found the set of ladderlike steps which had formerly been used to mount into the hay loft. These, fortunately, had been removed in one piece when Aunt Do had had them replaced by a less precipitous stairway, and with only a very little carpentering they were remodeled to suit our need. To make an easy access from the foot of this stairway across the gully to the peninsula, we built a narrow bridge of cedar stringers cut from the pasture topped with boards also rescued from the stack of refuse lumber.

The clearing of brush and sapling trees that cluttered the hollow and the adjoining ridge was the next chore on our agenda. This we did during the first winter, with the not-too-enthusiastic help of our children, though they did enjoy roasting potatoes and toasting marshmallows in the resulting bonfires. Linc also wished to cut down all the large trees on the peninsula so as to let in more light and air. He claimed their roots were taking all the nourishment from the soil and that nothing would grow beneath them. Considering the dense cover of weeds that clothed the ground under these trees, I found this hard to believe, and I fought the removal of every tree. Having been raised among sand dunes and potato fields, I regarded a tree—any tree—as something to be treasured, but Linc prevailed, and down they came, all but one maple near the lower end of the promontory, which was spared only because it was needed to support the far end of the clothes-line that stretched high above the driveway from a corner of the porch.

I will be the first to admit that a line full of flapping sheets and underwear does nothing to improve a garden landscape, but there was nowhere else anywhere near the house to put a line long enough for our enormous wash, and I am sufficiently penny pinching to begrudge the cost of an electric dryer, to say nothing of the cost of the power needed to run it, if God's wind and sun will do the job free.

In spring, as soon as the ground was bare of snow and suffi-ciently thawed to dig, we started to clear the accumulation of debris and weeds from the peninsula and that portion of the gully that lay between it and the high retaining wall. When the mass of rotting leaves was dug out of the hollow and carted off to our newly established compost pile, we discovered a moist runnel, hardly wider than a ditch, that circumscribed the base of the promontory. It could hardly be called a brook, as the seep of water that found its way through the stone wall that dammed the upper end of the gully was barely sufficient to wet the bottom, but we nevertheless cleared its entire length to the point where it rejoined the main stream at the foot of the peninsula.

The weeding which followed this initial cleanup was mainly my job. It required no brains or knowledge of plants, as every-thing was dispensable. Every moment I could spare from housework was spent on my knees on the muddy, still partially frozen ground. I was well bundled in layers of sweaters under an old lumber jacket with my nether extremities in sheepskin-lined rubber boots and a pair of old-fashioned ski pants—the warm, baggy variety resembling the bottom half of a baby's snowsuit; but even so it was a chilly business to crouch nearly motionless pecking away at the icy soil.

My implements were simple, a shovel for the heavy-rooted weeds, a claw made of three bent pieces of heavy-gauge wire fastened to a wooden handle—a tool I still consider indispensable when doing wholesale weeding—and my bare fingers. I have never been able to work in gloves, as I find touch almost as essential as sight for most garden chores, but I must admit I would have liked to have worn them when doing that job. My hands burned and ached from contact with the frigid dirt, the skin becoming so roughened and split, despite continual applications of hand cream, that they looked like lumps of raw hamburger held together with Band-Aids. But I was so proud; I could hardly wait to show Linc the few square yards of beautiful, clean, cultivated soil I had produced during a day's work. When he was home we worked together, and as the weather warmed up it became a pleasure to claw the weeds out of the soil. By the middle of May we had most of the area cleared and ready for planting.

As the soil in Norfolk is very acid, many of the plants which Linc had grown successfully in his rock garden there were not suitable to the limy soil around Millstream, but we were able to rescue quite a number of divisions and rooted layers from those which had no objection to lime. Most of the azaleas and rhododendrons had to be left in their nursery beds in Norfolk until we could prepare proper habitats for them up in the woods, where our soil is naturally acid. We did, however, bring a few of the older rhododendrons over the mountain and set them out under the pine trees next to the driveway. Linc had discovered an antique sawdust pile high on the slope across the stream from the house. This had been the site of a small engine-powered sawmill which, in an attempt to supplement the income from his herd of dairy cows, Carroll Miles had set up to replace the original water-driven mill, which had fallen into hopeless disrepair. This mill had long since vanished, but a deep bed of well-rotted pine sawdust marked the location, and Linc hoped this material would help to enrich and acidify the gravelly soil beneath the pines. He therefore carried down basketload after basketload of rotted sawdust, supplemented by further basketloads of duff scraped from under pines up in the woods, and incorporated this mixture into the soil in the bottom of every hole he dug.

Beneath the ash tree on the brink of the bank behind the pines, we placed a well-rooted layer of the shrubby horse chestnut *(Aesculus parviflora)* for the sake of its late-summer flowers. It is strange that it does well here in northwest Connecticut, as it is native only as far north as South Carolina, but we have seen it in a woodland garden in Utica, New York, and Linc brought the original plant to Millstream as a rooted layer from Norfolk, where he had grown it from seed. You can never be certain about winter-hardiness until you try. The Latin species name means "small-flowered," and it is true the individual flowers are very small compared to those of the other members of this group, being barely half an inch long. The flowers are tightly clustered on foot-long stiff spikes, however, so that when the shrub blooms in late July and early August, it looks as though it had been lit by hundreds of slender white candles. When examined closely these tapers appear bristled by the pinkish red stamens extending well out beyond the tufted petals, a feature which adds greatly to their charm. This low horse chestnut has one minor fault: it spreads, though slowly, as its outer branches touch the ground and take root, so that in time it may take up considerable space. But this fault has the advantage of supplying numerous layers, and we keep our plant within bounds by digging these up and transferring them up into the woodland garden where they can spread as far afield as they wish.

On the bank of the stream between the horse chestnut and the tip of the peninsula we placed a young shadblow *(Amelanchier canadensis)* for the sake of its ephemeral cloud of white blossom in early spring. In front of and between these two small multi-stemmed trees we planted a cluster of torch azalea *(Rhododendron kaempferi),* whose flowers, in early June, range from a deep orange-scarlet to a soft salmon rose.

These plantings shared the Pine Grove next to the parking area with our son Woody's collection of turtles, which were housed in a ramshackle pen that he had constructed out of scrap lumber. Half-buried tubs and sinks, scrounged from the village dump, occupied much of the area within the pen. These were kept filled with water from the hose and frequently overflowed so that the surrounding soil became progressively muddier and smellier as the turtle population grew. It seemed likely that this herpetorium would be part of our landscape for a while at least, so we made no attempt to improve the area beyond planting the shrubs and removing the rank growth of nettles. The area was not too unsightly, however, as the gill-over-the-ground and rapid celandine soon formed a dense ground cover between the shrubs and were quickly supplemented by self-sown seedlings of herb Robert *(Geranium robertianum)* and adventitious plants of common violet *(Viola papilionacea)* in both its purple-flowered and pale blue-gray forms, the latter known as Confederate violet *(V. priceana).* However, a few of the shrubs and all the herbaceous plants we brought over from Norfolk were reserved for the more open location on the rocky peninsula.

Here, a narrow path trails up the ascending spine of the ridge from the bridge across the top of the gully and loops around the crest before descending down stepping-stones set into the sharp incline to the floor of the hollow under the sycamore where it once again crosses the runnel on a wide board.

As an experiment, though we supposed the soil was really too limy, we planted a couple of *Rhododendron obtusum* var. *arnoldianum* about halfway along the crest of the peninsula where several large, craggy limestone rocks thrust up through the soil. These semievergreen azaleas are hybrids between the torch azalea and purple-flowered *R. amoenum* and in late May are covered with blossoms of a brilliant cerise. Surprisingly, they throve and grew apace, so much so in fact that eventually we had to move one to another site. They have in fact self-sown, producing offspring that resemble *R. kaempferi.*

Near them was placed a dwarf Alberta spruce *(Picea alberta conica),* and at their feet we planted a young *Cotoneaster adpressa* and a creeping juniper. This latter is a chance seedling grown from berries Linc had collected off a particularly flat specimen of *Juniperus horizontalis* and was even more prostrate than its parent; the ground-hugging mat of blue-green needles is only four to five inches deep. This plant layers down quite readily, and we now have many of its progeny scattered throughout the garden. Its seedlings, however, revert to the more upright habit of its ancestors.

This group of shrubs and rocks formed the focal point of the long oval bed encompassed by the circling path around the crest of the peninsula. Diagonally across the path from them, near the top of the slope, was placed another group of shrubs, among them a young mugho pine Linc had rescued out of a batch of normal seedlings he had grown for Ted Childs. Next to it is a mountain andromeda *(Pieris floribunda),* a native of the southern Appalachians. This evergreen shrub, usually called fetter-bush in its native haunts, is closely related to the more commonly grown Japanese andromeda *(Pieris japonica)* and has similar leaves, a little like those of laurel. It is a lower-growing plant, however, seldom attaining a height of over three feet, and it differs also from its Nipponese cousin in its blossoming habit. Its small, waxy white bells are borne on clusters of upright stems in late April or early May, earning it its alternative colloquial name, lily-of-the-valley shrub, while those of its Japanese relative hang in pendulous tassels. Below the pine and pieris we placed a boxleaf holly *(Ilex crenata convexa)* whose small, nearly round leaves provided a nice contrast to the needles of the pine and the glossy, pointed foliage of the andromeda. Though both ilex and pieris are, like the azaleas, reputedly acid-soil plants, they have done well on this ledge of limestone.

Farther down the slope, where it begins to level off, we planted a small Korean box *(Buxus koreana)*. This dwarf box, unlike its English relative, is completely hardy in our subzero winter temperatures, and though it never grows higher than two feet, it has, over the years, become nearly four feet across and resembles a fat green cushion. As the slender, supple branches slowly lengthen, they lean outward, partly of their own weight and partly as a result of snow piling over them. Occasionally after a very heavy winter the bush will be so flattened that the center is hollow and the shrub temporarily takes on the form of a doughnut. Though unsightly for a season or two, the hollowed center fills in with new growth. This is apparently a normal phenomenon and perhaps explains why Korean box grows wider and wider without growing taller.

Near the box, among the rocks at the brink of the runnel, we planted a well-rooted layer of *Daphne cneorum,* the garland flower. Another of these was planted at the top of the stepping-stones mounting to the top of the ridge. A third was placed in a deep pocket of soil near the blunt crest of the peninsula just behind the upthrust of ledge that supports the lower end of the promontory. These beautiful daphnes with their close-set, narrow, evergreen leaves and deep pink flowers that scent the air every May, grew apace and eventually spread out to cover many yards of ground, but eventually, after about twenty years, they started to go to pieces. A few straggling branches, which had rooted down around the periphery, still persist and may in time return to their former glory. In the meantime, herbaceous plants have sown into their midst to conceal the sprawling naked stems. We did discover that daphne cannot abide pruning back in the spring. We very nearly killed all three plants when they were only a few years old by trimming off the scorched, dead-looking branches that result from a hard, snowless winter. This only resulted in further die-back, and the plants shrank yearly. Then quite by chance one spring, I neglected to tidy up these "dead" branches and discovered that they sent out new leaves as soon as the weather warmed up. So now we withhold the pruning shears until late summer, when it is quite safe to cut out the obviously defunct sections which have by then become quite brittle. This daphne is not difficult to root by layering down a straggling branch, scratching the bark on the underside, and placing a stone on the wounded section to keep it in close contact with the soil beneath, but cuttings are hard to root unless they are cut after the first hard frost in autumn.

Near the daphne on the crest of the ridge we planted another Korean box and a dwarf chamaecyparis *(C. obtusa compacta)*. Its dense, fan-shaped clusters of twigs covered with close-set flat needles are a delight at any time of year. At a later date we added to this planting a rooted cutting which had been given to us under the name of *Juniperus squamata prostrata* but may actually be a *Juniperus procumbens nana*. These plants are so similar that it takes an expert to differentiate between them, but either one is a treasure. The trailing branches, thickly tufted with ascending branchlets, follow every rise, dip, and fall of contour as they spread over the ground in an ever-widening hummock of dense, rich green. We place our trailing juniper in a deep fissure filled with rich leaf mold at the very edge of the cliff so that its elongating branches cascade down the rock face.

Below the cliff, in a deep pocket of soil behind a portion of the cliff that had split away from the parent ledge and fallen askew at its base, we planted a rare native clematis *(Clematis verticillaris)*. Unlike the more common virgin's bower *(C. virginiana)*, which trails its white clusters of small, starry flowers over the shrubs in moist lowlands in late summer and early fall, *C. verticillaris* blooms in early spring and has large, blue-purple hanging bells. It is not as exuberant in its growth as its autumn-flowering sister and tends to grow in drier sites. True to its nature our clematis sent its sparse stems with its twining leaves clambering up the face of the cliff to mingle its pendulous lavender blooms with the pink flowers of the daphne above. It was a lovely combination but, unfortunately, after several years a family of mice nested one winter in the deep bed of leaves that had blown into the cleft from which it sprang and devoured it roots and all. And because we had every year with spendthrift generosity sent all its fluffy seed heads into the seed exchanges, we could not replace it with another. Some day perhaps we will find listed in one of the exchanges seed from the progeny of those we scattered around the world. Such is frequently the case with plants or seeds you give away—like bread crusts cast upon the waters, they return to you multiplied a hundredfold.

The far corner of the ledge which underlies the foot of the peninsula slopes downward and angles out into Deming Brook. During periods of high water the stream pours over the end of this jutting point to sweep away any leaf mold which might otherwise accumulate on its surface. This expanse of bare rock is deeply cleft in a few places, and we filled these crevices with soil so as to be able to plant in them mats of *Sedum spurium* and of the double form of the white-flowered rock cress *(Arabis albida flore-pleno)*. The sedum has since spread out in a thick carpet over the higher reaches of the ledge, but the arabis was swept away

during the flood of 1955 and has since been replaced by a dwarf
flowering quince *(Chaenomeles japonica alpina)* which grows only
a foot tall. Its twiggy branches and deep, searching roots have so
far withstood all flooding, and the shrub has now spread the
whole length of the eight-foot-long fissure, its glossy, somewhat
leathery leaves and orange-scarlet flowers stunning against the
rough gray stone. In fall it is decorated with golden quinces.

In addition to these shrubs and dwarf trees already mentioned,
we scattered over the promontory about eight alpenrosen *(Rhododendron hirsutum),* a small, bushy member of the ericaceous family
which, unlike most of its relatives, loves lime. These have done
well for us, though they do not unfurl their pink flowers in late
June unless they have had a fairly permanent snow cover the
previous winter. Accustomed as they are to the deep insulating
snows of the high-alpine regions of Europe, they have apparently
found it unnecessary for their flower buds to develop an ability
to withstand bitter temperatures such as those they must undergo
during our occasional snowless winter seasons.

To cover the ground between the shrubs and trees we used
divisions of Linc's selected forms and hybrids of ground phlox
and other lime-tolerant rock garden plants brought over from the
gardens and nursery beds in Norfolk. We also introduced a
number of native ferns and wildflowers.

There were, strangely enough, very few wildflowers in our
own woods across the stream from the house, probably because
the root systems of the big old trees in this mature forest, which
consisted mainly of sugar maples, pines, and hemlocks, absorbed
most of the nutriments and moisture in the soil, and the intertwined canopy of their leaves provided a shade so dense that even
many woodland natives could not thrive. Linc, however, owns
ten acres of second-growth woodland on a rocky east-facing
slope in South Norfolk. This is a treasury of wildflowers, and we

spent many a warm spring weekend on this hillside with the children, digging material out of the pockets of rich duffy soil between the rocks and transporting these back to Millstream to plant in what we were already calling the Shady Rock Garden.

Clumps of the two hepatica species, *Hepatica triloba* and *H. acutiloba,* were among these. We gently sifted the leaf mold between our fingers to find the plump clusters of pointed white grains from which sprang the frail, ferny leaves of Dutchman's breeches *(Dicentra cucullaria)* and the yellow grainlike tubers of squirrel corn *(Dicentra canadensis),* whose resemblance to yellow niblets of corn give the plant its name.

I discovered that I had to dig very deep and very carefully in order to retrieve the brown beanlike corm at the base of the long, slender, white underground stems of the two spring beauties, *Claytonia virginica* and *C. caroliniana;* stems so threadlike and fragile that they parted at the slightest touch. I couldn't help wondering how it was possible for such tender things to thrust their way up through eight to ten inches of rocky loam so as to raise into the light the twinned leaves and curled raceme of pink-veined blossoms.

We garnered mats of the beautiful white foamflower *(Tiarella cordifolia)* whose clusters of semievergreen, grapelike leaves on long, trailing stolons form a wonderful ground cover. Though it raises very few of its fluffy white spikes in its usual woodland sites, we found it bloomed profusely once transplanted into the garden in light shade. We also collected bishop's cap *(Mitella diphylla),* also known as miterwort or coolwort, probably by mistake as its leaves so closely resemble those of foamflower that I for one have difficulty telling them apart unless they are in bloom. But the slender blossoming spike that springs from the leafy mat of bishop's cap is a very different thing from that of foamflower, for the flowers are so minute and the greeny-white petals so finely cut as to make them almost invisible to the naked eye. Examined through a hand lens, however, these insignificant blossoms become things of exquisite beauty, as intricately cut and laced as a snowflake.

Among our finds were the eastern columbine *(Aquilegia canadensis)* with its scarlet-and-yellow blossoms beloved by hummingbirds, and the red-flowered *Trillium erectum,* sometimes called stinking benjamin because of the rotten-meat odor of its brownish red flowers. However, this smell, which attracts the flies and other carrion-loving insects that pollinate this flower, is not really obvious to the human nose except at very close quarters, and the plant is so handsome that it would be a shame to leave it out of a woodland garden for this reason. We also collected both species of the native baneberry, *Actaea rubra* and *Actaea pachypoda,* whose growth habit and showy heads of small white flowers are so similar. It is the fruit on these two plants which is so different and gives them their colloquial names. White baneberry *(A. pachypoda)* is known locally as doll's eyes because of the white berries, each with a conspicuous black dot at its apex; these ripen in September, two months after the shining, holly-red fruit of the red baneberry have been eaten or have dropped to the ground.

Despite the many plants we brought home, the effect was very sparse that first spring and summer, as the area we wished to cover was quite extensive. We believed, however, that it was better to prepare the entire area for planting than to leave part of it in weeds which would inevitably encroach on the cleared ground by stolon and seed. As it was I was kept busy scrabbling the soil around the plants with my wire claw to eliminate the weed seedlings that sprang in droves from the freshly turned soil. The real bane of our existence was the scouring rush, which sprouted persistently for three or four years from deep-set, wiry roots. Every day I would spend an hour or two on the knoll going over a small section of ground, thoroughly scratching up the soil and pulling off the tough tips of the scouring rush as soon as these protruded through the earth. This meticulous and time-consuming weeding program was carried out for the next year or two, though after the first year I hand-pulled all the weeds rather than using the claw, as this would have also destroyed the self-sown seedlings of the plants we were encouraging. It really paid off. By the end of two summers the ground was almost entirely weedless, and after four years even the scouring rush had given up and the area was so thickly cloaked with desirable plants that there was very little room for unwanted seedlings.

The hollow between the peninsula and the high retaining wall was almost completely taken up by the yews and the prickly masses of barberry. The latter we dug up and burned, the former we hacked back to stubs. We planned to use the flat area at the foot of the high retaining wall for those plants, such as primroses, that preferred moist, rich soil, and every day, between my hours of weeding on the peninsula and the household chores required to keep a family of six in food and clean clothes, I hacked at the jungle of weeds and cleared their roots from a few more feet of soil.

In addition to clearing this gully a sunnier location was necessary to accommodate some of the plants. Linc decided these could best be housed along the top of the wall above the tail-of-the-race, so with Aunt Do's blessing we dug out the row of privet and the matted tubers of the daylilies that preempted this spot. We had to replenish the soil, which disappeared along with the roots of the shrubs and plants we were removing. To fill this trough behind the top of the wall we cannibalized the vegetable garden on the other side of the road, wheeling barrow after barrow of soil up the hill until we had made a four-foot-wide bed that ran the full length of the top of the wall.

Right against the upper stones, where they could drape themselves over the rocks, we placed more of Linc's *Phlox subulata.* Behind these we replanted divisions of those few border perennials we had rescued out of Aunt Do's original planting and a few shrubs to give body and height to the border. Among these were several rooted layers of the apothecary's rose *(Rosa gallica),* which Linc had originally received years before as a gift from his philosophy professor at Williams College.

This lovely, single, deep red rose has been in cultivation since prehistory. It was originally brought to Europe from Asia Minor and Crete, where it was portrayed among the tangle of birds and flowers painted in fresco on house walls in Knossos. Pliny knew *Rosa gallica* as the red rose of miletus, and its deliciously fragrant petals were used for making perfume and as a royal carpet before the feet of honored guests. The Romans made it into garlands and delicate desserts and used the flowers to flavor wine in the belief that this permitted the imbiber to drink more before becoming drunk. The sugared petals have been used as a sweet, and even today this rose is sought as a major ingredient of potpourri, as its petals retain their scent and lovely color even when dried. When they bloom, the house and garden are filled with their delicate perfume. The plant is disease- and insect resistant—ours are never sprayed, and, though it is not ever-blooming, it has a long season. The only fault I can find with this rose is the difficulty of keeping it within bounds, for though its stiff, ascending branches seldom grow over three feet and never, as far as I know, root down, it spreads, though not rapidly, by very deep, underground root stolons.

In addition to this historic rose we put in several plants of *Rhododendron obtusum* which Linc hoped might be more tolerant of lime than most species. Though these survived in this bed for a number of years and even produced a few of their rosy lavender flowers every spring, they never thrived; perhaps it was the lime in the soil, or perhaps the site was too dry. In any case after about eight years we moved them up into the woods, where they have done much better.

More border perennials faced down these shrubs, and where the bed came in contact with the grass we planted lower things such as *Veronica latifolia* 'Crater Lake Blue', whose foot-high spikes are of that lake's extraordinary shade of glowing blue; chives *(Allium schoenoprasum)* for salads and for the sake of their round heads of pale purple flowers; catmint *(Nepeta × faasseni),* more commonly available as *N. mussinii,* with soft gray leaves and racemes of blue-violet blossoms. We also planted lavender *(Lavandula spica),* both the regular pale lavender-blue form and the 'Hidcote' variety with its deeper blue-purple flowers. Originally I intended to harvest the spines of bloom to put in among the sheets in the linen closet, but when the moment came I could not bear to cut them. Near these we planted clumps of spicy scented clove pinks *(Dianthus plumarius)* in all shades of white, rose, and pink, and more swatches of creeping phlox. It was something of a mishmash, but at least the bed housed those plants for which we had no other home, and we felt it was an improvement over the straggly privet in that it needed no clipping.

We also eliminated the privet hedge against the front of the house, replacing it with myrtle *(Vinca minor).* Though myrtle is usually considered a shade-loving plant, and though it will do well in deep shade—unlike pachysandra, that other ubiquitous ground cover, which does require shade—the vinca soon thickened into a glossy mat of green in that sunny site against the south side of the house. Right against the wall of the house we underplanted the myrtle with daffodils and iris. These eventually had to be removed to other quarters, as they did poorly in the smother of evergreen leaves and the limply fading daffodil foliage looked unsightly during much of the season.

At the corners of the main part of the house were placed two Christmasberries *(Photinia villosa)*. For years these throve and grew, eventually becoming almost treelike, but after fifteen years or so the one at the corner nearest the kitchen wing succumbed to fire blight and had to be cut down. The other is still in place. It is a delight all year. In spring its leafy branches are covered with clusters of little, white, single, roselike blossoms, which by fall have become shining red berries. The leaves turn orange and deep yellow in late autumn, and in winter the strong gray branches with their clusters of scarlet fruit make an attractive pattern against the wall of the house. The berries, however, are much favored by birds, and usually by Christmas they have been gobbled down by flocks of evening grosbeaks and cedar waxwings.

I I

All this clearing, planting, expanding, and redoing sounds rather like the labors of Sisyphus when written down, but for us it is not. A major portion of our great joy in gardening is the creation of our surrounding world, though admittedly we cannot pretend to control it except to a very minor extent. An artist friend for whom we were building a rock garden stated the problem very well. After watching us carefully place each rock and plant, he asked if it did not upset us to know that our meticulously executed plan would inevitably change. "It would certainly bother me if I thought, when I make a picture, that the lines would go wandering off on their own and the colors move about."

This, of course, is one of the frustrations of landscaping. Plants grow and change shape no matter how carefully trimmed and pruned; some inevitably die, others burgeon and smother their less aggressive neighbors. If you plant only with the present effect in mind you may soon find your landscape (and yourself) entangled in a jungle of greenery which only a major forestry operation will bring into control. Planning for future growth helps prevent such a contingency to some extent, but not completely, and occasionally it is necessary, even desirable, to plant closely with the intent of eventually removing every other one. It is when this latter chore is neglected that trouble ensues.

On the other hand, this very insistence on growth and proliferation which can so subtly and, at times drastically, change the effect originally intended has its great compensations. Without

Aquilegia scopulorum   In the Rocky Mountains it varies in height from six to ten inches.

it the prospect would be static, and one of the true joys of a garden is its dynamic dimension. Its quality varies with every hour. Each day the patterns and colors change. Each month it displays a new mutation, and as the years pass a well-cared-for landscape acquires a mature beauty which a newly made garden, no matter how carefully laid out, can never have.

Some of this rich loveliness is due to the plantings themselves: the subtle blending of color and texture as trees and shrubs fit their shapes to each other and the contours of the land and house and the flowering plants spread among their neighbors and self-sow into delightful combinations more appropriate to their character than man can devise. Some is the very patina of age: the creviced bark of old trees, the moss and lichens which pattern their trunks and soften the color and contour of rock and brick. But some is deliberately created by the owner of the garden by careful additions and removals, by pruning, weeding, and roguing. No other art, to such an extent, encourages, indeed demands, the active participation of the owner for its beauty. A painting may be hung well or badly, it may be kept from fading or becoming dimmed by dust and grime, but it will not turn into a different picture if left untouched, and to tamper with it is to destroy it. Quite the opposite is true of a garden. No matter how talented the landscape architect who conceived the original design, and no matter how faithfully it is carried out, constant tampering is necessary if it is to develop in beauty; though, of course, it may also be ruined by unsuitable modifications.

Every true gardener is forever making changes in his garden, some as simple as the addition of a plant or two or the trimming off of a single branch, some as major as the building of a whole new planting area or the complete revamping of a part of the established garden. This urge to improve and renew is perhaps one of the reasons for the frequent longevity of gardeners. Not only does the activity involved get them out into the fresh air and give them exercise to a greater or lesser degree depending on their ambition and strength—an essential for good health according to doctors, who now recommend mild but frequent exercise even for heart patients—but it creates a tremendous will to live. Any gardener, no matter how ailing, will fight off death like a veritable Horatius if only to see how a new planting of primroses will look when it blooms or whether the bulbs scattered so artfully under the old apple tree will give the effect intended. We have had gardening friends who were still sowing tree seeds at the age of eighty, though this is, perhaps, expecting too much of even the most persistent human frame. It is quite possible, however, that Methuselah yearly planted olive pits.

It is not essential, though, to reach the age of a Methuselah to have a lovely garden, particularly if you are fortunate enough to have a few well-placed, reasonably mature trees on your property. It is unfortunate that most real-estate developers and contractors have a passion for cutting down all the trees on the land they plan to use and frequently add to the destruction by bulldozing it into a featureless plain. Even the undistinguished little houses usually put up in such developments look quite presentable if shaded by a good-sized tree or two. Developers and contractors will reason that their behavior is practical and money-saving in that it simplifies building, but from a long-range point of view it seems foolishly extravagant to destroy the natural enhancements of a property in order to save dollars, some of which will then have to be spent to replace the sacrificed trees with spindly saplings of some cheap and frequently unsuitable species. It is a good idea, therefore, if you have any say in the matter, to take a long look at the trees on the property where you plan to build your house and then be very firm with the contractor about which ones you want kept unharmed. But even if you are the owner of treeless acreage, you need not despair; though you may never live to see that whip of a sapling grow into a hoary giant, it is astonishing how quickly it will become a very respectable feature in your landscape. But while you are about it, or rather, before you dig the hole or order the tree or trees, consider carefully their placement in relation to the house and surrounding land.

Too often a householder will plant evergreens against the house without considering the size and shape they will eventually attain. I lived for several years in a rented house so encased in a foundation planting of large and rather straggly arborvitae that hardly a breath of breeze could penetrate through the windows, and we groped about at midday in an impenetrable gloom. Eventually we persuaded our landlord to let us remove the trees and replace them with a border of low shrubs and herbaceous plants. It was astonishing, even to us, what an improvement it made both inside and out.

Lack of trees is not one of our problems here at Millstream; quite the contrary—we suffer rather from an overabundance. In the course of the landscaping work which we started as a summer vocation even before Linc retired from teaching in 1962, and which after that became our main source of livelihood, we were frequently asked to advise where and what to plant in the way of trees. Though this, of course, is largely a matter of personal taste and what is suitable to a particular house site or property, a few general suggestions may be helpful in making the final decision.

Deciduous trees to the south and west of a house will help keep it cool in summer by shading the roof and walls from the hottest sun and moderating the temperature of the air coming through the windows on that side of the house, yet the leafless branches will let the sun through to warm and cheer the rooms in winter;

shade over or to the west and south of a terrace will make it a pleasanter spot for hot-weather relaxation. Evergreen trees will not only provide a windbreak against prevailing winds of winter and blot out unwanted views, but, when thickly planted, will help deaden neighboring noise. They are better kept at some distance from the house, however, unless you like perpetual shade.

Although commonly used for this purpose, fir or spruce are not really suitable as lawn trees. Their stiff symmetry is unflattering to most houses and hard to blend into the average landscape, though they are often magnificent when used in a large mixed evergreen planting along the border of a property large enough to allow for a few lower deciduous trees in front of the evergreens to soften their somber green and unyielding posture. We have such a planting started along the edge of Under Mountain Road. As yet the trees are small, but they are beginning to shoot up and will eventually give us greater privacy from passing cars. Among these evergreens are one or two Colorado blue spruce *(Picea pungens),* a tree that has been planted to such triteness in suburban yards that it is hard to visualize it as other than a single specimen, a cone of blue-gray ensconced upon the lawn; yet rising among the varied greens of other spruces, fir, hemlock, and pine, its glaucous foliage no longer appears obtrusively artificial, and its noble proportions look at home.

Unfortunately, in present times, hemlocks can be used as a screen along the roadside only where the ground rises steeply up from the road; they are most susceptible to road salt, and many of the great Canada hemlocks *(Tsuga canadensis)* that graced our New England highways have been killed by the briny runoff and salt spray thrown up by trucks and automobiles speeding by. We hope the stone retaining wall that raises our hemlock hedge above road level is high enough to lift the branches and roots out of harm's way.

Spruce and fir seem more able to withstand salt, but, to me at least, the Norway spruce *(Picea abies),* so favored as a lawn tree throughout New England fifty or sixty years ago, is funereal and forbidding, and the black-green pendent branchlets have connotations of widow's weeds, of the infernal pits of Hades hung with stygian stalactites, and of the haunted forests that surrounded Draculean castles in the old horror films, where wisps of stealthy mist concealed the vampires moaning down the dark rides and werewolves hunting in slavering, silent packs.

Although deciduous trees, which let through the winter sun, are perhaps preferable near the house, pines, either singly or in groups, are not as somber as some of the other evergreens and, as they age, the horizontal structure of their branching is more becoming to most architecture. Their falling needles, however, are hard on a lawn. There are many sorts to choose from depending on site and climate, and the shape and texture desired. Some are tall and stately, others tend to twist into contorted angles reminiscent of Japanese prints. I am particularly fond of Scots pine *(Pinus sylvestris)* with its orange bark and short tufts of blue-green needles, but many of our native pines are most attractive.

The six white pines *(Pinus strobus)* planted to the southeast of our house, are now thirty-five to forty feet tall. They shade the graveled parking area and the plantings of ferns and wildflowers beneath them to create a cool, shady grove near the house and, in addition, provide a shelter belt against the noise and, at night, the glare of headlights coming down the road; but they are sufficiently distant from the house so that their branches will never cast a smothering shade upon our windows.

Be cautious about planting some of the more commonly used deciduous yard trees. The maple tribe, though excellent for shade, have their drawbacks. They are all greedy and send their surface-feeding roots to amazing distances in all directions, sucking up both food and moisture to the despair of growth in their vicinity. Very few plants, including lawn grasses, grow well under a maple.

This fact has been the cause of considerable altercation in our family. Sugar maple *(Acer saccharum)* is one of our most common native trees and constitutes a large proportion of the trees on our property. The great spreading ancients near the house have created endless controversy: Linc wants them down and states firmly that they will eventually reduce the garden to a maple desert; I have agreed to the removal of many of them but still refuse to part with them all, partly because of their particularly brilliant fall coloring and partly because of the shade they give us from the western sun. I must admit, however, that every tree removal to date has been an improvement.

Norway maple *(Acer platanoides)* has very little to recommend it except that it will grow practically anywhere and much farther south than will sugar maple, which does not do particularly well below New England except in the mountains. If anything, Norway maple is even greedier than sugar maple, and though its late-turning leaves become sunlight yellow in fall, it never produces the sumptuous autumn display typical of its American relatives. Swamp or red maple *(Acer rubrum),* though equally hungry, turns a gorgeous red in the fall and is not fussy as to climate or soil, for despite its name it does not insist on having its feet in a swamp. The silver maple *(Acer saccharinum)* has a graceful habit of growth not unlike that of the American elm and daintily cut, silvery leaves. These, however, never do more than turn a wan "greenery-yaller" in autumn, and the tree has the bad habit of shedding its brittle twigs and branches like a moulty hen.

The beeches *(Fagus grandifolia* and *F. sylvatica)* are also gluttonous, beautiful as they are, and should be planted with caution, though the sinewy, silver-gray trunks are handsome at all times of year, and the small, shining, pointed leaves create a wonderful canopy of shade. The beech is not common on our property, for they seem to prefer the north slopes of the mountain, but we have one or two young saplings up in the woods which we have allowed to stand. These are still sufficiently nubile to retain their dry foliage throughout the winter, and the little trees are an entrancing sight when the curled, pale gold leaves dance a twinkling entrechat in the winter wind. As they become more mature they will no longer produce this winter ballet, as beeches drop their leaves in fall once they are beyond adolescence.

The deep-searching roots of the oaks *(Quercus)* do not rob the surface soil of food and moisture, so it is possible to plant right up to the base of these handsome trees. The leaves of many turn beautiful muted shades of russet and old gold in autumn, and the foliage of a few species glows scarlet and crimson. Unfortunately they are all slow growing and create a cleanup problem when the acorns fall. We wish we had more oaks. There are none near the house, but we do treasure a few up in the woods garden where they make a perfect overstory for the azaleas and rhododendrons at their feet, providing a warm, crisp blanket that never sogs and which, as it decays, creates the acid leaf mold so necessary to the health and happiness of ericaceous plants.

I long for a horse chestnut *(Aesculus hippocastanum)* in the woods, though as a lawn tree it has grave disadvantages. Grass simply gives up beneath a horse chestnut, which may be just as well because the glossy brown nuts are hard indeed on a lawn mower. It is, however, a truly handsome tree, though difficult to acquire at most nurseries except as a very young tree, as its taproot has ambitions to reach China. Its dense dark head of fan-shaped, seven-fingered leaves, when lit with innumerable white candles of blossom in early summer, is a joy. There is also a hybrid form usually listed as *A. carnea,* with deep flesh-pink flowers, which is a cross between *A. hippocastanum* and *A. pavia.* This latter species is a small, shrubby tree with deep red flowers native to the southeastern United States and is a plant I would also be happy to have along with those other of our native shrubby American buckeyes, *A. octandra* and *A. discolor,* though all of these except the sweet buckeye *(A. octandra)* are southern and might not be winter-hardy in our area. Still it would be worth trying them here, as we have found that many trees and shrubs are hardier than might be supposed and grow perfectly satisfactorily in a more northern habitat than is their wont once they become established—as witness our success with that other southern buckeye, *Aesculus parviflora.*

How tragic it is that we have lost the American chestnut *(Castanea dentata).* It was, from all reports, one of our most magnificent trees, valued not only for its sweet nut but as a shade and lumber tree, wide spreading when grown in the open, tall and straight when forest grown, its wood straight grained and rot resistant. Many of the posts and rails still fencing our fields, the cabin in the woods, and the treads of our front stairway are made of chestnut, and until 1967 the gigantic trunk of an ancient chestnut stood in our woods garden, a great gray monolith. The branches and limbs had long since been cut off, and the trunk was almost entirely hollow, yet it stood firm. A pair of wood duck used it as their nesting tree. We had hoped it might stand for our lifetime knee deep in the rhododendron thicket we planted at its feet, its truncated limbs among the soft needles of the pines that had sprung up around it. It seemed so permanent, so indestructible, that it was with heart-wrenching unbelief that we noticed one afternoon in late winter the slight backward cant of its huge bole. It had lived many years and had stood, monumental in death, for many more; it was, as far as we knew, the last great chestnut still standing on all the mountain. Each week the massive trunk tilted a little more as the heavy roots lost their hold upon its base, but other than this slow, irreversible declination it showed no sign of its incipient downfall.

As soon as the ground thawed that spring we dug up and moved a swathe of rhododendrons from the path of its descent, glancing apprehensively as we did so at the enormous bole poised over our heads, though, before starting our labors, Linc had pushed against it with all his weight, and it had stood firm. Yet that night it fell. We heard the crash and went up next morning to see it lying hugely, split from end to end, in the slot we had prepared for it among the rhododendrons. There it will remain until it sinks into the soil, dissolved by decay.

Root sprouts from long-gone chestnuts still spring up in our woods and frequently reach burring size—thirty feet or more in height and ten or more inches in diameter. One year we had several of these trees covered with long pendent tassels of fluffy white flowers alive with pollinating insects, and that year we gathered several bushels of the nuts and had them for our Thanksgiving and Christmas dinners. But the blight had struck them, and the bark split and suppurated in the telltale sign of doom. Arborists are still working in an effort to produce a blight-resistant American chestnut and have hybridized it with the smaller, somewhat shrubby Chinese chestnut *(Castanea mollissima),* which is immune to the fungus, but though eventually this hybrid may become commonly available, it will not replace our native tree.

III

————

A sycamore dominates the whole lower garden. Its great double trunk rises out of the center of this area, and its limbs overstretch it. It was, perhaps, partly because of this magnificent tree that our first efforts were expended on that part of our land that is sheltered by its branches; it demanded a setting more suitable than brush and weeds. However, this section of the garden, the first we prepared and planted, has suffered many tribulations and has undergone more changes and renovations than any other.

After cutting down the maples on the peninsula and clearing it and the tail-of-the-race of its overburden of brush and weeds, trimming up the pines and whacking back Aunt Do's yews, we laid out the paths that circled the crest of the promontory and wove their way through the gully and Pine Grove into the D-Garden. These chores, plus our first plantings on the peninsula, took most of our spare time that first winter, spring, and summer. The next spring we moved some of Linc's rhododendrons and azaleas over from Norfolk. Most of them were planted across the brook in areas we had cleared of trees and brush the previous winter, our second at Millstream, but some were placed under the trees in the Pine Grove along with many ferns and wildflowers.

The long, wide bed at the foot of the high retaining wall that enclosed the tail-of-the-race had been almost completely taken up by the sprawling yews and some barberry. After digging up the barberry without a qualm and cutting back the yews, we found the earth was deep and rich with the decay of generations of leaves which had piled in under these shrubs. It was also very

Bruckenthalia spiculifolia   One of the most beautiful heathers and one of the
easiest to grow.

moist, almost mucky, because of seepage from the main brook. Linc was certain this was a perfect site for Japanese primroses *(Primula japonica),* and he sowed several flats full in anticipation of its clearing. Unfortunately, we discovered, once we had uprooted the shrubs which had grown against it, that the wall itself was most unsightly. Though apparently still firm, it bulged and sagged in a most alarming manner and obviously would not make an attractive background for the primroses. We therefore brought over from Norfolk a bunch of rooted stems of Baltic ivy *(Hedera helix baltica)* and planted these at the foot of the wall, hoping they would eventually mask, with a curtain of green, the skewed and crumbling stones. And in time they did just that, though it took almost five years for the ivy to conceal the wall to its very top.

The foundation of the mill was in much better condition, in fact the stonework was quite handsome, so we decided we would not cloak it with ivy. Instead we planted against its base a rooted layer of climbing hydrangea *(Hydrangea petiolaris).* In time it too clambered up the eight-foot wall, but never did the tracery of its heavy stems completely conceal the stones, as the large decidu-ous leaves and lacy white blossoms appeared mostly on the tips of short branches that sprang out of the twisting trunks that mounted the wall. These short protruding branchlets could easily be trimmed off where they became too obtrusive, but the top of the vine was left unpruned until, in about ten years, it attained the top of the foundation and rose above it to form a shrubby parapet about two feet high around its upper edge.

In the moist soil which we had cleared of brush we planted dozens and dozens and dozens of Linc's seedling Japanese prim-roses. For the first two or three seasons these had to be carefully weeded, as all kinds of noxious weeds sprang from the seeds that had lain dormant for years beneath the yews, but the primroses grew apace in the rich soil and self-sowed profusely to become a solid mass of lettuces which shaded out any remaining weed seedlings. In June these were a glory as the flowering stems rose higher and higher above the rosettes of leaves bearing whorl and whorl of white, pink, and crimson blossoms. They self-sowed everywhere the soil was moist and rich enough to suit them, their magnificent candelabras of bloom sometimes attaining a height of three feet.

Over the years we added to this planting of primroses species and hybrids of astilbe for the sake of their feathery leaves and late-summer bloom. Among these were *Astilbe chinensis,* whose stiff six- to twelve-inch-long spikes of bloom are a strange, luminous blue-pink; *Astilbe koreana,* with gracefully bending airy panicles of creamy flowers rising two feet above the mound of ferny leaves, and the innumerable hybrids known as *Astilbe* × *arendsii,* whose dense upright plumes may attain three feet and range in color from deepest crimson to carmine, from rose to pearly white.

Under the yews around the rotting stump of the ash we discovered a bed of lily-of-the-valley *(Convallaria majalis)* and blue bugle *(Ajuga reptans)* which had somehow persisted beneath the smothering shade of the yew. Though the plants were thinly scattered because of the growing conditions which they had endured, we knew they would soon thicken up now that they received light and air. We did not, however, want this area to become a solid mat of lily-of-the-valley and ajuga, so we introduced among them Canadian windflower *(Anemone canadensis),* which likes moist soil and, we were fairly certain, could compete. In this we were quite correct. The thin, black, threadlike roots of the anemone not only spread gleefully among the lily-of-the-valley and bugle but eventually invaded the dense bed of pachysandra that Aunt Do had planted at the foot of the euonymus that cloaked the corner of the wall where the stairway ascended to the terrace. In a matter of only a few years this end of the long bed under the wall danced with white windflowers every June. Canadian windflower, lovely as it is, spreads with great rapidity where it finds itself happy, and it would have moved in among the primroses without a qualm if we had not pulled up all the invasive forerunners as they appeared beyond the boundary of their allotted space. This is best done in midsummer when the rootstocks, which resemble knots of black thread, are mature and firmly attached to the base of the leaf stalks, but have not yet sent out a new set of underground stolons. It is, we found, quite possible in one season to completely eradicate this windflower from an area where it is not wanted by pulling up every shallow-rooted sprig. This might not work in heavy, stiff soil, but in our light soil each cluster of leaves comes up easily, roots and all.

A very narrow path threaded its way between this bed and the runnel, leading from the foot of the steps descending from the mill foundation to the handkerchief of lawn under the sycamore. The ditch side of this path was buttressed with heavy stones between which there was very little soil, but despite this lack of growing medium, ferns and self-sown seedlings of primroses, columbine, and miterwort found a foothold in the crannies and in only a few years fringed the edge of the ditch with leaves and flowers.

As the runnel approached the buttonwood, it veered off to skirt the foot of the promontory, leaving a wider space alongside the path. Here a group of rather scraggly upright yews shaded the runnel with their heavy boughs but, after very little deliberation, we cut these down and in their stead planted clumps of stately interrupted fern *(Osmunda claytonia)* and false hellebore *(Veratrum viride),* which produces its massive cluster of yellow-green starry flowers at the apex of the stout stem only every five to ten years. We planted it not for its rare blossoming, however, but for the sake of its handsome pyramid of large, heavily ribbed leaves. Among these we planted the white rhizomes of great Solomon's seal *(Polygonatum canaliculatum),* whose leafy, arching stems strung with dangling bells of pale greenish yellow grow four to five feet high.

At the feet of these tall plants we placed a few wide-leaved plantain lilies *(Hosta)* and mats of lily-turf *(Liriope spicata),* whose short spikes of white flowers appear in late summer among the dense rugs of narrow, straplike, dark, evergreen leaves. The running rhizomes of the large-flowered bellwort *(Uvularia grandiflora),* which in May carries two-inch-long bells at the tips of its leafy stems, were tucked in near the front edge of the bed, and on the very brink of the ditch, at the corner where the plank bridge gave access across to the lower end of the peninsula, we planted a clump of Japanese bugbane *(Cimicifuga simplex).* This is one of the smaller bugbanes and the last to bloom; its graceful three-foot wands of white blossoms do not appear above the finely cut foliage until October. The slender feather fronds of marsh fern *(Thelypteris palustris)* and the delicate whorls of maidenhair fern *(Adiantum pedatum)* completed this planting, which intentionally stressed leaf pattern rather than colorful bloom.

Across the short side path that led from the little lawn to the edge of the ditch, the soil directly under the buttonwood was composed mainly of crumbled bark fragments and was stiff with roots. We were uncertain what would grow in such a site, but of the various plants we tried a number survived. These we allowed to spread and self-sow to take the place of others which succumbed after a year or two to the nearly impossible growing conditions. Surprisingly winter aconite *(Eranthis hyemalis)* not only survived in this parlous spot but self-sowed to dot the bare, brown earth with its pale yellow coins in earliest spring. Blood-

leaves to find the curious red-brown flowers tipped on their sides like little earthenware jugs waiting for ants and other creeping insects to visit them.

Behind these ground-hugging plants we placed some taller ferns and flowers: wild geranium *(Geranium maculatum)* and among them *Phlox divaricata* so its pale blue-lavender blossoms could mingle with the rose-pink flowers of the geranium in May; the deep maroon *Trillium erectum* and, to add a spice of vivid scarlet and yellow, the native columbine *(Aquilegia canadensis)*. Here too were planted twisted stalk *(Streptopus amplexifolius)*, the zigzag pattern of its stems and leaves hung with pale yellow chimes, and Solomon's seal *(Polygonatum biflorum)* for its graceful laddered stalks and small pendent bells. Among these we placed a few of those other plants named for King Solomon: the starry Solomon's seal *(Smilacina stellata)* which carries on the tips of its leafy stems little constellations of white stars, and Solomon's plume *(Smilacina racemosa),* well named for its feathery show of spring bloom but even more exciting when these turn to clusters of red berries in autumn.

In addition to these native wildlings we planted wide swatches of the primroses Linc had brought over from Norfolk: the wild cowslip of Europe *(Primula veris),* with its multiflowered heads of small yellow blossoms each half hidden by the baggy green calyx, which upon occasion becomes petal-like. These aberrant forms that appear to have flowers growing inside their flowers have been given the name hose-in-hose by our English cousins. Nearer the path we planted the true primrose of English hedge-rows, *Primula vulgaris,* whose wide open blossoms of white, yellow, and soft rose rise one on each stem, in a tight tussy-mussy from the surrounding ruff of lettuce-green leaves, and the beloved polyanthus primrose, a hybrid of such ancient provenance that its lineage is uncertain. These primroses also included several patches of *P. juliani* hybrids, with clusters of dark crimson blossoms each centered by a yellow eye ring. To be truly international, we also planted the beautiful Japanese woodlander, *Primula sieboldii,* which has soft, green, crinkled leaves and snowflake blossoms in shades from deep pink to purest white. This Oriental primrose is much prized in its homeland, where hundreds of forms with more or less laced petals have been propagated and named. It spreads slowly in duffy soil by means of short underground stolons and will, in time, make a sizable swathe. It seems less fussy in our hot, dry summer weather than some of the other woodland primroses, which are frequently attacked by red spider mite. This pest turns their leaves to shriveled brown husks. *P. sieboldii* escapes this scourge by retiring underground in droughty weather and aestivating as a clump of small resting buds. This need not mean it leaves in its place an unsightly patch of bare ground, however, as *P. sieboldii* grows quite happily among other plants which will take over its area in the summer when the primrose has finished flowering and its leaves have vanished. It is wise, however, to mark the spot where it grows to prevent disturbing it when weeding.

Across the path from this planting, where the ground slopes up to the top of the retaining wall that surrounds the parking area, was a row of yews, but as these only extended partway down the path, there was room at the lower end of the bed near the Pine Grove for other plants. Linc thought it might be possible to maintain a low pH in this bed, as the back side was supported about three feet above the parking area by the wall, thus raising it above ground level. With this in mind he dug into the soil quantities of acid pine duff and rotted sawdust from the site of the old Miles sawmill across the brook. At its far end he sank a few carefully placed rocks to support the soil where the embankment terminated abruptly and where the supporting wall turned at right angles around the lower end of the parking area. Here the ground outside the wall sloped rapidly down toward the D-Garden next to the road, which is three feet or so below the leveled parking area.

On the lower end of this carefully prepared bed, Linc planted a small royal azalea *(Rhododendron schlippenbachii)*. Nearer the yews were placed several groups of the mayflower rhododendron *(R. racemosum)*. Linc had grown these delightful shrubs from seed collected off the original plant found in western China by George Forrest, the intrepid English collector who died in 1932 during the course of his seventh journey into the Chinese hinterland.

Rhododendron racemosum varies considerably in stature, form, and depth of flower color, and the species as a whole is not considered hardy in really cold climates. Mr. Forrest's introduction, known under the collection number 'Forrest 19404', is considerably hardier than some, lower growing and more compact, with flowers of a particularly delectable shade of clear pink. Of course all these desirable characteristics are duplicated precisely only in plants which have been vegetatively propagated from cuttings or layers of the original clone, and Linc's plants, being seedlings, were somewhat variable; but on the whole they displayed most of the characteristics of the clone. Some had proved to be more winter-hardy than others, and the rigorous winters in Norfolk, where they had been raised, had rogued these out of the batch of seedlings so only the hardiest remained. These were all delightful plants, never more than three feet tall, dense with typical small, oval, dark green leaves, and covered in mid-May with a profusion of clustering flower heads, each blossom about an inch across and of a delicate shell pink, the petals tipped with a deeper shade of clear, luminous rose. Under these shrubs were planted drifts of white and pale yellow primroses, several swatches of *Iris cristata,* and some clumps of lavender-flowered *Phlox divaricata.*

In the midst of helping Linc create a garden in the tail-of-the-race and on the promontory, I had found a few days to clean up the D-Garden. I dug out the weeds that were rapidly choking all the desirable plants that remained and cleared the paths, resetting the brick edging where necessary before spreading them with fresh gravel. As I had to take up most of the plants and tear them apart to pry out the weed roots that had invaded them, I ended up with enough divisions to almost refill the beds. Linc evinced no interest in all this tidying up, but once it was accomplished he willingly helped dig plants from the nursery beds in Norfolk to fill the remaining gaps. Though it hardly measured up to my dream of a perennial garden rich with bloom from spring to fall, the D-Garden was now at least recognizable as an intentional planting.

In addition to all this refurbishing and planting, we did, of course, spend considerable time just maintaining those sections we had already planted both around the house, in the vegetable garden, and in the areas up in the woods that we had cleared to make nursery beds for Linc's rhododendrons, azaleas, and other acid-loving plants. This in itself is an endless, time-consuming chore which must be done if your precious garden is not to sink back into its former weedy disarray. Fortunately I truly love to weed.

It may appear from these last few pages as though we spent our lives in the garden, and it is true that all our spare moments were so spent, but during these first years at Millstream we had many other things beside gardening to occupy our time.

Once Linc had achieved his masters degree, he was too deeply involved in teaching, preparing for classes, correcting the daily accumulation of papers, and handling the numerous extracurricular activities which are the lot of every high school teacher to do more than spend an occasional Sunday in the garden from Labor Day until the end of school in late June. In addition, during his two-month "summer vacation," in order to keep the family exchequer in the black, he spent another six weeks teaching natural history to children, their parents, and teacher trainees at the Vassar Summer Institute in Poughkeepsie, New York. As this included both day and evening classes, it meant he could only be home Saturday night and Sunday.

I too had a job during our first eight years of marriage, working two days a week and many evenings as assistant editor of our local paper, *The Lakeville Journal.* For two summers while our son Sheldon was at camp and the three older children had live-in summer jobs, I took extensions to my vacations from my editorial duties in order to join Linc and assist him in his teaching at Vassar, where we were known as "the nature people." I also managed to get myself involved in various town activities, among them a term as chairman of the local school board.

The time not preempted by these various activities was fairly well taken up by keeping house for what had become a family of seven, as for a number of years we had a series of teen-age boarders. The children helped as much as they could with the housework and such outside chores as lawn mowing, but none of them had the slightest interest in gardening. This is understandable, as gardening is fundamentally solitary work, and young people in their teens are mostly social creatures. They were, however, delighted to join us on plant-hunting expeditions in the neighborhood, and from 1953 to 1955 we went on a number of these, for despite our already rather full schedule we could not resist becoming involved in the preparation of *A Field Guide to the Ferns,* one of the Peterson Field Guide series, which was being written by a friend and neighbor, Boughton Cobb. We joined him on many of his local field trips and went on a few brief ones of our own to Vermont, Long Island, New Jersey, and West Virginia to search for some of the ferns and their relatives that were not to be found in our part of the world. Many of these plants are very rare, very local in habitat, and difficult to find, but it was necessary to collect living specimens to serve as models if I was to draw their portraits. It was great fun and had all the excitement of a treasure hunt. Many delightful people helped us in our search, and we had any number of fascinating excursions and some minor adventures, but the necessary research in old botanical records and herbaria, the days and weeks spent combing the countryside, and the hours spent at the drawing board left us very little time for gardening. Our forays did benefit our garden, however, in a manner we had not anticipated; most of the plants we brought home were planted at Millstream after they had served as models, and here many of them still thrive, spreading by spore and stolon into a very representative collection of species and variants and, because of their unusual propinquity, a rather extraordinary population of hybrids.

Most of these ferns went under the pine trees below the parking area, which had become less of a menagerie and more a part of the garden since Woody had returned his turtles to their native haunts and taken up snake collecting instead. These reptiles did not require outdoor quarters—from which they would probably have escaped anyway—as they could be kept healthier if not happier in cages and terrariums in Woody's bedroom. Thus, as a consequence of Woody's shift in interest, we were able to clear the weedy growth from the Pine Grove and replace it with, not only our growing collection of ferns, but many other shade-loving plants. These included Virginia bluebell *(Mertensia virginica),* with its lovely sky-blue bells, both red and white baneberries, woodland primroses, English wood anemones *(Anemone nemorosa),* yellow lady's slipper *(Cypripedium calceolus* var. *pubescens),* bloodroot, and many species of violets. Though the rhododendrons that Linc had planted under these pines were not exactly thriving, they were alive and beginning to bloom, and the whole area was taking on a settled and most attractive appearance. The Pine Grove also completed the lower garden, which gave us considerable satisfaction. It did, however, present us with a new problem, for Linc is a compulsive seed sower, and no matter how busy he is with other activities he always manages to find time to sow flats and pots of seeds, acquired by his own seed collecting or from numerous seed exchanges both in this country and abroad. This means space is needed for the numerous progeny that result.

In addition, the plants we had already introduced into the garden had been busily self-sowing, sometimes into the most unexpected crannies, while others had waxed so fat by vegetative growth that they were threatening to overrun their neighbors and had to be divided into bits and pieces which, when replanted, started new colonies. In the course of events the inevitable happened; the day came when Linc had several hundred seedlings of species he had never previously grown and not a place in the garden to plant them. Throwing away the seedlings, ripping out our present plantings to make room for the newcomers, or expanding the garden to create new sites in which to plant them seemed the only alternative solutions to this quandary. The first we did not even consider; the second we considered but discarded, thus leaving us—as any true gardener might have guessed—with only one remaining option.

The decision as to where this new garden was to be was easily made. For a number of years Linc had longed for an open sunny area in which he could grow those plants which did poorly or not at all in our shady garden under the boughs of the sycamore. We had already widened the bed along the top of the high retaining wall, and though this was adequate for a few low perennials, it was not at all what Linc had in mind. He wanted an extensive sunny rock garden. The rockfall below the dam which we had cleared so many years ago was certainly sunny enough, as it faced directly south. Here, after we had filled the worst of the holes and burrows among the loose tumble of stones, we had planted the sharp slope with such sturdy, ground-carpeting plants as basket-of-gold *(Alyssum saxatile)*, candytuft *(Iberis sempervirens)*, thymes of various kinds, blue bugle, and the coarse, strongly scented *Geranium macrorrhizum*, with its soft, velvety leaves and deep pink flowers; these, if not precisely choice, at least had the advantage of choking out most of the weeds that sowed down from the rough lawn above. But the rockfall was not an ideal site: it was a citadel for mice, who had a network of streets and apartment dwellings among the stones, and I, at least, was well aware that this area would need endless weeding once the carpeters were removed to make room for less aggressive plants, unless we removed the weedy sod above. If, we reasoned, this was necessary to make the rockfall viable, why not go whole hog and strip all the turf from the ground above? Not only would this destroy the weed source above the rockfall, it would give us a truly extensive area in full sun for Linc to play with. He was delighted with the prospect, and so, during the last two weeks of August after our return from Vassar, we set to work with spade, grub hoe, and digging fork to strip off the sod and shake it out. It was hot, dusty work and most satisfactory, but no sooner had we prepared the site and, the next spring, planted the first young plants, than nature intervened to solve Linc's problem of what to do with his excess seedlings.

IV

———

Almost every spring, and frequently in the late summer and early fall, Deming Brook would swell into a torrent, and the water would gradually rise to the top of the stone dike that blocked the gap between the mill foundation and the top of the peninsula. Occasionally the seething water would top the wall, slop over, and threaten to flood down through the lower reaches of the garden. The first few times this happened we manned the levee with pillow cases filled with sand dug out of Ben's high-jumping pit in the barnyard. This, though hard on the pillow cases, held back the major portion of the overflow so that little damage was done to the garden, but after this had happened several times we decided it would be wiser and less detrimental to the linen to raise the dike by adding several courses of stone to the top. This served admirably through several major spates, until, in 1955, came the deluge.

We were, we reluctantly admit, somewhat responsible for the 1955 flood; our only excuse is that like the sorcerer's apprentice we were novices with magic.

It had been an abnormally dry summer. The plants on the floor of the forest, even the leaves of the trees, had first wilted, then withered, and finally crisped under the pitiless sun that shone day after day, week after week. We spent many hours dragging hoses from place to place trying to carry the trickle of water still remaining in the stream to the young, drought-stricken plants that Linc had tucked so lovingly into our new sunny garden that spring. Fortunately the other demands on our water supply were

Calluna vulgaris   A single species with numerous forms and varieties.

small. Only Ben and our current boarder, Gordon, were home most of the time. Becky, who had just finished her first year at college, had a summer job on Long Island; Woody was boarding at a nearby farm where he was helping with the chores; and Shel had been shipped off to camp in New Hampshire, as we were both working at Vassar that summer and only returned home on Sundays to water the plants and check up on the older boys.

But even with sparing use the water in the reservoir dwindled weekly, until shortly after our stint at Vassar was over, the level behind the dam was so low that water no longer flowed through the pipe into the house, let alone through the hoses, and we were carrying water for washing and cooking from a neighbor's well. One of our problems, we realized, was that the reservoir leaked, for there was a trickle of water in the brook, but it oozed out of the pool nearly as fast as it dribbled in. We decided, therefore, to take advantage of the low water, clean out the reservoir, and, if possible, seal the bottom and sides. First we netted all the trout which milled around in the puddle of water that remained in the bottom of the reservoir and transferred them to a deeper pool below the road. Then, by using an old rain gutter, we caught what little inflow there was and led it directly to the gate in the bottom of the dam. This made it relatively easy to shovel out the accumulated debris of rocks, gravel, sand, and rotting leaves that had washed into the reservoir since its construction. Doing that proved to be quite a chore, as each water-saturated shovelful had to be thrown over the top of the dam, which when we were standing in the bottom was well above our heads, but eventually we swept up the last dustpanful of muck and sand to reveal the white marble basin of the underlying ledge. As we anticipated, there were several cracks, and these we plastered over with mortar, allowing it to set before closing the gate valve.

Ben and Gordon, accompanied by a friend, returned home one

afternoon shortly after we had completed our labor, and they came up to the reservoir bearing bottles of cold beer to help us admire the results of our work and measure the rise of water. This proved so imperceptible that the boys soon lost patience and suggested that a rain dance might speed things up. We discussed this possibility in a desultory fashion while we finished our beer but were too hot and tired to put it to test. Then Ben's friend, Mike, who was a classics scholar, proposed a sacrificial prayer to Zeus, god of storm and rain. This idea was more appealing in our present state of collapse than hopping about like Zunis, so while Mike practiced up on his Greek rain prayers, I fetched our best wine glasses, and Linc got out his precious bottle of brandy.

We were a bit uncertain about the protocol of such an occasion, but a procession seemed obligatory, so barefooted, glasses in one hand, and leafy twigs in the other we solemnly paraded three times around the reservoir and then climbed down inside and settled ourselves upon some dry rocks with our feet jammed together in the moist spot slowly spreading over the bottom. Linc doled out the brandy. The bottle was not even a quarter full, so our libations could not be generous, but to prove to Zeus we were holding nothing back Linc spilled the last spoonful into the pool at our feet. Crouched knee to knee, clutching our glasses and sacrificial branches, we waited expectantly for Mike to begin, but all he did was to continue muttering to himself until at last Ben complained that the brandy would evaporate if we sat there much longer; besides he wanted his supper.

But Mike was not to be hurried; he insisted, over our protests, that he had to get his construction right if Zeus was to know what he was talking about, and that, as mere assistants to the high priest, we would just jolly well have to be patient. Finally, however, he declared he was ready to begin. Gravely he requested that we stand, and as we stumbled to our feet he dipped the tip of his leafy twig into his glass of brandy and waved it over our heads as he intoned what we assumed was a prayer for rain. Linc added a Latin phrase or two to Jupiter Pluvius, and the rest of us chimed in raggedly in English. Solemnly we dipped our leafy twigs in brandy and waved them about, pouring a drop or two out of our glasses onto the rocks at our feet for good measure. After swallowing the remaining liquor and shaking the empty glasses upside down, we all sat down again, feeling a little silly. Then from the pristine sky above us came a spatter of heavy drops: only a few and only for the briefest moment, but we felt them on our arms and faces and saw the dark splashes on the bone-dry rocks around us; yet not a cloud marred the sky, and no bird or plane had flown over. We looked at each other, laughed self-consciously, and trooped down to the house for supper, carrying the empty glasses and the bottle.

No more rain fell that evening, and the next morning the sky was burnished blue, but before sundown clouds moved in from the south, and it started to drizzle. It rained all night—the sound of its falling patterned our dreams, and when we woke the sky was swollen with heavy moisture and a light rain still fell. Linc and I had to leave early that day on a long-planned visit to my mother's home on Long Island, and as we drove south and east, the windshield wipers slapping, we hoped that this was not just a coastal storm that would skirt northwestern Connecticut trailing only a few sparse showers across our mountains. It was still raining lightly when we reached my mother's. At cocktail time we eagerly turned on the radio to get the weather forecast and learned to our utter dismay that our corner of the world was the center of a deluge: streams were flooding to unparalleled heights, and people living along the rivers were being asked to evacuate their homes. We tried to call Millstream, but the phone was not answered, nor could we reach Linc's brother, who also lives in

Falls Village. Later newscasts did nothing to reassure us: hourly the toll of destruction and loss of life mounted. After several more unsuccessful attempts to reach someone in Falls Village by phone we decided there was nothing to be done that night, and we went to bed, planning to leave for home as soon as possible.

We spent a restless night, waking early to clearing skies. Our phone still did not answer, but it gave us some comfort that it rang at all and that the operator said it was not out of order. We did, however, manage to put a call through to Linc's brother, though he could add little to what we already knew. Yes, it was bad, he said; he had been unable to reach our boys by phone or by car, as the roads between our house and his were under torrents of water and most of the bridges across the small streams were out. He was not sure we could get home, for WTIC, the Hartford radio station, was announcing that all highways leading into the northwestern corner of Connecticut were impassable and closed to all traffic. He did report that it had stopped raining, however, and that we might be able to get through by midafternoon providing the bridges and roads now obscured by floodwater were not washed out.

The Long Island police could give us no information other than to say we could get to the Whitestone Bridge without trouble. The lines to the Connecticut State Police Barracks in Canaan were hopelessly jammed, and the operator told us there was no chance of making a connection for several hours at least. So with my mother's blessing and what little information we had curdling our stomachs, we started out.

I cannot remember the trip home except that the countryside was sparkling and rainwashed and looked perfectly normal until we were only a few miles from home. We had plotted our route carefully to avoid any low land, and we circled north and west up the Taconic Parkway through Millbrook, New York, to

Route 22 and Route 44, heading for Salisbury. We figured that we might be able to cross the Housatonic River via Dutcher's Bridge on Route 44, as it was a solid structure and fairly high above the river, but as we approached the bridge, the road vanished under a swirl of muddy water, and we were flagged to a stop by a group of rubber-booted men. We were lucky, though. One of them recognized us and said we might go through, but that as we were only the third car to cross the bridge he had better lead us, since there were several bad washouts hidden beneath the brown flood. He swished ahead through the foot-deep water and, when we arrived on solid ground, advised us how best to reach Route 7 and the foot of Under Mountain Road. He could not tell us, however, whether the bridges on our road were still intact, as it had been the small mountain streams which had done the most damage; then he wished us luck, hoped we'd find our house unharmed, and watched us drive off. We had no trouble. The three bridges between Route 7 and home were covered with debris but passable, and it was with great relief that we saw our house still stood firm as we descended the hill past the cemetery.

Ben and Gordon were in the kitchen peacefully eating a late lunch. They reported that they had had supper at Mike's house the previous evening and had gotten home quite late to sleep soundly through the height of the deluge, which certainly demonstrated the profundity of youthful slumber, as Mr. Cobb, who lived on one of the smaller brooks we had come across on our way home, told us later that the sound of the rocks crashing down his stream was reminiscent of a wartime bombardment. Our boys, on the other hand, were blissfully unaware of the turmoil of the night and were totally surprised next morning to discover that their cars, standing in the parking area, were hubcap deep in mud, gravel, and water. Nothing daunted, they had dug out their cars and after much pushing had started out in opposite directions to their jobs. They had not gone far. Gordon was turned back only a mile down the road by a ten-foot-wide gully brimming with rushing water where Wangum Lake Brook had jumped its banks and torn out Under Mountain Road. Ben had reached the valley only to discover that apparently the Housatonic River had changed its course and was flowing down Route 7. They were both rather gleeful over the success of our prayer to Zeus. It had not occurred to them to turn on the radio or try to call us on Long Island. As Ben pointed out, there was nothing we could have done anyway, and why get us upset?

He was right about the fact that there was nothing we could have done, and in many ways we were thankful that we had not been home to helplessly watch the advancing waters sweep toward the house and destroy our garden. The brook had missed the lower end of the house by a half a foot, and the garden was a shambles.

The stone dike across the top of the tail-of-the-race had vanished, and a portion of Deming Brook, though by now considerably subsided, still poured through the gap. Only the topmost reaches of the peninsula were still intact, the rest of the lower garden was a tumble of muddy rocks and trickling water, and the D-Garden was buried under two feet of mud and gravel. Though the yews and the sycamore in the tail-of-the-race and the pines below the driveway were still standing, their trunks were battered and torn, and their flayed roots sprawled naked, all cover of plants and soil swept away. The primrose bed at the foot of the high retaining wall had been gouged out to a depth of nearly two feet by the waterfall that had poured over the top of the mill foundation. All that remained in the lower garden was bare ledge, water-tossed boulders, and the splintered trunks and branches of uprooted trees torn loose from their moorings on the mountain.

We set to work. It took us the rest of the summer and fall to create some sort of order out of the chaos. Our first job was to rescue what plants could be found. The herbaceous material was almost a complete loss; only the liriope had come through unscathed. We found it still rooted firmly in position, though the green hummocks stood eighteen inches above the rubble of stones that surrounded them. Linc walked down the brook and retrieved the rhododendrons from the branches of the trees into which the floodwaters had flung them; these he heeled in temporarily in the sawdust nursery we had cleared up in the woods.

Our newly cemented reservoir was choked with rocks and gravel, and the gate valve had been smashed so we could not drain it, nor have we been able to since. We could see that the cage of heavy iron bars that had protected the end of the pipe through which the water flowed to the house had been wrenched and broken, and though we could not see the pipe itself, as it was buried under several feet of stones and gravel, we strongly suspected that the copper strainer that prevented trout and gravel from entering the pipe was crushed if not completely broken off. Water was flowing freely into the house, however, filtered apparently by the gravel around the end of the pipe, so we decided to leave well enough alone. It was not until the next summer that we dug out the reservoir again and replaced the strainer, which had indeed disappeared.

The boys spent their weekends trying to uncover the boards that closed the outlet of the swimming pool. This proved to be a slow and difficult task, as they had to work underwater. The rocks they rolled to one side. The gravel and sand they scooped out with an old pail with holes punched in the bottom so the water would drain out. They took turns, one underwater filling the pail, the other hauling it up with a rope and dumping the contents over the dam. They finally succeeded in freeing the top board, and after that, with the pool partially drained, they could use shovels to dig down around the outlet and pry the other two boards away from the opening. They dug out and dragged away the waterlogged limbs and tree trunks that the floodwaters had piled against the dam. We hoped that the high water of winter and spring thaws would flush out at least a portion of the remaining debris that clogged the pool, but this, as was later proved, turned out to be wishful thinking.

Before replacing the garden, we rebuilt the dike across the upper end of the tail-of-the-race, this time mortaring the stones and raising it two feet higher than before. We did not, however, close the gap completely, as we wished to keep some flow of water through the tail-of-the-race if possible. This proved relatively easy, as the flood had dug out the soil at the foot of the mill foundation to reveal the massive limestone ledge that underlay both this stonework and the peninsula. A deep cleft in this ledge acted as a natural sluice through which the water of Deming Brook now flowed into the gully, so we took advantage of this unsuspected feature and in building the wall incorporated into its base a four-inch iron pipe through which the water was led from the main stream into the slot in the ledge. This gave us an adequate but completely controlled source of water flowing as a narrow brook through the tail-of-the-race. With tumbled boulders left behind by the flood and gravel and mud dug from the parking area, we shaped and built the banks of our new streamlet.

A board over the mouth of the inlet pipe closes off the supply of water in winter so that ice will not build up in the bottom of the gully and cover the moraines we constructed on the bank of our little stream. After passing through the crevice in the ledge the water tumbles down a fall into a small round pool from which it hurries through the narrow channel that circles the base of the peninsula. Originally, as I have said, this little stream rejoined Deming Brook at the point of the promontory, but it now disappears into the deep chasm it has dug for itself over the years in the soft, porous bedrock.

We dug wheelbarrow- after wheelbarrowload of soil by hand out of the parking area and D-Garden and trundled them up a board ramp to fill in among the boulders we had set along the verges of our little side stream, and we spread a layer of it to cover the roots of the yews and sycamore. This soil was a little grittier than we would have preferred, some indeed was almost pure sand; it would have been helpful if we could have enriched it with generous quantities of humus, but we were in no position to be fussy, as our treasured compost heaps, along with the partially rotted sod we had hoarded when we dug up the lawn, had been close to the banks of the stream and had vanished down into the valley along with everything else.

We also had to replace the soil which had been swept off the lower slopes of the peninsula, and while we were about it we extended the cemented stone dike we had built across the top of the tail-of-the-race to make a stone bulkhead along the entire length of the promontory to protect the side of the Shady Rock Garden from erosion from future incursions of Deming Brook. We did not feel it was necessary to mortar this part of the wall, though it rose in some places eight feet above the bed of the brook; it was constructed of very large rocks and was, in addition, well supported from the back, as we rammed earth and stones into the space between the wall and the ledge that constitutes the foundation of the peninsula. This hard-packed fill rises to the level of the top of the wall so that the top of this three-foot-wide rampart can be used both as a planting site and a path which gives us easy access for weeding the steep back slope of the Shady Garden.

As we dug soil out of the parking area and transported it back to its former sites, we unearthed a number of plants which we thought we had lost permanently. Many were unrecognizable, but those we could identify, either by their roots or the few remaining macerated leaves that clung to their stems, were immediately replanted in the reconstructed beds, as much as possible in the same general area from which they had been ripped. Among these were three of the *Rhododendron racemosum* which had graced the top of the bed that had formerly sloped up against the wall of the parking area. As this section of the garden had not yet been rebuilt, we planted the battered shrubs near the foot of dwarf Alberta spruce on the unharmed crest of the promontory. It took them several years to recover from their traumatic experience (this species of rhododendron, unlike most of its tribe, resents transplanting), but they eventually settled down in their new site and remain there to this day, though they were not as flourishing as their progeny planted in the more acid soil of the woodland garden.

One of the rhododendrons we retrieved from the muck was an interesting hybrid, *Rhododendron myrtifolium,* which Linc had picked up several years before as a self-sown seedling on the property of a friend on Long Island. This rhododendron is thought to be a hybrid between *R. minus* and *R. hirsutum.* The latter, colloquially known as alpenrosen, is a dwarf shrub from the limestone mountains of Europe. *Rhododendron minus* is from the Appalachians and is a near relative and, according to some botanists, a form of the better-known *Rhododendron caroliniana.* It resembles the latter closely except that it is smaller in all its parts than the Carolina rhododendron and blooms later by nearly a month. I had long wished to have a small broadleaved evergreen at the base of the sycamore, and Linc rather hesitantly acceded to my request that we use the rescued rhododendron for this purpose. He agreed reluctantly that the soil at the foot of the bole might have been sufficiently acidified over the years by the annual accumulation of fallen bark to support an ericaceous plant, and though he thought the site was pretty dry and not at all fertile, he admitted that the network of the buttonwood's root system might form a barrier between the rhododendron's roots and the underlying limestone. All these predictions have proved true: though the shrub has not waxed fat on its lean diet, it has flourished and has never suffered from chlorosis, that fatal yellowing of the foliage which in ericaceous plants is symptomatic of too limy a situation. We knew, of course, that one of *R. myrtifolium*'s parents, alpenrosen, grows on limestone, and perhaps this tolerance for calcium had been passed on to its hybrid offspring. We also discovered, many years later, that its other parent, *Rhododendron minus,* heartily dislikes a rich diet and will, in fact, frequently die of indigestion if grown in too rich a soil. It is quite probable that these two characteristics had combined in our little hybrid plant and that, quite by luck, we had chosen a perfect site for it.

When we had first discovered the parking area and D–Garden brimming with gravel and mud, we thought we would have more than enough soil to rebuild the garden, but it was amazing how quickly this store dwindled away as we carted off load after load, and it soon became evident that we would not have enough to cover the roots of the pines between the parking area and the brook. As the cost of two or three loads of soil was not among the items included in our rather tight budget, and as we were afraid that the pines might not survive the winter unless we covered their torn roots, we at first thought the only solution would be to bring down from the woods basketloads of pine duff. Unfortunately we had already depleted the layers of fallen needles in the more easily accessible groves, so that it would have been necessary to scavenge far afield to collect an adequate supply.

We were gloomily considering whether we had the strength to face this herculean task when it suddenly dawned on us that maple, sycamore, and ash leaves would soon be falling in countless millions from the trees right around the house and would serve the same purpose. Heartened by this prescient stroke of genius, we decided to use our small remaining hoard of soil for a more constructive purpose: the filling of the deep hole dug by the pour of water as it plunged over the top of the mill foundation onto the primrose bed.

The flight of wooden steps leading up to the top of the foundation, and the little bridge crossing over to the upper end of the peninsula had, of course, been swept away in the maelstrom, and though eventually Ben and Gordon dredged them out of the debris in the swimming pool, they were too thoroughly smashed to be of any use. We decided, anyway, that we would prefer to replace them with stone steps and a one-span clapper bridge, these to be constructed to look as much as possible like a part of the ledge that had been exposed by the flood.

The steps from the floor of the gully to the top of the ledge and from there to the top of the foundation were relatively easy to build out of rocks garnered from the bed of Deming Brook. These were wedged into position with smaller stones to keep them firm, the interstices packed with some of our remaining precious soil plus some sand dug from the bottom of the swimming pool. It was a different matter, however, to find a flat stone large enough to span the cleft in the ledge. None of the boulders left in the gully or in the brook bed were suited to our purpose, so for days we combed the stone walls in the pastures below the house to find one the right size and shape. When we at last located the perfect stone, made, it would seem, to order, about the size of a card table top and about three inches thick, we realized that even with the help of Ben and Gordon, we could not possibly carry it up the half-mile slope to the road and from there over the rough ground to the spot where we wished to place it. How we wished for a stone boat and a pair of oxen. But, with our toboggan well padded with burlap sacks in lieu of the former, and Aunt Do's Jeep substituting for oxen, and by carefully skirting any protruding rocks in the pasture, we finally managed to skid it up the long, cow-cropped slope, across the road, and into the parking area to the foot of the steps leading into the tail-of-the-race. From here, over wobbling stringers and ramps of heavy oak planks, we manhandled it inch by inch with the help of logrollers and crowbars the length of the gully and up the newly laid steps to its final position. It made a perfect bridge and with smaller slabs, cushioned with soil, placed at its ends we made a level, continuous stone walk over the top of the ledge to the promontory, one side butting the stone dike, the other overhanging the top of the little waterfall made by our artificial brook as it plunged from the pipe into the pool below.

At first the stairway did not look as natural as we had hoped, but we planted tiny sprigs of creeping thyme *(Thymus serpyllum)* in the crevices between the stones, and after about three years these had grown to make a green carpet that completely concealed the joints in the stonework.

A few years later we also decided to try to plant the top of the dike. In order to do this we cemented rows of rocks to the inner and outer edges of its upper surface, creating a planting trough about eight inches deep along its entire length. We tried thyme in this trough, but after several severe years of drought it died. *Phlox subulata* survived, but barely, dying back badly during dry summers but spreading anew in normal seasons. Clove pinks, hybrids of *Dianthus plumarius,* throve, however, in this root-restricting, well-drained environment and, surprisingly, the dwarf white Japanese columbine *(Aquilegia flabellata nana alba)* self-sowed here and maintained itself better than in some other, richer sites. Basket-of-gold *(Alyssum saxatile)* in both the ordinary deep yellow form and the more choice pale yellow variety, *citrinum,* were obviously delighted by this trough and even self-sowed into hairline cracks in the mortar of the wall itself, and though the resultant seedlings never grew to be more than depauperate little clumps of gray-green foliage with scanty, few-flowered heads of blossom, they added greatly to the appearance of the dike. In addition to these herbaceous plants we put in a small, rooted layer of our creeping juniper. After a few years, during which it produced very little top growth, it settled in and sent out lengthening green streamers that flowed over the wall, clinging to its every contour as closely as if supplied with holdfasts. During our devastating six-year drought most of these extended branches died and had to be clipped off, but the plant itself survived and, as soon as we once again had normal precipitation, renewed its spread. Where its roots have reached by now would be hard to say: there is surely not enough soil in the shallow trough to support the exuberant sprawl of branches; perhaps they have secretly inserted themselves between the stones of the wall itself in their search for water and nourishment and may someday, to our dismay, pry the rocks apart and destroy the dike.

We are perpetually astounded by the power of growing things, though we have seen it demonstrated time and time again. A wisteria vine will tear a porch to pieces. Ivy will insert a tendril into an infinitesimal hairline crack and somehow work its way through a foot-thick masonry wall to produce, on the other side, a husky stem complete with leaves; given enough years it can dismantle the wall. Mushrooms and the tender, pale, flowering shoots of the common field horsetail *(Equisetum arvense)* will push overnight through asphalt. Hair-fine seedlings will pierce hard-baked clay to reach the light, and tree roots can split a granite ledge.

To reach the other end of the promontory from the narrow path that led from the patch of lawn under the sycamore to the edge of the brooklet, we at first used, as we had formerly, a plank bridge, but this was later replaced by a thick, flat rock to serve as a stepping-stone in the center of the narrow watercourse.

Cold weather and lack of soil put a stop to our endeavors soon after we had finished mulching the roots of the pines with fallen leaves. That winter Linc planted flats and flats of seeds with the foreknowledge that he would have plenty of planting sites to accommodate every seedling he could raise. These, plus divisions of the plants remaining on the crest of the peninsula, were set out the next spring, and we were pleasantly surprised by the number of plants that sprang unexpectedly from roots and corms which we had inadvertently planted along with the replaced soil, though some, of course, appeared in most unsuitable places and had to be moved. We were also happy to discover that the ferns we had collected while working on the fern book had mostly been spared. Though many of these had been planted under the pines below the parking area, the section directly below the wall which most of them had occupied had been protected from the worst of the floodwater by the wall itself, which had shunted the torrent off to one side.

All in all, considering the shambles of the previous autumn, the tail-of-the-race looked fairly well despite the expanses of bare, as yet unplanted soil. Of course we mourned the loss of those plants it would be difficult to replace, but even that first spring we could see that our enforced reconstruction, a job we never would have considered doing otherwise, would in the long run improve the lower garden.

The new little brook we had made through the garden was a

major improvement, and we immediately set to work to fill this area with plantings to hide and hold the freshly laid soil and naturalize its verges.

A wild rose was planted between the edge of the brook and the roots of the sycamore, a spot where its wandering underground stolons were safely confined. At its feet, with its roots in the water, we placed a large clump of Aunt Do's white-flowered *Iris sibirica,* where the long, slender leaves could dabble their tips in the stream and the delicate flowers shine in the deep shade. White blossoms, which so often can appear washed out in bright sunlight, seem enhanced by shade, in which they become themselves a source of light.

Around the base of the sycamore we replaced the ground cover of ferns, bloodroot, Jacob's ladder *(Polemonium caeruleum),* blue-flowered lungwort *(Pulmonaria angustifolia),* wild geranium *(Geranium maculatum),* and winter aconite *(Eranthis hyemalis),* all of which had done well prior to the flood despite the parlous growing conditions in this bed. To this conglomeration we added the white-flowered form of *Scilla sibirica* and some of Aunt Do's sweet woodruff *(Asperula odorata).*

Across the path from the sycamore we planted a Japanese maple *(Acer palmatum)* that Linc had grown from seed. It was a mere whip when we put it in, but it grew apace and soon became a stalwart young tree. We kept it pruned up to a single trunk as it grew, as this species tends to be shrubby and we wished to continue planting herbaceous material at its base. Here, too, we succeeded in replacing most of the plants which had previously done well in this bed, and in a few years it once more became a jungle of contrasting leaf shapes and textures.

On the lower reaches of the bank of the promontory we planted a number of ferns, mostly Christmas fern, evergreen woodfern and maidenhair fern, and a number of other woodland plants such as Dutchman's breeches *(Dicentra cucullaria),* hepatica, and the delicate little rue anemone *(Anemonella thalictroides).* Here, too, we put some trilliums, both the native one with blood-red flowers, *Trillium erectum,* and the beautiful white *Trillium grandiflorum.* At their feet we planted the yellow wood anemone *(Anemone ranunculoides)* from mid-Europe and the Caucasus, a delightful little plant that spreads slowly by means of twiglike underground rhizomes from which arise the ferny leaves and, on wiry stems in early spring, bright yellow buttercup flowers.

Among these plants on the promontory is a truly charming chickweed, the great star chickweed or starwort, *Stellaria silvatica,* by some botanists considered only a variety of *S. pubera.* It is thought to be quite rare, found only in rocky woodlands in the southern Appalachians, whereas *S. pubera* is quite a widespread plant from New Jersey south to northern Florida. Whether a species in its own right or only a variety, *Stellaria silvatica* is a handsome perennial plant and should be more commonly used in shaded or semishady gardens. We admired it greatly when we first saw it while fern hunting in the mountains of West Virginia where it made foot-high mounds of fresh green among the brown leaves on the forest floor, the wide, starry blossoms, nearly an inch across, scattered like snowflakes over the pile of foliage. We collected two or three plants which we transferred to our garden in the woods, where it self-sowed, providing progeny for transplanting onto the peninsula.

Close to the edge of the brook we planted the lovely white form of the Japanese woodland primrose, *Primula sieboldii.* We also, to our later regret, planted two species of forget-me-nots, the perennial *Myosotis sylvatica* and the biennial *Myosotis scorpioides.* The latter ended up by self-sowing itself into a nuisance. However, it is not difficult to yank it out of those places it is not wanted, and it does produce a wonderful sheet of sky blue in spring, most becoming with the misty pink of the *Primula frondosa,* the tiny bird's eye primrose we had planted in swatches on the banks of the brooklet.

At the base of the peninsula near the edge of the little stream we put in a number of the Eastern shooting-star, *Dodecatheon meadia,* which is tall enough to rise above the surrounding vegetation, as its stalwart stems, hung at the tip with a flight of white to red-purple inside-out blossoms, rise two feet above the upright basal cluster of wide, almost succulent leaves. As it happens those we planted are a rather washy pink and therefore do not stand out among the froth of other blossoms garlanding the brookside in May, but they are an attractive addition, nonetheless.

At the very verge of the little stream we put in several plants of the very rare native globeflower, *Trollius laxus.* It has been found in only a few scattered sites in the wild: in wooded swamps underlain by limestone in Michigan south to Pennsylvania, and in two or three spots here in northwestern Connecticut. We are fortunate to have it growing in our valley in the saturated soils along Wangum Lake Brook. It grows easily from freshly collected seed, and it was not too difficult to get it established along our little side stream, where it self-sows sparsely.

It blooms very early, sending up from the sodden soil a tight clump of heavy-textured, shining, buttercuplike leaves and fat round flower buds that slowly unfold their green petal-like sepals. The petals themselves are tiny, inconspicuous, bright yellow tabs nearly hidden beneath the green button of infolded immature stamens that fills the center of the flower. Gradually as the days warm up the basal leaves spread into a ruff of foliage around the base of the elongating leafy flower stems. The flowers open wider, and the overlapping sepals expand and lose their greenish hue and become a pale moonlight yellow delicately penciled with faint green veining, while the stamens spread ring on ring and the anthers become gold with pollen powder, until in early May the chalice is nearly two inches across and brimming with the puff of deep chrome-yellow stamens that surrounds the central green cone of clustered pistils.

Also on the very edge of the brooklet and around the little pool, with their roots actually in the water, we planted several marsh marigolds *(Caltha palustris)*. These were also collected in the swamps in the valley, and over the years they have self-sowed to fringe with green and gold both sides of the water along the entire length of the stream. We had at first great difficulty in trying to plant them. No sooner had we placed one in a hollow dug in the edge of the brook to cradle its long, stringy roots and slapped over it a shovelful of soil and gravel, than the swirl of water would dig it out and carry it off downstream. We finally solved the problem by plunking a largish stone on top of the plant in the hole and dumping the shovelful of earth upstream, whence it washed, we hoped, down among the roots. The plants looked rather pathetic with their bedraggled leaves and blossoms mostly underwater, splayed out around the edges of the rock like the legs of a squashed crab, but it worked; the following spring we were rewarded by husky marsh marigolds growing around the anchor rocks.

Linc also planted along the edge of the brook two white-flowered marsh marigolds which he had grown from Himalayan seed. According to the botanists it is the same species as our yellow-flowered northeastern American, although it varies from the native *Caltha palustris* not only in blossom color but in several other details. Its round leaves are more finely toothed around the margin and do not die down and vanish during the summer as do those of our plant. Also the white-flowered plants invariably bloom twice a year, once in spring and again every fall. It, too, self-sows, but more sparingly, and seedlings, even those grown from collected seed, are invariably white flowered.

The double-flowered *Caltha palustris* does not, of course, set seed, as all its stamens and pistils have been transformed into petals. To this we have no objection, as it is not, to our mind, a particularly attractive plant; the blossoms are lumpy and do not have the clear yellow shine of the single flowers. However, we grant our one plant house room beside the little pool because it is an oddity.

The Japanese primroses have reappeared on their own at the very edge of the little brook, where their sheaves of lettuce-green leaves tremble in the current and, in June, the banks are lined with their tall, stalwart stems whorled with tier on tier of crimson, rose, and white blossoms.

Around the edge of the little pond, and between the stream and the path running up the gully, we built a series of moraines of lean, gravelly soil with only a little leaf mold and soil admixed. The moraines were intended for precious and rare plants, and such were, indeed, the first inhabitants of these sites. Flat mats of the ferny, curled, furry leaves of that enchanting daisy from the Atlas Mountains of Africa, *Anacyclus depressus,* spread their foliage over the gravelly soil and in June covered themselves with glistening white daisies which, when closed in bud or in the evening, showed the bright crimson reverse of their petals. Here, too, Linc planted large patches of mossy saxifrages, mostly hybrids of *Saxifraga decipiens* and *S. caespitosa.* In May the sheets of crisp, mossy, evergreen foliage are afloat with delicate flowers on four- to six-inch stems, some glistening white with flashes of pale green, others with flowers that open deep red and fade to pale pink so that a blossoming plant shimmers with opalescence.

Here, too, we placed the dainty *Douglasia vitaliana* from the European Alps, a furry little mat of gray-green leaves on which

Among these slender orchids, grass of Parnassus *(Parnassia glauca)* opens its white cups veined with green. Why this little autumn-blooming plant should be called grass of Parnassus is a mystery. There is certainly nothing grasslike about the flower or the basal cluster of broad, heart-shaped, polished leaves, and though it has European counterparts, this humble species is a native of eastern America and has never gleamed among the sheep-cropped grasses on the rarefied heights of Mount Parnassus. The flower has a fringe of infertile stamenodes around the pollen-laden stamens and pistils in the center; bees landing on the broad white petals are thus prevented from sipping from the nectaries in the base of the flower unless they first surmount this frail barrier and brush against the fertile stamens and waiting pistils within.

Where the screes and moraines along the brook graded into the bed of taller plants under the Japanese maple, we put in plants of greater substance: some of the taller astilbes and a number of the handsome European globeflower, *Trollius europaeus.* Unlike its American relative across the brook, this is a fairly sizable plant, blooming much later, usually in late May or June; nor is it particularly rare in its native haunts, where moist alpine meadows may be as liberally gilded with its yellow blossoms as some ill-kept lawns are with dandelions. Its glossy, much-cut leaves make a sturdy clump above which rise on two-foot leafy stems the large lemon-yellow orbs, the petals of which are curled over the central boss of stamens. It has self-sown in the moraines, not profusely, but enough so that it has run out a number of the smaller plants.

Unfortunately, the tall globeflower is not the only plant which has found the moist moraines along the brook to their liking. Harebell *(Campanula rotundifolia),* lovely as it is with its showers of lavender-blue bells nodding at the tips of its slender, graceful

stems dight with narrow little leaves, has taken over in such
profusion in some places that it is a wonder anything else can
grow there. This we did not plant; it just appeared, sown in,
perhaps, from other parts of the garden or springing from little
filaments of root in the soil we had dug from the parking area.

Scarlet pimpernel *(Anagallis arvensis)* is another volunteer
that suddenly appeared and rapidly spread in the damp, gravelly
soil. This little plant, belonging to the same family as the primroses, is an annual with soft, threadlike stems set with little
round leaves not unlike those of the common chickweed. These
creep over the surface of the ground in a fine, jade-green filigree studded all summer long with minute jewel-like flowers of
such an intense vermilion that the ground seems dyed this brilliant color. I have had a tender spot for scarlet pimpernel ever
since my father read me the book of that name by Baroness
Orczy in which the hero, a foppish young Englishman, Sir
Percy Blakeney, under the pseudonym Scarlet Pimpernel, daringly rescues aristocrats whose lives are endangered by the
French Revolution. This little flower, which Blakeney left as a
signature, along with a mocking verse at the scene of his latest
rescue, immediately became for me a symbol of noble adven-
ture and mystery and has, even to this day, retained something
of this aura, so, though it is merely a common and widespread
little weed, I am more pleased than otherwise when it shows up
here and there in the garden. Linc does not completely share
my enthusiasm, however, particularly when it appears among
his more treasured miniature plants, so I do have to remove it
from beds dedicated to this purpose. But so attached am I to the
scarlet pimpernel that I frequently transplant it carefully to
some other spot where it will be more welcome rather than
tweak it out by the roots. We all have our peculiarities.

Another plant which is rapidly taking over some sections of

the moraines is ladies' mantle *(Alchemilla alpina)*. This we did purposefully plant, not realizing at the time its propensity to spread by both seed and stolon. Its flowers are mere nothings, tiny clusters of yellowish green, but I can highly recommend it as a lovely four- to six-inch-high ground cover for a sunny spot. The palmately lobed leaves are pleated and coated with fine, glistening white hair that fringes their rims and gives them a silvery sheen. Another delightful quality of the foliage is its ability to catch any moisture in the atmosphere and transform it into pearly drops that broider its edge and cluster in the hollows of the folds.

Replanting the tail-of-the-race, of course, took precedence over other jobs in the garden, but Linc had also grown many seedlings for the newly constructed alpine lawn, an expansive extension of the bed on the top of the high retaining wall. These, too, had to be set out as they were outgrowing the flats and pots into which they had been transplanted from the seed flats. And there was always weeding.

Never before had we had at any one time such expanses of newly cleared open soil, and in addition to the desirable plants which reappeared in the lower garden, hordes of weed seedlings sprang unbidden everywhere. Destroying these either by scrabbling the unplanted areas or handpicking among the young newly set transplants proved a heartbreaking chore. The abnormally cool, wet weather of April and May persisted into June that year, and every weed seed in the newly turned soil sprouted, and uprooted weedlings kept reestablishing themselves. No sooner was a bed cleaned and cultivated than it was once more filmed with green.

This was particularly aggravating as our time in the garden was more than usually limited that year because my mother had invited Linc, Woody, and me to travel with her in Europe that summer, and we were planning to sublet the house during the months of July and August while we were visiting gardens and botanizing in England, France, and Switzerland. This meant not only that we had to make arrangements for the housing and feeding of our other three children and the dog while we were away, but that the house had to be spic and span before we left, with every closet, cupboard, and bureau drawer clean and empty for the tenants. It also meant, of course, that the garden and nursery beds had to be whipped into shape so that they could be left to take care of themselves for two months.

Our son Ben, who would be boarding with friends in the neighborhood, had agreed to keep the grass mowed, but he would have neither the time nor the knowledge or desire to care for beds full of plants.

It all worked out in the end, however, and our trip was a glorious success, well worth every moment of our anticipatory worry and frantic preparations. Only very occasionally did we fret over our deserted children, dog, and garden as we climbed mountains, collected seed, toured gardens, chateaux, and picturesque villages, and used up yards and yards of film. It was not until we turned off Route 7 onto Under Mountain Road that anxiety about our neglected home overcame us, but this syndrome, we have learned, is perennial. Never matter how blithely we leave home and let slip from our minds—while we are gone—all concern for our children, our chores, our house, and our garden, never do we return, even after an absence of but a single day, without a feeling of trepidation as we turn onto Under Mountain Road and give a sigh of happy relief, as we reach the crest of the hill, to see our house still standing serenely in its accustomed place.

V

————

Although in the main all was well upon our return, the garden, as we had anticipated, had been engulfed by weeds. Fortunately these had mostly not yet gone to seed and, though it took us several weeks to clear them from the beds, the plants concealed among them had also grown apace and emerged unscathed by this temporary competition. We added the crop of weeds pulled from all our new beds to the partially rotted covering of leaves we had spread over the roots of the pines below the parking area, and that fall we piled on top of them another layer of fallen foliage.

One of the gardens we had visited in England is that fabulous piece of landscaping, Savill Gardens, created by Sir Eric Savill in Windsor Great Park for the royal family. We visited it again many years later in spring when it was rich with bloom and filled with birdsong, but even during the August doldrums of our first visit in 1956 it was truly an Eden. Because it was off-season for garden-admiring, and also because it was, perhaps, less well known then than it is now, the place was deserted. We had heard of it from Lanning Roper, whose book, *The Gardens in the Royal Park at Windsor,* was at that time in press, and he urged us to see it. We had a devil of a time finding anyone in Windsor who had even heard of it, much less could direct us to it, and we stumbled into it quite by accident by climbing a stile over an enormously high wire mesh fence. I do not think we saw another soul that whole day as we wandered entranced down the long grassy rides beside wide sheets of dark water as vista opened upon vista. We became lost in forests of rhododendrons, out of bloom that time

Daboecia cantabrica   A heathlike shrub with large hanging bells, it may need winter protection in the northeast.

of year, and discovered for ourselves the long raised beds of rare alpines at the foot of the great wall which had been built by German war prisoners from the mellow, rubbled bricks of London's bombing. The garden was fairly new then: it was not conceived until 1932, and prior to that time it had been a swampy thicket choked with undergrowth; but the magnificent ancient trees that are its framework are centuries old and even in its early years gave the garden a feeling of great permanence and antiquity.

The lilies were in pod that first year we visited it, which saddened us as we had heard of their beauty and, of course, as we had anticipated, the plantings of Asiatic primroses had long since gone to seed. There were thousands upon thousands of these plants, of every known species, their stalwart stems still raising the brown seed capsules above the rosettes of foliage. What a display they must have made in bloom, we thought, and wondered if it would do any harm to take a few seeds; surely there were enough, and already many of the pods had shattered and spilled their bounty. And so we did take a pinch from here and there and put them in an emptied cigarette box for safe keeping.

When we returned home, Linc sowed this mixed collection of primrose seed in flats, and by the middle of the next summer we had boxes and boxes of baby primroses sitting in a row on the top of the parking-area wall. It was obvious we were going to have to find a home for all these youngsters very soon, as they were fast outgrowing their quarters. The unplanted area in the Pine Grove was temptingly empty, and we had no other site ready to receive them, but the rather thin layer of half-decayed weeds and leaves over well-drained gravel seemed hardly ideal for greedy, moisture-loving primroses—we needed soil. As luck would have it, Aunt Do had recently constructed a small house down in the valley, and the dirt dug out for its shallow foundation still lay piled near the road. It was definitely not top quality;

about a quarter of the pile consisted of weedy sod and topsoil stripped from the surface of the foundation site, the rest being sand and clay subsoil. But we were in no position to be fussy, and Aunt Do was delighted at the prospect of our taking the dirt away and actually putting it to some use, so she offered us the Jeep for carting. It took many trips—as Aunt Do said, the Jeep only carried teaspoonsful—yet when we had it all piled in the driveway and compared the heap with the area it had to cover, it seemed like very little indeed. To add to its bulk and fertility we mixed with it a couple of Jeeploads of rotted sawdust and several loads of weedy cow manure from the farmer who pastured his dry cows in our fields. Gathering all this material together required a great deal of shuttling back and forth, but eventually we had enough of the amalgam to cover the pine roots with a layer about six inches deep with enough left over to rebuild the bed that had previously contained the *Rhododendron racemosum* against the wall of the parking area.

Somewhat to our surprise, the young primroses relished this rather strange diet. From seedlings barely an inch across when we set them out in August, they grew apace; a few even bloomed the next summer, and by the following spring the bed resembled a cabbage patch of succulent rosettes from which shot up a forest of blossoming stalks. Because the seeds we had originally planted had been a very mixed bag, and because we planted the seedlings as they came from the flats, the color combinations proved rather appalling. These ranged from the deep wine purple of *Primula pulverulenta* and the soft mauve-pink of *P. beesiana* to the crashing oranges and brilliant chromes of *P. aurantiaca* and *P.* x *bullesiana* hybrids. Among these towered eight-tiered giants of *Primula japonica* in white, magenta, madder, and rosy pink, while half hidden by its larger cousins, *Primula cockburniana* raised its delicate candelabras of glowing orange-scarlet flowers. It looked as though the foot of a rainbow had gone mad and touched down on the floor of the Pine Grove. But though these primroses grew rank and lush beneath the pines, they needed continual watering because of the porous fill beneath, and it was evident the site was really too dry to permanently suit them. After a couple of years we dug them up, sorted them into colors and heights, and transported them to moister areas we had prepared for them in the woods garden.

In their stead we planned to plant more ferns and other shade-loving plants, but as was almost inevitable, in removing the primroses we had also removed a large portion of the already rather thin layer of soil we had spread over the pine roots, and we had learned that even the wildest wildflowers required a good depth of humus-rich earth if they were to do well. So once again our problem was finding more soil.

While we had been in England we had seen, not only the raised beds built of stone at Savill Gardens, but also a few in which the low walls containing such beds were built of blocks of dried peat. As it happened Linc knew of a former bog several miles north of Falls Village which had been accidentally drained by nearby quarrying many years before and had been briefly mined for peat. This might solve our problem. Linc knew that commercial peat cutting had long ago ceased, as the area had not been large enough to support it, and that the property had since changed hands. We thought it might be worth investigating and soon discovered that we knew the present owner, who gave us permission to dig out as much of the remaining peat as we needed but warned us that the remnant was insignificant and had been left untouched only because it was perched on the very lip of the quarry.

We promised to be very cautious and set out, axes and sharpened spades in hand. Once we found the peat, after hacking our way to the end of a nearly obliterated, brushy track, it was not too difficult to cut out with our spades chunks about the size and shape of cement blocks. The peat was dry and consequently very light, and we stacked it roof high in the back extension of the Jeep and secured it with a network of old clothesline. We did creep cautiously to the brink of the quarry to peer down its precipitous white walls hung with vines and the stunted trees which had managed to find a foothold in the crevices. It put me in mind of a great underground palace or temple, unroofed now and in ruins, more suited to Yucatan than Connecticut.

We laid the blocks only one, or at most two, courses high, varying this occasionally with stone, in a wide oval circumscribed by a narrow path that circled around the central group of pines. On each side of this path were other, quite narrow beds, one against the wall of the parking area, the other backed by the remaining kaempferi azalea along the bank of Deming Brook. Rather than waste any of our precious layer of composted soil, we lowered these paths by digging them down to the underlying gravel, adding the earth thus garnered to that already in the beds. To this we added quantities of broken-up peat and the summer's accumulation of compost to form a foot-deep layer of spongy material that was the color and consistency of rich chocolate cake. The plants we inserted into this delectable mixture flourished, and in a few years carpeted the ground. This miniature woodland has needed, after the first few years of weeding, very little care. It has become so thick with flowers that unwanted plants have very little chance of sowing in.

It is a pleasant spot of sheltered green all through the growing season. In early spring small clusters of *Scilla sibirica* splash the ground with intense blue as they thrust their nodding bells from among the crinkled lettuce-green leaves of *Primula vulgaris,* both in the species and in hybrid forms. These are mostly in shades of yellow and creamy white, but we have one patch in all tones of blue from velvety purple to palest azure and another where the white and cream of the blossoms is suffused with rose and pink.

Among the primroses shine the dazzling evanescent cups of bloodroot, which has self-sown here so profusely as to have become almost a weed.

Among these are a few of the double-flowered bloodroot *(Sanguinaria canadensis multiplex)* with globe-shaped blossoms like miniature water lilies. As the pistils and golden stamens have been transformed to petals, the flowers are sterile and consequently do not shatter as quickly as do those of the single form. Found only once in a woodland near Dayton, Ohio, the original plants were propagated and sent to various botanical gardens, whence they have been spread to grace our gardens. As it sets no seed, this form can only be propagated by dividing the stout roots, but this presents no difficulty and is, in fact, beneficial to the plants, as the rhizomes tend to crowd and override each other and rot, as do those of iris, unless they are separated and replanted from time to time.

Before the last flowers on the early primroses fade, after nearly three weeks of bloom, *Primula polyanthus* opens its first blossoms, and the taller stalks of the cowslips *(P. veris)* are hung with puffy calyces and shy yellow bells. Now is the season when violets open, and their flowers sweep under the pines in colors of white, blue-purple, and yellow. Most thickly spread of all this clan is *Viola canadensis,* which has self-sown along the paths in wide sheets of heart-shaped leaves and slender white flowers with a mauve reverse. The ground is white with their blossoming in spring, and they give us scatterings of bloom all summer. Among them are the deep piercing blues of lungwort *(Pulmonaria angustifolia),* the forget-me-not–flowered *Anchusa myosotidiflora,* and the lovely blue-eyed Mary *(Omphalodes verna),* which spreads its low tufts of dark green leaves and cobalt stars by means of strawberrylike runners. Above these rise the softer sky-blue showers of Virginia bluebells *(Mertensia virginica)* on tall wand-

like stalks, and the ground between is spangled with the white
and blue multirayed flowers of the English wood anemone set
close above the clustering mats of daintily cut leaves. Twinleaf
(Jeffersonia diphylla) from the southern Appalachians spread their
two-parted leaves like angels' wings under the pines and open
glistening white cups that shatter all too soon and change to seed
pods shaped like small cornucopias, while nearby their Japanese
counterpart *(Jeffersonia dubia)* raises amethystine goblets above the
garnet curl of its unfurling foliage.

From late April until mid-June the vermilion flowers of the
red lungwort *(Pulmonaria montana rubra)* kindle among its rough,
hairy leaves. Threading over the dark peat blocks is twinflower,
named *Linnaea borealis* after Linnaeus, the famous Swedish father
of modern botany, who claimed it among his favorites. The
self-effacing twinflower's slender stems, set with small round
leaves, creep unobtrusively among the mosses, but in early summer when it hangs its miniature pairs of bells of palest pink by
the multitude on three- to six-inch hair-thin stems, the air beneath the pines is redolent with its delicious fragrance.

Above this carpet of flowers and varitextured leaves the stalwart stems of *Trillium grandiflorum* hold high great, white, three-
petaled chalices above the trinity of leaves. We are also most
fortunate in having a clump of the double-flowered form with
flowers like gardenias though not sweetly scented. Unfortunately
this beautiful trillium is not so easily propagated as is bloodroot.
We impatiently wait for the slow, natural increase of the rhizomes, but we have been told that some gardeners, more coura-
geous than we are, have cut nicks in the short rootstock to force
it into producing more numerous offsets, or have even chopped
it into pieces for this purpose.

Groups of western trout lilies *(Erythronium)* thrust up their lily
bells of smoky pink, soft yellow, and opalescent white above the

surrounding herbage, and the tenderly unfurling, ferny clumps of
Epimedium are decorated with dainty sprays of varicolored, intricately formed flowers. The downy clustered spikes of the yellow
lady's slipper *(Cypripedium calceolus* var. *pubescens)* erupt into
sheaves of ribbed leaves bearing glossy yellow pouches each
mustached with wonderfully twisted, reddish waxy spikes that
would shame Dali.

As May slips by, the fern crosiers uncurl, and the rainbow of
color beneath the pines subsides. But even as the summer comes,
the yellow and orange poppy cups of Welsh poppies *(Meconopsis
cambrica)* open to nod and flutter among the ferns.

Allegheny vine *(Adlumia fungosa)* trails its slender, twining
stems and froth of pale foliage over and among the ferns and
other plants. This dainty vine may extend ten, even twenty, feet
in a season. It has sent its streamers to the top of the utility pole
that stands by the roadside near the Pine Grove. All summer long
the fragile runners lengthen, putting forth cluster upon cluster of
pale "bleeding hearts" as they clamber, light as foam, over their
more stalwart neighbors until, in autumn, they wither away to
a snarl of brittle, pale threads. Both Allegheny vine and Welsh
poppy are monocarpic and usually biennial, producing only a
single season of bloom before they die, but in the rich duffy soil
in the shade of our small grove of pines, they self-sow profusely
and yearly provide us with summer blossom.

Other invaluable summer-blooming plants for shade are those
of the astilbe clan. Those we have planted beneath the pines are
only the ordinary sorts, white and pale pink, but their fluffy spires
are a pleasant addition to the green sea of foliage that laps the
base of the trees. Later still the great pink bells of the hardy
amaryllis *(Lycoris squamigera)* chime out unexpectedly above the
tall ferns. This plant never fails to startle us with its sudden
appearance. Sometimes called the naked lily, it produces a great
sheaf of straplike leaves that come up in early spring and are gone

by June. Then in late summer the thick, leafless, flowering stalk shoots up almost overnight, it seems, bearing on its tip a spreading umbel of large, flesh-pink trumpets. This naked, gawky, two- to three-foot stalk is oddly unattractive unless clothed by the verdure of surrounding plants, and tall ferns are ideal for this purpose, as both like the same growing conditions.

As everyone who lives with a rock garden knows, there are months of backbreaking labor and days of heartbreaking catastrophes, but also hours of unmitigated bliss when the weather is perfect, and the garden is at its loveliest, and everything seems right in one's little world. And even those hours of hard labor when muscles scream in protest and joints crack with strain as you dig up more beds and prepare more sites for more plants are not unmixed with that certain blissful feeling of accomplishment that accompanies any act of creation. For surely building a rock garden is as much an act of creation as painting a picture, writing a book, or carving a sculpture. For a brief while, as the garden takes shape, one feels a very god, creating a small world to one's own specifications.

There is a deep glow of satisfaction that comes to those who create their own landscape, the child of their own imagination, molded by their own labor and nurtured by the care of their own hands. Linc and I have often wondered, when we planned, built, and planted gardens for others, whether we were not somehow cheating our clients of that special feeling of making their own thing. Perhaps so. I know in some cases, and I suspect in most, that the moment our backs were turned the owners hastened to place their own imprint on the new landscape, perhaps by adding a rose bush to that corner and a clump of daffodils over there, or by moving or removing a shrub, which to their eye was planted in the wrong place. And who is to say them nay? The garden is ours while we construct it, but once we are gone it becomes the property of those who live and work in it.

No landscaper can expect a garden to remain exactly as he saw it in his mind's eye. Whether or not the present or future owners change it, a garden will change itself. Gardens, unlike most artifacts, are not immutable. Rocks, no matter how carefully placed and firmly set, will shift and tilt as the frost levers them from below. They may sink to half their height or disappear completely into tunnels delved beneath them by moles and mice, or they may be left stranded like beached whales on the surface as the soil is washed from around them by rain and snow melt. Trees, shrubs, and herbaceous plants are living, growing entities with wills of their own, developing new shapes and textures as well as new proportions. They can be battered and broken and occasionally uprooted by ice storms and wind. They can sicken and die or burgeon so mightily as to swallow huge rocks and obliterate paths, walls, fences, and vistas. They cannibalize their neighbors and will, indeed, engulf the garden itself unless restrained, pruned, trimmed, or removed. Gardens, therefore, invite, indeed demand, tinkering if they are to remain gardens, and who has a better right to tinker than the gardener who lives with the garden?

It is hard now to remember the exact sequence of how our garden spread from its initial beginnings. It seemed to take on a life of its own. Like quack grass it spread by seed and stolon. New colonies formed in distant areas, and plantings followed paths between these new bits of garden, filling the intervening space only to leap forward into new territory beyond the periphery set as the garden's boundary. Seedlings sprouted in pots and flats that jostled each other on the top of the parking-area wall. They sprouted in vacant spaces between the plants in the beds, they burgeoned in paths and threatened to block them. Tiny, delicate cotyledons grew into yard-wide specimens crying for space and yet more space.

"No more seedlings," promised Linc, as he tried to jam one

more potful into the frames. But the seed lists flowed into the mail box, and who could resist those lists of unknown plants pregnant with possibilities? We built more frames.

"Please, no more beds," I cried. "I can't keep up with the weeding." But seedlings outgrew their pots. We made nursery beds. The plants in the nursery grew into mats of tangled verdure. We dug them up and separated them and divided them and made new beds to house the overflow. We gave them to seedling sales and plant sales. We gave them to friends who came to visit. We gave them as house presents when we went visiting. It didn't help. Our friends brought us twice as many to replace them.

We enlarged the beds we had. We brought up rocks from the valley and built more retaining walls along the brook so we could plant right to the edge of the stream. We brought up more rocks, made more soil, and tore down the old dam to make a ledge and talus slope. We filled in the former millpond. An end of the high retaining wall that bordered one side of the tail-of-the-race collapsed, and we rebuilt that into a planted wall with a moraine at its base.

We spent every winter cutting down trees in the woods, at first with a great long two-man saw, later with a power saw. Most of the logs and limbs were split and hauled down to the woodshed next to the sugarhouse, some for the fireplaces, but most of them to fuel the sap boiler. Some were given to our farmer friend who heated his house with a wood-burning furnace. But there was still the brush and the smaller branches to dispose of, and these were dragged and piled in heaps huge enough to cremate a Viking chief and set afire. In those days no one was worried about clean air, and as long as the snow lay on the ground the fires burned day and night, and our clothes and hair reeked of woodsmoke. Nowadays we haul the brush off to make long piles that go snaking along the boundaries of the garden into the woods.

In the new openings in the woods more beds were dug in which to line out baby rhododendrons and azaleas. Linc was once more dabbing pollen, and a potful of seedlings soon required a quarter of an acre. He was hybridizing herbaceous plants as well: primroses, phlox, and saxifrages mostly. When our children were all grown and had moved away, we sold the sap works, tore the roof off the sugarhouse, enclosed it with plastic, installed fans in either end, and turned it into an alpine house. Here Linc could stand upright and work in relative comfort during the cold days of late winter and very early spring without the competition of bees and flies. His hybrid progeny soon overflowed the benches, and suitable quarters had to be found for their comfort, so more beds had to be made. And of course there were more seed-exchange seedlings. Like the sorcerer's apprentice, we had started something we could not stop; plants kept multiplying by geometric progression, like fruit flies.

Something had to be done to siphon off this overflow. I resigned my part-time job as reporter and assistant editor at the local paper, Linc resigned from school teaching, and we went into landscaping work, building gardens for others in order to house the superfluous plants crowding the nursery beds. It did help, but building and planting gardens for others and simultaneously trying to care for our own, presented us with a new set of problems. It was just too much of a muchness. Our backs gave out, we developed housemaid's knees and tennis elbows, and our own plants and garden suffered from neglect. After twelve years we finally called it quits and once again concentrated our energies on Millstream.

It was wonderful at first being able to work full time in our own garden, but it meant, inevitably, that we were tempted into future expansions. Though Linc had vowed to cut down on his seed sowing, and he did, there were always unknown plants listed in the seed exchanges to tempt us. And friends and friends of friends sent us seed collected in far-off places. We discovered new areas in the garden that were much too attractive to leave in trees and weeds, and special beds had to be made for special plants. Linc's hybrid rhododendrons and azaleas were growing apace and needed more room, and all these areas had to be weeded.

Linc has always mowed all the grass, sowed the seed, and cared for all the pots of seedlings. He decided where to put them. He has also done most of the clearing up in the woods and the policing of established shrub plantings, pulling up or lopping off the tree seedlings and sprouts and pulling off the tops of heavy weeds. He also does most of the weeding in the nursery beds of small rhododendron transplants, though I have helped with these chores when they threatened to get ahead of him. For many years we worked together in planting, laying out, and constructing new sections of the garden, but as the plantings expanded up in the woods, Linc took over this job almost entirely, while I concentrated on the upkeep of the herbaceous plantings.

This had always been my responsibility, and I found that by weeding the established beds very thoroughly once a year and new beds every week or so, I could do all the herbaceous areas and their peripheries during one growing season. But as the garden gradually became more extensive, I realized I was falling further and further behind schedule, until finally I was still weeding an area for the first time in late October when I should have been helping to rake leaves. Eventually time completely caught up with me, and several of the older sections of the garden were still untouched by the end of the season.

I truly enjoy weeding. I am at my happiest hunkered down over a bed with my fingers deep in the soil sorting out weed root from plant root, immersed in the sight and scent of foliage and flowers. But there is an obverse to this enjoyment. A bed choked with weeds makes me feel guilty and physically uncomfortable, so much so that I will avoid the area unless I can do something about it. Linc calls me a compulsive weeder. He can walk past a bed full of gigantic weeds and apparently never see them, whereas if I see a weed I have to bend over and dig it out. This drives Linc crazy on the few occasions when we walk through the garden for a sightseeing tour together. If I am walking in front of him he is always tripping over me as I bend down to snatch up a weed. On the other hand, if I walk to the rear and stop to remove a weed, I almost invariably see others that need immediate attention, with the result that Linc walks on without me. If I am left to my own devices, hours will go by before I come up for air, and Linc, having finished our walk, picks me up on his way back down to the house.

Linc has found that being married to a compulsive weeder has other drawbacks. He likes his meals on time, and I am usually deep in the bushes up in the woods when he wants to eat. I never used to wear a watch, but finally in desperation Linc gave me an old one of his. It doesn't help, as I forget to look at it or if I do and I discover I still have half an hour until lunch, instead of hurrying down to the house to fix it, I try to finish the last few square feet of unweeded bed—and lunch is late again.

As more and more weeds appeared in the more mature areas of the garden, I became more and more desperate. It became increasingly obvious that I was unable to weed the new beds as often and as meticulously as necessary and also keep up with what needed doing in the older sections. At last Linc noticed that the herbaceous plantings were getting out of hand and, though weeding is not his favorite occupation, he has recently taken on quite a bit of the upkeep in many herbaceous beds in the woods garden. This has a double benefit, as it means he no longer has quite as much time to make new beds, and the garden is therefore not expanding quite so quickly. Even so, as we become older and work more slowly, the garden is not quite so well kept up as in former years, and this despite the expert help once a week these past few summers from Tamsin Goggin. It would be far worse without her presence. The garden has just grown too big.

As we depend rather heavily on self-sowing, our rock garden, perhaps more than most, tends to do its own thing. Though it is Linc, in the main, who decides which plants to introduce and where they should go, it is the garden itself, with its climates, macro and micro, and its various soils and degrees of moisture, shade, and sun that makes the final determination. Some species simply will not do for us. They sicken and die or vanish without warning perhaps down the gullet of one of our resident critters. We mourn such plants, but if after we have put in several years of trying to please them in a variety of sites they still declare their discontent by disappearing, we give them up. Why should we continue to murder them? Others of Linc's introductions thrive, and in most cases, though not all, I rejoice when their seeds have found a place to their liking where they can sprout and grow and make seedlings of their own. It is only then that I think they truly feel at home and have become a permanent feature of our land-scape. Other advantages of the self-sown method of plant propa-gation are the particularly good forms and occasional hybrids that sometimes occur.

Perhaps Linc's greatest pleasure is a leisurely tour of the garden, admiring what he has wrought, checking up on his plants, and planning future plantings. He doesn't understand why I, too, do not spend several hours each day just wandering and looking. He has accused me of not appreciating the garden—even, upon occasion, of disliking it, because he believes all it represents to me is work and yet more work. He claims all I see are the weeds.

This is not strictly true. There are many areas, particularly in the woods, where weeds such as wood aster and ragwort are a major and most attractive constituent of the ground cover; it is only when these invade the beds of more choice plants that I object to them. In such places they make my fingers itch, and I long to get at them. Housework and kitchen work are a frustrating waste of time from my point of view, but when I spend a day working in the garden I feel that I have accomplished something, and I am refreshed and feel relaxed and at ease with myself. Working in the garden is to me a major part of my absorption and pleasure in it, and means far more to me than a brief admiring stroll along its paths.

As I move from one work area to another, I can be as transfixed by the way a vista opens up to reveal a familiar view suddenly transformed to a scene of exquisite beauty by a change of light as I would be if I had purposely sought it out, even more so. When I bend to weed I am close enough to really enjoy the intricate patterns of leaf and flower and the feeling of the various textures of the soil. And all the while I am working I am deeply immersed in the evanescent fragrances that drift around me and the blend of brook sounds and leaf sounds and birdsong. As I work, unlike a visitor to the garden, I become an integral part of it.

Although my role in the garden is the rather subsidiary one of helping with its upkeep, this gives me the privilege of nurturing the plants within it and to some extent the opportunity to guide their growth. As I free them from encroaching weeds, I choose which plants to encourage and which to restrain, which need freedom from competition and which prefer close company. In so doing I too have a hand in the creation of our garden; I become an essential part of its life, and it, in turn, has become a part of mine. Without the garden and the work I do in it, I would be sadly diminished.

L.L.F.

II

PLANT PORTRAITS

AMERICAN PLANTS
FOR THE
WOODLAND GARDEN

The flora of the eastern portion of the North American continent from the Canadian provinces to Florida has a large component of woodland plants because of the generally forested nature of the terrain. Except for beaver meadows, sandy coastal plains, bogs, and a few mountain summits, the region was originally completely forested in postglacial times. Deciduous hardwoods predominate in the south and coniferous evergreens in the north. To the west of the central plains are also vast areas of mostly coniferous forests.

Within these forests, which exhibit a wide range of climate and topography and diversity of soil types, there has developed a rich array of herbaceous plants, many of which are admirably suited to cultivation in the shady woodland portions of our gardens. Though few of our shade-tolerant plants have the tight cushion habit of the classic alpine, many form extensive mats of elegant foliage and sparkling flowers, and some bear, in addition, showy fruits.

Many rock gardens have sections which are shaded. Being human, we like to get into the shade ourselves once in a while, so we have shady areas around our habitations. We want to plant these up, so we use woodland plants. In the wild many of these plants grow in dense shade, but it is amazing how adaptable many of them are to an increase in the amount of insolation. Many actually flourish better under such conditions. They also frequently flourish better because of reduced root competition for moisture and nutrients with the overstory trees.

There are still many woodland plants worthy of introduction.

Even among those that have been introduced, there are selections to be made. We haven't learned to look for the superior cultivars among our native plants, nor have we learned to propagate and disseminate them among gardeners.

I will start with plants I consider ground covers and will then move to some that are more discrete plants and even some that are fairly large but accommodate themselves in the shade of trees.

Among ground-covering, shade-loving plants is *Maianthemum canadense,* an eastern species of wild lily-of-the-valley. There is also a western species *M. bifolium. Isopyrum biternatum,* a little anemone relative, is really a plant of calcareous soils in the wild, but I don't think it is that fussy in cultivation. It will stand fairly deep shade, but actually grows better at the edge of woodlands. There is a western species, *I. stipitatum,* which is rather similar and suited to the same conditions. The foliage is delicate. The plant is easy to propagate by division, and once established, actually self-sows rather abundantly.

One of the loveliest of the ground covers is the circumpolar *Linnaea borealis.* There are slight differences in the American forms as distinct from the European forms of *Linnaea.* In the East, it establishes itself in rather dense forest, frequently under evergreens. It grows rather lushly in the White Mountains of New Hampshire on fallen logs. Once established, it roots as it runs, so that it is very easy to propagate by taking off rooted runners. This twinflower is notable for its rapid spread and dangling, paired, funnelform pink flowers so sweetly scented as to perfume the air. A delicious plant.

An excellent companion for *Linnaea* is that stunning woodland phlox from Oregon *Phlox adsurgens.* It is more demanding than its eastern counterpart *P. stolonifera.* The latter will expand its mats in a wide range of woodland soils and display its sumptuous flowers of various colors even in considerable sun.

There are many *Synthyris*. Some of them are true alpines at high elevations above the trees. There are also woodland species such as *S. missurica, S. reniformis,* and others—not showy plants but with elegant foliage and very early bloom.

Our eastern *Oxalis,* closely related to the European *O. aceto-cella,* has been separated off as *O. montana.* There is an even more handsome one growing in the forests of the West: *O. oregana.* We find it not hardy in the Northeast. I wish it were, because it's a huskier plant than *O. montana* with magnificent pink flowers.

Sedums we rarely think of as being woodland plants, but there are a few woodland species. A rather nice white one which blooms for a long period and grows in the southern Appalachians is *Sedum glaucophyllum,* previously known as *S. nevii.* There is a close similarity between this and a more common sedum, *S. ternatum* from the same area. Also white flowered, it climbs over mossy rocks in the fairly deep shade of deciduous forests.

The *Chimaphila* are a puzzling group: closely related to the *Ericaceae,* elegant in foliage, evergreen, with hanging bells of waxy texture. They are propagated mostly from cuttings, though every seed capsule is stuffed with thousands of tiny seeds. I don't know of anybody who has ever gotten them to germinate. Has anybody experimented? Is there any information? They must self-sow in the wild. I don't think they depend on vegetative reproduction. There is *Chimaphila umbellata; C. maculata,* with spotted and patterned leaves; and the western *C. menziesii,* a slightly huskier one.

Closely related to the chimaphilas are the pyrolas, with many species both east and west. *Pyrola picta* has rather handsome, fleshy foliage, well marked with incised veins. It is a plant difficult to dig up and establish. It must be treated more or less as a cutting. I gather that the best time to do this is when it is actually in flower.

Moneses is a genus intermediate, actually, between *Chimaphila* and *Pyrola*. *Moneses uniflora* is a plant that everybody loves, although those who have tried to grow it have almost invariably failed. I don't know why. The only place we find it growing, at least in the Northeast, is in the shade of white pine. I suspect that there is some kind of mycorrhizal association at the roots of *Moneses* which is even more sensitive than the roots themselves, so that if the fungus is destroyed, the plant dies. This is just speculation.

There are many species of *Asarum*. Our eastern *A. canadense,* a deciduous species blooming very early, is fertilized by beetles. I understand that studies have shown that the interiors of the deep purply-red, meaty blossoms are many degrees higher in temperature in spring when they bloom than the surrounding area, so that beetles crawl in to get warm, and hence do their business. The leaves unfold and make quite a canopy, creeping rapidly across the ground. The plant self-sows abundantly in the garden when happy in shade and will move out into considerable sun. There are also some western deciduous species, such as *A. caudatum,* with plain green leaves. The interesting thing about this species is that each division of the corolla has a long tail that sticks out handsomely, like a mouse's tail. Another notable asarum is the handsome *A. hartwegii,* which is beautifully mottled in the foliage. We also have mottled-foliaged evergreen species in the Southeast, which have been separated off by many botanists into the genus *Hexastylis.* There are six species distinguished by fine characteristics of size and shape of blossom and to some degree also by their very handsome foliage, which is of thick texture.

A little northeastern plant that I believe is monotypic in its genus, if you want to separate it from *Rubus,* is *Dalibarda repens.* It has rubuslike blossoms and is a very handsome plant that makes a carpet with time but is slow to spread. Interestingly enough, it's frequently known as the false violet; it doesn't look like a violet, and I wonder how it ever got that name. The only similarity *D. repens* has to a violet is that it produces cleistogamic flowers during the summer. At the base of the plant it develops the self-fertilized flowers without petals, which set seed.

Most of the polygalas grow in open soil, and some are annual. *Polygala paucifolia,* the fringed polygala, is a completely perennial woodland species. Its normal color is pink, but occasionally you find it in pure white. This, of course, is what always delights the gardener: to find an aberrant form. The pink is very beautiful, but how much choicer it is to have a white one, which is so rare!

Mitchella repens, with its very flat, compact spread of small, round, evergreen foliage, is found in acid soils and frequently beneath conifers. It provides a double display with sweet-scented, twinned flower trumpets followed by berries of glowing red, or glistening white in the rare *leucocarpa* form.

The red fruits of carpeting *Gaultheria procumbens,* which develop from the waxy flower urns, are wintergreen flavored, as are the white fruits of the snowberry, *G. hispidula. Gaultheria procumbens* grows in highly acid, usually well drained, sandy soil in woodlands, pine plains and similar areas. It's rather open—that is, the individual clumps are at some distance from one another— and it runs underground and makes new clumps of foliage. It blossoms late in summer, and its berries last through the winter. If it is grown in more sun, its carpet becomes denser and denser, and it flowers and fruits better. It is much easier to grow in the East than its western compatriots *G. ovatifolia* and *G. humifusa.*

Cornus canadensis, bunchberry, is widespread. In moister, more humusy acid soils, it forms mats of largish whorls of leaves. From the center of each whorl arises a cluster of small yellow flowers subtended by four showy white bracts to be followed by a clump of scarlet fruit against the fall coloring of the foliage. In the

Northeast it comes down all the way to West Virginia at high elevations. With us, in Connecticut, it's at about the southern limit of its natural distribution below the really high elevations. It doesn't bloom very well with us and rarely sets fruit even if it does bloom. However, as you move north along the eastern seaboard and get up, for instance, into the Gaspé, it becomes a roadside plant, heavily flowered and richly fruited. The foliage, especially in the sun, turns a very handsome color.

The fabulous trailing arbutus, *Epigaea repens,* has woody stems, leathery leaves, and fragrant blossoms. Some very good forms have deep pink or large white flowers and large leaves. It is an excellent plant. It prefers good drainage and is frequently found in poor acid soils containing much sand or rock. In the wild it tends to grow on north slopes at the edge of woods and is especially common along old wood roads where the soil has been disturbed and the seeds have a chance to germinate.

With us in the East, *Epigaea repens* will grow in full sun in acid, well-drained, sandy soils. Once established, it grows rapidly. Don't be greedy in transplanting *E. repens;* don't try to dig up a large clump. The plant keeps spreading in one direction, and the main root may be far from the cluster of foliage and flowers. If you can find a small, round clump, you are safe to dig it up, but why bother? This is an easy plant to propagate by cuttings. Take cuttings of the current year's growth just as it is beginning to harden, about mid- to late July. Propagate by laying down a bed of live sphagnum moss on a piece of plastic. Put the cuttings on the moss, roll up the plastic, plunge it into a plastic bag, tie it up, and hang it in shade where it doesn't get full sun. In about six weeks open up the bag, roll out the sphagnum, and snip between the cuttings because they will be full of roots.

If I were to select a group of the top fifty, or twenty, or even ten American woodland plants, near the head of that list would certainly be *Shortia galacifolia.* Rare in nature, this evergreen

carpeter is adaptable in almost any climate so long as it is provided with an acid, humusy soil in light to dense shade. The early,
fringed white bells, sometimes tinged with pink, are almost an
inch across. They are carried singly and abundantly on 4- to
5-inch reddish scapes above the rug of rounded, heavy-textured,
evergreen leaves, which turn wonderful shades of red in winter.

Shortia galacifolia was discovered back in the eighteenth century by the French botanist Michaux. He took back a specimen
with leaves and seed capsule (he never saw the flower) and
entered it in his herbarium as *Plantae incognitae,* discovered on the
mountains of the Carolinas. Professor Asa Gray, one of the
grandfathers of American botany, saw the herbarium specimen
when he was in Europe, and drew a picture of the flower as he
thought it would look. Gray looked for the plant for years in
the high mountains, going up into the Smokies in the Carolinas,
but it's not up there. It's down in the Blue Ridge, in the valleys,
along the rivers, in a very small area in the corner of South
Carolina and Georgia. It remained lost for many years. When
finally found, by a person out collecting herbs, the flower actually
matched Dr. Gray's drawing.

Unfortunately, the type site and the area of much of the
distribution of *Shortia galacifolia* have been disturbed. There was
a large power dam put in, and much of the area was flooded along
the streams. The plant has not naturally moved out of its area.
I have a theory that the reason *S. galacifolia* never spread north
again after the last glaciation is that the seed has to be very fresh
to germinate. By the time it ripens down in those valleys, it can't
get out because conditions up on the ridges are too dry for the
seed to germinate. It's easy to propagate by division or by cuttings, and if it is moved north, it does self-sow. There is a Japanese
species, *Shortia uniflora,* which we must admit is even more
handsome.

A related and more common plant from the same area is *Galax aphylla.* The galax, an excellent ground cover for similar situations, carries its small white flowers in a dense wandlike raceme during early summer. It, too, is most readily propagated by division. Galax grows abundantly in the Southeast. In fact, it used to be collected literally by the railroad carload and shipped to city centers such as Philadelphia and New York for use by florists. The leaves turn a lovely russet red in the fall and are very permanent, appearing almost shellacked or lacquered. They were much used in floral decorations, especially for funerals. In the fancier restaurants one always got grapefruit served on galax leaves.

We move now from ground-covering plants to a few very choice woodlanders which do not spread by stolons or underground runners. The hepaticas are among my favorites. In the Northeast we have two species. *Hepatica triloba* var. *americana* is similar to *Hepatica nobilis (H. triloba)* in Europe but tends to be somewhat paler in blossom. Each of the three scallops on the leaves is rounded, whereas on our other species, *Hepatica acutiloba,* the leaf segments are sharp pointed. There is a double form which is extremely rare. For many years I looked for a deep pink one. I found a plant and propagated it by division and was bold enough to give it a clonal name 'Millstream Pink'. I wrote it up in the ARGS *Bulletin,* and hardly had the issue been published before I got an order from Mr. Henry Du Pont by mail, saying, "Would you be willing to send me five hundred of your pink 'Millstream' *Hepatica acutiloba?*" He did things that way.

The bloodroot, *Sanguinaria canadensis,* of the evanescent poppy family, is a very handsome plant. Its blossoms are closed early in the morning, then they open wide and last, really, for just a day. While the plant blooms, the leaves are curled up around the base of the stem. Then they elongate and become umbrellalike above the faded blossoms and the seed capsules. I've kept looking for a pure pink *S. canadensis.* Why? Well, I just want something different. It has been recorded, actually. *Gray's Botany* lists *S. c.* forma *rosea,* which is pink throughout. The handsomest bloodroot, of course, is the double *S. c.* forma *multiplex.* Because it is sterile, it has the advantage of being less fleeting than the single form; it is never fertilized and therefore it does not set seed. It can be easily and properly divided every three years or so to avoid soil depletion and other mysterious ravages of long-established clumps.

There are two species of woodland spring beauty in the East. *Claytonia virginica* has long, thin leaves; *C. caroliniana* has shorter, blunter leaves. Both have pink-striped white flowers. I have not seen, but have heard of and have received seed of, a pure yellow form of *C. caroliniana.* Whether it comes true from seed I don't know, as the seeds have germinated but the plants have not bloomed. *Claytonia virginica* and *C. caroliniana* are matched by similar western species such as *C. lanceolata,* which blooms a little earlier.

Jeffersonia diphylla is another of our natives that has a counterpart in Japan: the perhaps more beautiful *J. dubia. Jeffersonia diphylla* has lovely leaves which are a delicious color. These "angel wing" leaves open very early, before the hepaticalike blossoms. I tried for years to obtain a plant by getting seed from the exchanges and planting it over and over and over and over again in pots. Nothing germinated. Finally, in desperation, I sowed some in the open soil and got a couple of plants. An interesting thing I have found about both species is that once you have a plant, they'll self-sow. Some plants send off some compound or other agent that inhibits seeding nearby, but *Jeffersonia* and a few others seem to encourage germination of the seed that's right around them. Maybe it's the mother's skirts. A study ought to be made of this effect.

Dentaria (Cardamine), the toothworts, are not enough used. They're nice woodland plants. We have *Dentaria laciniata* and two or three other species in the East. The western *D. tenella* is a fairly good pink, and *D. gemmata* is purple.

During the early part of the year, the dicentras begin a display that in some species carries on well into the summer. I'm fond of dicentras because of their foliage and their lovely blossoms, and because when their bloom is over they get out of the way. Planted among ferns, they are finished by the time the ferns begin to grow up. *Dicentra cucullaria,* which grows from a small cluster of ball-like tubers, is a close relative of the eastern *D. canadensis.* It is almost impossible to distinguish between the two in foliage. The difference is in the position of the spurs and, of course, in the bulbs or tubers at the root. When the two handsome western species *D. oregana* and *D. formosa* are growing together in the garden, I understand, there is such a mixture, such a progeny of hybrids, that it is difficult to tell them apart. That odd little fellow with the steer's-head flower, *D. uniflora,* is also from the West. There are other delicious species. The eastern *D. eximia,* generally bearing pink to purple flowers but especially beautiful in the white clone, produces a succession of bloom on scapes about a foot tall. In Virginia, Dr. Wherry discovered a pure white, a true albino form, which comes true from seed. I believe it was given an Award of Merit in England.

Dr. Marion Ownbey crossed a western species, *Dicentra nevadensis,* with that very difficult Japanese species *D. peregrina* and produced a whole series of hybrids which he was about to introduce at the time of his death. They have the characteristic sort of steer's horns of *D. peregrina* and the vigor of *D. nevadensis.* Many of them have gotten into gardens, and very handsome they are.

Amidst the general throng mentioned above, there must be

found room for the early-flowering woodland anemones: *Anemone quinquefolia* and *A. caroliniana* of the East, and the superior westerners such as white *A. deltoides* and blue and pink *A. oregana.*

Closely related to the anemones are the anemonellas or rue anemones, so-called because of the ruelike foliage. The typical form of *Anemonella thalictroides* grows at the edge of woodlands. A man by the name of Oscar Schoaf once found a bold pink form in a graveyard in Minnesota. He dug it up and took it home. Think what might have happened if he had not done that. We wouldn't have the pink *A. thalictroides* in our gardens today, I'm sure: in no time at all a grave would have been dug right on the same spot, and the plant would have been destroyed. Mr. Schoaf's discovery merits a conspicuous place in the garden because of its singular elegance, its long season of bloom, and its ease of propagation. All that's necessary is breaking up the small dahlialike tubers from which it sends forth its airy foliage and pompon flowers.

Weaving through the mixture of bulbs, corms, tubers, and ferns in a woodland garden, there should always be the open carpets and the discrete clumps of tiarellas, the foamflowers, lending an airy grace. Especially useful are the spreading *Tiarella cordifolia* in a selected clone, and *T. wherryi* for its long season of bloom and restrained growth habit, and for the charming tints of its fall foliage.

For a difference of foliage effect, we might wish to include species of *Silene* in our acid-soil woodland. In the East we have the cespitose *Silene caroliniana* and its subspecies, all with good pink flowers. *S. c.* var. *wherryi* tends to be a little more vigorous, but *S. caroliniana* can have forms of a magnificent deep color. These are easily propagated from cuttings. The handsomest is the more erect *S. virginica* with its firecracker burst of bloom. In the West is the showy Cascadian *S. hookeri*. Then, of course, there is the spectacular *S. h.* var. *bolanderi* introduced by Crocker and Kline.

There is one woodland *Carex, C. fraseri,* now moved by most botanists into a separate genus, *Cymophyllus.* It is very primitive, a relict genus closely related to the sedge, as can be seen by the large flowers and big, fleshy, straplike leaves. It is found in the southern Appalachians, and makes a handsome plant for the woodland garden. Unfortunately for me, *C. fraseri* is also a favorite browse for the deer.

You know that ubiquitous plant from Japan, *Pachysandra terminalis,* which is much used as ground cover. Every suburban area has it by the hundreds and thousands. The American *Pachysandra procumbens,* from the southern Appalachians, is a much more handsome plant and is really worth growing.

The earliest of the violets with us is *Viola rotundifolia.* It hardly looks round in foliage when it blooms, because the leaves are just beginning to unfold. Later the highly polished, deep green leaves will be as large as butter plates. I'll tell you a secret about this violet: its buds are delicious to eat—a spring tonic! *Viola canadensis* is fairly prolific. Its blossoms come above leafy stems, and their petals are blue on the back and quite handsome. It blooms for a long period, frequently having a late-summer second blooming. I hesitate to include *Viola pedata,* though with us it will grow in light oak shade, sometimes in scrub pine areas. It wants very acid sandy soil and will indeed grow in full sun. It comes in a variety of forms. The pure albino form tends, at least with me, to self-sow true to form.

The genus *Iris* also provides us with woodland species of varying stature and habit. Of easy culture and rapid increase is the southeastern *Iris cristata.* It has short, deciduous, daggerlike foliage and short-stemmed, gold-crested flowers in good shades of blue and violet, and rarely, pure white. From the same regions, more difficult of cultivation and even more handsome, is the evergreen-leaved *I. verna.* It does not run by stolons, but has fibrous roots and spreads very, very slowly. It wants an acid soil and half shade, certainly not deep shade. Its more rigid and erect blooms tend to be intense hues of blue or purple with a striking orange median band. There is a magnificent white form, very rare in the wild and only beginning to get into cultivation. The western woodlands provide us with an even more varied array of iris species from *I. tenuis* (which self-sows abundantly for me) to taller species such as *I. bracteata, I. chrysophilla, I. innominata,* and *I. tenax.* Most are from rather dry, open woodlands.

One would like to be able to describe in detail the various genera of the lily family that offer a rich array for the woodland garden: in such genera as *Clintonia, Smilacina, Streptopus, Maianthemum, Disporum, Xerophyllum,* and the woodland lilies themselves.

Erythronium grandiflorum, from the higher mountains of the West, will grow in shade as well as in open meadows. We have in the East: *E. americanum* and *E. albidum. Erythronium americanum* has spotted leaves and, normally, yellow flowers. It frequently makes a great deal of foliage without very much blossom. A similar Midwestern species, the nodding *E. mesochoreum,* never fails to bloom.

A small eastern woodland lily which is very rare is *Lilium grayi.* We have others: *L. canadensis,* which grows in moist meadows or in open woodlands, and the magnificent upward-facing *L. philadelphicum.*

The clintonias make very good woodland plants in acid soil. The fruit of *C. borealis,* our northeastern clintonia, is a magnificent robin's-egg blue and long lasting. Others are *C. umbellata,* with white blossoms and black fruit, and the western *C. uniflora.*

Also followed by handsome berries are the blossoms of a

number of species of *Disporum* and *Streptopus,* such as *S. rosea,* with its very shiny red berries.

Two more woodland members of the lily family are *Xerophyllum* and *Chamaelirium.* Our eastern beargrass, sometimes called turkey grass, is *Xerophyllum asphodeloides.* The western one, the great beargrass, *X. tenax,* grows near the edge of woods at higher elevations. *Chamaelirium luteum,* its blossoms in pale spikes, grows in open meadows but is also a woodland plant frequently found in limestone.

Diphylleia cymosa is an eastern plant with rather large but handsome foliage. The blossoms are white and are followed by handsome blue berries. The plant grows up to 3½ or 4 feet. Also with blue berries is *Caulophyllum thalictroides.* Its foliage is very much like that of a thalictrum. The blossoms are not conspicuous, but it blooms very early.

Trollius laxus, I have discovered, is growing in a shady swamp at the foot of my own hill. (We are preparing to give a small piece of the land there to the state to preserve at least this site for the endangered species.) It makes a handsome plant in cultivation and will stand some sun if it has moisture. The eastern form normally grows in deciduous swamps. There is also a western form.

We do have a very handsome clematis in the woodlands of limestone areas in the East. It is *Clematis verticillaris,* which blooms early in the spring.

Lobelia cardinalis, that magnificent plant for late in the summer, grows along our stream sides but doesn't really require running water to make it flower. It will grow in the shady rock garden.

To be combined with the many charming native herbaceous flowering plants under deciduous trees that allow for ample light in spring and shade in the heat of summer, there is a rich variety of ferns to provide summer textures and shapes. Among them are the less aggressive ferns such as the woodferns, the woodsias, and the maidenhairs.

There are many other genera from diverse families that should properly be included in our shaded gardens: all-summer-blooming *Chrysogonum virginianum,* the brightly fruited *Actaea,* the mat-making *Coptis* and *Trientalis,* stalwart *Cimicifuga,* greeny-yellow-fruited *Podophyllum,* the foot-high carpets of *Vancouveria hexandra, Petasites frigidus,* and so many others.

Too often we tend to overlook our own natives. We pine for the brilliant cushions of the high alpines and anguish over their intransigence in our lowland gardens. We have in the woodlands of America a fabulous treasure trove of garden-adaptable plants. I would like to urge that we search out superior clones of these wonderful wildlings, learn to propagate and tame them, and share them with our fellow gardeners.

H.L.F.

ADONIS

Dorothea DeVault writes that she has growing in her garden the perennial adonis of the *Ranunculaceae,* "that glimpse of sunlight with two-inch golden buttercups," in her words.

"When and where my husband and I purchased it eludes me. That I covet many more plants is a fact. That it is difficult to find and purchase them is also a fact.

"We never had seed from our plant," she continues, "so one fall we finally had the courage to split our single adonis (after consultation with H. Lincoln Foster) into three sections. The following spring our three plants produced more than thirty glistening yellow flowers. The blooming began in February, earlier than usual due to the mild winter. The flower stems and feathery leaves gradually elongated for several weeks of bloom, and after the flowers faded the leaves remained until late summer. Then, as the leaves too faded and collapsed, we marked the area, for this plant disappears until the following spring.

"The plants thrive in half sun in ordinary soil which is probably slightly acid. It does take several years of growing before the plants become truly spectacular.

"Whether the plant was *Adonis amurensis* or *A. vernalis* we could not remember at the time, and, of course, the label was gone. So we decided to consult the authorities. First to *Rock Gardening,* by H. Lincoln Foster; then to *All About Rock Gardens and Plants,* by Walter Kolaga, which had a black and white photograph of *A. vernalis;* next on to *Collins Guide to Alpines,* by Anna Griffith, which boasted a colored picture of *A. amurensis;* finally to the *Royal Horticultural Society Dictionary of Gardening,* which contained a black and white sketch of *A. amurensis* and detailed descriptions of several other adonis. Unfortunately our taxonomic knowledge was sadly limited, but we think our perennial is *A. amurensis.* But don't press me."

Mrs. DeVault is probably right; her plant is almost certainly *A. amurensis* if it bloomed as early as February, even with a mild winter and early spring. Usually this species blooms in March in Connecticut, whereas *A. vernalis,* despite the specific name, generally delays its blossoming until late April or even May in this area.

Both species are long lived in the garden and develop multiple crowns with numerous long, heavy, ramifying, brown roots. They seem to be tolerant of either limy or acid conditions; *A. vernalis* grows in limy soil in nature. Both prefer a deep, fairly light soil. Though both species will grow in light shade, they are at their best in full sun. They will survive some competition but do better without severe overcrowding.

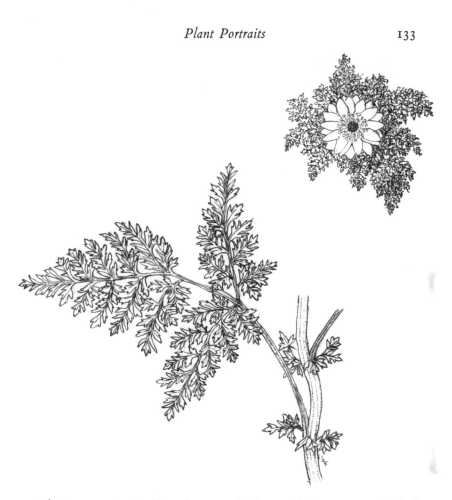

Adonis amurensis   Looking down on the flower of *A. amurensis* with leaf fully expanded.

Unfortunately, the two photographs used by Mrs. DeVault in her attempt to identify her plant are somewhat misleading. The adonis pictured in Walter Kolaga's book is labeled *A. vernalis,* but the photograph, though an excellent one, seems to be of *A. amurensis,* while the adonis pictured in *Collins Guide to Alpines,* which is captioned *A. amurensis,* appears to be *A. vernalis,* though it is difficult to be sure, as the details of the leafage are not easy to see. The drawing in the *RHS Dictionary of Gardening* is more helpful in that it delineates the foliage of *A. amurensis* more accurately.

Although superficially similar, the two species are quite different in appearance if one observes them closely. Both plants grow from six to eighteen inches tall, elongating their flowering stems and foliage as they mature. Both are clothed with finely dissected leaves and large, solitary, many-petaled buttercup-yellow flowers at the tip of each leafy flowering stem. *Adonis amurensis,* however, has branching stems, and its leaves all have stout stalks almost as long as the leaf blades. These spring from little frills of laciniated leafy bracts set along the flowering stem. Each leaf is broadly triangular and is divided into three major divisions which are then further dissected into numerous flat segments, resembling flat-leaved Italian parsley.

In earliest spring, when *A. amurensis* first thrusts through the cold, wet soil, the leaves are deep red and still furled when the first flowers open. Later these leaves become green, and the blades bend out at an angle to form a lacy green doily just below the later blossoms, which will continue to open for several weeks. Those dilatory blossoms are particularly welcome as the first ones are frequently blasted by frost.

Adonis vernalis, on the other hand, usually has unbranched stems, and the leaves have no stalks but are merely fringed clusters of branching threadlike segments springing from the main stem. These give the plant the fluffy appearance of a green form of *Artemisia* 'Silver Mound'. Though more delicate in appearance than *A. amurensis, A. vernalis* does not vanish completely after its flowering season as does the Oriental species, but lingers through the summer. In fact, the old stalks of *A. vernalis* with leaves still attached can be found the following spring spread upon the ground as attenuated, flattened shadows of their former selves.

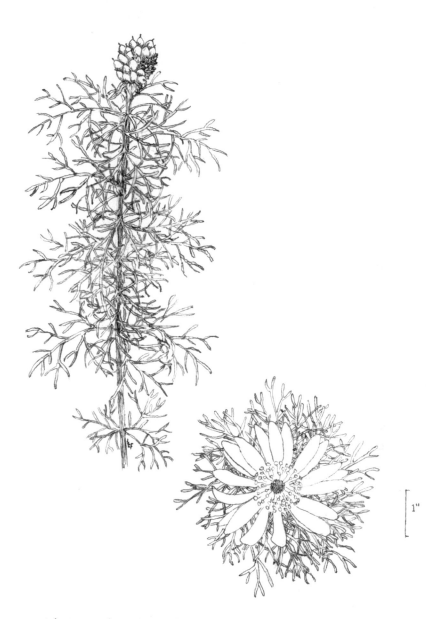

1"

<u>Adonis vernalis</u>   Large golden flowers; one of the best of the species.

The flowers of the two species of adonis are very similar, but here, too, there is a difference. Both usually have blossoms of shining yellow, but those of *A. amurensis* have a deeper bronzy sheen on the reverse of the petals and in some forms may have white, rose, or red-streaked flowers. Comparing the size of the flowers can be misleading because of individual variations, but on the whole those of *A. vernalis* are the larger, up to three inches across, whereas the flowers of *A. amurensis* seldom exceed two inches. The flowers of *A. amurensis* make up for their smaller size, however, by carrying many more petals, from twenty to as many as fifty, which overlap in several years. *Adonis vernalis* usually has between ten and twenty petals, and though they overlap to some extent when the flower is fresh, they tend to gape as the blossom ages.

Of the two species, *A. amurensis* is the easier to propagate by division. This can be done either in early spring or fall, as Mrs. DeVault discovered, but it is perhaps best done in the later summer or fall since the plants start growth so early in the spring, frequently while there is still snow on the ground. *Adonis vernalis,* on the other hand, deeply resents disturbance and often takes several years to recover.

It is usually recommended that adonis be propagated by seed, but there's the rub. Viable seed is very difficult to obtain unless you already have plants. Seed should be absolutely fresh, and it may take two, sometimes three, seasons of low temperatures before seed dormancy is broken. Even in those conditions, germination is chancy and sporadic. We have had *A. vernalis* self-sow around the mother plant where competition is not too heavy. It is possible that fresh seed sown directly into the ground might germinate better than seeds sown in pots.

There are also a number of annual adonis. Widespread in Europe from England to the Near East are two species, both called pheasant's eye. Both are sparingly branched plants from one to two feet tall with feathery, rather sparse foliage resembling that of dill or love-in-the-mist *(Nigella damascena). Adonis annua (autumnalis)* has small, ¾-inch flowers of scarlet to crimson with black anthers. Unfortunately, the blossoms open only partially. As we grew *A. annua* from exchange seed, we found it disappointing because of its spindly growth habit and small, partially closed flowers, despite its dramatic blossom color. Perhaps if grown *en masse* it would prove a more exciting garden plant.

The other pheasant's eye, *A. aestivalis,* blooms in June. We have not grown this plant. Its blossoms are reputedly larger than those of *A. annua,* reaching 1 to 1½ inches in diameter, and they open fully. They also are usually red but do not have the dark central eye. A citron-yellow form is sometimes found. Two other annual adonis are listed, both sounding better than the above: *A. aleppica,* from Syria, with 1½- to 2-inch blood-red flowers that open wide; and *A. flammea,* from central Europe, with scarlet blossoms 1½ inches across and blotched black at the base of each petal.

From our somewhat limited knowledge of this genus (named for the legendary handsome young mortal beloved by the goddess Aphrodite, who transformed his blood into this flower when he was gored to death by a wild boar), we think the perennial species are well worth seeking out. Though difficult to obtain initially, they are long lived in the garden. Their glorious shining blossoms, framed in the delicate halo of frilled foliage, make a stunning addition to the early-spring rock garden.

L.L.F.

THE DOUBLE PINK RUE ANEMONE
Anemonella thalictroides

Anemonella thalictroides is a delicate early-spring plant of open woodlands in eastern North America. In neutral soils, rich in organic material, moist but well drained, this monotypic genus has an elfin, if rather fleeting, charm. The five to ten white, petal-like sepals cup a cluster of fine stamens and pistils. The flowers are arranged in an open umbel on thin, wiry stems with involucral leaflets forming an airy collar beneath. The leaflets are repeated more generously on the ruelike, leafy stems which arise, with the flowers, from the cluster of tuberous roots and persist after the sepals have fallen. The overall height is usually under one foot.

In its range, from southwestern Maine westward to Minnesota and southward to northern Florida, Alabama, Arkansas, and Oklahoma, *Anemonella thalictroides* tends to vary in color, showing more and more pink in the blossom in its western extension. Whole stands in Arkansas and Oklahoma are almost raspberry in color. These color variations are worth searching for and introducing into cultivation.

Besides the color variations, there are forms in which the stamens and pistils have been transformed into sepals, giving the plant the flore-pleno type doubling so sought after by gardeners. The double white form has been christened forma *favilliana* after its discoverer. It has a beauty and even greater lasting quality than the fully double bloodroot, *Sanguinaria canadensis multiplex*. Think what a fully double *pink* rue anemone would be like! And it is no dream wish. Such a plant has been discovered, has been propagated, and is being distributed.

The rose-pink pompons last for well over a month on *A*.

thalictroides, and when the plant is well grown, each umbel produces secondary umbels of fresh flowers from early spring into
July. Because there are no sexually functioning parts to the
flower, it does not quickly shatter by being fertilized, nor does
it, of course, set any seed. Fortunately the cluster of tuberous
roots, just beneath the surface of the soil, provides a sure and easy
method of increase.

Such a choice plant, originating as a chance genetic sport,
would not be likely to reproduce in nature by division except
by extraordinary coincidence. A burrowing mole, or inquisitive
squirrel might perhaps dislodge and transport one of the clustered
tubers. More likely, however, would be the complete extinction
of this choice double pink rue anemone by the inevitable change
of environment which would "swamp out" this one-in-a-million
genetic accident.

Fortunately for us, Oscar Schoaf, the gentleman who spotted
this beautiful freak in a small graveyard in Owatonna, Minnesota,
amidst a wave of the common single variety, recognized its
distinction. In honor of his discovery about twenty years ago, I
would like to propose the name *Anemonella thalictroides* 'Schoaf's
Double Pink' for this extraordinary form. There seems to be no
technical name assigned to this form in botanical literature.

When this clone was given an award in England, the authorities argued that because the original plant was found in the wild
and not in a garden it could have a commemorative clonal name.
The award was presented to the plant as *A. thalictroides rosea
flore-pleno.* To have been technically consistent, they might have
used the botanical name, *A. thalictroides* forma *favilliana.*

To Mrs. Louise Koehler of Bixby, Minnesota, we owe the
introduction of this wonderful plant into general horticulture.
To quote from a letter from Mrs. Koehler: "I knew nothing
about this *Anemonella* until one spring when my husband went

to pick up his seed corn at the dealers. I rode with him. While I was waiting for him to finish his business, I watched a neighbor across the driveway working in his garden. When I saw mounds of pink along the border I got out of the car and walked over to see what those mounds of pink were. It was then that the gardener gave me two of the plants. He said they could be increased by dividing the tubers, which I did the latter part of July when they had finished blooming.

"This gentleman's name is Oscar Schoaf. He tried to sell the *Anemonellas* to a nursery, at a price, but never succeeded. He left his plants in large clumps and seldom divided them. I divided mine regularly and soon had them by the hundreds. I felt I should not sell mine until he had had a reasonable length of time to find a nursery to take his. I don't know what price he demanded for them. After twelve years I started selling my plants. Everybody who saw them wanted to buy some. I sent plants to the University of Minnesota Arboretum, to Mrs. Mary G. Henry, Gladwyne, Pennsylvania, and to several friends who had wildflower gardens."

Through the generosity of Mrs. Koehler the plant is slowly getting into wide circulation. All those who have it are, I am sure, grateful to Mr. Schoaf and Mrs. Koehler and to others who have extended its introduction by skillful division and generous sharing. It is thus, slowly to be sure, that choice plants arrive in our gardens. The three essential steps are a keen and discriminating eye to spot the plant, skill and willingness to propagate, and finally a love of sharing such beauty with others.

This multiplex form of *Anemonella* seems more vigorous than the ordinary white. Under good cultivation it may be divided annually after flowering when the foliage begins to pale. Each single tuber in the cluster, up to as many as ten, will produce a plant the following spring, some of which will flower. All will flower abundantly and for a long season the second year.

Transplanting may be done in very early spring or in fall. A location on a slope with adequate moisture and soil rich in leaf mold will produce an abundance of flowers, especially if the site is sheltered from sharp winds and provided with constant high, deciduous shade. Division every other year will ensure a good display of flowers and rapid increase of *Anemonella thalictroides* 'Schoaf's Double Pink'.

H.L.F.

ARISAEMAS

The fossil record of herbaceous plants is meager, primarily because their soft structures are not readily preserved. Therefore we cannot say much about the sequence of development in the extraordinary variation of plant form and the flowering design among the angiosperms, the modern plants with seeds in an enclosed ovary. So far as we know comparatively rapid diversity was the rule when land plants and insects proliferated together during the Cretaceous period.

We cannot say, however, whether plants like arisaemas and others in the arum family, with their sex organs arranged on a spadix enclosed in a leafy spathe, are more primitive than plants with stamens and pistil exposed within a corolla of showy petals. Somehow they *look* more primitive, but that is only because we are most accustomed to think of flowers in the familiar pattern of the petunia, rose, or lily.

Plants in the arum family, the *Araceae,* have their own kind of architectural elegance—some of them, such as calla and lysichiton, are even considered beautiful. Although most of the arisaemas, the jack-in-the-pulpit plants, are rather demurely plain, others are strikingly handsome. In fact, some in my garden, when in flower, attract almost universal attention and admiration. This is especially true of *A. sikokianum* and *A. candidissimum,* but even

Arisaema candidissima   A Chinese species with large white spathe.

the less flamboyant members of the genus attract notice by intricacies of pattern and structure.

I suspect that the general feeling about the arums is that they are rather quaint, in the sense that they are skillfully wrought. Some are startling by virtue of intricate patterns of color on the leaf, spathe, or stem; others are curiously decorated by long appendages on the spadix, on the tip of the spathe, and occasionally on the tips of the leaflets.

The purpose of these long, frequently threadlike appendages is obscure. We are taught that all such features serve an adaptive role and as they have evolved help the plant survive. These filaments may carry scents undetected by the human nostril but alluring to insects useful in pollination. Since most are associated with species from areas of monsoon rains, the threads may act as water spouts. I suspect, however, that they are merely expressions of a natural exuberance I seem to detect in many plants. They appear endlessly to diversify and experiment until the exuberant modification becomes lethal in its extremity.

However this may be, the genus *Arisaema* is a vast one. There are about 150 species, chiefly in tropical and temperate eastern Asia with a few in Africa and North America. Depending on the taxonomist consulted, there are up to forty species in Japan alone. With their widespread distribution and variation of form, the arisaemas all share certain generic characteristics. They all arise from a depressed-globose tuber, the tuber tending to be more onion shaped and pointed in youth, but shortening and splaying at the hips with age. A few even become so spread out that they become rhizomatous. This underground storage organ is primarily starchy and might serve as a source for human food except that it is heavily laced with poisonous alkaloids and contains spicules of calcium oxalate. One name for our American arisaemas is Indian turnip. It is unclear whether the Indians actually ate the tubers or whether they were given this pejorative name by the white settlers because they looked so edible but weren't and were therefore associated with a benighted people. It is reported that though they are not made edible even by boiling in a succession of waters, the tubers may be rendered harmless by some months of drying.

Since our interest is more horticultural than culinary, we turn from the arisaemas' root to the flower. The flower, as we have indicated, is composed of a central fleshy column, the spadix, enclosed within a spathe, the cylindrical leafy tube that flares in various ways to make a hood over, or a flag above, the spadix.

The sex organs develop in discrete zones surrounding the spadix. Around the lower portion are ovaries with receptive stigmas, and in the ring above are the male stamens. This would appear to be an ideal arrangement for ready pollination and assured seed development. But, as with other plants, the arisaemas employ strategies to assure a mixing of genetic material. Most species tend to abort either the male or female organs on a particular plant to enhance cross pollination. Hence most are designated as dioecious, that is, they have functioning male and female parts on separate plants.

The arisaemas play interesting games with this arrangement, however. Studies made both in America and Japan have demonstrated that at one stage in its life history an individual tuber will produce a flower that carries viable male organs only, and at another stage will produce one that carries functional female organs only; the same tuber may, indeed, sometimes produce a hermaphroditic flower, one with both sexes functional. So much for women's lib and male chauvinism!

When, either with insect help from plant to plant or from rare self-pollination, the ovaries are fertilized, there is developed near the base of the spadix a cone-shaped cluster of berrylike fruits containing one to five seeds. As the spathe withers away and these fruits swell, they slowly change from a shining green to a gleaming red. Where the fruit clusters are carried aloft on tall stems, they frequently grow too heavy for the stalk and are swayed earthward even before they fully ripen. Those species that carry their flowers near the ground on stout stems present in autumn a marvelous display of a fiery red cone of berries—an exciting ornament in the landscape of the dying year.

These appetizing-looking fruits are as heavily laden, with poisons and mouth-tingling spicules as are the arisaemas' tubers. They cling for a long time, avoided by birds and rodents, until various soil and airborne agents of decomposition break down the outer coat. Thus the seed will frequently lie moist and cool for spring germination right where the fruit cone has fallen, and we find a tight cluster of single-leaved seedlings in the spring fighting for dominance. At other times late-foraging ants carry off the partially fermented berries, or rodents and birds are tempted to disperse the seeds, or the heaving of moist soils with the help of gravity spreads them about during the winter.

If you would grow these seeds for your own delight, collect and leave them in their fleshy wrappings until ready to sow. I find that soaking the berries in water for a few days breaks down the pulp, which can then be readily separated from the seeds. If the seeds are sowed immediately and given a warm temperature, they will germinate in short order. If seeds are stored dry for any length of time, germination may be delayed up to two years.

One year I sowed fresh seed of *A. sikokianum* in December under lights in the basement. They sprouted quickly and grew well until late April, when the small plants all withered. On inspection I found that each had developed a small onionlike tuber, quite viable looking. I put these in moist peat in a sealed plastic bag. This went into the butter-saver compartment in the door of the refrigerator for two months. The tubers were then planted in humusy soil in a small plastic flat, about one inch below the surface and about one inch apart. They all soon sent up new vigorous plants, completing by fall two years' growth in one. They bloomed after another full year in the garden. Under normal conditions it takes from four to six years from seed to flowering.

I have since tried this procedure with a couple of Chinese species without the same results, probably because I tried to hasten the process at one stage or another.

The tubers of some *Arisaema* species have not been easy for me to grow in pots. When potted up in the fall and carried over in the alpine house, tubers of *A. sikokianum* and *A. candidissimum* did not appear in the spring. I found that they had rotted, and suspect I watered them too consistently, under the impression that because many grow naturally in really moist situations they could not stand a dry soil in winter. Now, if I plan to carry over in pots new tubers, either received as gifts in a dormant state, or doubtfully hardy ones grown from seed, I keep them just barely moist through the winter, and preferably in a situation just a bit above freezing.

Though, as I have indicated, many species do grow in moist to swampy conditions in nature, they will thrive even better, I think, in rich woodland soil, even on the dryish side under high shade. It is possible that many are found in wet spots because that's the preferred situation for seed germination.

Here are some of the species of arisaemas that I have grown, with a few comments about each, arranged alphabetically for convenience.

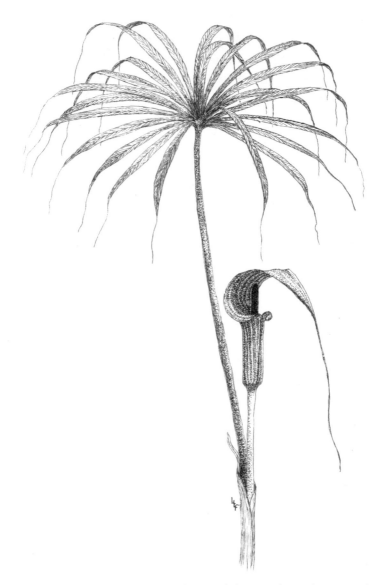

Arisaema consanguineum   From China and the Himalayas, this species has a green spathe.

A. atrorubens

This is our common jack-in-the-pulpit, with a wide distribution in rich woodlands of eastern North America. The broad spathe arches horizontally well above the spadix and may be solid green or deep reddish purple, variously striped. The large leaves, from one to three on each plant, are generally composed of three leaflets, but in especially vigorous plants may carry up to five. The heavy cone of glistening, large red berries is a prominent feature of the autumn garden. The tuber will multiply by offsets.

A. candidissimum

This species, from western China, is one of the handsomest in the genus. Rather late coming up in the spring, it rapidly develops a single large, heavily veined, three-parted leaf, each segment rounded and overlapping its neighbors. Simultaneously, on a separate shoot, is unfurled a great, shell-like, erect spathe of a diaphanous white suffused with pink and frequently with deeper pink ribs running from a broad base to an acutely pointed tip. Some forms tend to have the spathe tinted with pale green in combination with the pink, while others are pure white. Against this showy backdrop stands the erect, blunt, reddish purple spadix. Because the tuber is marginally hardy in severe-climate areas, it is suggested that it be planted about four inches deep and mulched for the winter. As it grows on rocky banks in open sites in its native home, this species does not want a heavy wet soil or deep shade.

A. consanguineum

This, I think, was the first arisaema I grew from seed, probably at least ten years ago. I can't remember how many seeds I got from one of the exchanges, but today I have only a solitary plant.

Coming from temperate eastern Asia and Yunnan, it is described in the *Royal Horticultural Society Dictionary* as "nearly hardy." Mine is planted near a rock and very close to a path in the upper woods garden under tall white pines in company with other arisaemas. Every year I fear that it is never going to show above ground or that it has been stepped on by someone plunging off the path to get a closer look at the blooming arisaemas behind it. But so far each year it has thrust up, about the last week in June, an asparaguslike spear that then shoots up at an astonishing rate. Within a week it has erected a slender mottled stalk three to four feet high. At the tip it unfurls a startling, umbrellalike, solitary leaf, deeply slit into long narrow segments elegantly pleated down the center. The literature describes the segments as ten to twenty-one in number. Last year mine displayed twenty-six leaflets. At the tip of each leaflet is a long, threadlike appendage. Just below this intricate leaf is a short side shoot bearing a rather small but typical flower, composed of a concealed spadix and a narrow mottled spathe, here distinguished by a long, threadlike appendage at the tip, which sweeps down almost to the ground. So tall and slender is the whole plant that if it sets a crop of seed it becomes top heavy and flops to the ground. I have a friend who planted his right at the base of a dwarf rhododendron and urges it to grow up through the branches for support.

For many years my plant produced only a leaf, like a pinwheel on a tall staff. For the past three years it has flowered, and perhaps next year the tuber will split up and send up a clump of small, more juvenile plants.

A. *dracontium*

Here we return to eastern North America. This species, colloquially called green dragon, is readily distinguished from other American arisaemas both in leaf and flower. Here the solitary leaf is composed of five to fifteen fanlike leaflets. The flower is made up of a rather pinched green spathe and a curious spadix that extends its green tapering tip well beyond the spathe and shoots skyward. The spadix in this species is frequently hermaphroditic. The green dragon has a generally Southeastern distribution, and is found most commonly on flood plains.

A. flavum

So far as I can discover, this is the runt of the litter. The plant, growing from a small tuber, is eight to ten inches tall with one or two leaves pedately divided into five or more divisions. As these leaves unfurl the curious blossom looks like a small blinking owl atop the green peduncle. The bisexual spadix is totally concealed within the spathe, which is squat and ovoid and does not produce a tubular elongation before forming the hoodlike blade. The blade narrows to a prominent point and bends down against the base. The hood is yellow, while the ovoid base is banded yellow and dark purple. The owlish effect is produced by the globose spathe forming a body; the pointed tip of the hood forming the beak; and the two dark hollows below the two earlike flares where the spathe bends abruptly downward forming the owl's half-shut eyes. The color in the flowers, I gather from reading, is variable from plant to plant, frequently with no yellow pigment apparent.

This species, found from Afghanistan through the Himalaya to western China, is borderline hardy. I lost my earliest seedlings by premature and shallow planting. Three-year-old tubers buried three to four inches deep under high pine shade have survived our most severe winter.

A. ringens

This species, from Japan and Korea, is readily distinguished from others, primarily by the pair of tripartite green leaves of a lus-

Arisaema flavum   Native from the Mediterranean region to the Himalayas.

trous, thick, waxy texture, each leaflet with an abrupt, sharp point. The cobralike inflorescence on a short stalk is also distinctive. The strongly ridged spathe is greenish or purple, with a short tube. Instead of ending in the more usual point at its apex, the deeply curved hood carries a dark purple, rippled extension that hangs down across the opening like a curtain. Like *A. candidissimum* and *A. consanguineum,* this species tries one's patience by its tardy appearance in the spring, sometimes as late as the first of July.

A. robustum

Late in the winter some years ago, I received from a friend in Japan a plump, apple-sized tuber of this species. At that time I had no alpine house, and it was impossible to plant the tuber outdoors. I potted it up and kept it gently watered in a cool end of the living room against a pair of north-facing French doors. Within two weeks it began to grow, and once begun it grew like a stalk of corn on a hot July night. You could daily perceive its climb from mullion to mullion of the door. It finally expanded a five-foliate leaf and an undistinguished, typical inflorescence, rather insignificant looking atop the three-foot-high, thick, shining, almost black main stem. It has had a checkered career since. Planted out its first summer in a moistish spot under an oak tree in the upper garden, it retired underground in appropriate fashion. The next spring, perhaps triggered by its domestic treatment, it pushed its eager shoot with the first fake whisper of spring and was, of course, frozen to a pulp. I thought that was the end of *A. robustum*. The following spring it reappeared only slightly later and was again frozen. The third spring was more favorable, and it sent up a majestic ebony stem, flowered, and set fruit which was nipped off by a deer while still green. Since then it has split its bulb and produced a clump of nonflowering, shorter plants. I should get around to digging them up and giving them fresh soil. A small grove of *A. robustum* might be rather impressive.

A. sikokianum

This species, strictly Japanese in distribution, is in my estimation the most glorious of the genus, *A. candidissimum* notwithstanding. In fact it is named by some Japanese botanists *A. magnificum*. In every respect it declares its beauty, from the elegant silver markings on the leaves and the flamboyant spathe to the ivory drumstick of the spadix. It is not very tall, only about twelve inches the first year of its bloom, and it is rather delicate in appearance, though it becomes taller and more robust as it puts on years. The spathe is a deep eggplant purple, lightly striped with green on the outside, its interior lined with white porcelain. The blade does not bend over, but stands erect with a jaunty flare to reveal the knobbed white spadix standing proudly within. As the inflorescence ages, the white lining of the spathe becomes suffused with pink as though tinted by the deep purple dye of the outside, and the blade becomes limp and folds forward to conceal the berries forming inside. Though these would undoubtedly turn scarlet outdoors if allowed to remain on the plant, they ripen so slowly that I have always picked off the cone of fruit, sometimes as late as November, while they are still green, and allowed them to ripen indoors in a warm place.

A. stewardsonii

This rarely encountered eastern North American species is tardy to spring into growth and resides in really wet, unfrequented swamps and bogs. It resembles our common species in growth habit and shape of flower and is distinguished not only by its lateness, but by the prominently corrugated conformation of its

Arisaema ringens   A low-growing robust Japanese species.

spathe, which has highly raised ridges of a sparkling white against the green to purple background. I have found in the garden that it will grow in sites far drier than those of its native home, and it is prone to rather rapid production of tuber offsets. It has not set seed in the garden.

A. thunbergii var. *urashima*

Like others in the genus this Japanese taxon suffers at the hands of the Nippon taxonomists. Messers. Hara and Makino at one time assigned it varietal status under *A. thunbergii.* At yet another time Messers. Hara and Nakai created a separate genus, *Flagellarisaema,* with species *urashima* attached. Most recently, in my available literature, Mr. Owhi accepts it on Mr. Hara's authority as a separate species: *A. urashima.* Take your choice.

Whatever its status, this arisaema is something unique. It is a squat plant as I grow it, with a solitary leaf of many leaflets. The bronze to reddish purple spathe is handsome, with a long tail-like point. What makes it startling is the flagellate tip of the spadix, which snakes out across the ground for forty to sixty centimeters. That's a thin worm 1½ to two feet long. Quite something to see in any garden.

A. triphyllum

We end with a technical difference. For years the primary species of American jack-in-the-pulpit was known as *A. triphyllum,* and for years I supposed this was the accepted name. Even such an esteemed botanist as W. H. Camp, when he was doing his paper "Sex in *Arisaema triphyllum*" back in the 1920s, considered it the primary species. The plants he dealt with would now be assigned to *A. atrorubens.* This species, *A. triphyllum* (of three leaves), tends to be smaller, with distinction in the leaflet shape and in the tube of the spathe. Its natural distribution is essentially coastal eastern

botanists placed in a separate genus *Hexastylis* (meaning six-styled) on the authority of that early wayward plantsman, Rafinesque, who based his decision on the quite different arrangement of the sexual parts. Europe provides two evergreen species of wild gingers, and Asia a group of deciduous ones.

A. canadense, found in rich woodland sites from eastern Canada to Minnesota south to North Carolina, Kentucky, and Illinois, begins to unfold its pungent, crumpled, membranaceous leaves very early in the spring, sending forth also in that same chilly season the solitary flowers at the base of a pair of leaf stalks, these opening frequently beneath the carpet of tree leaves deep and fluffy from the fall of the previous autumn. Especially in its early stages the whole plant is downed with soft pubescence. Later the heavy-textured leaves spread their long-stemmed blades, broadly acuminate at the tip and deeply heart shaped below. The flowers of the typical species are composed of a fleshy three-parted calyx forming a tublike wrapping about the basal ovary. This flagon, purplish green and woolly outside, is smooth and creamy within. The three-parted lip is enameled on its inner surface with a deep plum-purple glaze that runs in three thin lines from the partings of the calyx into the base of the cup where it forms a hexagonal band around the ring of twelve rich maroon stamens. These spring from the flattened top of the ovary, which is embedded in the fleshy base of the flower. The pointed tip of each stout filament extends well above the elongated anther that clings to its out-facing surface. The six pistils, fused into a short thick column, rise within these encircling menhirs.

This secret and dungeon flower, in the chilly spring days, by its ability to raise its temperature, lures into its darkened halls early flylike insects to perform the rites of fertilization as they move from one intoxicating tavern to another to ensure the mingling of genes from a diversity of individual plants.

Although on superficial inspection all specimens of *A. cana-*

dense look identical, botanists have created three varieties, in addition to the typical, based on the shape and carriage of the pointed calyx lobes: *acuminatum, reflexum,* and *ambiguum.*

In many ways even more exotic are the blossoms of the western deciduous asarums: *A. hartwegii* and *A. caudatum.* Here the lobes of the three-parted calyx are elongated into attenuated curlicues, and the whole greenish purple flask is long persistent until the fat, thick seeds burst forth from the enclosed ovary. Ants, doubtless attracted by the eventual breakdown of the seed envelopes, may play a role in the distribution of the seeds. There is no information about this in the literature available, but the fact that various species have self-sown in my garden at a distance from the original plants rather beyond mere gravitational effects suggests a possible auxiliary agent.

The two westerners have more glossy leaves than their eastern cousin, and *A. hartwegii* is especially attractive in having its polished green leaves splashed with ample silvery splotches. One wonders, sometimes, why silvery markings on the leaves, as in the Rex begonias and other plants, hold such an allure for gardeners. Photosynthesis must be reduced in those areas of the leaves so decorated, and presence of the colors should therefore be negatively selected. It is worth pondering.

For beauty of foliage the *Hexastylis* species in the southeast United States are preeminent, and there the common name for the wild gingers is more often heart leaf. The leaves, on long, stout, brownish petioles, are broadly heart shaped to rounded spear shaped, thick and leathery. They are a light green beneath with prominent veins and much darker on the upper surface, tinged occasionally with dark red and frequently decorated with an intricate pattern of lighter reticulations and maculations. These leaf variations occur in all the different species, some being almost kidney shaped while one, *H. arifolia,* has arrow-shaped leaves.

Hexastylis (Asarum) virginica   A southern woodlander; one of the wild
gingers.

Based on the size and shape of the flowers, with special attention to the length of the three calyx lobes, the authors of the
Manual of the Vascular Flora of the Carolinas recognize eight
distinct species, somewhat more than other botanists. Except
possibly in the case of *H. arifolia,* it is probably sufficient for
horticultural purposes to make two principal separations based on
the size of the flowers, remembering that the urnlike blossom is
really a calyx with three pointed lobes. In one group we may
include *HH. virginica, maniflora, minus,* and *heterophylla.* In these
the calyx is 1 to 2½ centimeters long. In the other group, which
includes *HH. shuttleworthii* and *lewisii,* the calyx is from 2½ to
5 centimeters long. Time of bloom may also play some part in
this division, *H. shuttleworthii* blooming much later in the season,
in June and July in our New England garden, rather than in late
April and May as does its look-alike *H. virginica.*

The larger flowers of these last two species are especially
striking when they are explored after a probing beneath the
leathery leaves; fat, thick-textured, streaked with green and maroon on their outer surface, they last long, late into the season
before decaying to release the seeds. Their flaring three-parted lips
are most marvelously speckled and dotted on their inner surface
with subtle colors against the sueded tan to mulberry-purple hide.
Deeper in, these jugs are variously ridged with fleshy vermicula-
tions. Amidst them one can visualize strange gnomish rites, secret
and seductive. Or, as one observer said about a mature plant that
had a close-packed clutch of blossoms at its base, "It looks like
a nestful of baby birds with gaping beaks." A hill-country man
native to the woods where these gingers flourish is reported to
have commented, "A real passel of young sarpints coiled up and
ready to bite."

To return briefly to botany and taxonomy while on the subject
of the blossoms of wild ginger, the flowers of *Hexastylis,* unlike

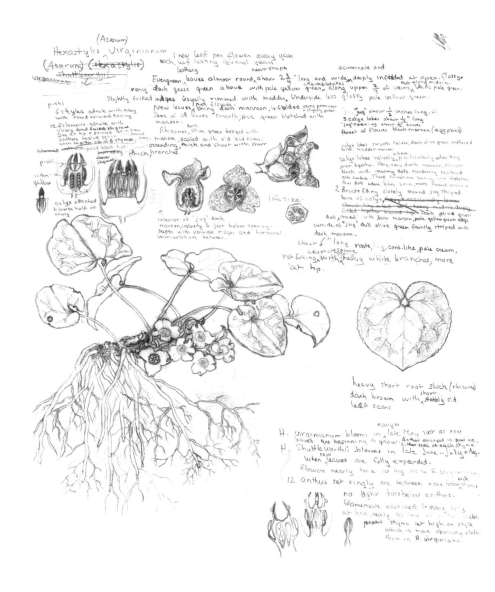

Hexastylis (Asarum) virginianum   Working sketch. The final pen-and-ink
illustration appears on page 160.

those of *Asarum,* carry their hemispherical stigmas facing outward near the apex of the six styles. These are pointed at the tips,
which are more or less split into two parts. These styles, instead
of being united into a single column rising from the center of
the top of the ovary as in the asarums, are fused to the sides of
the ovary and enclose it. The filaments of the twelve stamens are
in turn fastened to the basal portion of this crown of styles, their
anthers pressed tightly against it.

Less exciting flowers, but decorative leaves, mark two evergreen asarum of Europe: *AA. europaeum* and *causasicum,* with
blunt, open heart- to kidney-shaped leaves of lesser substance than
those of the American *Hexastylis.* In Asia the species tend to be
deciduous and similar to *A. canadense,* though one species, *A.
sieboldii,* is so variously mottled in the leaves that Japanese fanciers once recorded up to seventy variants. Some of these also
have flowers of considerable interest, *A. macranthum* of eastern
China and Formosa, having rich purple-brown blossoms two
inches across with wide, wavy, yellow-margined lobes, and *A.
caudigerum,* having lobes extended into curly tails an inch or more
long. Unfortunately neither of these is hardy.

The wild gingers are not plants that elicit exclamations from
your garden visitors, but are for display to the observant few.
A collection of the deciduous and evergreen species along some
shaded path in the woodland garden provides occasion for a
close examination, with a discerning friend or on your own, of
the varied leaf shapes and textures and the discreet display of
flowers. This inevitably leads to those friendly disputes about
distinctions among species. The final gesture, of course, is to
extract a rooted rhizome with attendant leaves and a solitary
flower and, as you tuck it into the plastic bag, to toss off a
remark like: "I find this one particularly pleasant. I believe it's
Asarum—or if you prefer—*Hexastylis lewisii,* but I can't be

sure. At any rate I think you'll like the foliage, and the flowers are worth scrabbling for."

All the species of *Asarum/Hexastylis* are readily propagated by division at any time during the period of active growth. They thrive best in duffy soil, well shaded. In fact, they are among the few of our woodlanders that will flower well even in dense shade. The various species tend to self-sow, but experiment shows that one must wait two years for seed to germinate and another two for seedlings to give good account of themselves. I think the wait is worth it.

H.L.F.

ASTER LINARIIFOLIUS

Although the tribe of eastern American asters is vast and botanically confusing, and although asters are a prominent and glorious ornament of roadsides and meadows and woodlands throughout the late summer and autumn, very few are of a stature or carriage fit for a place in the rock garden.

In recent years there have been developed some dwarf, showy hybrid Michaelmas daisies with much of the New England and New York asters in their genetic background. The blossoms are large and copious, ranging in color from deep lavender through blues and pinks to white. They have found their proper role as magnificent mounds of color in the foreground of the perennial border in late summer, just before the early chrysanthemums. They have also been planted in rock gardens to bring some of the late color, eagerly sought, to carry along after the show of spring and early summer. But it must be confessed that, for the same reason that fat-faced pansies are ruled out where wild violas are admitted, these hybrid asters look dowdy and dumpy, over-dressed and ostentatious in the rock garden. They are also gross feeders and require almost annual division to keep them thriving.

None of these complaints can be lodged against *Aster linariifolius,* the savory-leaved aster. Here is a composite that not only has the subtle mark of untamed breeding, but possesses many virtues as a rock garden plant. It blossoms at a time of year—from late August until frost—when there is little else flowering on the sunny ledges of the garden. It will grow in a variety of sites and soils, is reliably perennial, and yet never ramps or crowds its neighbors.

Aster linariifolius (with leaves like *Linaria,* the toadflax), grows wild in dry, open soils, on ledges and rocky or sandy banks from New Brunswick to southern Minnesota, down through New England, and south to northwestern Florida and eastern Texas. It forms a rather stiff, raspy tussock of erect stems from four to twenty-four inches tall with narrow, bristly leaves somewhat on the order of the leaves of summer savory, but not pungent. The inch-broad flowers have numerous conspicuous rays, or ligules, generally lavender, but sometimes white, surrounding the golden disk in the center. There are usually from two to five flowers in a loose head near the tips of the stems.

Because this aster dies down to the ground in winter and is late to send up its sheaf of stalks, it may be grown generously amidst early-flowering and low plants, slowly to take their place as the season advances. If grown in ample numbers, it will form a very pleasing lavender haze across the garden as the autumn days grow shorter. It appears to be indifferent to the pH of the soil, and will thrive in any well-drained site, even in the poorest stony soil. In fact, a starvation diet keeps the stems short and dense, and the blossoms bright.

There are, moreover, inherent differences of stature, of blossom size, and color. Good, dense, dwarf forms with large and brilliant flowers occasionally appear in any large colony. Here at Millstream, where we have permitted this aster to self-sow abundantly (as it will do if the seed heads are not removed before dispersal), one or two plants of superior quality have appeared. When they are in bloom in September and on into October, I promise myself that I shall try propagating them vegetatively. Each spring—the proper time to divide them, or take cuttings— my attention has been distracted elsewhere. Next year I shall try to remember, and I urge others who know this aster in the wild, or grow it in the garden, to search for fine forms. It may be quite easily transplanted in early spring, or while in flower, and it comes readily from fresh seed.

Here is another of our American natives infrequently seen in gardens. It is not in immediate danger of extinction in the wild, but it is certainly worth bringing into more general cultivation.

H.L.F.

CALLIRHOE INVOLUCRATA

When the flush of spring bloom has left the rock garden, and the long, hot days of summer are ripening the seed of earlier- flowering plants, there is one that will just be coming into its own, a plant of our own short-grass prairies and the sandy dry soils along roadsides and railroad embankments in the West and Midwest: *Callirhoe involucrata.*

Starting its blossoming season in June and continuing on through the summer until frost, this member of the *Malvaceae* is variously called buffalo rose, poppy mallow, and wine cups and is found from Minnesota to Missouri westward through North Dakota and Oklahoma to eastern Wyoming and Colorado and down into Mexico, its tough, hairy, vinelike branches trailing across the parched, sun-baked soil. Unaccountably and perhaps inappropriately the generic name of this dry-lands plant honors Callirrhoë, the daughter of Achelous, a minor Greek river god.

Callirhoe involucrata   The brilliant red poppy mallow blooms all summer.

Perhaps this nymph was banished from her riverine home to the desert for some grave misdemeanor, or perhaps, like some of our young people today, she became impatient of or sickened by the easy life along her father's river bank and ran off to make her own way in a more challenging world. The specific name of this plant is, however, more pertinent. It is earned by the three involucral bracts directly beneath the five-parted calyx.

The leaves of poppy mallow are intricately and deeply cut into lanceolate lobes that are themselves cleft into slender-pointed segments. They are covered with short, stiff hairs and are dark green with pale veining. Though the leaves are handsome in themselves, it is the blossoms that float above them that are the plant's true glory: great satiny cups, up to two inches across, and of a rich, glowing magenta. Yes, magenta. But don't be put off by this frequently derogatory color word; even the most adamant magentaphobes succumb to the blossoms of *Callirhoe involucrata*. They are sumptuous, whether the five wedge-shaped petals are entirely dyed this pure deep color or whether, as they sometimes do, they pale at the base to immaculate white.

Within this salver of Oriental splendor is set a column of stamens, their filaments fused to form a tube studded with creamy white anthers that, as they ripen, sift pearly grains of pollen over the inner surface of the petals. Later, after the pollen is shed, the pistil springs upward through the opening at the summit of the stamen column, the style split into ten to twenty threadlike branches, each with a stigma on its inner surface. As these rise they spread and curl like the slender arms of a sea anemone.

The seed head of wine cups resembles the "cheeses" of the weedy *Malva neglecta* which, as children, we crunched between our teeth with such relish. The seeds, each enclosed in a carpel, are set in a ring around the remains of the stamen column. They germinate easily and may be sown in either spring or fall. In fact,

C. involucrata will usually self-sow to provide progeny for transplanting, though it has not done so profusely in our Connecticut
garden. Seedlings should be transplanted early into their permanent site, as even in infancy they have a deep, searching taproot
that thickens and elongates rapidly as they mature, a great advantage in the droughty, hard-baked soils of their native habitat.
Seed seems to be the only way in which to propagate these plants
as, to my knowledge, no one has succeeded in increasing them
by division or root or stem cuttings.

In the garden, wine cups do best in a well-drained, rather sandy
loam in a sun-drenched site. This plant needs elbow room. It
should not be overrun by taller plants, neither should it be placed
too near small and delicate neighbors, for though in early spring
it displays only a neat winter rosette of evergreen leaves, its leafy
flowering stems will sprawl eighteen to thirty-six inches out from
the crown by midsummer. *C. involucrata* does well when planted
at the top of a wall where its trailing branches can fall in a curtain
of interlaced leaves and brilliant flowers, and it grows well on
the flat, as the trailing branches are not smothering and will
weave among and over such stalwart plants as penstemons, dwarf
iris, and pulsatillas. Its glowing blossoms are particularly lovely
when mingled with the soft lavender-blue bells of *Campanula
carpatica* and *C. rotundifolia*.

I have never had the heart to trim back the flowering stems,
which are studded with new buds at the elongating tips, but I am
told they may be cut back quite severely in midsummer to make
a more compact and floriferous mat.

Britton and Brown lists seven species of *Callirhoe* in the
United States and Mexico, mostly perennial, upright plants with
showy flowers of magenta, pink, or white. A few, perhaps best
suited to the border as they sound a bit tall for the average rock
garden, are *CC. alcaeoides, digitata, papaver,* and *triangulata*.

L.L.F.

CAMPANULA PLANIFLORA
Confusion Confounded

Off and on for a number of years I have grown a neat little campanula that I have always called *Campanula planiflora*. The first time I saw this plant was many years ago in the wonderful garden of Mrs. Florens DeBevoise at Cronamere, in Green Farms, Connecticut. She called it, as I remember, *C. nitida*. Either *planiflora* or *nitida* are apt names, the former describing the flatness of the large round blossoms close held to the six- to eight-inch stem, the latter describing the shining, polished luster of the small, dentate, basal leaves.

It is a curious plant in many ways. When the species is grown from seed, not all the plants in the same batch will be typical. In fact, most of them are not, but the difference can be quickly detected even before the plants are old enough to send up flowering stems. Those that will be true to the description of *planiflora (nitida)* will have very firm, glossy leaves, regularly, but not deeply, serrate. All the others will have thinner, paler leaves quite definitely long and tapering. The ones with the long leaves will eventually flower in a manner which makes them indistinguishable from *C. persicifolia*.

Because I do grow *C. persicifolia* in other parts of my garden, for a long time I thought perhaps miscegenation had taken place and that the taller ones were from hybrid seed which had selfsowed at the base of and among the dwarf *C. planiflora*. So I began to investigate the literature.

What I found is bewildering. H. Clifford Crook in *Campanulas* lists *C. planiflora* among synonyms in the back of the book thus: "planiflora, Engelm.—parryi; planiflora, Lam.—pyramidalis (or nitida); planiflora, Willd.—versicolor; planiflora (see p. 148)." Page 148 is under Crook's consideration of *C. planiflora*. He says in part, "A form occurred recently, and was named 'Telham Beauty', which due to a doubling of chromosome content, is larger in all its parts and a stronger grower, while a pygmy form (technically a Mendelian recessive) is often referred to as *C. planiflora* or *C. nitida.*" We shall return to Mr. Crook later.

In *Hortus Second,* Bailey says, "*C. planiflora:* probably *C. versicolor* is meant; the American *C. planiflora* is *C. parryi.*" So I looked at his *C. versicolor.* Here is the description: "To 4ft— glabrous: lvs. ovate to ovate-lanceolate, toothed, the lower long-stalked: fls. pale blue with violet throat, in long spike-like racemes. Greece." This is obviously not our dwarf with flat blossoms. Bailey's description of *C. parryi* is thus: "Erect, 3–10 in., glabrous: lvs. narrow-lanceolate or spatulate, upper ones linear, entire or slightly denticulate: fls. usually single erect, broad, about 1 in. across, violet. Rocky Mts., subalpine.—This is the *C. planiflora* of American botanists." Again this is obviously not our plant. *C. parryi* is entirely different, as you know if you have seen its open habit of growth with long trailing stems.

But let us see what T. C. Mansfield says in *Alpines in Colour and Cultivation:* "*C. planiflora* (Bearing flat flowers). N. America. Rosettes of foliage of deep shining green with 'deckled edges' giving a short, stout spire of flat, bland, open flowers of cool powder-blue. Succeeds best in rich soil in position where plenty of sunlight is incident." Ah! This is clearly our plant, but the author makes no mention of its peculiar habits, of its either dying out or suddenly changing its identity. And note that he asserts without question, "N. America." He is not confusing the plant with *C. parryi* in his description, but because of the synonym he has assigned it to the wrong niche.

Or, what is more likely, Mansfield is repeating the original confusion of our *C. planiflora* with the *C. parryi* synonym which Farrer included in *The English Rock Garden,* where he says, "*C. planiflora,* an interesting and valuable thing from North America, rather obscure in its history and confused in catalogues, which sometimes call it *C. nitida,* and have at other times even placed it doubtfully as a dwarf form of *C. pyramidalis.* But this last is not an American plant at all; nor has *C. planiflora* any resemblance to it, being much more approximate to a stunted development of *C. latiloba.* It has a marked personality, being stiff and stocky, about 9 inches to a foot in height, with smooth hard and leathery foliage, narrow-oblong and scalloped; while on the stem sit tight the big fat flowers, round and flat and rather stolid-looking, of cool powder-blue (or white). It is quite easy of culture in any ordinary place, suggesting most of all, perhaps, a much condensed and blank-faced form of *C. persicifolia.* It has a look of Spartan sturdiness and character, and might justly be described in the words of an eminent authority as 'a very dressy little alpine.' "

Once again this is obviously our plant, more vividly and precisely described than we can do, but that expression "blank-faced" has a touch of the patronizing tone Farrer generally employed for American plants, and he clearly thought of it as an American species, probably because of the *C. parryi* synonym. He does, to be sure, note its similarity to a much-condensed *C. persicifolia.*

What prompted further search, however, was Farrer's phrase, "more approximate to a stunted development of *C. latiloba.*" That is an entirely new suggestion. So back to Mr. Crook. *C. latiloba* is for him a synonym of *C. grandis,* which he describes thusly: "This species is a useful, if rather coarse and stiff, border plant whose home is in Siberia. It forms a mat of rosettes of long, glabrous, undulate, strap-shaped, widely and coarsely dentate leaves, narrowed at both ends. The leaves are longer & coarser

than those of *C. persicifolia* to which the present species is closely
akin and from each rosette springs a stiff flower spike, up to three
feet in height. The lower third of this stem is furnished with
leaves similar to those of the rosette, diminishing gradually in size
as they ascend, the upper part with large, flat, saucer-shaped
flowers about two inches across in blue or white and either singly
or in threes, which, being carried on very short pedicels, produce
a solid and formal effect."

The excellent picture of *C. grandis* in Crook's book and the
description are very like a tall-growing version of our *C. planiflora*. Wheels within wheels!

Is it possible that we have in the inconstant *C. planiflora* a
Mendelian recessive form of *C. persicifolia* further complicated by
some unrecorded crossing with *C. grandis?* If any of the few
plants I have left send up short stems with "blank-faced" blossoms, I shall scrutinize them from radix to calyx for any clues
of their possible parentage or puzzling behavior.

H.L.F.

To add to the confusion about *Campanula persicifolia* forma
planiflora among rock gardeners and donors of seed to our exchanges, a number of authorities have in the past assigned the
name *C. planiflora* to several species of campanulas, among them
C. parryi, a native of the Rocky Mountains. It is, perhaps, this
muddle which has led many horticultural authors, including such
authorities as Farrer, Bailey, and Mansfield, either to assign the
wrong plant to the name *C. planiflora* or give the wrong provenance to the correctly described and named plant.

The true *C. parryi* of the Rockies grows from a running root
which produces numerous tuffets of coarsely dentate, strap-
shaped leaves. Similar leaves adorn the rather trailing stems from
which rise slender, upright, leafy pedicels bearing at their tips the
usually single, deep lavender-blue, open funnelform flowers.

These are cut into rather starry segments at least halfway to the base. On the other hand, *C. persicifolia* forma *planiflora,* described correctly above, neither runs nor trails but stays put in a compact clump.

Anyone with a keen eye, who grows the typical form of *C. persicifolia* and permits it to self-sow, may occasionally run into a seedling of *C.p. planiflora.* As a Mendelian recessive, the gene for dwarfism is probably present, though masked, in a number of plants of *C. persicifolia* of quite normal appearance. It should be possible, by persistent roguing of all normal *C. persicifolia* that grow in the neighborhood of the dwarf form, to eventually produce a *C.p. planiflora* that comes 100 percent true from seed, for even without such Draconian measures a fair percentage of the seed of *C.p. planiflora* will produce the dwarf plant.

It is possible, but unlikely, that this dwarf form of *C. persicifolia* was first noticed in a garden in this country. If so, this would certainly have strengthened or even started the misconception that *C.p. planiflora* is of American origin. However, because its progenitor is a native of southern Europe, we really cannot, with a clear conscience, claim it as our own.

L.L.F.

CHRYSOGONUM VIRGINIANUM

Farrer, in his inimitable way and with that slight touch of scorn he usually nourished toward American plants, portrays *Chrysogonum virginianum* L. as: "a very popular and much praised composite of curious unattractiveness, though useful; forming under any treatment, masses of low foliage on which all summer through appears a profusion of yellow flowers with rays so few and broad as to look like five-pointed stars not belonging to the Compositae at all."

Chrysogonum virginianum var. *australe*   An accommodating and cheerful United States native.

Despite Farrer's first phrase about its popularity, the plant is rarely mentioned by other rock gardening authors, either American or British, and it is very little seen in gardens today, whatever its vogue may have been in former times. Nor is it a really common plant in the wild.

It is found in nature from southern Pennsylvania southward to Florida and Louisiana, in rich woods and on shaded rocks. Over its range it tends to diversify into two recognized varieties: the typical variety, a clumpy but rather gawky plant with small, gap-toothed flowers on stems up to sixteen inches tall; and var. *australe,* forming a spreading, stoloniferous, densely leafy carpet with large, broad-rayed flowers on stems of six to eight inches at the most. Our own Ed Alexander described this latter as a separate species and assigned the epithet *australe,* which it now bears as a variety. This is an appropriate name, because in the Carolinas, where the two varieties are found, the typical one is centered in North Carolina and var. *australe* in South Carolina.

The stoloniferous variety is far superior as a garden plant, and the best forms of it are easily propagated by simple division of the clump. As is suggested by its natural habitat, *Chrysogonum,* known by the colloquial name green-and-gold and occasionally as golden aster (a name more commonly assigned to the genus *Chrysopsis*), thrives best in cultivation with a bit of light shade. It will grow, as Farrer suggested, even in full sun and dryish sites, but there, in midsummer, it tends to wilt in hot weather.

The complex golden flowers are borne on short stems arising at the joints between pairs of leaves: hence the name *Chrysogonum,* from the Greek *chrysos*—golden and *gonu*—knee or joint, which Linnaeus borrowed for this American plant from the Greek name for some obscure herb.

The flower head is composed of five (and occasionally six)

yellow ray flowers and a dense cluster of disk flowers in the center. Each ray flower carries at the base a yellow, divided pistil which eventually produces in the ovary that adheres to the involucral bracts blackish nutlike seeds without the typical composite feathery pappus. The disk flowers, developing first unevenly about the rim, are complete little flowers with tiny yellow petals and numerous stamens and pistils, but the pistils are sterile.

As these composite flowers develop, they change from day to day. And all through the season until frost, new ones are unfolding as the old ones pass away. Not a spectacular plant, but certainly useful, as Farrer grudgingly admits. W. H. H. Preece, in that rare book published in 1937, *North American Rock Plants (First Series),* analyzed the singular charm that *Chrysogonum* holds for those who have grown it.

I must admit that I do not quite know why I am so fond of this little plant: it has neither splendour nor prodigality of blossom; it gives forth no intriguing perfume; it has neither airy grace nor stately form; the rather coarse foliage is produced with abandon, the dainty golden blossoms with considerable restraint; its habit is humble and lowly; just the same, to grow it is to love it. Sometimes you meet an attractive girl; you analyze her features and find she has not one good point, then you consider the *tout ensemble* and find her altogether adorable; so it is with *C. virginianum,* though, in addition to its indefinable charm, it does have some very good points. Its most endearing quality, perhaps, is its persistency in blooming, for though it never covers itself with a garment of Midas, there is rarely a day from mid-March to late November when you cannot find a few five-pointed, golden stars gleaming amidst the olive-green foliage.

H.L.F.

CLAYTONIA

Two species of the genus *Claytonia* grow naturally in Connecticut: *C. virginica* and *C. caroliniana*. Both are called spring beauty, an apt name for these lowly herbs that grace the vernal woodlands and copses with pale pink or white five-starred flowers striped with deep pink lines. Sensitive and transient as they are, expanding only when the spring sun shines, they do persist for an extended period of days in the halting spring weather. Each blossom on the upward-advancing raceme of the inflorescence itself persists for more than a day, unlike some other more evanescent flowers within this same purslane family, the *Portulacaceae*.

In fact these two plants merit in the august pages of Gray's *Manual of Botany* a marvelous and rare exclamation point after the phrase "Corolla rose-color with deeper veins, opening for more than one day!" It is not the color of the corolla that was being exclaimed at, I'm sure; the point was to signal the delight that these delicate-seeming purslanes persisted for more than one day. It does warm the heart to know that the botanist who inserted that punctuation was as pleased with *Claytonia*'s flowering persistence in nature as he was with the taxonomic features he had to delineate from dried specimens.

In the usually arid pages of the taxonomic floras the eastern spring beauty is described as a low perennial plant with somewhat fleshy leaves arising from a small, deep tuber, up to four stems and a few basal leaves from each tuber. The flowering stems bear a pair of opposite leaves and a loose raceme of flowers on fairly long pedicels. There are five petals with five stamens adhering to the short claws of the petals. The style is three-cleft at the apex. The three-valved pod is enclosed between two ovate persistent sepals. The three to six small seeds are a shiny red-brown. The distinction between the two species is based primarily on the leaves. In *C. virginica* the leaves are linear-lanceolate, 7 to 15 centimeters long, whereas in *C. caroliniana* they are spatulate—oblong, 2½ to 5 centimeters long, and with a conspicuous petiole. Where they grow together the latter blooms about a week earlier and has fewer flowers in a shorter, tighter raceme. Because of this dense arrangement of flowers, *C. caroliniana* has a slight advantage as a garden plant.

These two species are rarely found growing together in nature, however, a fact that raises some interesting questions of distribution. In the *Manual of Flowering Plants of Connecticut, C. virginica* is described as being "occasional or frequent in the southwestern part of the state, rare or local elsewhere." *C. caroliniana* is characterized as rare or local throughout, recorded mostly from the northwestern portion of the state.

Homer House, in the *Wild Flowers of New York,* says that *C. caroliniana* is abundant throughout the state, while *C. virginica* is mostly coastal.

The overall ranges of the two species are not entirely the same, though they overlap for a considerable portion. *C. caroliniana* appears to have a somewhat more northerly and westerly distribution extending from Saskatchewan at one extreme to the mountains of North Carolina and Tennessee at the other. *C. virginica* is found from Quebec to Minnesota in the north, and south as far as Georgia, Louisiana, and Texas.

Both species grow in moist but well-drained sites, mostly in wooded areas, though *C. virginica* may be found also in moist meadows. In fact Dr. Rickett, in *Wild Flowers of the United States,* makes the curious statement about *Claytonia:* "A favorite spring flower, decorating lawns, borders of parkways and other suburban precincts." That remark suggests that spring beauty is almost a weed, keeping company with such as dandelion and wild onion. Such denigration is hardly softened by Dr. R.'s unverified assertion that it is a "favorite" spring flower.

To be sure, in a congenial site the spring beauty will self-sow and eventually form large, showy patches, but I have never seen a woodland garden beset by *Claytonia* to the point where it becomes a weed. Because of the delicacy of its growth habit and the depth and small size of the tuber, these plants never interfere with associates. Since they are delicate and do die down completely fairly early in the season, they are best planted in drifts amidst other kinds of plants that will furnish the area all through the summer. The spring beauties are admirable companions for any of the woodland primroses.

If perchance the spring beauty ever becomes a problem weed in your garden, it is easy to amend the situation. Dig and eat them. Dr. Steyermark in the *Flora of Missouri* says, "The young plants of Spring Beauty, in regions of abundance, may be eaten as a cooked vegetable, while the thick, round, underground corms, when boiled in salted water, resemble the taste of chestnuts."

There are other species of *Claytonia* in the western United States, some quite similar to our eastern representatives and two especially beautiful alpine species: *C. megarrhiza* and *C. montana*.

The genus name commemorates John Clayton, one of America's earliest botanists, who in the eighteenth century sent much material to Europe to J. F. Gronovius for his *Flora Virginica*.

H.L.F.

COLLINSIA VERNA IN THE GARDEN

The pure deep blue of a winter sky on a halcyon day is rare and treasured in flowers, and it is perhaps this color that brings

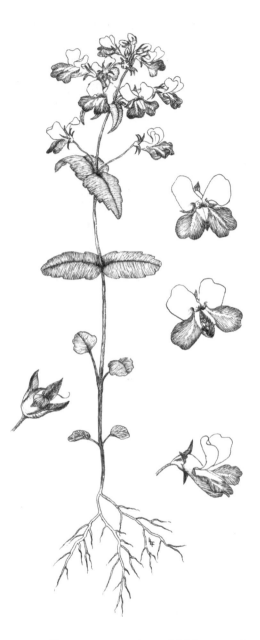

Collinsia verna   A beautiful blue annual.

exclamations of delight from those who see a drift of *Collinsia verna* shimmering in the spring wind. And it is in a colony of close-set plants, growing as they are found in their natural habitat, that these flowers do and look their best.

As single plants these annuals, named after a Philadelphian, Zaccheus Collins, an early nineteenth-century botanist, are rather skimpy. The slender eight- to sixteen-inch stem, with widely spaced leaf pairs with short petioles, the upper ones stemless, is topped by a few blossoming whorls of up to six flowers splaying out on long pedicels, each flower only about half an inch across. In shape the flowers are somewhat reminiscent of penstemon; the upper lip is divided into two upstanding segments and is usually white but occasionally very pale blue. The lower lip is three-lobed, but from the front appears formed of only two petals, as the central segment is tucked under and behind the two flaring outer lobes and folded in half longitudinally around the cluster of stamens. This lower lip is a rich azure, and it is perhaps the combination of the white and blue in the flower that gives it such a lively sparkle.

Each flower produces up to four seeds which drop very quickly from the ovoid capsule as soon as ripe. It is not surprising that these seeds are favored by mice, but it is surprising that they do not retain their viability for long: they are almost nutlike, shaped rather like eggs deeply dented on one side, comparatively large (up to three millimeters long), and dark brown. A colony of plants is perhaps best established by scattering the seeds and patting them into a patch of bare soil that has been lightly cultivated. They should then be allowed to self-sow.

Although quite widespread in distribution from New York out to eastern Wisconsin and south to West Virginia and Kentucky, *Collinsia verna* is apparently not frequently seen in the wild. It seems to favor a neutral to limy soil in rich woods and thickets near stream sides, though it does not appear to require a great deal of moisture. Here at Millstream it does least well in the thin acid soil of the woods garden, where it tends to peter out. But it has maintained itself for about five years in limy soil among wild strawberries despite the root competition of a large sugar maple which shades it from the north. In very acid soil a sprinkling of lime might be salutary.

Early blooming, as its specific name indicates, *Collinsia verna* is quick to vanish as soon as it sheds its seeds, and by early summer the patch of plants, which gave us such a show in May, has disappeared without a trace.

L.L.F.

CORNUS CANADENSIS

The specific name *canadensis,* shared frequently by other native American plants, was used by early botanists to indicate that such plants are most at home in the northern parts of the American continent. This epithet is verified further by the observation that, though in nature *Cornus canadensis* is found from Greenland to Labrador, across the north to Alaska, and southward in the mountains to West Virginia and California, this plant flowers and fruits abundantly only in its northern haunts. It may be persuaded, by careful site selection, to grow in more southern lowland gardens, but here it never puts on such a display of flower. And even when it does flower, it sets fruit poorly or not at all.

This behavior may be solely controlled by temperature, but it is more likely a response to day length. I remember how struck I was seeing great beds of this dwarf cornel, densely set with glistening clusters of red fruit, growing in full sun as a roadside ground cover in the Gaspé and again seeing it heavily fruited, though not so dense, in deep, moist shade in New Hampshire.

How different it looks in the few native patches I have found in the northwestern hills of Connecticut, where *C. canadensis* flowers sparsely and never develops good, full clusters of berries. I used to wonder whether in the southern part of its range an insect pollinator was scarce or even absent, or possibly, whether some fungus destructive to the flower buds proliferated in warmer climates to diminish fruit set. These two factors may play a role, but I now incline to think that day length may be the controlling influence. Here is an area of investigation for some graduate student of botany at a university where there is equipment to control all aspects of a plant's environment.

Yet, though this plant fails to perform in many of our gardens as superbly as it does in the northern wilds, it is still a most worthy candidate for inclusion.

Cornus canadensis forms a rapidly spreading ground cover by way of its forking underground rhizomes, and from these ramifications rather sparse feeding roots wriggle down into the acid, duffy, moist soil it prefers. At periodic intervals from the upper surface of the rhizome arise the leaf-bearing stalks, four to eight inches tall. The opposite leaves, of sufficient substance to be evergreen when not tattered by an open winter and suffused in fall with shades of orange and cerise, tend to cluster in a whorl near the summit. Broadly flaring at the middle, the leaves narrow abruptly at both ends and are conspicuously veined. From the center of the leaf whorl grows a short flower stalk that carries what appears to be a solitary flower with four white petals and a yellow-green center. Actually the center is a cluster of small, four-petaled flowers that eventually produce the clump of red berries giving this plant one of its colloquial names: bunchberry. The four white petal-like structures are bracts just as in the flowering dogwood tree, the closely related arborescent species of *Cornus*.

Because of the similarity of the flowering and fruiting of the treelike *Cornus florida* and the herbaceous, ground-hugging *C. canadensis,* one is curious about their evolutionary history. This curiosity is further piqued by the fact that in the lower reaches of the *C. canadensis* range in the West, there is a parallel treelike species, *C. nuttallii,* though this usually sports six bracts around the cluster of flowers rather than four. Is there in the Orient now or in records of the past a ground-covering species to make a balanced pair with the tree form, *C. kousa?* There is not now in Europe a treelike companion for the herbaceous *C. suecica,* a near relative of *C. canadensis.*

One gets lured away easily into these speculations when one tries to capture the "feel" of the plant itself and remembers a tree or two of *C. florida* that presented problems in a controlled landscape because they persisted in sending out rather herbaceous stolons in a skirt all about the base of the trunk—wonderful fodder for deer, but never assuming treelike stance. Is it even possible that we could cross fertilize *C. canadensis* or *C. suecica* with *C. florida, C. nuttallii,* or *C. kousa* to hark back to some previous evolutionary forms? Probably not. Too many genetic changes have taken place to allow such miscegenation.

To return from our wayward speculations, it is accurate to say that the flower clusters set off by the white bracts are truly handsome in *C. canadensis* and are sometimes even more exotic in having the bracts purple tipped or even roseate throughout, as in *C. canadensis* forma *purpurescens,* again duplicating the color patterns of *C. florida* with its commonly cultivated *rubra* form. The scarlet berries, huddled in a tight bunch, are certainly as notable as the flowers. Each fleshy berry contains a single plump, nutlike seed, but the berry has enough flesh around the seed to encourage eating.

That the fruit is indeed edible is attested to by some of its

Cornus canadensis   Bunchberry is a diminutive relative of the flowering dogwood.

common names: crackerberry and puddingberry. Linnaeus, in his account in *Travels in Lapland,* reports that the Lapps made what he called a "dainty" from a mixture of the berries of *C. suecica* which they boiled down until as thick as "flummery." This pudding is eaten with milk or cream, rather easier to mouth if the seeds have been strained out earlier in the process. Cow's milk and whey may be as satisfactory here as the milk of reindeer that the Lapps depended upon. It might be wise also if using *C. canadensis* to add a dash of lemon juice or other flavoring to the mixture, because its berries are rather insipid, while those of the European *C. suecica* are in themselves pleasantly tart.

The current enthusiasm for the nutritional value of our native and imported flora should not exclude, I think, aesthetic virtues. *C. canadensis* does possess this latter quality in sufficient degree to prompt us to try to introduce it into a moist, acid corner of our garden for a long season of display. It is definitely not an easy plant to transfer from nature to the garden, but it may be propagated by careful separation of a subterranean rhizome from the plant, treating this as a cutting in a sand-peat frame or pot until it has made new roots. Seedling plants are even more readily established if you are willing to wait two years for the seeds to germinate after at least one spell of freezing.

Because the flower structure of this ground cover is somewhat different from that of the various other shrubby species of *Cornus,* some botanists have christened it with a separate genetic name: mouth-filling *Chamaepericlymenum.* There is plenty of sound authority, however, to warrant retaining the simpler nomenclature.

Cornus suecica is very similar to *C. canadensis* but is in appearance a leafier plant. It has a considerable number of larger opposite pairs of leaves on the upright stem below the terminal whorl. The blossoms are very like those of its New World cousin, though not so large. The creamy bracts are smaller, and the cluster of flowers in the center is dark purple instead of pale yellow. Though considered primarily a European plant, *C. suecica* is circumpolar and comes across from Siberia into Alaska and thence east across the Canadian arctic.

H.L.F.

PINK MOCCASIN
Cypripedium acaule

One of the most sumptuous and appealing flowers of our native flora is *Cypripedium acaule*, the pink lady's slipper. That it has borne more common names than perhaps any other native plant tells us of its universal allure. The first foreign visitors to these American shores must have been impressed with this pink version of what they knew in Europe as "Venus shoe," the yellow-flowered *Cypripedium calceolus*.

Linnaeus created the Latinized name for the genus from *Cypris*—Venus, hence Aphrodite, and *pedilon*, the Greek for shoe. Purists may wish to write the genus name *Cypripedilum*, with excellent authority. But Linnaeus may have had in mind the goddess's foot within the shoe, from the Latin *pes, pedis*. Or as he created that great new catalogue of plants the name may have been truncated for convenience of pronunciation. The species name, *acaule*, is a Latin adjective meaning stemless. Unlike other species of *Cypripedium* it does not carry its flower at the top of a leafy stem, but produces two basal leaves from the crown, and also from the crown a single leafless peduncle bearing the solitary blossom or rarely two blossoms.

In this country, where *C. acaule* is found wild over an extensive area, it has been christened with a host of colloquial names: pink lady's slipper, stemless lady's slipper, two-leaved lady's slipper, dwarf umbil, Noah's ark, valerian, whippoorwill shoe, squirrel shoe, purple slipper, rose-vein moccasin, hare's lip, brown lady's slipper, old goose, camel's foot, and in Quebec, *sabot de la Vierge.*

This shoe of the Virgin has an interesting distribution. It is found from Newfoundland and Nova Scotia west to Alberta, through the Great Lakes area to Ohio, and south along the east coast to Georgia and Alabama. It is not found in the Ozarks of Missouri or in our western mountains. Within its defined range it favors a variety of sites, always intensely acid. In the southern part of its distribution it is found most commonly in rather dry, sandy locations, and in the north in moister, even boggy situations. In the northeastern portion of its extension it frequently produces pure albino forms, rare in other sections. So far as the available literature declares, there are no recognized subspecific divisions of the species except in forma *albiflorum;* yet the habitat preferences may coincide with considerable genetic variability. There may even be local races more amenable to cultivation.

Prescriptions for growing this lovely plant in the garden are always tentative and buffered by so many caveats that one may safely conclude that most gardeners and all garden advisors have failed to bring this native orchid into cultivation. Usually there is resort to an account of the success of a friend, which on further investigation generally means that the plants introduced existed solely as supplements to natural stands already in existence. Or, because the pink lady's slipper has the ability to survive for one, two, or occasionally even three years (though dwindling yearly) after transplanting, it is likely that the optimistic gardener has rejoiced and bragged about his success too soon. Such gardeners too often, when faced with their plant's eventual demise, lay the blame on a mouse or some other accident and again import into their gardens the longed-for plant, not realizing that they are condemning it to a lingering death from starvation.

I'm sure a few people have, indeed, succeeded in introducing

C. acaule into a virgin site by transplanting the plant with a large chunk of its native soil into a situation where the plants would naturally grow, such as a well-drained, acid, rather sterile soil beneath an old stand of pine trees. Under such circumstances the micorrhizal fungus so essential for the plant's nourishment would also have found a congenial home for its own survival and could perform its symbiotic role with the roots of the *Cypripedium*.

It is important to note, I think, that the fleshy white roots of all *Cypripedium* species splay out from the crown very near the surface. They always inhabit a layer of recently decomposed vegetation, especially well supplied with ambient air.

An established plant will send forth its white spaghetti roots for some distance and develop subsidiary crowns until a colony may eventually carry up to ten stalwart blossoming stalks in a neat clump. Generally, though, the increase is slow, and solitary plants may flower year after year without increase, or may even, if conditions are unfavorable, remain underground for a year or more and then reappear to flourish and flower as before, perhaps as their symbionts have regenerated. Injured roots may suffer fungus infection, and this may be fatal to a newly transplanted specimen.

It is only fair to say that *Cypripedium acaule,* beautiful as she is, is an untamable Shakespearean Kate. Her reluctance to be tamed must not, however, turn us away from admiration of her essential and intricate beauty and her marvelous devices for fertilization.

The flower of the pink moccasin is composed of several disparate parts. To the tip of the scape is attached the long, curved, heavily ribbed, green, pubescent ovary surmounted by a floral bract that bends down over the top of the blossom partially hiding the capsule and frequently resting on the dorsal sepal that in turn leans over the flower in a graceful curve. Beneath the

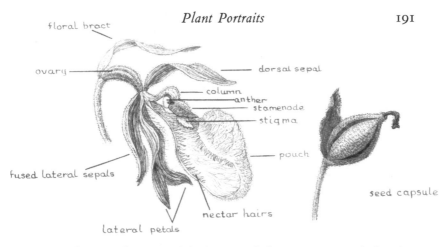

floral bract

ovary

dorsal sepal

column

anther

stamenode

stigma

pouch

fused lateral sepals

nectar hairs

lateral petals

seed capsule

Cypripedium acaule   The lady's slipper orchid is native to North America.

pouch are two more sepals, but they are so fused that they appear to be only one. These sepals are yellow green to greenish brown and more or less marked with maroon striations. The two long, acuminate lateral petals, more waxy than the sepals and densely clothed with long silky hairs, spring out with a spiral twist from just behind the pouch and are also longitudinally veined with purple, madder, and maroon on a yellowish green base.

But it is the third petal of this orchid, the silken pouch formed by the inflated lip, delicately veined with rose and velvety with soft pubescence, be it white, pink, or nearly crimson, that is the cynosure that tempts the gardener. It is also, and more importantly, part of a live trap for insects, a trap designed to ensure cross fertilization.

The inner floor of this pouch is downy with hairs that exude a sweet nectar, the bait that lures the insect in. The entrance is the longitudinal split in the upper surface of the pouch, the edges of which are infolded and fringed on their inner surface with long, stiff, crystalline white hairs. The lips of the split are pressed tightly together throughout most of its length, but at the base of the blossom they part to form an oval opening just under and partially blocked by the overhanging column made up of the stout curved style of the pistil, which expands at its tip into a broad, concave stigma covered on its underside with rigid, sharp, forward-pointing papillae which become sticky when the pistil is receptive.

On either side of the column and attached to it at the base are the two stamens with thick white filaments and large yellow anthers protruding out and down into the gaps on either side of the style. These, when ripe, are covered with a mass of granular pollen called "pollonia." Attached to the top of the base of the column is a broadly triangular petal-like sterile stamen called a "stamenode," which expands over the stigma, serving to some extent as an umbrella to shield the sexual parts from the rain. It also acts as a curtain that conceals and partially blocks the opening at the base of the pouch, thus discouraging and even preventing all but very small insects from using it as an entrance into the pouch; in order to reach the nectar hairs most insects must force a passage through the closed lips of the slot.

Once having sipped its fill, however, an insect finds it cannot exit through the same fissure because of the tightly fitting, in-rolled edges guarded by the interlaced fringes of hair. Seeking an escape, it is attracted by the light coming through the opening under the column. To reach this exit, however, it must crawl up the narrow throat of the pouch. To do so it must first creep under the protruding stigma, scraping its head and back against the stiff papillae that literally comb off any pollen adhering to the insect's body. Once it has negotiated the narrow passage beyond, it must squeeze through one of the gaps on either side of the column, rubbing against one or the other anther and thus picking up a new load of pollen to carry to the next lady's slipper it visits.

If, by chance, a luckless insect fails to find the partially blocked aperture or is too large to force its way through the narrow tunnel to reach the opening, it is doomed to die sealed within the luxurious chamber unless, as some do, it can gnaw its way through the side of the pouch to freedom.

In certain years very few of the blossoms produce seed capsules. Some authorities think late frosts may damage the flowers just as they mature, preventing fertilization of the ovules, but that cannot be the case in this corner of northwest Connecticut, as we seldom have frosts at the end of May when this plant customarily blooms. It would seem, therefore, that failure to set seed is more likely from a lack in some seasons of the particular insects needed to transfer the pollen from anther to stigma. Those fortunate enough to have *Cypripedium acaule* and wishing to increase their stand can, with the aid of a toothpick or even a handy twig from the forest floor, play the insect's role and thus ensure pollination. This is a form of rape and as such is necessarily a bit brutal. Grasp a mature flower firmly by the throat between thumb and middle finger and, with the index finger, lift the stamenode. Extract the waxy lump of pollen from an anther with the tip of the twig and, seizing a flower on a neighboring plant in the same fashion, scrape the pollen off onto the underside of its stigma, after which you can remove its pollonia in turn for further transfer. The flowers are a bit battered after this operation, but it is amazing how many fat seed capsules result.

One would like to be able to advise that you may propagate these Venus shoes by carefully separating the crowns and their intertwining fleshy roots and carefully planting each separation into an appropriate site, as one can with many of the other *Cypripedium*s. There are a few who have succeeded in so doing in a stand where the whippoorwill shoe is established. But I advise against it. Let well enough alone. If you have one or a hundred established *sabots de la Vierge,* be thankful, admire them inordi-

nately, pollinate them as gently as possible, and scatter the seeds
with a blessing.

H.L.F.

CREEPING DALIBARDA
Dalibarda repens

This shy plant of the northern woods forms an unspectacular
carpet of elegant evergreen foliage, sparingly but charmingly
decorated for a long period in summer with short-stemmed,
small, full-petaled flowers of purest white. Belonging as it does
to the *Rosaceae,* it has the five petals and numerous stamens of
the family, very like those of running blackberries or strawberries, but the flowers sit more neatly on the tuffet of dense dark
green leaves.

Like other, even more common wildflowers, the creeping
dalibarda has more than one vernacular name. For a long time
it was known as false violet, christened probably by a botanist
who knew of its cleistogamic habit, but carried on by those who
then saw a similarity between the leaves of the dalibarda and those
of various woodland violets. One could hardly be misled when
the showy flowers are in bloom, however. A less frequent name,
of uncertain origin or application, is robin-run-away. Current
books on wildflowers are more likely to use the colloquial name
dew drop, applied either because of the spattering of glistening
white flowers just above the foliage or because under certain
conditions drops of dew are caught in the short, bristly, white
hairs that cover both surfaces of the leaves.

The scientific name *Dalibarda repens* was given to the plant by
Linnaeus; the genus name to commemorate a contemporary
French botanist, Thomas François Dalibard, and the species name
to describe the plant's growth habit. Though the plant has occa-

apatalous flower

fruit

drupe

petaliferous flower

bud

calyx

Dalibarda repens An excellent ground cover in the woodland garden.

sionally been placed by botanists in the large genus *Rubus,* it is sufficiently distinctive so that most modern botanists retain it in its own separate genus with but this single species.

A distinctive feature of *Dalibarda* is its flowering and seeding habit. The showy five-petaled flowers on upright peduncles with their numerous pistils and conspicuous white stamens are generally infertile. One author erroneously describes the central boss of stamens as golden, and the peduncle has been described as red. I have never noticed this red characteristic, though the sepals may be tinged with madder.

Before the showy flowers develop—and along with them at a later season—are to be found on short, curved peduncles below the leaves numerous fertile apetalous flowers with five to ten ovaries which become dry, seedlike drupes. This method of producing seed in "blind" flowers, found also among violets and a few other genera, is called cleistogamy. The word derives from two Greek words: *kleistos* (closed) and *gamos* (marriage).

This seed-producing device so intrigued the author Neltje Blanchan that he wrote of creeping dalibarda in the *New Nature Library,* Volume 8, Part 1, titled "Wild Flowers: An Aid to Knowledge of Our Wild Flowers and Their Insect Visitors":

> This delicate blossom, which one might mistake for a white violet among a low tuft of violet-like leaves, shows its rose kinship by its rule of five and its numerous stamens. Like the violet again, however, it bears curious little economical flowers near the ground, flowers which never open, and so save pollen. These, requiring no insects to fertilize them, waste no energy in putting forth petals to advertise for visitors. Nevertheless, to save the species from degeneracy from close inbreeding, this little plant needs must display a few showy blossoms to insure cross-fertilized seed;

for the offspring of such defeats the offspring of self-fertilized plants in the struggle for existence.

When you have unraveled the grammar of the final sentence,
you may wish to ponder the sentiment so clumsily expressed. It
seems doubtful that *Dalibarda repens* "needs must" raise those
perfect and sterile flowers, but we do welcome them. The showy
flowers are intricately composed, beginning in the bud with the
five unequal sepals, variously cut at the tip, erect about the
unfolding petals. As the blossom expands the sepals turn down
to clasp the stem, the petals lie back from the horizontal, and the
white stamens spray up around the short white pistils in their very
center attached to the multiple ovary. Because for some reason
these flowers are not fertilized, the blossoms remain in good
condition for an extended period, making up thus for their rather
sparse production.

The plant itself is slowly stoloniferous, sending out new stems
on or just beneath the surface, at the tips of which new rosettes
of leaves develop. New roots, few in number, are sent down from
the stolons to feed and anchor the new growth. For propagation
the plant may be carefully lifted and cut apart into as many
divisions as there are stolons with developed roots. Because the
roots are few and delicate, however, it is wise to treat each
division with care. Treat it as a newly rooted cutting till strong
roots develop, or if a cut stolon is put in a permanent planting
site, keep it well watered until it is established.

Since the plant is generally found in moist, but not wet, acid
woodlands, for best success it should have in the garden a duffy
acid soil in a site not exposed to full sun. Individual plants may
in time become as much as a foot across, but are slow to reach
such dimensions. A group of small plants set close together will
form a charming carpet for the woodland garden.

Because the seed is found in the well-concealed cleistogamic flowers, it is rarely gathered, and so far as I can discover has never been offered in the seed lists, nor is there any information about how to grow plants from seed. Here is a challenge for someone to experiment with.

In the wild, *Dalibarda repens* is reported from Quebec south through New England to northwestern Connecticut, and then in the mountains of West Virginia and North Carolina. It has been recorded as found in three towns in Connecticut: Colebrook, Norfolk, and Winchester.

H.L.F.

DIAPENSIA LAPPONICA

The name, *Diapensia lapponica*, rolls readily and liquidly off the tongue, and one expects to find that the genus was christened by Linnaeus after some mythical nymph or dryad; Diapensia to dance along with Andromeda and Cassiope. Not so; the genus name derives by some quirk of the Swedish mind from the ancient Greek name for a weed, a *Sanicula*—gross, fleshy, and practically flowerless.

One can only suppose that Linné conjured up this title from some dried herbarium specimen before he had met the plant face to face, as he must have in his tour of Lapland. There is certainly nothing gross or fleshy or flowerless about this hard tussock of a plant graced by milk-white flowers, elegantly proportioned.

Actually a shrub of condensed and consolidated posture, *Diapensia lapponica* forms a rocklike convex mound of congested twigs, each clad at the slow-growing tip with a thatched rosette of coriaceous, deep green, spatulate leaves polished to a glossy finish. In fall, before they are beaten by winds and snow, the

Diapensia lapponica　A handsome and challenging alpine.

leaves take on a burnished warm mahogany glow beneath the pale, ghostly seed capsules and tattered sepals.

In the late and hasty spring of its mountain heights, out of the center of each rosette rises up a short-stemmed flower stalk, unfurling a few green bracts beneath the five-lobed calyx. Within the sepals, in turn, expand the pearl-like buds to open five glistening white overlapping petals that finally bend their separate blades horizontally out. Between each pair of petals stands a joined pair of golden stamens forming a ring around the expectant central pistil. And now the greening tussock glows as with a dusting of late snow.

In its mountain home on Mount Washington, New Hampshire, and on a few other northeastern American peaks, this handsome member of the small *Diapensiaceae* family asserts its noble and elusive charm. It gives its name to a curious and specialized family which includes four very specialized genera in eastern United States. One of these, *Diapensia,* spills over into Europe and has outliers in eastern Asia. Two, *Galax* and *Pyxidanthera,* are unique to our region. *Shortia,* including the possibly separate *Schizocodon,* is represented both in eastern North America and in eastern Asia.

What an elegant family! Through the puzzling processes of evolution, its members have become so specialized in their adaptation that the whole group is in danger of extinction. One is tempted to see parallels with the House of the Seven Gables.

Diapensia itself (it may be significant that it bears no common name) has been bred to endure a spartan diet in a fierce environment. The upper reaches of Mount Washington are subjected to the wildest extremes of climate to be found anywhere in the world. These conditions are doubtless duplicated, if not so completely recorded, on Mount Katahdin in Maine, another haunt of *Diapensia.* Those who have climbed these mountains know that there can be from mid-May until mid-August days of spangling sunshine and endless visibility. Plants basking in this clear air and intense light respond with a racing metabolism as the photosynthetic mills work full tilt in the long day. But even within this season there are many days when clouds shroud the mountains, winds roar, hail beats down. During these not infrequent spells, as mountain climbers hasten to seek shelter, the plants hunker down, brace against the wind, and absorb essential moisture.

Rapid as they are to spring into flower when days lengthen and the frozen soils slowly melt, the plants must also hasten to seed. The summer visitor sees only the huddled foliage and the straw-colored persistent sepals. By August the seed has ripened in the three-parted capsule. As the sutures open and the locules spread, the fine brown seed is ready to be scattered by the winds. Even at that season wild winds may suddenly rise to blow the seeds to the Atlantic Ocean or into the intervening valleys of forest where no *Diapensia* would deign to grow. A few seeds may be caught in the tangle of a low *Rhododendron lapponicum* or *Loiseleuria procumbens*. These provide a possible nursery for the seedlings that germinate the following spring. (Or perhaps hastily in late summer. Who knows?)

If conditions are favorable over a number of years, the seedling may increase rosette by rosette until it forms a jeweled ruff about the base of an ancient gnarled dwarf rhododendron, or it may mingle its flowers among the tangled, prostrate stems of the alpine azalea. Or, in crevices of the rocky pavement where pockets of peaty detritus have been lodged by wind and the running meltwater, a sprouting seed may in many, many years become a foot-wide solid crust of foliage studded in its solitary splendor with the largest and most abundant blossoming.

How one wishes it were possible to have such a miracle in one's own rock garden. Collected plants, with their flower buds for the next year already set by August, have been brought down to our lowland gardens and have bloomed. A few have persisted, flowerless and dejected, for a year or two longer. One by one the rosettes generally turn brown and crumble from the woody stems. No new rosettes are set forth around the periphery, and soon the whole plant perishes.

There may be more adaptable strains of this species: var. *obovata* of northern Japan, Kamchatka, and northeastern Siberia is said to be somewhat more amenable to cultivation in British gardens. But even the arctic conditions must be as severe as on our mountain peaks. One thing certainly these various sites have in common is a low average annual temperature and no periods of really high temperatures.

The illness to which *D. lapponica* succumbs in lowland rock gardens has its onset during prolonged spells of high temperature and high humidity. Perhaps because the pathogens that cause the die-back and eventual demise of the plant are not able to flourish in arctic conditions, there has never been any genetic selection for tolerance of this subtle blight.

Is it possible that we might be able to devise growing conditions to inhibit the pathogens even though we cannot provide the arctic-alpine weather? It occurs to me that the *Pyxidanthera* relative endures high temperature and high humidity, but it grows in a very acid, almost sterile sand. It might be worth experimenting with growing *D. lapponica* in pure Pine Barren sand.

If this proves successful we might find in the future that someone will introduce from the Sino-Himalayan regions three other species of *Diapensia: himalaica, purpurea,* and *wardii,* whose flowers are rose purple, lilac, or yellow, as well as white. What an attraction those would be on the show bench.

H.L.F.

SOME DICENTRAS

Fleeting but elegant are the two species of dicentra that grace the early-spring flora of eastern United States: *D. cucullaria* and *D. canadensis*. Similar they are to the point of confusion, with only slight above-ground and yet conspicuous below-ground differences.

D. cucullaria, most commonly known as Dutchman's breeches, has green ferny foliage early in the spring topped by a one-sided raceme of nodding, white, dancing flowers most curiously formed. The structure of the blossom is intricately arranged, with the four pleated and folded petals assuming such unlikely postures that their basic poppy relationship is not only concealed but flouted. Instead of raising a cup of crinkled petals upward to bask in the sun, *D. cucullaria* wraps two of its petals upward to form puffed, wide-spreading horns—yes, like an up-side-down pair of Dutch pantaloons—suspended by an almost invisible pedicel and filled only with air. Two other petals curl down to form a pouch that expands at the mouth into two cupped wings tipped with gold. Wrapped within are the functional stamens and pistils. These blossoms dance for a week or so in earliest spring above the lacy platform of deeply cut, slightly glaucous green foliage. Then, after this ballet, all collapses with remarkable suddenness; the ballerinas sink as they sway, their garments shriveling to tawdry brown. Black seeds within the horned pods of the ovary extension harden and glaze. The pod bursts. The seeds extrude. The foliage fades from green to yellow, glimmering down gently to leave no remnants, and the underground base of this ballet of blossoms is called upon to carry on the life processes unseen until another performance the following spring. These underground parts consist of a short rootstock bearing a cluster of pinkish white ricelike tubers, huddled into a scaly bulb.

In *Dicentra canadensis* the subterranean rhizome carries loosely held, golden, grainlike tubers. It is this feature that gives this plant its colloquial name, squirrel corn. The foliage is quite impossible to distinguish from that of Dutchman's breeches, though it appears a bit later in the spring and persists for a week or two longer. Squirrel corn blossoms are carried in a manner similar to those of Dutchman's breeches, but the individual flowers, though superficially similar, are quite differently shaped. Here the upward-pointed furled petals form shorter, more rounded spurs, parallel rather than divergent, looking, indeed, like the erect ears of a baby rabbit, and the wings on either side of the mouth are pinkish rather than yellow as in *D. cucullaria*.

These two dicentras, similar as they are, possess other less obvious differences. Though their ranges overlap to a large extent, they do not hybridize, as they have different chromosome numbers and there appear to be subtle differences in their site preferences.

Dicentra cucullaria has a slightly more extensive range south and west, extending from Quebec west to North Dakota and south to Alabama and Missouri with a curious disjunct population, distinguished as var. *occidentalis,* in Oregon, Washington, and Idaho. Where its range overlaps with that of the less widespread *D. canadensis,* the two are occasionally found growing together in rich woodlands, but in all state floras squirrel corn is described as much rarer than Dutchman's breeches.

Neither of these dicentras is commonly encountered in rock gardens despite their intrinsic beauty and the fact that most rock garden texts list at least *D. cucullaria.* For some years I thought these two charmers were difficult to establish in cultivation, even though *D. cucullaria* is locally abundant in certain natural settings.

These seemed almost invariably to be at the base of rocky slopes in woodlands, most always where the rock was acidic. Investigation showed that the tubers lie close to the surface in pockets of almost pure humus.

Efforts to move a few clumps of Dutchman's breeches from an area along a major highway where expansion of the road was impinging on the rocky slope were successful to the extent that some leaves appeared the following year, but no blossoms. My site, though rocky and shaded by high trees, was amidst rocks of Stockbridge marble, an ancient metamorphosed limestone. Meanwhile I had purchased from a "wildflower nursery"—that usually means one providing plants collected in the wild—some tubers of squirrel corn. These I put in a nearby spot under some Kaempferi azaleas. For a year or two there were a few sprigs of dicentra foliage and no real display of blossoms, so I tried moving a few corms of each species up into the acid soil of the woodland garden.

Then, I think it was the third year, there was a fine burst of early Dutchman's breeches blooms along the path amidst the limestone rocks. And year by year their numbers increase, and they have spread into the most unlikely and enticing pockets: amidst ferns, primulas, mertensias, arisaemas, all huddled together, with the Dutchman's breeches generally leading the parade of flowers. They appear to thrive on competition and, conversely, never interfere with the most delicate neighbors.

After about five years I suddenly became aware that at the very end of the blooming season for the Dutchman's breeches, there was a great flush of flowers on an expanding bed of squirrel corn which had been quietly multiplying unnoticed beneath the Kaempferi azaleas.

What I begin to think is that you need patience and fresh seed. The cluster of tubers usually breaks up in the transplanting, and

H. LINCOLN FOSTER

*A group of plants in the Cliff Bed, including a superb clump of Dodecatheons
(foreground), emblem of the American Rock Garden Society.*

H. LINCOLN FOSTER

*The raised beds surrounding the gravel pathway behind Millstream House.
Visitors would often enter the garden by these steps.*

May at Millstream Garden; a view from the terrace looking up the hillside toward the Alpine Lawn in the middle distance. The Phlox Bank (right background) is in full bloom.

The Cliff Bed in May. The Alpine House can just be seen in the background.

Lewisia cotyledon: *one specimen of a large and breathtaking collection developed by the Fosters.*

H. LINCOLN FOSTER

BUFFY PARKER

ABOVE LEFT *Superb specimens of* Arisaema sikokianum, *one of Linc Foster's favorite plants. A sheet of* Primula abschasica *blooms in the background.*

H. LINCOLN FOSTER

ABOVE *A stand of* Primula sieboldii *is backed by a clump of* Trillium grandiflorum *in the woodland garden. The pink blossoms are of the native azalea.*

Millstream House on a May day, viewed from the Alpine Lawn.

August at Millstream, with candelabra primulas flowering near Demming Brook.

H. LINCOLN FOSTER

The Dell looking toward Demming Brook with kaempferi
azaleas in bloom.

HUMPHREY SUTTON

Linc and Timmy Foster in their element.

The falls created by the Old Dam across Demming Brook.

Calthas along the Tail of the Race.

By strange and wonderful accidents sometimes their written descriptions were misread, and names became garbled. If the copier of the early Linnean nomination had misread the specific instead of the generic name, he might have dropped out one "l" and arrived at *cuculus,* the Latin for lark. Let your mind play with that as those white blossoms take flight into a blue sky. But the first error was not there, alas. *Dicentra* was misread as *Diclytra.*

There is no such Greek word. Emendations later composed it to *Dielytra,* not very much happier except for its resemblance to *dialuo* and its relatives having to do with dissolving. Eventually someone untangled this confusion and came back to what was apparently Linnaeus's intention: *Dicentra,* double-spurred. Some later botanists, off on another track and unhappy with the *dielytra* syndrome, christened the genus *Bikukulla* and *Bicuculla,* twice-hooded. But now we are back with what we suppose was Linnaeus's original idea, and it does make sense.

Under no such constraints are the inventors of the "common" names. Here the play of free association is at liberty. Who first noted that *Dicentra cucullaria* blossoms did indeed look like puffy Dutchman's breeches hanging waist down along the arching stem? And how, one wonders, did this sudden inspiration become accepted and perpetuated? Yet I find in the "Catalogue of the Flowering Plants and Ferns of Connecticut" these other colloquial names listed: kitten breeches, little-boy's breeches, white eardrops, white hearts, soldier's cap, and boys-and-girls. Not one of these seems somehow quite as precise, and certainly none has been so persistent.

Other members of the genus have earned equally apt common names. *D. eximia,* bleeding heart; and *D. uniflora,* steer's head, each of these from the shape of the blossoms. *D. canadensis* gets its commonest colloquial name, squirrel corn, from the cluster of yellow tubers out of which the plant springs. I am sure that the Japanese have a descriptive name for that exotic and ungrowable

D. peregrina. Peregrina, by the way, means exotic or foreign. Is this an occidental bias sneaking into taxonomy?

But to return to our own *D. cucullaria,* which set me chasing down through reference after reference all the way back to the bare skeleton of my old Greek dictionary, I would make a tentative nomination for this as the emblem of the Connecticut Chapter of the ARGS if we were to have one, for indigenous as it is, it is a dwarf, perennial, wild plant that looks "right" in the rock garden. It is distinctive and easily recognized, and a challenge to grow. Yet who of us at home tries to grow it? We neglect it just because it is a Connecticut native.

I know one area along Route 7 just north of Danbury where at the foot of a steep slope facing to the east amidst a massive tumble of blocks of gray, hard rock on an early May morning at the base of scattered oaks there used to dance thousands of Dutchman's breeches. Most of the area is now bulldozed flat, and a line of gaudy shops for wares of all sorts blocks whatever may be left of the plants from the view of the passing motorist, too busy anyway to glimpse them, dodging as he must the in-shooting and out-shooting shoppers. I do regret today, as I pass by, that I did not dig clutches of those white tuberous roots before they were buried alive to perish beneath the topping of cement and asphalt.

You must know of sites equally prolific with the subtle, dazzling charm of *Dicentra cucullaria,* white ballerinas poised and glistening above a shimmer of glaucous green foliage. As brief as a ballet and as bewitching. Before they are all bulldozed and buried, let us learn to grow and cherish them.

I shall return in another chapter with some notions about growing and propagating this charmer. Meanwhile, do I hear a second to the nomination?

H.L.F.

Dicentra cucullaria Revisited

Recently I wrote of *Dicentra cucullaria* and the history of its naming, going so far as to describe the elegant features of the plant that made it a worthy candidate for an emblem of the Connecticut Chapter. And I think I threatened to write about it again in horticultural terms.

Let me begin by quoting from *The Rock Garden,* by Louise Beebe Wilder, published in 1935: *"D. cucullaria,* the little Dutchman's-breeches, now called *Bicuculla cucullaria,* is a choice delight for a woodsy corner in loose and fibrous leaf soil. Not always easy to establish, though growing most freely in a wild state in such localities as it elects to grace." In these two sentences Mrs. Wilder precisely sums up the challenge of its cultivation. And I am not sure that since that date we have learned much more.

It is curious that this elfin species, possessing as it does all the qualities that allure the passionate rock gardener, is rarely found in rock gardens, or alpine houses, on the show bench, or even described accurately in the rock garden literature. It is dwarf, beautiful, and difficult, all that a rock gardener can ask.

To be sure it is generally listed in those copious catalogues of alpine plants that are found in most British rock gardening books, but often the language suggests that the author is merely passing on secondhand information. Could Mr. Mansfield ever have seen the true plant when he describes it in his wonderful book, *Alpines in Colour and Cultivation* thus: "Very dwarf, very grey, very small and a very divided foliage, with flowers of pale pearl-like appearance." The color of the blossom is right, but not its shape, and the foliage is not very gray. Henry Correvon, that grand old man, in his *Rock Garden and Alpine Plants* gave the color of the blossoms as "light rose." Even Farrer, who, if he knew *Dicentra cucullaria,* would have gone into rapturous descriptive prose, dismisses it *"D. cucullaria* is a finer [than eximia] frailer thing in the way of *D. formosa,* but only 4 inches high or so, with flowers of pale pearly white, most delicate."

And if you contrast the cursory description of *Dicentra cucullaria* with that of *D. peregrina* in Heath's *Collector's Alpines,* it seems apparent which species he knew firsthand or at least which won his attention.

There is in Anna Griffith's *Collins Guide to Alpines* a poorly reproduced picture of a well-grown plant in a pot, and her description is obviously from life. To her eyes though, instead of breeches, "the soft creamy flowers, yellow-tipped, really more truly suggest a flight of small moths above the ferny foliage." I like that phrasing, and it does prove that at least occasionally this lovely American is persuaded to grow and flower in the British garden.

So far as I can remember, seed of *Dicentra cucullaria* has not been offered in the seed exchanges of any society devoted to plants for the rock garden. Maybe I am alone in my admiration for this plant. Maybe it is a rare and difficult plant in cultivation. Maybe it is ignored because the seed is so early to escape and so is overlooked at the time when the general run of rock garden plants are still bursting with bloom.

The Dutchman's breeches are early, modest in their way, and even their foliage disappears quickly. They are gone by the time we are down on our knees doing the post-spring weeding. Out of sight, out of mind. They ask, therefore, for companion plants to fill the space left by their disappearance.

It is true, as it is of any plant of delicate and modest mien, that this charmer should be planted in masses to make it effective, as it is in nature. As Mrs. Wilder says, it grows in abundance in those sites it elects to grace, and there it is generally followed by annuals, frequently of a weedy sort, or late-arising perennials.

In the wild I have generally found them flourishing in pockets among large neutral to acidic rocks or cradled in the large buttress roots of some deep-rooting deciduous tree, where, in either situation, humus of a fibrous and well-drained lightness tends to accumulate and rain water trickles down the rocks or tree trunk. The plant arises from and stores its nourishment in a curious collection of white bulblike tubers that cluster around a sort of central rootstock. These are always lightly held in this fluffy humus, never down in the mineral or compacted soil. Light and well drained as the compost is, it is rarely utterly dry, certainly not during the period of active growth. It is the lower reaches of long slopes toward which moisture works that house the richest and most floriferous colonies.

In the garden then, if we can rely upon the clues from nature, *Dicentra cucullaria* would seem to have its best chances of success in a deep pocket of well-drained leaf mold in a downslope location. With a rise of rock behind it, the site need not be overhung by trees. To plant it, in fact, among the moisture-demanding roots of many trees is to defeat the purpose.

Plants may be grown from seed, but it will be three or four years before the tubers have reached flowering size. The seed, as in most of the *Fumariaceae,* are small and shining black, with a small, white, fleshy aril at the point of attachment. Because of this aril, the seed, if exposed to drying, soon loses its viability. This suggests that the seed be sowed as promptly as possible.

Collected or purchased dormant plants frequently have the tenuously united cluster of small tubers torn asunder, which may explain why so often such material takes a few years to settle down and flower. This also suggests that it is wise to be careful, when the plants are dormant, not to disturb them. It also indicates that an excellent way to propagate Dutchman's breeches is to deliberately break up the clustering tubers and replant them just under the surface of leaf mold. A feeding with bone meal will tend to increase flowering.

Dicentra cucullaria in the wild is an uncommonly constant species, with only one recorded form: *purpuritincta,* in which the calyx is deep purple, the corolla pink, and the flexure deep orange. There is a rare West Coast variety, *D. cucullaria* var. *occidentalis,* reportedly somewhat more robust than the eastern one, but otherwise quite similar.

Dutchman's breeches are not known to hybridize with the other two eastern species of *Dicentra.* This fact is not unexpected, however, since the chromosome numbers are different: $n = 8$ for *D. eximia, n = 16* for *D. cucullaria, n = 32* for *D. canadensis.*

H.L.F.

DRYAS

When Linnaeus christened the Dryas, he chose the name because of the resemblance of the plant's evergreen leaves to small leaves of oak, and the oak was sacred to the dryads or wood nymphs. The fancied resemblance to woodland dryads of the white blossoms of feathery seed heads dancing on slender pedicels at the windy heights among the mountains is but a happy coincidence. These are no children of the woods, but of the sun and open air; true mountain dwellers around the world in the northern Hemisphere.

Not so happy is the coincidence that these gorgeous, creeping shrubs have been given the common name of mountain avens, suggesting a similarity to those other avens, the geums. To be sure, they both belong to the rose family, and both carry feathery styles on the ripening achenes in the seed head, but there the likeness ceases.

The showiest of the three *Dryas* species is *D. octopetala,* which displays for a long season in late spring and early summer its glistening flowers of eight to ten petals. These begin to show their white color, peeking from the swollen, hairy sepals, when the slender pedicels are just beginning to arise from the evergreen mat of foliage. As the pedicels elongate, reaching three to six inches, the overlapping petals expand into an open cup filled with a stout tassel of golden stamens embracing a paintbrush of many pistils. In the sunlight, the reflection of gold from this central tassel gilds the inner depths of the chalice and glows through the petals.

When bees have found and ravished this goblet and have slathered themselves with the heavy silken pollen till their legs are bowed and wings lag, then the workmanlike styles swirl in spirals and slowly unwind their feathers into a tousled head. As the seeds ripen, the feathery styles begin to brown. Then, when they pull away easily, you may collect them for immediate sowing.

After sowing, the seeds may germinate within two weeks, or you may have to wait until the following spring for signs of life. At last, maybe even two patient years from capture and sowing, there will appear an unmistakable dryas. (All species apparently behave the same, if they behave at all.) But this is only the first of your devotions to the dryads.

These plants are not quickly or easily established upon the earth—though once so founded they flourish forever. Seedlings are slow and curiously sensitive to transplanting. Unlike many plants that send reaching roots into all corners of the seeding mixture, these seem to wish to settle in by sending only one wandering root down into the earth source. If you can wait until this wild gravitational urge is stilled into the formation of side-feeding rootlets, then you may transplant to a deep pot of open, gravelly soil, or direct to the sunny scree, or open, well-drained rock garden. No heavy clay, no dark corners, no close shade against the sustaining sun. Even in favorable conditions the seed-lings may sadly shrivel and succumb.

It is easier to allow an established plant to supply the material for propagation. Cuttings, with a flush of new growth and a base of last year's wood, will, in August, rapidly root in a shaded, moisture-constant, sandy rooting medium. Or, if the urge is upon you in May when the leaves, echoing the unfolding oaks in the woods, are beginning to expand beneath the elongating blossom stems, find a naturally layered woody branch, sever it with clip-pers, and dig it carefully. Here is an established side arm of an established plant. But severed away from the grandfather root, it rarely flourishes on its own immediately. Better to cosset it in a partially shaded bed of sand until new roots have formed and complete independence is declared. Then you are free to move it where you will. But let the spot where you place it (not tenderly now, but firmly) be in the eye of the sun, in well-drained soil, not necessarily either limy or acid, as long as it has room to ramp and root. These prescriptions hold true, as far as I know, for *Dryas octopetala* and its varieties and for *D. drummondii,* the shyly nodding yellow species, and for the rare but scarcely dis-tinct *D. tomentosa* of the Canadian Rockies.

Dryas octopetala, the most widespread of the species, has varied as it moved about the world since prehistoric times. (Its leaf patterns are marked in ancient deposits.) There is the somewhat standard form; a ground-hugging woody plant, rooting as it spreads, found frequently in limy soils in alpine regions of the world. The leaves are about one inch long, gray-tomentose be-neath, shining green above, rounded dentate along the edges, like those of the white oak in miniature, generally subcordate at the base. In severe winters without snow cover in the softer world of the lowland garden, many of the leaves may be blasted by sun. But most will green again, and on bare stems new ones will spring forth to replace them even before the blossoms unfold. Even beneath snow the old leaves become tarnished, but the dull brown of the winter foliage miraculously greens in the spring.

There are varieties of this species to be found in the American Rockies and on some isolated cliffs of Great Britain in which the leaves, flowers, and the whole habit of growth have been diminished by half. This is var. *minor;* choice and elegant for the small rock garden, but not so easy to establish or propagate. Other forms or varieties are locally recognized: var. *lanata* with grayish hairs on the upper surface of the leaf as well as beneath; var. *integrifolia,* or *tenella* (these are perhaps not really synonymous). Var. *integrifolia* is smaller in all parts, but differs from var. *minor* by appearing to have no indentations on the leaf margins. This is because of an underfolding of the small leaf to prevent excessive transpiration in sites of diminished moisture. Var. *tenella* is neither revolute, nor unindented on the margins of the leaves, nor does it have the uniformly diminutive character of var. *minor.* At least in cultivation, where conditions may be more luxurious than in its native home, it carries fully expanded, oak-shaped leaves; narrower and bronzed more noticeably in winter than the normal species.

But, as always, I make these assertions about the varieties on the basis of the plant, or plants, I have known under these names. In the case of var. *tenella,* it is a single plant grown from seed pinched from George Schenk's garden in Seattle where the plant was labeled *D. tenella.* Whatever it is, it is not the same as the *D. octopetala* var. *integrifolia* I used to grow that came from the White Mountains of New Hampshire; nor is it the same miniature *D. octopetala* I saw and coveted on top of Mount Lolo in the Bitterroot Mountains of Montana. A small rooted layer of this last form could not be quickly nursed in sand, and succumbed. The few seeds collected were probably not quite ripe, or not fertile. At any rate they never germinated.

Seed of all the *Dryas* variants is tricky to handle. Once again this is a snap judgment without careful and controlled testing. Like many achene-form seeds with tail-like styles persisting, they do seem quickly to lose their viability. Sowed as soon as thoroughly ripe, some seeds do, indeed, germinate. Three years to flowering is precocious. Nor does the rampaging parent plant, which, once established, will go sprawling in almost any site, seem to spread its progeny by self-sowing. In fifteen years of growing *D. octopetala* in many sites in the garden at Millstream, I have found only one volunteer seedling, unflowered after three full growing seasons since I recognized it as a vagrant on its own.

Dryas drummondii, the yellow-flowered species, elegant in growth habit, but pinched and shy of bloom, has all the same recalcitrance of propagation. It is, moreover, even as a growing plant, less easy to move, or divide, or strike from cuttings, than *D. octopetala,* nor does it ramp and roam so readily.

I remember my first sight of this plant in the wild. This was on the gravel bars in the Grande Rivière of the Gaspé, to which we had been transported in the shallop of a French-Canadian farm boy who found us slithering along the steep, muddy banks of the river. Amidst the stones and pebbles and sands of the extensive midstream bars, which must be several feet under water in the spring, were sizable mats of dryas, past flowering. The leaves were slightly smaller than those of *D. octopetala* and cuneate at the base. Quite silver gray beneath, they were a smoky pinkish tan on the upper surface and conspicuously covered with an open mat of long, silky hairs, completely adpressed. We were finally able to locate two small seedling plants, easy to dig amidst the gravel. Transported dry in sealed plastic bags, these survived four days on the road, plus an inspection in the office of the Plant Inspector in Quebec, and have become established in the gravelly soil of a raised bed in our garden. It was three years before they showed a yellow blossom, a lovely soft color but disappointing because the petals do not open wide at the end of the nodding pedicels.

Franz Suendermann used *D. octopetala* as the seed parent for a hybrid with *D. drummondii,* producing what is known as the *D.* ✕ *suendermannii.* This is reputed to have a habit like the seed parent with flowers slightly nodding and yellowish in bud. Plants I have purchased under this name have been indistinguishable from vigorous forms of *D. octopetala.* Perhaps a cross in the opposite direction would make a more interesting hybrid.

The chief species in themselves are rock garden plants whose beauty increases with age, year by year, once they are established, and the small-leaved forms of *D. octopetala* are real gems.

H.L.F.

EPIGAEA REPENS

Trailing arbutus (*Epigaea repens*): what is more redolent, not only of its own delicious perfume, but also with the aroma of myth? This was once the very symbol of a New England spring, and bouquets of its enchanting flowers were hawked in the streets by young boys and girls. Those youthful forays into the secret haunts of trailing arbutus, I fear, are no longer popular. Nor is the plant so abundant as it once was, though I do know some great swatches of it spreading its elegantly textured evergreen foliage on the shoulders of some ancient abandoned woodland roads. Moreover, if you have the right site—acid, well-drained soil on a north-facing slope—it may flourish and even self-sow in your garden.

Although not confined to Connecticut, *Epigaea repens* is strictly an eastern, and chiefly a northeastern, American plant. Except for its sister in Japan, *Epigaea asiatica,* and its cousin *Orphanidesia* of Asia Minor, it does stand alone.

To propagate *Epigaea repens* is not really very difficult. If you already have it growing, the easiest method is to induce layering, a process the species practices naturally. In the wild a seedling plant will begin to send out from the central root woody runners in various directions across the ground: hence the name *Epigaea* (upon the ground), *repens* (creeping). These stems tend to be most numerous in the direction of proper light, and they usually run downhill if the plant grows on a slope. Where the soil is right, young feeding roots are sent off from the woody runners, and in time the older basal portions lose their leaves and renewal comes only at the tips. If you wish to make an independent propagation, choose a shoot or shoots with vigorous growth. Just back of the flower cluster, scrape the bark from the lower side of the stem, bury the stem with a mixture of half peat and half sand, and put on top of it a small stone. New leafy growth will form at the tip beyond the flowers. In September, cut the woody stem back of the stone. By June of the following year you should have a well-rooted independent plant ready to move to a new site, or, if no roots were formed, you have merely pruned the mother plant.

Another method is to wait until a new leafy shoot has made its full growth, generally in early July, and use this as a green-wood cutting. Clip the shoot at the base of the new growth. Strip off the lowest leaves of the shoot, wrap around it a thick wad of sphagnum moss, and insert this into a pot full of half acid leaf mold (or peat) and half sand that is well moistened but not dripping. You can, of course, insert more than one cutting. Enclose the pot in a plastic bag tied with a wire-twist fastener at the top. Set in a light but not sunny spot. Roots should be formed by September. Then you may harden off the rooted cuttings by opening the top of the plastic bag for a week or two, or you may transplant to a new pot of acid sand and leaf mold, enclose for a few days in a plastic bag, then harden by exposure. You may even set the rooted cutting in a properly prepared site—acid, peaty, sandy, north slope—water well and place over the newly rooted cutting a large glass jar for a few days. Then harden by removing the jar, but cover the whole plant, leaves and all, with a fluffy covering of pine needles.

Such a pine needle or oak leaf covering, left on the plant for as long as six months, is advisable whenever you set a new plant of trailing arbutus, either a small plant collected from the wild, or a rooted cutting, or a seedling.

Speaking of seedlings, growing *E. repens* from seed is not impossible, but it is tricky for two reasons. First, as is said about any shy game, catch the seed. Seed of *Epigaea repens* is formed, if the blossoms are fertilized, on the surface of a white berrylike fruit, after the fashion of the strawberry. Entomologists will have to tell you what insects accomplish the carrying of pollen from one blossom to another. Some years they are apparently not busy enough, whoever they are. To assist them, if you are concerned about fruit and seed, you may have to crawl about with a camel's hair paintbrush or a small wad of cotton on a toothpick to transport the pollen "by hand." It is unnecessary to buzz like a bee.

The fruit will slowly swell (if you or the insects have done the job) within the embracing, elongating calyx of the blossoms. There is a pregnant swelling detectable for a protracted period, and then suddenly the sepals curl back, generally in July, to reveal the white, fleshy fruit peppered over with tiny brown seed. Ants, chipmunks, and mice have been waiting for this moment. Before you can say *Epigaea repens* the fruit is likely to be devoured. The fruit is delicious, tasting rather like a cross between a strawberry and wintergreen.

By combing all the branch tips you may find some that escaped the wild raiders, and at this point you can collect even those still wrapped in the calyx. Let the fruit dry for about a week in a paper sack, and the fine seeds can be rubbed off. These should be sown within a week because they lose viability rapidly. Sow them thinly and without covering on the surface of a potful of acid sandy soil. Germination is sometimes speeded by sowing the seed on about a ½-inch layer of milled sphagnum moss above the soil. Thoroughly water the soil and sphagnum by immersion after sowing. Drain briefly and place the pot in a plastic bag, seal, and put in a well-lighted spot out of the sun.

Seedlings, very tiny to begin with, should be visible in about three weeks. Open the top of the plastic bag or remove the whole pot. Keep the seedlings growing without transplanting if possible till the following spring by carrying them through the winter in a frame or alpine house. Plants have been brought to flower in three years from seed.

Plants grown from layers, cuttings, or seeds will generally establish much more readily than those collected in the wild. To get them well established water frequently and shade; then they will endure full exposure and add year-round beauty to an acid pocket in the rock garden.

H.L.F.

THE EASTERN ERYTHRONIUMS

It is generally known that in the evolution of plant structures bulbs were developed, according to doctrine, as underground storage organs for plants that were subject to prolonged periods of drought. In fact (or is this just a conceit?) most bulbous or cormous plants inhabit areas of the world where there are definite dry seasons. One thinks, for instance, of the flora of the Mediterranean world where, following the fall and winter rains with an early-spring flush of growth, the vegetation generally recedes below ground into food-storage plant segments that are bulbous or rhizomatous. This scheme makes proper sense, and becomes especially advantageous given the added stress of sheep and goat grazing.

But how do we explain that in eastern North America the plants that have evolved bulbous or rhizomatous structures generally are not plants of rapidly drained and droughty sites, but almost exclusively inhabit moist sites along stream banks or even in swampy ground? One thinks of *Lilium canadense* and *Lilium superbum,* and then there is our eastern trout lily, *Erythronium americanum,* also known as fawn lily or dog tooth violet.

By whichever name, this last is a curious plant. It is not uncommon in moist woods and along stream banks over a very wide geographical area from New Brunswick west to Minnesota and south to Florida and Oklahoma. Where it grows it usually produces extensive carpets of mottled lanceform leaves with here and there clusters of yellow lilylike flowers nodding and solitary.

It is not entirely clear why in a large, dense colony of this bulbous plant of the lily family, even where the colony is known to have existed for a number of years, there are so many one-leaved, nonflowering plants. These do not appear to be merely immature seedlings that will eventually blossom; if they were, established colonies would in time, as the bulb matured, produce more and more flowers each year. But this is not observed to occur.

Nor does the explanation seem to be in the splitting up of the bulb after flowering, as happens in some tulips.

It is known, however, that as the leaves are withering, one or more long, white, fleshy stolons grow from the base of the bulb, each producing upon its tip a new bulb. In deep, easily penetrated soils these new bulbs may be produced more deeply each year into less and less fertile layers of soil. It is certainly true that when one attempts to dig bulbs from the wild, one finds that most of the bulbs, where conditions permit, are as much as a foot beneath the surface.

Somewhat west of the range of *Erythronium americanum* is a white-flowered species, *E. albidum,* with a dry-site var. *mesochoreum.* This variety in the wild has a much higher proportion of flowering to nonflowering plants in a colony than either the straight species or *E. americanum.* It may be significant that this variety, unlike either *E. albidum* or *E. americanum,* produces its new bulb at the base of the old one, not on a stolon.

To encourage more abundant development of bulbs of *E. albidum* or *E. americanum* capable of producing the two-leaved flowering plant, various schemes have been devised with varying but never consistent success. One grower buried a short wooden plank about six inches beneath the surface and planted collected bulbs of the fawn lily just above the plank. This was to discourage new bulbs from going deeper and deeper. He reported some temporary increase in flowering. Planting above a large flat rock or tree roots also seems (at least temporarily) to increase flowering.

Another grower, knowing that the wild bulbs were always found deep and believing that the secret of flowering was lack of fertility at greater depth, dug a foot-deep trench and placed in the bottom some well-rotted manure. On the manure he put a layer of rich soil in which he planted bulbs of collected *E. americanum.* The second year there was a fair display of flowers, but thereafter the proportion of flowering to nonflowering plants diminished.

There may be room for more experiments to encourage this charming spring wildling to grace our gardens with more abundant flowers. But it may be possible that there has evolved in this species such a successful method of vegetative propagation of offspring that it cannot be readily diverted to the usual method of increase by flower and seed.

H.L.F.

GALAX APHYLLA

The *Diapensiaceae* is a family of elegance and sensitive tolerance, closely related to the more resilient *Primulaceae* on the one hand and the far-ranging *Ericaceae* on the other. It does, however, contain one monotypic genus, *Galax,* that displays the sort of plebeian tendencies we find in the odd member of most aristocratic genealogy.

Galax aphylla has its own stalwart originality. What it lacks in beauty of flower it compensates for in grandeur of leaf and in reasonable temperament. From a fairly fleshy underground system of stoloniferous rhizomes it sends up from each growing tip a cluster of leaves and a potential flowering spike. It must be confessed that it tends more to leaf than flower, and I cannot discover by inspection of any particular bud at the tip of a rhizome whether it is to become merely leaves or a leaf plus flower. In other members of this family, as also in the *Ericaceae,* by autumn one can distinguish between the purely leaf-bearing bud and the flowering bud. *Galax* blooms rather late in the season, though, and it is just possible that preliminary decisions have not been made by fall.

Along the below-ground rhizome, in addition to the budlike tips surrounded by a few mature evergreen leaves, are many incipient spurs to develop perhaps into leaf-bearing side shoots, elongating rhizomes, or even thwarted nodes that merely develop feeding roots. To discover the mysterious ways of the plant one

Galax aphylla   A fine foliage plant for the woodland with handsome fall
color.

should burrow like a mole, dig the plant monthly for inspection, or indulge in unverified speculation.

What is presented to the casual eye is a collection of glossy, long-petioled leaves and a few spikes of summer-flowering white flowers. Few of us, I think, take the second look. On closer inspection we see that the leathery, rounded leaf blade is definitely cordate at the base, with large but somewhat irregular serrations around the edge of the somewhat scalloped outline. The leaf petiole is attached at the junction of the radiating prominent veins where they meet at the base of the sinus. This petiole, up to eight inches long, holds the leaf stiffly erect persisting for many years. In deep shade the foliage remains green during the winter, but in sunnier sites the leaves take on brilliant crimson and purple hues in the fall and hold the color well into spring. Then magically these same leaves turn once again to a burnished apple green.

So long lasting are the leaves when separated from the living plant that there used to be a thriving business in them for the florist trade. Mountain folk in the southern Appalachians annually gathered the *Galax* foliage in such abundance that boxcar loads were shipped to the florists of major cities for flower and fruit arrangements. They were even used in fancy hotels and restaurants as a decoration beneath a half grapefruit served in those silver goblets of crushed ice. With changing habits in the mountain country this trade has fallen off. And city customs have changed.

The white flowers, which open in June and July in our area, are arranged in a dense spike or raceme on the upper three to four inches of the fairly heavy, rigid, leafless scape that carries them well above the foliage. These flower stems with dried sepals and empty seed capsules may persist for two years. The individual flowers in the spike look like small pyxie flowers, somewhat gap-toothed in the corolla but so thickly set along the stem that the effect is rather splendid. In a rich woodland situation, with acid soil, a large colony of the bold, glistening foliage decorated with white spires is a handsome sight.

Plebeian and rugged as it may be compared with the other more specialized members of the family, *Galax* merits our warm regard for its vigorous constitution, for its own special beauty of foliage and flower, and for its late season of bloom.

It does have a few cultural requirements: *Galax* needs an acid soil, preferably in some shade, and is at its best in duffy open soil. Yet all of these site factors may be ignored within reason, and *Galax* will still thrive. I have seen it growing in heavy red clay. It will persist in a site quite exposed to the sun. How much lime it will tolerate I cannot say. I suspect it might perish, and certainly would not thrive, in a sunny, clayey, limy situation. Most gardeners can, however, find some location where *Galax* will be content, and the gardener who finds a location for it will soon, I am convinced, become a devoted admirer of *Galax,* if not its passionate lover.

It is easy to propagate by division. Once established, cautiously at first, but more daringly as the plant spreads with age, portions may be chopped away from the edges of the increasing clump at almost any time of year (best in early spring or fall) and set immediately in a new section of the garden as you more and more appreciate the splendid qualities of *Galax aphylla.*

The genus name *Galax* is rather obscure, but most likely derives from the Greek word for milk, in recognition of its milk-white blossoms. The species name, *aphylla,* straightforwardly asserts that the flowering spike is without leaves.

H.L.F.

RED, WHITE, AND GREEN
Gaultheria

There are two species of plants in the eastern United States that have a great deal of charm but live under the shadow of some confusion for those who wish to make reference to them horticulturally or botanically. The confusion lies more in the area of their names than in their botanical or horticultural reality.

I refer to *Gaultheria procumbens* and *Gaultheria hispidula*. And right away in my reference I must stutter over the spelling of the generic name for both, and then stumble over the second from a deeper and related confusion about whether the two belong to the same genus or in different genera. Who is to decide? What is the authority? What does it matter to the plant or its genes, or even to the rock gardener in his approach to the world of plants, or to those who want to grow one or the other of them?

Let us then deal with these entities as discrete and admirable plants without coming to grips with what is both a taxonomic and a historical problem. (Both problems, however, do offer a level of involvement that lends an added dimension to our already intoxicating pursuit of growing.)

Gaultheria procumbens has a fairly clear bill of lading as to name. The genus name commemorates a naturalist and court physician at Quebec, Jean-François Gaultier, whose name, after the fashion of the times, was also spelled Gaulthier, Gauthier, and Gautier. He is believed to have been born in 1708 and to have died in 1756, but there is some uncertainty in these dates. It may have been that this adventurous naturalist sent to Linnaeus the North American plant that the Swedish botanist christened in the Frenchman's honor, a name which, in turn, is the generic title of about thirty species in North and South America, Asia, Australia, and New Zealand. They are all evergreen shrubs of varied stature, with small, fleshy, hanging, campanulate flowers that are white frequently tinged with pink or red. The fruit is a fleshy berrylike capsule, generally bright and conspicuous, pure white, blue, or red. Many of the species are difficult to grow, and some are definitely not hardy, at least in the Northeast.

The charge of tenderness, however, cannot be brought against *Gaultheria procumbens,* which is found growing wild in rather sterile acid soil, in sun or shade, from Canada south to Georgia and as far west as Minnesota. Its specific name is not entirely appropriate, because the plants are not really procumbent, or prostrate, though some plants may produce a carpetlike effect by the density of the erect stems. These flowering branches, which carry a cluster of dark green, hard and coriaceous leaves, may be six inches tall. To be sure there are other leafless branches that do creep either on the surface or just beneath to enlarge the colony.

The leaves produce a volatile oil of wintergreen and have long been distilled for use in medicine and as flavoring. The young leaves, which are tender and slightly ruddy of color, are especially delicious when chomped between the teeth and do wonders for a thirsty hiker in the wooded hills. There is some medical opinion that, in addition, the plant contains substances inhibitive of cancer. The pulpy, rather dry white flesh of the fruit, wrapped in a crisp crimson skin, is equally delicious, permeated as it is with the same mystical flavors and principles.

Some of these qualities, plus its distinctive characters may, years ago, have led Dr. Gaulthier to this plant that bears his name. The same characters must also have given *G. procumbens* a special position in local lore, as recorded in colloquial names. The very number of these names may be a measure of its prominence. How many plants can support as diverse or as many common names: aromatic wintergreen, teaberry, checkerberry, mountain-tea, petit thé des bois, boxberry, ivory plum?

Aside from its place in the pharmacopoeia and lore, the beautiful *G. procumbens* is acknowledged even in the august pages of the *Royal Horticultural Society Dictionary of Gardening* in its discussion of the *Gaultheria* genus as "One of the most useful, decorative, vigorous, and hardy species."

Though slow to establish after being collected in the wild, the plant eventually will make a sizable carpet. In order to encourage a good root system and rapid establishment, it is wise to handle collected plants as cuttings in a mixture of peat and sand in a frame or pot. Indeed, *G. procumbens* makes a superb specimen in a pot, where because of confinement, growth is dense and flowering and fruiting encouraged.

As is true with many natives, I suspect, the checkerberry fares better in cultivation than in nature. Enjoying in the garden a more nourishing diet than its normal fare, it returns a reward in richer foliage, lustier growth, and a far superior display of flowers and fruit. On its own in the wild, because it does not fight easily against competition, it is relegated, like many of the meek of the earth, either to poverty-stricken, sandy, arid soils or to the leaf-strewn floor of oak or conifer forest. Here, because of its tolerance of very acid soils and slowly decaying and acid leaf cover, it struggles and persists but does not have the sustenance to blossom and fruit abundantly. In the garden, however, if given a rich acid diet, relieved of weedy competition, and housed in the fullest sunshine short of dryness and baking, this aromatic wintergreen will grow lush and dense with a resplendent display of waxen flowers in late summer and before winter be beautifully decked with fleshy crimson fruits. Though of modest mien in the wild, *Gaultheria procumbens* is another of our neglected natives that deserves not only a welcome but a fanfare as a rock garden plant.

Its sibling, if we are to accept the latest taxonomic determinations, *G. hispidula,* occupies some of the same geographic range as *G. procumbens*. But it, the creeping snowberry, moxieplum, capillaire, maidenhair-berry, petit thé de perdrix, or petits oeufs de perdrix, does not roam far south; yet it does range widely in the north from Labrador to British Columbia. The creeping snowberry has a rather narrow site tolerance, however, and it is found only in mossy moist spots, frequently beneath coniferous trees, and in the southern part of its range almost exclusively in the wooded fringes of sphagnum bogs. In such moist, acid spots, especially on the elongated moss-covered mound where fallen logs or stumps are slowly decaying, the plant will weave an intricate flat mat. The mat is composed of long, wire-stemmed branches with only sparse feeding roots on the lower side. These interwoven branches are densely decorated with small, ovate leaves, firm and bristly, arranged in an alternate pattern.

Here and there over a mature mat will hang out from leaf axils on short, nodding stems small white crystalline lanterns of blossoms, which when fertilized become in fall snow-white berries with a clasping, fleshy, white calyx. These berries are deliciously juicy with a delicate, aromatic wintergreen or black birch flavor.

This pert and charming mat former is not easily moved from the wild to the garden. Roots are delicate and sparse, constantly moist in sphagnum or rotting acid duff. There is some evidence, however, that its obligatory site in nature may be determined more by requirements of a constantly moist medium for seed germination than for mature growth. It can be propagated by layers, cuttings, or seed, and when growing well in a carefully controlled situation, can be transferred successfully to less moist, acid duffy soil in the garden, although it should always remain in the shade. In sun it cringes, shrivels, and dies, except perhaps in a northern bog. I have never seen it in an open bog, always in the wooded fringe.

The fact that we have in snowberry a *Gaultheria*-like plant with a white fruit which has a range full across the northern part of the American continent raises a nice set of questions. Is it, perhaps, another preglacial Holarctic plant which ties the flora of the eastern United States with that of Asia? By way of *G. humifusa* and *G. ovatifolia,* with red fruit, does it have ties with white-fruited *G. miqueliana* of Japan and the blue-fruited *G. trichophylla* of the Himalaya?

Is it, in fact, a *Gaultheria* at all, or does it more properly merit a separate genus, as it did until recently under the name *Chiogenes?*

Though Jacob Bigelow (1787–1879), Boston physician and botanist, proposed many years ago that this plant belonged in the *Gaultheria* genus despite its more berrylike than capsular fruit, it long bore the name *Chiogenes* (from the Greek *chion* = snow and *geonos* = of spring). There it rested in a separate genus in standard floras right through the first seven editions of *Gray's Manual of Botany.* In the massive revision of Gray's bible undertaken by Merritt L. Fernald, the name was shifted from *Chiogenes* to *Gaultheria* with Bigelow as authority, and was so published in the long-awaited and now standard edition of *Gray's Manual* of 1950. Since that date regional floras have accepted this designation, and even eccentric H. W. Rickett uses *Gaultheria* for this taxon in the New York Botanical Garden's monumental series *Wild Flowers of the United States.*

Like many eastern native herbs these two *Gaultheria*s, as is clear from some of their colloquial names, served as a substitute for tea. One wonders, though, about the source of the colloquial "moxie-plum."

H.L.F.

HEPATICAS

Like Wordsworth's Lucy, "Fair as a star, when only one is shining in the sky," the early blooms of hepatica have the stage to themselves. Invidious as I have always considered Wordsworth's lines to Lucy, it is certainly true that the hepatica calls to itself every merited attention by leading the parade of spring blossoms and by gleaming "among the untrodden ways beside the springs of Dove," without rival.

There on the forest floor, generally on a slope, with a mixture of deciduous trees above, in the pure light of early spring, suddenly the hepaticas' blossoms burst into bloom amidst the dun and dreary fallen leaves, with barely a sprig of green to compete.

It is not entirely, I think, sentimental associations with the first warm ambient air or the tingle of unobtrusive but noted birdsong that win our affection to the translucent loveliness of the "liverleaf in bloom". It is a thoroughly admirable plant.

In America, this genus of *Ranunculaceae* is separated into two species on the basis of leaf shape: *H. americana,* with three rounded lobes to the leaf blade, each lobe usually broader than long; *H. acutiloba,* with the three leaf lobes ending in a point and generally longer than broad. Occasionally the two species (if they are separable genetically) intergrade in areas where the two grow close together. Puzzling intergrades certainly exist under circumstances where the two extremes are recognizable and contiguous.

There are also a few nonscientific differences, at least between the extremes of the two species. *H. americana* generally has shorter, more hairy flowering scapes. The leaves are not often more than tripartite, whereas in *H. acutiloba* subdivisions of the three lobes are not uncommon. The flower color in *H. americana* is generally in shades of blue or white, while *H. acutiloba* tends away from blue to white and pink. At least these are casual observations in northwestern Connecticut. The texture and color of the foliage in *H. acutiloba,* despite variety in lobing, is uniformly shiny, coriaceous, and unmottled. In *H. americana,* the hairier leaves may vary considerably in size at maturity, with actual pygmies consistently growing as local clones. Likewise mottling of the leaves may occur in *H. americana.* In both species the flowers open before the new leaves uncurl their soft green, but the old leaves usually persist.

There seems to be no difference in the blooming seasons of the two species, and since both will thrive in identical sites in the garden, even a mixed planting of the two will bring a very early display of bright blossoms of varied hues. The cuplike flowers open in the late morning, gradually dilating until they are almost flat. They move with the sunlight, even in shady corners, and close by evening. Shade is their preferred site in nature. In rich soil full of leaf mold, they may be grown in positions that receive up to 50 percent full sun. In fact, in open sites, if the soil is not parched and is enriched with old manure, the plants will assume massive proportions with myriad blossoms on long stems.

When grown in sizable groups, the hepaticas are a delight at all seasons. The leaves are evergreen, firm-textured, and elegantly proportioned. As fall approaches, the polished green of the foliage assumes warm tints of ox blood and dark wine. The shape and autumn color were once thought, in fact, to be the Creator's mark upon hepaticas as a fitting cure for complaints of the liver. For centuries, which we look back on as less pragmatic than our own, plants and their study would be justified only as they were thought to be practically useful to man. Now, thankfully, we can accept hepaticas and such as existing in their own being, beautiful and irrelevant in nature. We bring them into the garden, balm not so much for a crippled liver as for the impoverished spirit.

Nor are we limited to the two American species, varied as they are. In Europe there are likewise two species: *H. triloba (nobilis)* and *H. transsilvanica (angulosa).* The former, which may also be listed as *Anemone hepatica,* is hardly to be distinguished from the American species, coming very close to an intermediate between our two species. This one ranges in all the temperate European woods, into parts of Asia and on around the globe to America (some botanists classify *H. americana* as a variety of *H. triloba [nobilis]*). But there are wide gaps in Asia and western America where no hepaticas are found.

In the Near East appears the other species, *H. transsilvanica (angulosa).* These can be readily distinguished by the leaves, which have each shallow, broad lobe pinked at the tip into a series of blunt notches. The notable clone *H.* × *media* 'Ballard's var.', or *H.* × *ballardii,* is vigorous in foliage and has large sky-blue flowers. It is purported to be a hybrid of the two European species.

It is possible to suggest, however, that this horticultural clone is merely a selection of *H. transsilvanica (angulosa),* which it more nearly resembles. Moreover, it is possible that all hepaticas are but variants of a single circumpolar species with local variations of leaf pattern. Color variations in the blossom are abundant in nature, more so, perhaps, in one "species" than another, or one locality than another. Soil preferences indicated in some botany books where, for instance, *H. acutiloba* is assigned to calcareous soils and *H. americana* to acid soils, do not appear to stand up in the wild in northwestern Connecticut and are of no significance in the garden.

Color forms have been recognized and selected and vegetatively propagated, as have multisepaled and double forms. Others have been selected for size of blossom or shape, size, and color of foliage. Desirable as all of these are for garden purposes, the hepaticas are not so frequently seen in cultivation as they deserve, and there are many questions about them that are not answered in the available horticultural literature.

For instance, is there a chromosome difference among so-called species? What is the soil pH tolerance of the European and American hepaticas? What is the best time to divide plants of desirable forms which can be reproduced only vegetatively? Is there any other method of vegetative reproduction besides the slow method of division? Hepaticas are divisible not more than every other year under normal growing conditions. How long do seeds take to germinate?

This last question is one that baffles me on the basis of personal experience. I do know that hepatica seed falls green and remarkably soon after flowering. I do know also that young plants, with only the two oval cotyledons apparent, are found around mature plants in nature at various times: from early spring to late summer. Yet I have not had sowed seeds germinate in pots, flats, or open ground. Fresh green seed has been sowed. Some has been subjected to artificial freezing. But so far not a plumule.

The search for desirable forms in the wild is not only a pleasant springtime enterprise (if rock gardeners can ever be torn away from the garden in spring), but may also result in the introduction of unrecorded forms before our changing environment snuffs them out. So far as I can discover no fully double forms of the American species have been listed. Pale blues, whites, and pale pinks of varying flower size are to be found in any considerable patch of hepaticas. The back cover of the Cranbrook Institute of Science *News Letter* for April 1958 shows colored pictures of ninety variants in one woodlot in Oakland County, Michigan.

Good, strong, clear blues, real pinks, and pure whites of substance and size are all to be sought; and, of course, the illusive true doubles. If found, these are all quite easy to transplant in full flower. Merely put them in a woodsy site with a rich, well-drained soil; water them well at transplanting. If they measure up as outstanding when grown side by side with the best, treasure them, divide them, share them.

It has taken ten years to build up a stock and introduce into the gardens of friends *H. acutiloba* 'Millstream Pink'. This is a vigorous plant with large blossoms of vivid deep pink, an outstanding individual in any collection. Distributed now into many gardens, this solitary plant, found after long search amidst hosts of plants in many sites, will perhaps persist in cultivation. It might have been destroyed in the wild!

H.L.F.

HOUSTONIA CAERULEA

To see a run-down upland meadow or pasture in New England misted with sheets of bluets in flower is an annual joy in early May. So common and so lovely are they in their natural setting that we rarely think of them as worthy of rock garden culture. Not so in England or other parts of the world where they are not native.

The principal flush of flowers in nature is preceded by a few of the earliest blossoms of spring, and all summer into fall there are scattered flowers to be found on the neat tuffets of evergreen foliage.

So valued is the plant in England that Farrer exclaims: "a creeping treasure with spreading tufts that emit all the summer through (but especially in May) an incredible and plant-hiding profusion of exquisite little pale-blue four rayed stars borne singly on fine stems of 3 or 4 inches."

Even in that English book devoted exclusively to the aristocrats of rock garden plants, *Collectors' Alpines,* Royton Heath writes of *Houstonia:* "a genus of plants which has two species *(caerulea* and *serpyllifolia)* that can be used for pan culture, and these are well known, but somehow the Bluets are not so easy to grow into large specimens, for they seem to have the tendency to die away after two years or so."

The august pages of the *R.H.S. Dictionary of Gardening* contain this recommendation: *"H. caerulea* forms a good pot plant under cold frame treatment or for the alpine house, and may be used for surfacing soil in pots in which bare-stemmed hardy plants are grown."

Our lovely pasture plant has not been entirely neglected, however, for at least one perceptive rock garden author in America has appreciated it. That doyenne of American rock gardening, Louise Beebe Wilder, in a work long out of print and sadly overlooked, *The Rock Garden,* is worth quoting in full:

> Houstonia is a most precious small native, the daintiest and most engaging of fairies—and sometimes the most elusive. Not by any means are these little Quaker Ladies to be led by the nose. In some places they will dwell and in some they will not. We may set them out in a pleasantly shaded and cool spot, but we need not be surprised if the next season this choice locality is quite deserted, and to find away along the edges of the starved paths, on precarious ledges, or from the midst of tight wads of Saxifrages, in all sorts of unexpected places, little gatherings of demure Quaker Ladies, quite gleeful and heady with liberty. Gradually they will increase, choosing their own neighborhoods, until there are throngs of the charming creatures, and one is glad to be alive just to look at them.

The winsome and capricious *Houstonia caerulea* grows wild from Nova Scotia, Ontario, and Wisconsin, south to Georgia,

Alabama, and Missouri. In the northern part of its range it tends to inhabit open turfy slopes and fields, while to the south it is more likely to grow in shady thickets and woods. In its middle range, in Connecticut, it thrives either in sun or shade so long as the site does not become parched. Though perhaps more common and vigorous on acid than on limy soils, it certainly does not entirely shun the latter.

The *Houstonia*s, of which there are a number of species in temperate North America, belong to the *Rubiaceae,* the madder family. The family is chiefly tropical, containing the coffee and Peruvian bark trees, and our genus is named by Linnaeus for Dr. William Houston, an English botanist who specialized in tropical American plants.

Our bluets, also called innocence or Quaker ladies, form small pads of delicate small-leaved tufts joined together by short threadlike rhizomes, which remain green over the winter but do not reach large dimensions. Particular plants may be only annual in duration or may persist for a few years, but in congenial sites they self-sow readily and reach flowering size within a year. An individual plant calls to mind an old-fashioned brooch of intricate gold filigree jeweled with tiny brilliant green leaves and delicate flowers of enamel. From even the smallest tuffet of foliage there springs up as the season warms a dense tangle of wiry, threadlike stems branching as they go with a few tiny leaves paired along the stems, each filiform branch carrying a single four-petaled, salverform blossom. These guileless flowers in their jostled cluster show a range of blue from the palest almost-white to deep sky blue, all with a yellow eye. They range in size from only 2½ to 4 full millimeters across.

In England a form of Quaker ladies has been selected for its large flowers of deep blue color and nominated 'Millard's Variety'. This has been for years propagated vegetatively by division and by cuttings and even tends to come fairly true from seed of segregated plants. In the wild, pure white forms have been found and are listed as forma *albiflora.*

The range of flower size and color suggests a program for an enterprising plantsman. By collecting the largest flowered and deepest colored forms and growing them in segregation from the general run, seedlings from these plants by selection could doubtless in a very few generations produce a superior strain for garden culture.

There is also the possibility that this species as commonly found can be crossed with the var. *faxonorum,* found only in alpine regions of the White Mountains of New Hampshire and on the borders of streams on the islands of Saint Pierre and Miquelon off the southern coast of Newfoundland. This handsome variety has large pure white flowers with a deep golden center produced on plants of firmer substance throughout. Var. *faxonorum* appears to be reliably perennial in nature but is not easy to grow in more lowland gardens. Hybrids might have ease of culture with increased size and substance.

Yet another possibility is a program of hybridizing with the more southern species, *H. serpyllifolia,* the creeping, thyme-leaved bluet. This species, a good garden plant in its own right, forms large mats of close-packed, deep green, small foliage and is certainly a long-lived perennial. The flowers, on characteristic wiry stems, are always a good, intense blue, but they are not as thickly set as are those of *H. caerulea.* The southern mat former is found in really moist soils along streams in the mountains of Pennsylvania and West Virginia to Georgia and Tennessee. Hybrids between the two species could possibly combine the virtues of both.

There are other quite different species within the genus, a group of garden-worthy upright perennials up to two feet in height, bearing opposite leaves up the stiff stems and tubular pink flowers in clusters at the apex. In all, this is a genus of native plants worthy of more attention than has so far been given it by American rock gardeners.

H.L.F.

IRIS CRISTATA AND IRIS VERNA

It is surprising how frequently, when one has ordered *Iris verna,* particularly from a wildflower nursery, one receives *Iris cristata* instead. Though both are low-growing iris native to the southeastern United States, of approximately the same height and general coloration, ranging from deep violet blue through lavenders to albino forms, they are very different plants.

Iris cristata is, to begin with, a crested iris, as its name implies, carrying on its falls one to three parallel rows of fleshy, yellow to white lobes rather like crumpled ribbons or long, narrow cockscombs. *Iris verna,* on the other hand, has smooth falls, though the central orange-yellow blotch is likely to be more pronounced than in *Iris cristata.*

Though both species are rhizomatous, the rhizomes of *Iris verna* are chunky throughout their length, fairly deep-lying in the soil, and with very short branches so the plant remains quite compact. *Iris cristata,* on the other hand, has long, very slender rhizomes, slightly thickened at the nodes. These sprawl widely on or very close to the surface; each plant, therefore, will quite rapidly make a fairly large mat. Where competition is not too heavy and the soil is light and humusy, a single plant may eventually fill a circle six feet across or more.

The leaves of *Iris cristata,* though upright when they first emerge from the soil in spring, soon lose their youthful arrogance and bow over so that the flowering stems rise above them. As the

Iris verna   For moist woodland places.

season advances and they elongate slightly, these flexed leaves in a pure stand will form a dense, rippling, light green carpet of foliage. In fall this carpet turns pale creamy tan and shrivels away into a threadbare covering for the tangled web of rhizomes below. The foliage of *Iris verna,* on the other hand, is evergreen and will last through several seasons though the leaves become progressively more discolored and tattered as they age. They are more slender for their height than those of *Iris cristata* and more upright, usually slightly taller than the flowering stems at anthesis, but tend to arch gracefully away from the blossoms as if to frame rather than conceal them.

Both species seem to prefer a site on the edge of thin woods where they receive plenty of light but can be somewhat shaded during the hottest part of the day. Both do well in light, humusy soil. *Iris cristata* will accept a somewhat heavier soil and appears indifferent to pH, whereas *Iris verna* requires acid soil and seems to need slightly sharper drainage. Both species can withstand considerable drought. Division of the rhizomes is the easiest method of increase, and either species may be grown from seed unless a particular color form is desired.

The effects of the two in the garden are quite different, and not only because of their dissimilar growth habit. *Iris verna* has a restrained elegance; its slender leaves have a more graceful carriage, and its flowers not only tend to be richer in coloration but have a certain aristocratic bearing and refined clarity of outline that is not as manifest in *Iris cristata.* It is the difference between a court beauty and a bevy of pretty milkmaids.

L.L.F.

JEFFERSONIA

The third President of the United States has many commemorations: architectural, legal, philatelic, political, and social. One wonders, though, as he turns beneath the Watergates in his sainted shroud, whether he does not take some quiet and particular pleasure in the fact that there are two lovely perennial plants that spring early from the soil of the southeastern states and eastern Asia, respectively, year after year and bear his name: *Jeffersonia diphylla* and *Jeffersonia dubia.* This botanical and horticultural commemoration, I can only hope, comforts his shade as it delights our souls.

These two widely separated species have much in common besides their namesake. Early in the spring, as bloodroot, spring beauty, and other harbingers break into sudden and reassuring flower, these two entrancing members of the complex *Berberidaceae* family begin their resurrection by expanding above the moist floor of their woodland haunts a veritable flutter of unfurling leaves. Rather like humpbacked elves, the hunched leaves, of rare iridescence, begin to rise up and unfold their winglike foliage.

The American species, *J. diphylla,* carries on its unfurling leaves only a slight overlay of reds and purples, which as they expand fade to a pale green foliage so divided as to make each leaf appear like a pair of angelic wings and give to the plant its common name, twinleaf. Rising soon above the expanded leaves on naked stems are pure white flowers rather suggestive of a narrow-petaled bloodroot or a lofty hepatica. Of rather short duration and with the eight petals too widely spaced to be entirely elegant, the blossoms, nevertheless, do gleam in purest white against the green of the winglike leaves.

The Asian relative, *J. dubia,* glows with an ethereal light in both leaf and blossom, and by comparison outshines its relative for utter beauty. The leaves spring up folded like butterfly wings, garnet red with darker veins and darker margins where the veins end in spiny tips. As the leaves unfold and begin to shade with green, the full-petaled blossoms, iridescent amethyst, stand clustered above the ruff and complement the foliage. This species has only six petals, but each is large and overlaps its neighbor. The corolla in both species carries these true petals above a quickly vanishing set of brown sepals.

Beautiful as are the blossoms and leaves of both species, the seed capsules add a second dimension of structural beauty as they ripen in late June. At this stage the American species surpasses the Oriental in size and elegance. (Is there, perchance, some hidden significance here?) The swollen, channeled capsule of *J. diphylla,* up to an inch in length, changes from a waxen, pitted, leathery object with the texture of shriveled lemon peel. A prominent suture develops, and the lid folds back to reveal a cornucopia full of two rows of large seeds attached by a fleshy aril to the longitudinal placenta. The pod of *J. dubia* is smaller and more pinched, twisting as it ripens to roll the seeds out onto the long tonguelike lid of the capsule.

The seeds falling about the mother plant will germinate abundantly the following spring. It takes up to three years for the seedlings to develop what becomes a great tangled mop of rather fleshy white roots and before the plant is ready to begin blooming. Many of these self-sown seedlings cannot compete with the husky root growth of the long-lived parent and must perish. But there is no better way to establish a colony of either species than to let them self-sow and transplant the young seedlings in an increasing circle about the parent plant or plants.

As with some other species, *Jeffersonia dubia* appears to be subject to a colonizing urge, and seeds germinate best in near association with established relatives. It is possible, on the other hand, that the important consideration for self-sown seed is that it is fresh, and the fleshy aril does not dry out. It took me years of trying seed from the exchanges before I finally got germination of *J. dubia.* Beg fresh seed if you can, and sow it directly in the ground in a prepared woodland site, and in three years you may have one of the most exalting sights of spring, a clump of flowering *Jeffersonia dubia.*

Though some botanists have proposed a separate genus, *Plagiorhegma,* for the Asian species, the many similarities of the two certainly suggest a common ancestry and a fairly recent evolutionary differentiation. No hybrids between the two species have been recorded, but they are likely to appear at any time where the two species are grown in close proximity.

H.L.F.

KALMIOPSIS LEACHIANA

Kalmiopsis leachiana has an elfin charm, being a diminutive near relative of our Connecticut *Kalmia latifolia,* whose proportions of leaf to woody stem and flower to leaf are absolutely classic. Because it is found wild in only two rather small areas in the Siskiyou Mountains of Oregon, Kalmiopsis was unknown to botanists until comparatively recently, as such things go, until a Mrs. Leach discovered it early in the present century.

After its discovery it was first called *Rhododendron leacheanum,* but when the resemblance of the blossoms to those of *Kalmia* was noted, a separate genus was created to register the likeness. It is, however, distinguished from that genus by the absence of the little pleats in the corolla in which the true *Kalmia*'s stamens are held until released by the tramp of a bee.

One cannot help wondering how this now-unique member of the vast ericaceous tribe evolved and became isolated in the Umpqua area. Has its evolution endowed it also with such specialized needs that it has been impeded from colonizing new territories? It does, I know, produce an abundance of seed, fine seed that could be transported readily by winds. Nor does the seed appear to be of only brief viability, as is true with some other narrowly distributed plants such as the *Shortia*s. Seed from the ARGS seed exchange has germinated reasonably well even when sown in late spring from the previous year's gathering.

Indeed the seed appears to require rather high temperatures for germination, and it is just possible that at the season in the Siskiyous when the temperature becomes warm enough, the weather becomes excessively dry, and the tiny seedlings perish except in the plant's home territory.

Seedlings, even well tended, are very slow in growth and are, therefore, best left in the seed pan during the first winter and protected against extreme low temperatures. It is advisable, however, to move them on during the second year because they do not establish easily, in my experience, after root disturbance.

I now have four blooming-size plants from seed sowing of 1967. One, planted among low rhododendrons on a shaded rocky slope facing west, has reached eight inches high and about six inches across, and is rather erect in habit. It flowered in 1970, the first year after being set in its present site, but has not flowered since.

The other three plants were set in a clump on a rather dry rocky knoll with plenty of light, being in the sun for about three hours. These three are flatter growing with slightly smaller leaves. They are all three inches high, the largest eight inches across and the smallest only four inches in diameter. These did not bloom until 1971 but have done so each year since. These three were given a light covering of pine boughs last winter, more to discourage deer browsing than to offer protection from the cold. This act may have been beneficial during a recent winter's snowless cold spells; even with protection a few flower buds were blasted. The pine bough covering will be a regular routine from now on because, like other Siskiyou Mountain plants that normally enjoy a persistent snow cover, Kalmiopsis flower buds, I suspect, will not endure temperatures below zero.

I have had two plants, either divisions or cutting-grown, from Siskiyou Rare Plant Nursery and, though both are still alive, neither has grown thriftily, and one has had its top frozen back rather consistently. Maybe the seedlings got an early acclimatization, or maybe the four that survived beyond the seedling stage were stalwarts of the litter.

As a rock garden plant for acid soil, *Kalmiopsis* has few peers among shrubs for excellence of carriage and elegance of flower. It is certainly well worth the slow process of growing from seed to see if we can develop a strain adapted to Connecticut gardens. Once such a hardy and adaptable clone is developed, it can be made available to other gardeners, because *Kalmiopsis* can be propagated from cuttings.

H.L.F.

LINNAEA BOREALIS

Jan Fredrik Gronovius, an eminent early botanist, dedicated the European twinflower, *Linnaea borealis,* to the revered Linnaeus, who was especially fond of this sweetly scented little creeper. The type species is found widely in northern Eurasia and Alaska where it overlaps *L. borealis* var. *americana.* This American variety has its own extensive range, running in the west from Alaska to northern California and in the east from Greenland south to the mountains of West Virginia. Within this extensive range it tends to be rare because of its preference for cool, acid sites, common only in some northern woodlands and upland peat beds, where it may form large, flat carpets, rambling over fallen logs and stumps, weaving among such plants as bunchberry, creeping snowberry, wineleaf cinquefoil and lingonberry.

The thin woody runners, downy with fine hairs, are thickly set with opposite, rounded oval leaves with shallow crenations and short petioles. These evergreen leaves are frequently russet tinged on the upper surface, much paler green beneath, beset on both surfaces with scattered hairs. The trailing stems advance rapidly in congenial sites, branching and rooting down as they progress.

At periodic intervals along the woody runners arise short, erect shoots with overlapping leaves from the tip of which spring the flowering stems in June. The flowering stem or peduncle, about two inches tall, is very thin and wiry, dark green above, tinted with madder in the basal portion. At the summit the peduncle divides into two divergent pedicels, each bearing a delicate nodding flower, strongly almond scented. The plant belongs in the honeysuckle family, the *Caprifoliaceae*.

These blossoms, rather long lasting and densely arranged on a mature established carpet, dance in an elfin way, moved by the slightest breeze on their filiform stems. Occasionally more than two divergent blossoms to a stem are reported, but the very name, twinflower, tells us that two is the usual pattern. The pair of flowers, held elegantly apart yet on one plane, are beautiful *en masse* but are so nobly proportioned and so handsomely shaped as to demand close inspection. They are narrowly flaring bells, less tubby and longer in the American variety than in the European species, up to fifteen millimeters in var. *americana*. There are five equal lobes at the mouth of the bell and a small five-parted calyx at the base, below which is a small bristly ovary clasped in two bracts. The fleshy corolla has an alabaster white base all splashed and streaked with pink on its outer surface, more deeply dotted and flecked with reddish pink within, intensified by an interior fringing of pink hairs. The center of the flower is graced with a slender white pistil and four unequal stamens, whose filaments are white and anthers very pale yellow.

The three-parted ovary becomes a fuzzy brown ball as it matures the solitary seed.

To propagate this woodland elf one need not rely on the few seeds. It is more rapid and far surer to take off rooted runners, or to make cuttings of the short, erect, sterile shoots or tips of the runners. Cuttings, especially if taken early in the growing season, root rapidly and may be potted up to be held in a frame or alpine house for setting out the following spring. If twin-flower is given a shady situation in moist, acid, peaty soil, in three years there should be a spacious rug well set in June with the sweetly fragrant, dancing twin bells.

Ralph Waldo Emerson made his own commemoration of the twinflower and the man to whom it was dedicated:

> He saw beneath dim aisles, in odorous beds,
> The slight Linnaea hang its twin-born heads,
> And blessed the monument of the man of flowers,
> Which breathes his sweet fame through northern bowers.

Emerson was, I fear, a better essayist than poet.

H.L.F.

MITCHELLA REPENS

Dr. John Mitchell of Virginia, who lived to the age of ninety-two (1676–1768), as few except doctors and botanists did in those days, and who was an early correspondent from the Colonies to Linnaeus in Sweden, is nobly commemorated by the woodland carpeter of eastern America, the prosaic but elegant partridge-berry, *Mitchella repens.* Who could wish for a more apt memorial than a plant that, though it may be a bit fussy about its milieu, bears evergreen foliage delicately penciled with palest green at the midvein, intricate flowers endowed with a delicious fra-grance, and brilliant scarlet fruit that persists frequently through the winter even as the next crop of flowers is forthcoming in mid-June?

Mitchella repens is worthy of close scrutiny at all seasons and in its mythical aspects. Its colloquial names, like those of other American plants, are redolent of folklore. Partridgeberry is the most widely accepted of these everyday names here and in Can-ada, where the plant is frequently abundant, and where it is also called pain de perdrix (the bread of the wood grouse). Other colloquial names less frequently heard and sometimes of rather precious botanical origin, are two-eyed berry, running box, and squawberry. The last name, I suspect, is a case of cultural denigra-tion, suggesting, because the fruit is edible and perhaps nutritional but certainly not tasty, that it was suitable fodder for Indians.

The fact that it is generally known as partridgeberry likewise gives rise to speculation. The mealy fruit is edible, as attested by literature and my own experiment (I am still alive); some crea-tures must therefore find it palatable. God never created an aimless beauty. Partridge do live where *Mitchella* thrives; there-fore, partridge must eat the berries.

When I was a hunter, in my more sprightly days, I hunted our native ruffed grouse and occasionally shot one. While plucking and dressing any sparse bag of partridge, I always inspected the crop of the bird (and I use the singular in admission of my poor marksmanship) to see what it had most recently eaten and thus get a clue as to the most likely sites for the quarry. Never did I find a fruit or leaf of *Mitchella* in the crop amidst the undigested strawberry leaves, fruits of barberry and hawthorn, and apple seeds. But it is pleasant to visualize a handsome male grouse strutting across a carpet of *Mitchella repens* in sites congenial to both plant and bird, punctuating his march by a quick gobble of a partridgeberry or two.

To turn from speculation about the mundane food value of *Mitchella* to the plant itself, I am struck by the marvelous morphology of both the flowers and the fruits. Yet I cannot leave its nutritional or at least gustatory attributes without wondering, since it is a member of the *Rubiaceae* and hence related to coffee and cinchona, whether if we roasted the nutlets within the fruits and steeped these in boiling water, we might not brew a potion as seductive as coffee and perhaps more closely approaching the celestial elixir. I plan to experiment.

To return then once again to the growing plant.

We read that *Mitchella repens* is to be found from Florida and Texas northward to Quebec, Ontario, and Minnesota. Yet off in the fringes of its extension it is authoritatively reported from many sections of Missouri, and obviously it will thrive out of its usual range. The specific sites where it is found are cited as "dry or moist knolls in woods" by one authority and "rich or low deciduous woods" by another. In my own area of southern New England, where it is a frequent or common component of the ground flora of rich woods, it tends to favor acid sites, frequently under hemlocks, where there is an open, duffy soil into which the fine, shallow roots may penetrate. These feeding roots, never more than about two inches long in their extensions, are sent down by the rambling vinelike runners of the plant at the base of the nodes from which the opposite, rounded, evergreen leaves are borne. There is no central rootstock as may be found in some ground ramblers. Each ramifying runner may be separated from the parent plant and, if not permitted to dry out, will become an independent plant, soon sending forth its own colonizing runners. Various clones of *Mitchella* have different patterns of branching. Some tend to send forth branches at every node and hence make dense, compact pads, while others send forth rather extensive runners with few side branches. For terrarium use, to which the partridgeberry lends itself commonly and successfully, or as a neat carpet at the foot of a bonsaied evergreen, the compact small-leaved, many-branched forms are most desirable. For large spaces in outdoor gardens, the bigger-leaved, rapidly spreading clones, especially if prolific of flowers and fruits, are more useful.

The flowering and fruiting of *Mitchella* deserve special attention. The flowers, which develop from pearl-like valvate buds sometimes deeply tinged with pink, are always borne in pairs on a single short scape. The ovaries of each pair are united and form the two eyes on the fruit. Each flower in the pair, waxy white when expanded in June and July, is composed of a trumpetlike tube and four spreading corolla lobes, densely bearded with crystalline hairs inside. These sweetly scented blossoms, quite similar to those of *Daphne,* are dimorphic in their sexual organs.

All the flowers on a given plant will have a single style split at the tip into four stigmas, which will be exserted while the stamens are included within the tube, while on another plant it will be the stamens which will be exserted and the pistil included. This arrangement, shared by many *Primulas,* is a useful device to prevent self-fertilization, but it may also account for the fact that in some patches of partridgeberry, because the plants have the same morphology, there will be very little fruit.

If the ovaries are fertilized, small green berries begin to form in late July and grow plump, waxy, and brilliant scarlet in September. Each ovary in a fused pair contains four small nutlike white seeds. Fully developed fruits frequently persist through the winter and are to be found on the carpet when the new flowers expand, creating a stunning picture of red berries and fuzzy white trumpet flowers close among the round-ovate, shining green leaves which themselves are handsomely variegated with pale lines.

There is a rare form of *Mitchella repens,* forma *leucocarpa,* whose fruits are ivory white, and it seems to be a consistent fruiter.

It is a simple process to increase the supply of selected clones by division at almost any time of year, or by soft stem cuttings in May or June. Seeds take two years to germinate.

In the Japanese forests there is another *Mitchella* species of similar growth habit, *M. undulata,* whose long-tubed, fringed, and bearded white flowers arise from prominent boat-shaped bracts.

H.L.F.

NEGLECTED
Omphalodes verna

Why is *Omphalodes verna* so seldom seen in rock gardens, or any gardens for that matter, particularly in the northeastern United States, for whose gardens it is eminently suited? It is an easily grown plant in shade or semishade, a pleasant ground cover though not evergreen, and hardy to about −20 Fahrenheit. It ignores hot, muggy spells of summer, and has a rather spectacular bonus of brilliant true-blue blossoms for two or three weeks in early spring.

It is an easy plant to propagate, producing short, stout stolons that root down at the tip to produce new rosettes. These can be left on the parent plant to ramble among rocks or to form a cluster and eventually a tight ground cover on open ground. The mature plants can easily be divided, or the stolons may be rooted to form new colonies. It perhaps prefers alkaline soil, but seems to grow quite readily, if not so lushly, in acid conditions and, though it does well in reasonably moist soil, seems to be impervious to drought.

A member of the *Boraginaceae, O. verna* declares its affiliation to that family by its clusters of forget-me-not–shaped flowers, though the flowers here are of a much deeper, brighter blue, and is indeed sometimes known as the creeping forget-me-not. It is also called blue-eyed Mary and by the rather unprepossessing names of navelwort or navel-seed. Its botanical name is derived from the Greek *omphalos,* meaning navel. The round, nutlike seeds, indented on one side, do to some degree resemble the human navel. Or so we are told. Our plant has never set seed.

Omphalodes verna is very occasionally listed in the seed exchanges. There are also listed, along with a few other species, two forms: *O. verna* 'Alba', which is reputed to be very handsome, and *O. verna* 'Anthea Bloom', with sky-blue blossoms.

The type plant grows to eight inches or less in height, with dark green, heart-shaped, somewhat fuzzy leaves that seem not to be attractive to insects or slugs and so remain in good condition throughout the season.

By some, *O. verna* is not thought as beautiful as *O. luciliae,* which is considered the queen of the genus with glabrous gray leaves and sky-blue flowers. It is, however, a miffy plant, not nearly as cold-hardy as *O. verna* and tending to sudden departure.

Perhaps this is the problem. A lovely plant in its own right, *O. verna* may be too amenable and is therefore scorned as an "easy" plant by rock gardeners who sometimes seem to equate a plant's difficulty of culture with its desirability. It does seem a shame, though, not to include *O. verna* among the constituents of a shady bed if only for the scilla-blue of its flowers.

L.L.F.

PARNASSIA

The autumn-blooming, moisture-loving grass of Parnassus is neither a grass nor does it grow on Mount Parnassus in Greece. It is known that Dioscorides, one of the earliest and most respected of botanical authors, did write of a Greek plant he called grass of Parnassus, and later botanists, familiar with the flower we know as *Parnassia palustris* (then without a technical name), assumed, for some reasons now obscure, that their plant was the same as the one named by Dioscorides.

Linnaeus, in his whimsical Swedish way and devoted as he was to classical names, permanently assigned the scientific generic name *Parnassia* to a group of plants that includes the European grass of Parnassus. There are actually twelve or more species of this genus of *Saxifragaceae,* ranging from the North American continent, through Europe, to India and China.

One cannot avoid being impressed, whenever one pauses to look into the differentiation and distribution of our flowering plants, by the stunning evolutionary mysteries involved. Here is a genus of wide-ranging plants that shares among its species a remarkable similarity, to the extent that a person familiar with *Parnassia glauca* of the northeastern United States would not fail to mutter to himself, "Grass of Parnassus" if he were to run into *P. nubicola* in wet washes of the Himalayas, or even yellow-

Parnassia glauca   The eastern native, typical of the genus.

petaled *P. wightiana* of India. Have they all wandered off from some primitive common ancestor (perhaps, indeed, on Mount Parnassus), each wearing the mark of their lineage, or has there been some parallel evolution involved?

However it is, all parnassias share a subtle beauty somewhat lost amidst the rich diversity of herbage that attends their late blooming. By this very late blooming the plant suffers also an unmerited neglect among gardeners. With a full rosette of succulent green leaves, they begin to assert their presence early in the season. Then, rather tardily to be sure, they send up one-flowered scapes ranging from six to twelve inches, bearing a midscape leaf and at the summit of each scape a large, five-petaled, crisp, white blossom delicately laced with green lines. In two or three species the petals are even elegantly fringed.

In America botanists recognize at least nine species of *Parnassia,* divided neatly into those that have basal leaves that are only membranaceous (rather thin and translucent) and those that have coriaceous leaves (leathery and dense). Other features, such as the structure of the stamenodes and the shape of the basal leaves (which range from an elongate oval to a kidney shape), separate the species within the two groups.

For those concerned with the botanical aspects of these plants, it might be interesting to point out that the stamens in each individual flower ripen one at a time, starting as five short, plump tabs tightly pressed against the central, pear-shaped, as yet undeveloped ovary, which bears at its apex the four fleshy stigmas. As each stamen matures, the filament elongates out between the petals, bearing on its tip two large ovoid anthers which shrink somewhat as they ripen, their bases pulling away from the filament until they are but tenuously attached. In fact, no sooner have they split and discharged their burden of pollen than they fall away. The needlelike filaments, however, along with the stamenodes, can still be found fringing the base of the fat seed pod long after it is dry and emptied of its numerous seeds.

The stamenodes are placed directly above the petals. These are somewhat fan shaped in outline and are cleft more or less deeply, depending on the species. They may be merely thickened scales scalloped at the apex, as in *P. fimbriata,* or may be slivered nearly to the base into long, slender, spreading filaments each tipped with a pseudo-anther and greatly exceeding the true stamens in length, as in *P. grandiflora.* There may be as few as three of these blades to the fan, as in *P. glauca,* or as many as twenty-five, as in *P. californica.*

For the gardener it is only necessary to say that here is a group of species worthy of further consideration, belonging as it does to the *Saxifragaceae,* which gives us so many other plants of outstanding quality.

Parnassias come readily from seed and once established in a congenial, moist site will self-sow to form colonies that provide a quiet, yet heartwarming, display in the late days of summer and early fall. In fact, one remembers grass of Parnassus, at least in the Northeast, chiefly as a partner in that restrained display of roadside ditches during the last months of the flowering season when *P. glauca* and *Gentiana crinita* dance sedately among the roadside grasses against a background of tumbles of New England and New York asters and other late flowers less known to us than to goldfinches and botanists.

In nature most of the eastern American species of *Parnassia* are found growing in wet calcareous soils, but the presence of lime does not seem to be essential for their successful cultivation. The western American species are found in very wet, mostly acidic sites. *P. fimbriata,* with the lateral edges of each petal elegantly fringed and frilled, frequently grows right down in the cool waters of small brooks and rills. This handsome species has so far resisted my few efforts to get it established in my Connecticut garden, but I shall continue to try.

The European species, *P. palustris,* grown from Czech seed, has established itself nicely, self-sowing among vernales primroses, and producing its green-striated white flowers for a long period beginning in July, at least a month ahead of our native *P. glauca.*

The grass of Parnassus, also locally called bog stars, may also be increased by division as the plants begin their growth in the spring.

H.L.F.

THE NAILWORTS
Paronychia

Like some stalwart friends, there are plants that win our lasting affection by an unpretentious and reliable serviceability. One such is the genus *Paronychia.* They win our affection also by their quiet historical significance, an ancient coat-of-arms never flamboyantly displayed and discovered only by dint of accident.

The common name of the family is whitlow-wort. A whitlow is an inflammation of the finger, a malady not so common as apparently it once was. The Greeks knew it and had a name for it. Two genera of plants were thought to be curative when made into a poultice to ease the bursting pain and to promote cure: *Draba* (whitlow grass); *Paronychia* (whitlow-wort). The Greeks knew this inflammation of the finger as *paronychia.* When the botanist Philip Mills assigned the name to the genus, he may have been aware of the already existent pharmaceutical myth or, in accordance with the doctrine of signatures, he may have assigned the name because of the conspicuous white bracts in most species of the genus, bracts which suggest a pale, papery fingernail (one of the symptoms accompanying a whitlow or felon). The whitlow-wort may be called, in common parlance, nailwort. (May the fingers that hold this pencil not evoke, by an inadvertent slighting of the ancient disease, or of early botanists, a visitation of the whitlows tonight, or tomorrow, or ever!)

If such an untoward visitation should occur, I shall be quite willing to steep a few stems of *P. argentea* or *P. canadensis,* both of which we have growing here. We grow them, not for pharmaceutical purposes, but because they are winsome plants.

P. argentea is a carpeter. The growth pattern is that of a rather tenuous thyme, small-leaved and never smothering. At the tips of the widely ramifying branches and in the leaf axils are compact clusters of small golden flowers without petals. These are embraced by conspicuous, white, papery stipules or bracts which last all summer and, diminishing in brilliance, into the winter. The effect is like a soft dusting of glistening snow over an openweave tawny carpet. Though native to the Mediterranean, *Paronychia* is resolutely hardy.

It is a plant most admirably adapted to lace a rock, or with its tracery to cover dwarf bulbs. The species we have, which is tentatively given the name *argentea,* I originally grew from seed labeled *P. nivea.* This latter, as described in *Hortus,* is more erect, from a woody base, and having larger bracts. The picture in Farrer, labeled *P. argentea,* is more like the word description of *P. nivea.* But whatever it is that we have, it is a delight. It may even be *P. serpyllifolia* of nurseries.

This nailwort will grow in the hottest and driest site or in partial shade, so long as it has good drainage and preferably a rocky surface to sprawl upon. Increase is simple by lifting rooted pieces at almost any season.

There is an Eastern American species, *P. argyrocoma,* with

which I have just recently become acquainted. A plant was presented to me in October by a friend who had collected it on Pilot
Knob in North Carolina. It was a tufty little cushion on the order
of a western bun phlox, but there was something about the white,
scarious tips of the awl-shaped leaves that was not phloxlike. In
the absence of blossoms, however, I had no clues. So I sent a sprig
to Dr. Wherry in Philadelphia.

Though he was still confined after an attack of pneumonia, and
without reference books or herbarium material, Dr. Wherry
made a tentative identification:

> The plant you sent looks more like silverling, *Paronychia
> argyrocoma,* than anything else familiar to me. That plant is
> rather common on North Carolina peaks, and makes such
> magnificent mats on the bare rocks that it is a perennial
> source of wonder that it has not been introduced to rock
> gardening. (Maybe it has, in England.) The flowers, to be
> sure, are incredibly invisible, but after all, silvery foliage has
> ornamental value. This plant is manifestly winter hardy, the
> N.C. peaks not being winter-resorts, and moreover a variant
> of it was once found in New Hampshire and adjacent
> Maine. If it gets written up, however, one point must be
> mentioned—it needs really acid soil, and cannot be expected
> to thrive in limestone rock gardens.

How fortunate we are to have great men like Dr. Wherry, full
of knowledge and lore of plants, modest withal and always
willing to assist.

The tiny tuffet of *P. argyrocoma* is perched in a pot in the alpine
house for the winter, with a few shoots rooting in acid sand. This
should be another quiet but utterly pleasing little plant in an acid,
rocky scree. I look forward to seeing the papery blossoms, and

someday I hope to locate *P. pulvinata,* from Colorado, Wyoming, and Utah, which sounds rather like it.

The other whitlow-wort which we have grown for many years in the shady rock garden is even less pretentious, but equally serviceable. This is *Paronychia canadensis.* It is an annual, one of the few annuals admitted to our garden, aside from the dandelions and the like that sneak in until their presence is discovered by my wife, the weeder. This one was invited in, and we look forward to it year after year as it self-sows among the primroses and other early bloomers. It shows not a vestige until early June. Then, like magic, the lazy seeds sprout, and in a brief period a delicate sea of green has risen six to eight inches above the ground.

On wire-fine stems, which divide and divide like an arterial system, are thickly set the small, elliptical leaves, which diminish in size up the stems. Though thin and entire, the emerald greenness of the tiny leaves is a shimmer of sea light as they move in the slightest breeze, or appear to shimmer even in the stillest air. The minute, petalless flowers are like tiny green beads, turning, as fall approaches, to a dusky brown before the whole plant collapses and evaporates with the first frost, as suddenly as it has sprung. Never so heavy as to be smothering even among the most delicate of woodland flowers, the plant is so lightly rooted that it can be easily twitched out where not wanted.

P. canadensis is native to acid, rocky woods in eastern North America, but will self-sow in any garden site not open to full sun. In fact, it is probably better suited to growing among primroses and other cultivated plants in shady or semishaded sites in the garden than among the rough and tumble of weedy competition in the wild. Never flamboyant, never greedy, self-sufficient and demurely lovely, *P. canadensis* will be reborn here in our garden year after year, we pray.

H.L.F.

SORTING OUT THE FINE PHLOXES

The genus *Phlox* is almost exclusively American; there is one, *P. sibirica,* that sneaks over into Russia. It's an impossible one to grow, probably because our soil is somehow different from Russian soil.

There are, depending upon the experts you consult, anywhere from eighty to sixty to ten species in the genus, a genus which probably gives the greatest difficulty to the taxonomist. I couldn't begin to straighten out the problems. In a brief space, I can't even tell you how to grow these phloxes, but with that caveat, I'll try to give you a brief taxonomic and horticultural survey of some of the species.

One of the difficulties is that the species don't make a nice clean separation. Even within what botanists recognize as a species, there is a wide range of differences, and they overlap. If you're in the field, it may help you in classifying phloxes to know where you are, because for this genus botanists seem able to separate the species on geography better than on morphology.

The difficulty is that nobody has come up with a good key, especially to the dwarf *Phlox,* the little cushion *Phlox,* the buns, those Dr. Wherry calls *Microphlox.* In his great monograph *The Genus Phlox,* Dr. Wherry attempted to deal with all the phloxes in North America, and this is a massive job. His monograph is based on herbarium specimens and field work and is an excellent achievement, although it has some weaknesses, as in the key for the *Microphlox.*

A key which seems to work for some of the *Microphlox* in the Northwest is the one developed by Cronquist in that great work by Hitchcock, Cronquist, et al., *Vascular Plants of the Pacific Northwest,* but don't forget that he had a more limited area than Dr. Wherry to worry about.

Another difficulty is that when you bring phloxes into cultivation they behave very differently, so that if you send a cultivated phlox to an expert like Dr. Wherry, you may get a very different determination from the result if you sent one collected in the wild.

Having grown many of these phloxes from seed, I suspect that the taxonomists have missed the boat. I wish I were younger and had the time to collect the seeds of all these so-called species and look at them under a scanning microscope. Even under a hand lens, the seeds of those species I've seen are all different and have the most beautiful sculpturing. I'm sure that if somebody were to work on the sculpturing, shape, and size of the seeds, we might be able to come up with a clearer notion of the species of *Phlox*.

All phloxes have five petals. They belong to the *Polemoniaceae*. Most of them have an eye ring, sometimes a sort of double eye ring, and many have striae that go onto the petals. They all have a tube and a flat arrangement of petals. The stamens, attached to the tube, are sometimes long and actually exsert through the mouth of the blossom. Their placement is helpful in determining species. Dr. Wherry also considers the length of the style an important feature for purposes of determination. The calyx itself is an important clue. It has folds, the carinae, with segments in between, and it may have hairs. Whether the hairs have glands or not is important. But you also have to look at the growth habit and the foliage. Putting all these into a key is almost impossible.

Despite these difficulties of taxonomy, the genus *Phlox* presents us with handsome and variable species adapted in nature to a wide range of habitats and in the garden to every available situation. Yet we must select among them, because some have become so specialized in their adaptation that they may present serious problems in cultivation.

The plebeian, utilitarian easterner *P. subulata* must certainly

lead any list of phloxes and would stand high in the ranks of rock
garden plants in general, but its ease of culture in a wide variety
of sites and its prodigal display of flowers have won it such
popularity as to render it stale and trite. Yet it is no dandelion.
It is not a common weed in nature, where it occupies rather sterile
soil on open, rocky, gravelly, and sandy slopes in the eastern
United States. There are extensive natural stands on serpentine
barrens in southeastern Pennsylvania and on shale barrens in
Virginia. In some cases the plants in these colonies form a dense
intertwined carpet. In other cases they are quite scattered.

Unfortunately, in many gardens you'll see that awful gas-
station pink. I don't know who found and introduced that clone,
as you seldom see that dreadful color in the wild, where the usual
color range runs from pure white through shades of lilac and pink
to purples.

The species varies also in the size, density, and texture of the
needlelike foliage as well as in growth habit. Literally hundreds
of forms have been selected and named and readily propagated
by simple division of the rooting prostrate shoots. Some of the
more handsome clones that have been developed in cultivation
may be hybrids with other species of eastern and western cushion
phloxes, too many to name or give preference to.

Another eastern species, though not coastal, is *P. bifida,* called
the ten-point phlox by Dr. Wherry, as each of the five petals is
deeply cleft. It is a plant of dry cliffs, bluffs, and sand hills west
of the Appalachians, ranging from Michigan to Oklahoma. It
forms tussocks eight to ten inches high with stiff, long, linear
leaves well supported by the woody base of the plant. Rather
than sprawling and rooting like *P. subulata,* it forms a billowing
sheaf of stems topped by a solid dome of starry blossoms ranging
in color from a good blue through lavender to white. The plant
may be propagated from soft-wood cuttings or layered by work-

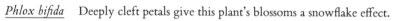

Phlox bifida   Deeply cleft petals give this plant's blossoms a snowflake effect.

ing a sandy soil mixture among the numerous stems that rise from the crown.

In richer woodland soils of the eastern United States are two species of *Phlox* most worthy of inclusion in the rock garden: *P. divaricata* and *P. stolonifera*.

P. stolonifera is a true rambler, sending out in all directions from each flowering crown a spider web of leafy stolons to form new flowering rosettes until it becomes an extensive carpet. During May and June each mature rosette displays an erect flowering shoot six to ten inches high, topped by a cluster of open-faced, full-petaled blossoms. The ample dark green leaves at the base make a fine carpet to set off the pale pink to violet to purple flowers, each with a prominent golden center of exserted anthers. There are lovely color forms of this stoloniferous *Phlox* found in the wild from southern Pennsylvania into the wooded Appalachians south to Georgia. Some fine named clones are 'Blue Ridge', 'Pink Ridge', and 'Sherwood Purple'. The last, a deep violet-purple not commonly seen in the wild, is a much slower spreader than most. It was found in Henry Fuller's garden on Sherwood Lane in Easton, Connecticut.

A long search for a white *P. stolonifera* ended finally about ten years ago when Mrs. Thomas Shinn, of Asheville, North Carolina, discovered in the wild a true albino without the tinge of purple on the tube that had marred previously found white ones. It was introduced by Harold Epstein and given the name 'Ariane', but it can also be obtained as *P. stolonifera alba*. It is a husky, fast-spreading form.

Phlox divaricata, the so-called blue phlox, seeds itself with such abandon in some gardens that it creates, in late spring, a pleasing and delicate sea of blossom in lightly shaded areas. The plant forms a decumbent clump of node-rooting, persistent shoots sending up flowering stems to a foot or a little more. Flowers with full, rounded petal lobes and others with notched petals are recognized as separate varieties but flourish amicably in the garden and are all of the same general effect and color range—not a true blue, but a good violet running to lavender. There is one outstanding clone, of purest white notched-petaled flowers and strong growth, known as 'Fuller's White'. It is quite superior to the washy white occasionally found in the wild.

There's a great dispute about the blue, maroon-eyed *P.* 'Chattahoochee'. When it was first discovered by Mrs. Henry (down in northern Florida, I believe), she thought it was a *P. divaricata*. However, if you grow seedlings from *P.* 'Chattahoochee', you get a range of colors, and the flowers don't have the dark eye, so I suspect *P.* 'Chattahoochee' is either a natural hybrid between *P. divaricata* and *P. pilosa* or, more likely, a color form of *P. pilosa*. All seedlings certainly look and behave like *P. pilosa,* a handsome but short-lived plant that does not root down at the nodes of decumbent shoots.

There's a very rare *Phlox* in the East that grows only in one small triangle in West Virginia. This is called *P. buckleyi,* a handsome, clear pink *Phlox* that varies somewhat in color. One of its characteristics is that each twelve- to fourteen-inch blossom stalk rises from a cluster of grasslike leaves that looks like a sedge. It's one of the few phloxes I know that spreads by underground stolons, sending up at considerable distance more tufts of sedge-like leaves and flowering stalks. It grows under special conditions in shale barrens, but I have been able to grow it quite successfully in ordinary garden soil in part shade.

Another of the taller phloxes, and we have quite a number of these in the East, is *P. ovata*. There is difficulty separating *P. ovata* from some of its relatives. Dr. Wherry has named a number of species in the *P. ovata* group. All have fairly large leaves, and none is as tall as the so-called border phlox, *P. paniculata,* though they approach those dimensions. There is a small one in this group, however, called *P. ovata pulchra* (*pulchra* meaning beautiful) because of its handsome clear pink color.

Another group of the taller phloxes, this one with rather swordlike leaves, is the *P. carolina* complex. There are at least five species in this confusing group. As you move west, you find relatives with more swordlike leaves and better blossom color; one in the Ozarks is known as *P. ozarkiana.*

P. amoena is another of our eastern species. Unfortunately, the name *amoena* was assigned long ago to a hybrid between *P. subulata* and *P. stolonifera,* but the true species is an erect-growing phlox found quite far south. It can be distinguished immediately because it is the only *Phlox* that has, close under the cluster of blossoms, a real fan of bracts.

In his monograph, Dr. Wherry set up the subgeneric section called *Microphlox.* The many species within it are all of western North America and are characterized by low stature, small leaves, and sparse inflorescences, generally with a solitary flower on each shoot. This division of the genus is quite readily recognized in the field (especially if you know you are in the West) and is quite satisfactory for herbarium specimens with adequate geographical designation. It is when one begins to give more specific definition to the western cushion phloxes that confusion reigns. Then, even knowing where a specific *Microphlox* grows does not always help. Some taxonomists have been tempted to suggest that all the various taxa which have been given specific names might be lumped into a single species of considerable variation. At the other extreme, Dr. Wherry creates for the *Microphlox* seven subsections and forty-eight species and subspecies. Under the circumstances, I hesitate to attempt even the following brief summary of these confusing and difficult-to-tame (at least in the East) *Microphlox.*

Overlooking Missoula, Montana, is a huge gravelly mound known as Waterworks Hill. This is the type site for *P. missoulensis,* a plant I had longed to see in the wild. We were there in July; everything was dried up. The phlox were there, but dormant, crisped and brown and thick with seed capsules. *P. missoulensis* has quite long leaves, in fact, probably the longest leaves of any of the microphloxes. Dr. Wherry describes the blossoms as bluish, but all I have seen or grown from seed have been white.

One of the problems of growing these in our eastern gardens is that it doesn't stop raining long enough for them to go into the kind of summer dormancy they have on Waterworks Hill. I have grown them in the garden and bloomed them, but the plants are not as compact and hard as in the wild.

In the same area are other phloxes with blossoms very like those of *P. missoulensis* but with leaves not quite so long. These could be *P. multiflora* or *P. caespitosa* or that very convenient catch-all, *P. variabilis,* the variable phlox.

Also from the same area is *P. viscida,* with foliage a little broader. Its blossoms look like those of *P. missoulensis* but are of varying color, some with an eye ring, some pink, some white, some on the lavender side. Fortunately, the gland-tipped hairs on the leaves and calyx identify *P. viscida.*

In *P. multiflora,* the leaves are lax and linear and may be slightly downy or hairless, though if it has hairs, they are never glandular. It is of wide distribution and fairly easy in cultivation. The hairs on the very similar *P. variabilis* can be either glandular or glandless.

P. muscoides, or probably more properly, *P. hoodii muscoides,* is an intermontane taxon forming a mat of compact stems with tiny, tightly adpressed, woolly leaves.

P. salina, a subspecies of *P. kelseyi,* is a rather succulent little plant that grows in alkali seeps. You will know it if you find it in such a site.

P. alyssifolia, coming from the eastern foothills of the Rockies, the Black Hills, and the high plains, is fairly easy even in eastern gardens. Its large, round, clear pink or white blossoms are scattered over a loose mat that increases by underground stolons. These can be severed from the main plant for propagation.

The *P. longifolia* complex has a wide geographical distribution in the intermontane region. It has long, narrow leaves and is fairly erect.

P. andicola is like a tight bonsaied tree with firm, hairy leaves. It comes from South Dakota and elsewhere in the Great Plains.

P. hoodii, a tiny mound of short, rather broad leaves, comes from the northern Rockies and Great Plains.

P. caespitosa is a high alpine in the Rocky Mountains, with rounded smallish flowers on compact tuffets of leaves.

If you see a mat-forming *Phlox* on the west side of the Cascades, you can be almost sure you have *P. diffusa.* It varies considerably in size, shape, and color of blossom and in the ease with which it grows in the garden.

Not all of the western *Phlox* are *Microphlox,* however. *P. speciosa* is a tall, almost shrubby plant that grows on brushy, dry hillsides and in open, rocky woods on both sides of the Cascades. Its epithet *speciosa* (meaning showy or spectacular) is earned by the good-sized bright pink flowers, generally with a strong white eye ring and contrasting striae on the somewhat notched petals. It is a stinker to grow. It just won't transplant. I've had plants grown from seed for ten years and nary a blossom.

P. speciosa is closely challenged, if not surpassed, in loveliness of flower by *P. triovulata,* that wayward species from the southwestern United States and northern Mexico. The species is sometimes split into three: *P. triovulata, P. nana,* and *P. mesoleuca,* the last name being the one given to that beautiful form introduced into England many years ago. The common provenance, habit, and floral characters of these plants certainly declare them closer relatives than kissing cousins. Whatever the relationship, these phloxes are found in rocky soil on rather dry slopes, usually in open woods or among brush, sometimes at considerable altitudes where winters are severe. From a deep-seated, ramifying, woody rootstock, thin vegetative shoots may rise as high as a foot in seasons of ample rain. They tend to be rather floppy and produce, for a long period from late spring onward, an inflorescence of three to six flowers. The flowers are large, the broad petals generally of a brilliant hue from purple to clear pink with a prominent white to yellow eye ring and occasionally darker stripes. This is not an easy plant to grow in the garden, though it is sometimes successful for a few years in a large, deep pot where, in an alpine house or frame, it can be given winter protection and an essential summer dormancy.

Indeed, all of the western phloxes that live in sites of rapid drainage or summer drought rest rather thoroughly after flowering early in the season. In our moister gardens, they cry out for more and more drainage and a lean diet. This is not true, however, of what is perhaps the handsomest of all the creeping phloxes, *P. adsurgens,* from the mountains of Oregon.

P. adsurgens stands close to *P. stolonifera* in growth habit and in flower arrangement, and indeed, Dr. Wherry brought them together in one of his subsections of the phlox genus, *Stoloniferae.* Yet these two spread their carpets on opposite sides of the vast North American continent. *P. adsurgens* has a limited range in Oregon and northern California west of the Cascades. There, on shaded slopes in both duffy and sterile soils, it spreads its ramifying, rooting stems and sends up six- to eight-inch flowering shoots soon after the snows disappear from the hills. What gives this species its particular charm and distinction is the brilliance of the blossom color and the pattern of rings and stripes that enhance the corolla. There are rare pure albinos, but the common color is a vivid salmony pink with a deeper stripe down each blade and a paler eye ring.

P. adsurgens generally spends a long winter beneath a blanket of snow. In consequence, it has not proved a very satisfactory plant in the Northeast where winters are fickle and severe. I have made hybrids between the eastern *P. stolonifera* and its western relative which seem hardier in our northeastern climate but to date have not bloomed as profusely as either parent. These hybrids are very like *P. adsurgens* in growth habit and flower color. A cross between *P. stolonifera* and *P. a.* 'Wagon Wheels' has even inherited the narrow petals of its western parent, though other hybrids have the typical broader petals.

In closing, I'll mention a few other hybrids and some forms of *Phlox* species.

Phlox 'Laura', named after my granddaughter, has round, full flowers of a lovely shade of soft pink. It is a cross between *P. subulata* and one of the western phloxes whose identity I don't know, as a bee did the work.

P. 'Millstream Jupiter' is a *P. subulata* crossed with a good blue *P. bifida* which gives the flower of the hybrid its deep periwinkle blue color and notched petals. It has the rooting stoloniferous habit of *P. subulata*.

An extraordinary and attractive little *Phlox* is *P.* 'Star Bright', a form of *P. bifida* found in the wild by Mrs. Mina Colvin of Nashville, Indiana.

I gave the name 'White Star' to a pure white, very compact *Phlox* with deeply cleft petals that appeared in my garden. It may be a *P. bifida* form or perhaps a hybrid, as the upright stems will root down to some extent.

A *P. subulata* form with broad white petals and a deep coral, almost crimson eye that bleeds slightly into the petals also appeared in the garden and has been named P. 'Millstream Coraleye'. From a distance, the color of the flower is a soft salmon pink.

Another *Phlox* hybrid, or perhaps a *P. subulata* form, I named 'Unique'. It is very compact and slow to spread, and it is composed of such close-packed upright shoots that when it first blooms it has no petals, only the pistil and stamens extruding from the calyx in a sort of brush. Eventually, however, the petals do expand, and the flowers look like those of a silene.

Yet another *P. subulata* selection found in our garden I named 'Daphne' because of the vivid color of the flowers. It's a very compact plant with deep green foliage.

But I am proudest of a cross between *P. subulata* and *P. stolonifera* with large blossoms of a deep, clear rose. It is very floriferous and thrives in sun or shade. When Dr. Wherry first saw it, he said, "This is so different, in color at any rate, from those found in the wild that I think it should be named," and he called it *Phlox* × *procumbens* 'Millstream'.

H.L.F.

LOOK AGAIN AT THE GROUND PHLOX

A catchy or stirring tune, if played over and over again, soon becomes trite and annoying; so with some plants. By repetition in garden after garden even the most exciting flower may soon begin to tumble into banality and out of fashion. Moreover, there is in most keen gardeners a touch of the snob. Not for them is the ordinary and easy, lovely as it may be in its own right. And again is proved the old adage that beauty is in the eye of the beholder.

I have actually heard people say, "I hate ground phlox," or "I loathe moss pinks." What they probably mean is that *Phlox subulata* is so commonly used and so badly used that they cannot think how they could tolerate it in their gardens because of the unpleasant associations with which it is mixed in their minds. And it must be admitted that it does have some tawdry associations.

For years and years a rather dirty form of *P. subulata,* a rabid magenta which fades to a soiled raspberry, was the common form. It hung faded and limp over the edges of strawberry baskets at every wayside flower stand like a rather messy, unlaced bodice. Even today, that same tired form is being chopped up and passed around instead of being erased from the earth to make way for the finer color forms of *P. subulata* and its hybrids.

Moreover, these same glaring forms were planted in the most unnatural settings. They made unkempt rugs on untended graves, or were spotted higgledy-piggledy amidst lumpish cobblestones on those awkward embankments between the sidewalk and the house in city lots. Despite the trampling of dogs and children, the litter of paper, and the competition of dandelions and grass, the ground phlox persisted year after year with a spattering of blossoms; a monument to its vigorous determination, but a sorry travesty of its beauty.

In nature, *Phlox subulata* grows on open, rocky, gravelly and sandy slopes, generally in rather sterile soils. It ranges throughout Pennsylvania to eastern Ohio and lower Michigan, up into western New York, and spottily in New Jersey. Acres of serpentine barrens in southeastern Pennsylvania are sheeted with blossoms in late April, a dazzling sight and in no way garish. Here there is a subtle blending of purples, pinks, and whites; rarely a harsh magenta or dirty pink. Many delicious colors have been selected by discriminating eyes both in nature and from self-sown seedlings in cultivation. Some of these, especially among the latter, are probably hybrids with some other species: *PP. nivalis, bifida,* and the western creeping phlox species.

During the last twenty-five years, amateur gardeners and nurserymen have selected and named hundreds of forms, based principally on flower color and size. There is also wide variation in growth habit and leaf character. It would be almost impossible to list and describe the various named clones, and it would be invidious to try to select the best. There are clones of soft lavender blue, many of pale pink, with or without darker eye markings, deep pinks, red-purples (with 'Scarlet Flame' almost a pure red), also some fine pure whites; these last sometimes with eye markings of various colors. That all of these have been easy to perpetuate by simple division or cuttings means that they pass from garden to garden and from nursery to nursery with consequent confusion in names, or loss of names, and rechristenings.

Starting with a selection of named sorts with a range of color, it is possible to reproduce from seed just about any color variation that has already been named, and many that have not. After raising several thousand seedlings I have found that just about the whole range of color possibilities has been exhausted, without the introduction of new genetic material from other species.

For ease of culture, ease of propagation, and for flower display there are very few plants superior to *Phlox subulata*. It may be used as a single brilliant splash in the rock garden, as a tapestry of various shades on a steep bank, or as a carpet draped over a soil-banked retaining wall. It has the added advantage of forming a dense evergreen turf when out of flower.

If used in the rock garden it should be so placed that it does not overrun frailer, smaller plants; yet it may be restrained as vigorously as you wish by clipping back the mat after flowering. Moreover, there does seem to be a maximum limit to the spread of a single plant even if permitted to root down along the ground-hugging stems. Maximum size may be up to three feet in diameter, but it is generally less and in some forms is not more than one foot.

Plants with dense, restrained growth habit, with bright, clear-colored blossoms, and with full, rounded petals are still the ideal. Though there are forms that approach these qualifications, there are still many possibilities open to those who wish to explore further the genetic variations in this species. Of even greater potential is to work toward hybridizing a phlox which combines the ease of cultivation of *P. subulata* with the tight bun habit of the phloxes of western United States.

Two subspecies of true *P. subulata* are found south of the species range; *P. subulata australis* and *P. s. brittonii.* The former differs little from the species except in technical details in the glandularity of the inflorescence. The latter has come into gardens as *Phlox brittonii rosea,* and a very charming plant it is. It forms close, rather hard cushions, with the short, needlelike leaves tight upon the radiating stems. The flowers of pale pink are somewhat starry in effect with each of the five petals conspicuously notched.

It is possible that the cushion phloxes, which have been developed in England and named "Douglasii hybrids," contain some genetic material from *P. subulata,* but this is uncertain. They do have a tight cushion growth similar to some of the western phlox, such as *P. douglasii,* but they do root down along the stem and are easily propagated by division. This characteristic is a feature of *P. subulata,* but not generally of the westerners, which tend to spring from a single taproot.

There are, however, two definite hybrids of *P. subulata,* both choice plants for the garden. One is a cross with *Phlox bifida,* the prairie or ten-point phlox, a native to the country south of Lake Michigan. This species has long, pointed leaves on the rather erect stems which grow from a central rootstock. The tall cushion of the plant is a solid mound of color as the blossoms open in early May, each petal so deeply cleft as to appear like two. In nature this species is generally white flowered, but there are occasionally good light blues with no taint of purple. A hybrid of a good blue

clone of *P. bifida* crossed with *P. subulata* has produced P. ×
'Millstream Jupiter'. This is a prostrate plant, rooting sparingly
along the stems, like *P. subulata,* but with long and relatively
broad pointed leaves. The flowers are a strong lavender blue,
large and deeply notched.

A plant known for many years in the nursery trade as *Phlox
amoena* is really a hybrid of *P. subulata* and *P. stolonifera,* and
should be called *P.* × *procumbens.* There is a true *P. amoena* of
quite different habit which is probably not in cultivation. The
hybrid, which has been grown for many years, carries clusterlike
heads of *P. stolonifera* on clumpy, nonstoloniferous plants, with
flowers of purple-pink. This same cross has recently been repeated
using light-colored *P. stolonifera,* with the result that the flowers
are a clear, true pink. This clone is known as *P.* × *procumbens*
'Millstream'. It forms an open mat of rooting runners with leaves
combining the features of the two parents. It has a long blooming
season through the month of May and will grow in either full
sun or light shade.

Since this cross between *P. subulata* and *P. stolonifera* has
occurred more than once, it is to be hoped that eventually *P.
subulata* may be crossed with *P. adsurgens.* Because *P. adsurgens*
belongs in the same section as *P. stolonifera,* this should not be an
impossible hybrid, and has great potential. The hardiness and ease
of *P. subulata* combined with the habit, flower size, and flower
color of *P. adsurgens* would be something very desirable.

When Reginald Farrer wrote in *The English Rock Garden,*
"The day that saw the introduction, more than a century ago, of
Ph. subulata, ought indeed be kept as a horticultural festival," it
was a real accolade from a man who had little praise for most
American plants. How much more would *P. subulata* merit his
acclaim today, since the introduction of superior forms and hybrids which in 1919 he could not have known.

H.L.F.

FRINGED POLYGALA
Polygala paucifolia

The fringed polygala, *Polygala paucifolia,* carries its intricate, showy, rose-colored flowers two or three together on leafy flowering shoots in light woodland soils from eastern Canada southward to Georgia. As it marches southward it seeks the highlands and cooler reaches where it associates with other eastern woodlanders so intimately a part of our natural background. There, in company with the earlier-flowering hepaticas and Dutchman's breeches and the late-flowering wintergreen, by virtue of its carriage and jaunty air it calls for close inspection to account for the superficial resemblance to a tiny orchid or a brilliant large-winged insect.

Each flower is composed of a five-parted calyx and a three-petaled corolla, but modifications and transformations disguise this division of the floral parts. Two lateral sepals of the calyx are enlarged and colored like the petals, forming the wings that give the plant its colloquial names, gay wings or bird-on-the-wing. The three petals are fused into a tube with the lowest one rather canoe shaped and crested with a contrasting white fringe at the tip. Hence the name fringed polygala.

The generic name, *Polygala,* was assigned to this widespread genus by Linnaeus, borrowed from Dioscorides, who had assigned it to some low shrub reputed to increase lactation. The name is composed of the Greek *polys* (much) and *gala* (milk). The rather inept specific name *paucifolia* (sometimes mistaken as *pauciflora*) was applied by Carl Ludwig Willdenow to this plant because the leaves, except for those just beneath the inflorescence, are so small and scalelike as to be inconspicuous. We must rely on the more colorful colloquial names to hint at the essential quality and charm of this woodland carpeter.

Polygala paucifolia   The species found in the eastern United States is a trailing plant with rose-purple blossoms.

Fringed polygala in its typical form makes sparse mats of leafless subterranean stolons loosely anchored by fine roots. Along the stolons are four- to eight-inch shoots that carry at the top a tight cluster of petioled, ovate, evergreen leaves, deep green above and reddish purple beneath. This stoloniferous growth habit, rather like that of the shinleaf tribe, with scattered feeding roots does make transplanting slightly tricky. If you find a small, compact plant and dig it as a sod with no disturbance of the roots, and transfer it to a well-drained woodland site, it should pose no problem. On the other hand, if you attempt to lift a large patch from the kind of open soils the plant seems to favor, then, because of the tenuous root structure, you will have a limp spaghettilike tangle of stolons difficult to untangle and replant successfully. The simplest and safest procedure is to take a few foliage clusters with a length of stolon for each and treat them as cuttings in individual pots to be set out later near together when they have formed independent root systems. Even top cuttings, without stolon attached, will root quite readily.

This is certainly the best conservation method to use, especially for the very rare and very beautiful pure-white–flowered form. The foliage of forma *alba,* though similar to the type in size and shape, is distinctly paler green and carries no reddish cast on the under surface.

While the showy flowers of fringed polygala produce few seeds, throughout the summer and autumn there are produced small cleistogamous flowers on subterranean branches. As the two–parted seed capsules mature, they are thrust up through the surface of the soil to ripen above ground.

H.L.F.

PRIMULA CARNIOLICA

Occasionally there turns up in the seed lists a species that has hovered for years on one's want list, not exactly the sort of plant one goes to extremes to acquire, just one of those plants one would like to see in the flesh. So it was about six or seven years ago there appeared in one of the seed lists (I can't now remember which) *Primula carniolica,* collected in Yugoslavia.

I always mark immediately on the lists good species collected in the wild, and since it was a primula I had never seen and from an area where I thought it was native, I double-starred my list on the first go-through. I guess I probably underlined more than once in red its number in the sequence of squares on my request form. I got the seed. How many seeds I received and how I handled them I cannot now remember. Because I have never disciplined myself, nor really found the time or the inclination, to keep scrupulous records of seeds sowed, with all the attendant and valuable information, I now regretfully rely solely on an ancient, fallible memory.

I think there were three seedlings the spring after sowing, or was it the second spring? They were doubtless planted on in small plastic rose pots in my standard mix along with hundreds of others at that busy season sometime in June. They probably jostled along with other transplants for a week or so on the barn floor near the wide north-facing doors, were watered regularly, and then were transferred to the long, deep frame with plastic net shading.

I must admit that I don't remember them particularly during this routine and sometimes cursory procedure. I do distinctly recollect setting out two small plants of *Primula carniolica* from pots at the time in August about five years ago when I constructed a small limestone bed near the back terrace to receive new saxi-

frage propagations, some good seedling ramondas, and a few
other specialties. There, I know, I put one *Primula carniolica,*
which flowered miserably the next spring. Another I set in a new
bed in a wide, deep fissure atop a big rock in the remote, upper,
acid-soil rock garden alongside some lewisia seedlings from
Czech seed. There the Yugoslavian primrose did rather better.
There were two rosettes and two rather spindly clusters of flowers. *P. carniolica* appeared as a rather fascinating plant because of
its foliage, unique in the Auricula Section, narrow and long,
without meal, and for its smoky rose flowers, a bit more tubular
than most auriculas and with a dust of meal in the white-ringed
throat.

But the plant began to droop as the summer heat advanced,
and on sunny days it languished sadly. In the fall I decided to give
this plant a do-or-die treatment. I potted it up in a good, rich
soil mixture with good bottom drainage and, because it had an
ample root system, into a ten-inch pot. I carried it through the
winter in the alpine house.

I did this not only because of its halting growth where it was
but also because of a recollection of a visit to Keillour Castle
garden in Scotland following the 1971 International Rock Garden Plant Conference at Harrogate. While we were there Mrs.
Knox-Finlay, despite her quite reasonable annoyance that we had
not come on the bus trip before the conference, graciously let us
wander through the garden and did rather proudly display in the
alpine house a pot of *Primula carniolica* with two flowering
stems—which, she announced, she was taking "up to London for
the Rock Plant Committee" for an award, because she had discovered by going back through the records that it was a species
that had never received an award and had probably never even
been submitted before. As I remember reading later in the *AGS
Bulletin,* she did get an award of merit.

My plant in the alpine house fattened up beautifully over the

grown seed of *P.* × *venusta* once offered in an exchange, and there was a vast range of forms, some indeed very splendid.

If that plant does bloom next spring I now am determined to go back to a primary cross and start again.

H.L.F.

PYXIDANTHERA BARBULATA

The pyxie moss of the New Jersey Pine Barrens is most aptly named. The elfin white flowers bursting in early April from the pearl-like buds appear to dance on a magic carpet in the mysterious shade of scattered pines or tangled shrubs on the fine white sands of the Barrens.

This dense carpet of narrow, hair-fringed leaves is just beginning, at the time of flowering, to revert again in the annual cycle from the reds of fall and winter to the green of summer. The carpets in the sun, which turn in the fall to the most brilliant reds, still retain mahogany colors when the reddish sepals expand, and

Pyxidanthera barbulata   Thrives in sandy soil.

the almost stemless blossoms open their white petals. Who then can escape the association with the pyxie of folklore?

The origin of the word "pixy" or "pixie" (which goes back before 1600) is apparently lost in the dim past. The Oxford Dictionary, which can usually discover with the aid of its erudite researchers some plausible derivation for the most obscure word, falls short here and confesses "derivation obsc." The definition of "pixy" is "fairy" or "elf." There is an expansion into the word "pixy-led," which I assume to be the forerunner of "pixilated" to describe someone bewitched and obsessed. This could, I suppose, characterize the state of obsession of the deeply devoted rock gardener.

No other plant, as far as I know, has its common name with all its attendant associations so curiously allied to the scientific name. The name *Pyxidanthera,* invented by Michaux, the French explorer of the eastern American flora, is actually a combination (as is so often true of botanical names) of the Greek word *pyxis* (a small box) and *anthera* (new Latin for anther), describing the fact that the anther opens as if it had a lid like a small box. Nothing at all to do with the folklore word "pixie," but how congruent.

Think of the common name wandflower or beetleweed for *Galax,* which derives from the Greek *galax* for milk, or any number of other names you want to conjure up. Or the name Dutchman's breeches, which is as descriptive of its plant as pyxie moss is of its, yet in no way echoes *Dicentra* as pyxie does *Pyxidanthera.*

What a charmer this rare plant is! It forms a mosslike carpet, frequently elongating branches out in all directions like a starfish against the white sand. It is to be found growing only in the sandy pine barrens of the coastal plain from New Jersey to South Carolina. Abundant in some locations, it is nevertheless absent from many areas of the coastal plain even where conditions appear appropriate. For instance, it has never been found in the sand plains of Long Island. It grows, not in the wettest, nor the driest sites, but always in pure silica sand, dry on the surface but moist beneath by virtue of a high water table. Plants will succeed in full sun or partial shade, and in sun it produces its solitary and stemless flowers most abundantly. The five regular petals splayed out beyond the tube are more separated than are the rounded, overlapping petals of *Diapensia,* and hence give a less solid and substantial appearance, even though they clearly declare the family resemblance.

The leaves of the pyxie also differ from those of its relative the diapensia. Here the leaves are thinner in texture, of lighter green, narrower in outline, terminating in an awl-like point and with a slight fringe of hairs on the margin at the base. Hence the specific name *barbulata*—bearded, of exaggerated importance, I think. The leaves arrange themselves in loose clumps but not in dense rosettes. There may be a common ancestor of *Pyxidanthera* and *Diapensia,* unrecorded. One can almost compose it in imagination as midway between these two extremes. As its descendants moved to the fierce environment of mountain top and arctic regions, the leaves lost their fragile tips, grew thick and hard in texture, huddled into dense rosettes; whereas the Atlantic coastal plain descendant became more tenuous in all respects, growing less hard and woody and rooting down more readily along the advancing ground-hugging stems. Flowers of pyxie are less flamboyant and glistening than those of diapensia, though they are similar and indeed beautiful to the human eye. In the former, the flower is no doubt essential for the attraction of insect fertilizers, which are more abundant in the Pine Barrens than on the mountain peaks where *Diapensia* grows.

That pyxie is so comparatively narrow in its distribution suggests that it is not an easy plant to grow in conditions other than those in which it makes its home. In general this is true. In some gardens, to be sure, it has flourished for a number of years, generally in pockets of pine-barren sand imported about the root ball, and it is only safely moved by careful digging with a ball of wet sand.

One cannot resist at this point quoting from *The New Nature Library,* Volume VIII, Part One, devoted to Wild Flowers and prefaced by the author, Neltje Blanchan, March 1900:

> In earliest spring, when Lenten penitents, jaded with winter's frivolities in the large cities, seek the salubrious pine lands of southern New Jersey and beyond, they are amazed and delighted to find the abundant little evergreen mounds of pyxie already starred with blossoms. The dense mossy cushions, plentifully sprinkled with pink buds and white flowers, are so beautiful, one cannot resist taking a few tuffets home to naturalize in the rock garden. Planted in a mixture of clear sand and leaf-mould, with exposure to the morning sun, pyxie will smile up at us from under our very windows, spring after spring, with increased charms; whereas the arbutus, that untamable wildling, carried home from the pine-woods at the same time, soon sulks itself to death.

Though not as easily grown as Neltje suggests, pyxie can be grown from cuttings, and rooted layers (treated as cuttings) will establish quite quickly in the sterile, very acid conditions needed by this plant. So far as I am aware it has not been grown successfully from seed even by the "Lenten penitents." It is quite possible that seed must be very fresh to germinate, and this may be the explanation for pyxie's failure to move out of its limited range, as I am sure it is in the case of its relative, *Shortia.*

There is, moreover, a *Pyxidanthera* that grows in drier sites in the Carolina coastal pine lands, sometimes distinguished as a separate species, *P. brevifolia,* or as *P. barbulata* var. *brevifolia,* or, more generally, swallowed up in the species *barbulata.* Far be it from me to enter the taxonomic fray. Plants collected in these drier Carolinian sites have a combination of features distinctive at a simple level. The flowers are smaller in all respects, more gap toothed in the petals, hairier in the leaf, almost like a slightly degenerate offspring in a human family. One would think that perhaps this offshoot into the drier pine lands might be more inclined to grow in ordinary rock garden conditions. It must be reported that a few experiments, thanks to collections by Neil Haas some years ago from an area being rapidly overrun by a camper site, were briefly successful but not rewarding. I remember a twelve-inch sod of a plant that grew two years in a pan and billowed over the edges. Sliced in two with a spade and repotted, the two halves grew on for a year in pots, one here and one given to a friend. When each of us tried them in what we thought were appropriate locations in the garden, they lived and flowered but were soon ignored and overrun. They just didn't have "quality." The blame, if blame is what we have to assign, may be more in the eyes than in the plant and its will to live. *Pyxidanthera barbulata* itself measures up in all respects, a challenge but not impossible.

H.L.F.

SANGUINARIA CANADENSIS

Bloodroot, *Sanguinaria canadensis,* is an eminently satisfactory rock garden plant, particularly charming in a clump at the base of a large gray rock and in company with ferns. The waxy white flowers with their tassel of yellow stamens come early, before the leaves have expanded to full size, in March at the southern end of its range in Kentucky and Missouri, as late as May in Quebec, where it is called Sang-Dragon. It is known in its southern territory as the red puccoon, an Indian name for a red dye which is also found in *Lithospermum canescens,* also called puccoon.

After flowering, the long-pointed seed pod of bloodroot is overtopped by the large, lobed leaves, the irregular lobes themselves coarsely and irregularly toothed. Some botanists recognize in the southern part of its range, even into Florida and Texas, a form with leaves barely lobed or toothed, known as var. *rotundifolia.*

As the seeds ripen, the long, slender pod splits its full length to expose large brown seeds each with a conspicuous transparent gelatinous crest. This crest is apparently attractive to ants who help in the distribution of the seed. Mice and chipmunks also carry off the seed, frequently hoarding them in clusters in the soft humusy soil where they eventually sprout as a tight sheaf. Once bloodroot is established in a congenial site, self-sowing is abundant, frequently even into gravel paths and narrow pockets among rocks.

There is a pink-flowered form, named by Benke in 1933 for its discoverer, Earl H. Colby, forma *Colbyorum.* So far as I know this form is not in cultivation, though I keep hoping that one day there will appear at Millstream a really pink seedling. Bloodroot self-sows here generously, and we do have a few plants with petals quite pink on the back, very lovely in the early morning before the flower opens to display the golden stamens and pure white inner surface of the petals.

A few years back I became intrigued by the idea of trying to discover where the double bloodroot had originally been found and by whom. I had heard over the years from various gardeners conflicting reports, usually that the wild plant had been found in Michigan, though occasionally someone named a different state. Finally I chased down every reference under *Sanguinaria canadensis* in the card index at the New York Botanical Garden library, and in one of these references (I can't remember which one now) I picked up a couple of clues that pointed in two directions: the Arnold Arboretum and a Mr. von Webern of Dayton, Ohio.

Correspondence with the staff of the Arnold Arboretum brought in some information, mostly negative. I wrote to the only person I knew in Dayton, Harry Butler, who subsequently became president of ARGS, and asked him if he could uncover any information about Mr. von Webern and the double blood-root. By clever detective work he located von Webern's widow, now a Mrs. Thomas, living in Florida. Correspondence between Mr. Butler and Mrs. Thomas supplied much of the missing information.

By putting together the various pieces of the puzzle, I thought I had finally gotten the true picture of the discovery in the wild and the introduction into horticulture of this handsome form of the common bloodroot. I wrote up my findings in an article for the magazine of the American Horticultural Society, the substance of which is reprinted here. The publication of the article brought in some added facts that refuted some of my deductions and clarified the whole situation. These corrections are here included in a recasting of the original article:

Mr. Guido von Webern had a perceptive eye and a love of nature. In 1916 he was attracted by a seven acre tract of land at the corner of North Main Street and Turner Road in Dayton, Ohio, about four miles north of the center of the city. He bought the property because of the beauty of its terrain, which included a steep slope covered with splendid trees, a site likely as the setting for wild flowers, a particular delight of his.

In spring when he inspected what he had purchased, he discovered to his joy, among a clump of *Sanguinaria canadensis,* a solitary plant with fully doubled blossoms. Because of his acquaintance with the native flora and his amateur knowledge of botany, Mr. von Webern realized that he had spotted an unusual mutation. It was a small, spindly plant; so, without disturbing it, he marked its location and protected it. By 1919 the plant had increased to a vigorous clump, large enough to divide. Mr. von Webern sent a division of the plant to the Arnold Arboretum in the autumn of that year.

In the *Gardeners Chronicle,* series 3, vol. 73, p. 283, May 1923, H. E. Wilson, director of the Arnold Arboretum, described this plant, the Double Bloodroot, as *Sanguinaria canadensis* var. *multiplex.* In 1931 Weatherby made it a form rather than a variety and in botanical literature today it would be listed: *Sanguinaria canadensis* Linnaeus forma *multiplex* (Wilson) Weatherby.

In his article Wilson mentioned that Dillenius in 1732 had illustrated a *"Sanguinaria major flore pleno"* in his *Hortus Elthamensis,* vol. 2, p. 334, plate 252, fig. 326. This plant apparently had 14–16 petals, only double the normal number, whereas Mr. von Webern's plant had the multiplication of the petals carried to a greater extent so that even the stamens and carpels were transformed into petals. Wilson also says that the plant named *S. canadensis* (var.) *plena* by Weston in *The Universal Botanist and Nurseryman* vol. 3, p. 610 (1772) is the same as Dillenius's plant, since Weston sited the Dillenius reference in synonymy when he coined the name *plena.*

Mr. von Webern's plant is no longer growing at the Arnold Arboretum, nor was the plant apparently formally accessioned in the Arboretum collections, but Mr. von Webern's widow, presently Mrs. Thomas, has preserved the letter of acknowledgment from the Arboretum. She reported recently that the original plant on the Dayton property suffered either from neglect or depredations of one kind or another until it ceased to exist in 1966.

After his gift to the Arnold Arboretum and before the demise of the plant in Dayton, Mr. von Webern gave divisions to two friends. One of the plants soon died and the fate of the other has not been traced, but from neither source is it likely that the plant got into general horticulture.

(Here is where I went off the track and was led to make the following assumption.)

The Arnold Arboretum has no record of having distributed the plant, but this seems the most likely origin of the completely double-blossomed form of the Bloodroot that is found here and there in connoisseurs' gardens.

(Soon after the last statement was published, I received a letter from M. Henry Teuscher, Emeritus Director of the Montreal Botanical Garden. In the letter this great plantsman identified himself as the second friend to whom von Webern had sent a division of his prized *Sanguinaria.* It was Henry Teuscher who propagated this original clone and distributed it to various arboreta and horticulturists in America and abroad, and it is to him that all gardeners owe a debt, not only for this generous action but for many others before and after.)

No record exits of the fully double Bloodroot's having been found in the wild either before or since Mr. von Webern's discovery on his newly purchased property in Dayton, Ohio, in 1916.

(But here again as a result of the article, I received a letter from a Mrs. Thomas A. Benzinger of Sparks, Maryland. She wrote: "Twice within the past year specimens of the double Bloodroot from the wild have been brought to me for identification—one along the roadside a few miles away from my home and the other from Pennsylvania. I believe the person who brought that dug up the plant. If so, it was planted on my grounds, and I will report in the spring." I did not hear from Mrs. Benzinger thereafter, but this past year, still wondering about the whole question, I wrote her to inquire about the double bloodroot. The letter was returned to me stamped starkly "Deceased" on the envelope.)

Occasionally the plant is offered in nursery catalogues or written about in garden books or magazines. In these publications it is usually referred to either as *Sanguinaria canadensis flore pleno* or 'Flora Plena', or 'Flore Pleno' or *plena*. Since, so far as can be determined, all fully double specimens in cultivation ultimately derive from Mr. von Webern's original plant, they should properly be designated *Sanguinaria canadensis multiplex,* a name which would cover any fully double forms similar to von Webern's that might have been or may be discovered in the future. Because Dillenius used the name *flore pleno* to describe a form with only some extra petals and because such forms are sometimes found in the wild and may be introduced, confusion might be avoided if horticulturists would consistently use the Wilson name *multiplex* for the fully double form of *Sanguinaria canadensis*.

By whatever name, it is a handsome plant with an advantage for garden purposes over the single form because it holds its petals for many days. The single or even many-petaled forms quickly drop their petals as soon as the blossom is fertilized. The *multiplex* form has no sexually functioning organs; hence the blossoms are infertile, and the petals more persistent.

That it cannot set seed and hence reproduce itself by self-sowing, as the fertile forms also readily do, does mean that its distribution depends on gardeners. Fortunately, in both the typical and double forms of bloodroot, the thick, prostrate rhizomes which are just beneath ground surface naturally divide and produce new growing points. A single rhizome planted in rich humus soil, preferably not strongly acid, in an area highly shaded, never parched nor soggy, will in a few years produce a sizable clump of flowering shoots. Because the rhizomes do tend to double back, and old rhizomes decay, it is wise to divide the clumps and replant about every three years to ensure vigor and avoid excessive rotting.

H.L.F.

SOME SAXIFRAGES

The last book devoted exclusively to saxifrages was written by Walter Irving and Reginald Maltby and published in England in 1914. Since then there have been short articles in various journals, and Winton Hardy did a series of articles for the *Quarterly Bulletin of the Alpine Garden Society* in 1969 and 1970 dealing with the genus in its various sections, a series later published as an AGS Guide.

It is curious in many ways that horticultural authors have been timid about dealing with a genus that Farrer characterized as the backbone of rock gardening. There are, probably, a number of reasons for this reluctance.

The genus in the wild presents even trained botanists with critical problems, and until the taxonomists have settled their confusions, the horticulturists tend to flounder—always years behind. But look at the horticultural literature dealing with rhododendrons and with orchids, two genera equally complicated.

Likewise, as with rhododendrons, the saxifrages are rather free in hybridizing, not only in nature, but certainly in the garden; hence few garden saxifrages represent what taxonomists would recognize as true species. This is most certainly true among the "Encrusteds and the Mossies," and to a large extent among the Kabschia-Engleria complex, currently lumped in the Porophyllum Section by many botanists.

At one time, primarily during the first three decades of this century, saxifrages of all sorts were extremely popular among the horticultural cognoscenti because they made a good display in pots at competitive shows and because they were at the same time slightly tricky to cultivate well. Hence every keen competitor tried to grow the largest and floweriest pan of saxifrages for the shows, and every nurseryman was as furiously creating new hybrids to lure the pence and marks from the grower. This was the time when new named hybrids, particularly in the most popular sections of the genus—the Kabschia-Englerias, the Encrusteds, the Mossies—were filling the nurserymen's catalogues and prancing their way to the show benches.

As new species were introduced, they were forthwith made the subject of devoted hybridizing, not only by the nurserymen but by enthusiastic amateurs. Among the leaders of this swarm of hybridizers were Farrer, Irving, Boyd, and Pritchard of England and Suendermann of Germany. Many of their hybrids and selected forms of species are still in cultivation—commemorating a fine frenzy and an admirable devotion.

Then there came about what must be looked upon as a mini–Dark Age in the creation and culture of the saxifrages. The First and Second World Wars took their obvious toll. But I suspect that the principal reason for the decline was a combination of things. There was a limit to the size of a full-flowered pan of saxifrages, and beyond a certain point there was no competitive impetus. Very few new species were turning up in the wild to enrich the hybridists, while at the same time primulas, meconopsis, rhododendrons, et al. were swarming in from the plant explorers. The new plants presented a new challenge, and the saxifrages became more and more deja-vu; plantsmen are as fashion prone as food addicts and the clothes conscious. Moreover some of the old clones of saxifrages appeared to lose vigor, either from that mysterious tiredness that plantsmen assign to continued vegetative propagation, or more probably from a susceptibility to such soil organisms as nematodes that had evolved along with the dwindling rate for saxifrages.

There was a definite waning of enthusiasm in England, and German horticulturists were not prepared to take over the work of Papa Suendermann. At the same period after the wars, however, in America and interestingly enough in Czechoslovakia, there was a renaissance of interest in the saxifrages.

By then there were only a few nurseries still listing species and hybrids. Names had become increasingly muddled, and more often than not the same plant was sent out under two different names, or different plants had become tagged with the same name. Seedlings of hybrids were occasionally grown and old names reassigned. Confusion was compounded.

That same confusion still generally reigns. Dr. Radvan Horny, a paleontologist at the Museum in Prague, Czechoslovakia, became enamored of the Kabschia-Engleria saxifrages and grew successfully as many as he could lay his hands on. His garden, outside Prague, on a steep limestone slope, provided an ideal setting. Some of his fellow rock gardeners in Prague and surrounds, all of them keen and expert gardeners, had already been bringing back into cultivation by hook or by crook many of the old-time saxifrages from England and Germany. Their lists were impressive, their enthusiasm endless, and their growing skill mighty. But Dr. Horny, a highly disciplined scientist trained in taxonomic paleontology, was naturally distressed by the confusion among the Kabschias (which in the meantime botanists had combined with the closely allied Englerias) and especially puzzled by the utter welter of hybrids. With the encouragement and assistance of some of his colleagues, he determined to try to bring order out of the chaos.

He tried a number of approaches. First he attempted to sort

out the hybrids by looking at what was in cultivation under all their names. Then he searched the literature, such as it was, in gardening articles and nursery catalogues and through personal correspondence. He then started at the very base with the wild species, poring over all the old and latest information in the scientific writings. These he checked by as many personal field explorations as he was able to undertake. On the basis of his research he has devised a system of grouping all the named hybrids and cultivars around the basic species into a set of what might be called "grex" and "super-grex." Dr. Horny and his associates will, I am sure, finally be able to bring some order out of the confusion, and God bless him.

If we follow Dr. Horny's system, so elegantly devised, we shall have to make a few adjustments in cultivar names commonly in use, but the effort will help to clarify genetic relationships. For instance, the reliable old favorite we have known as *S. 'Irvingii'* has been rechristened 'Walter Irving' to conform to the code of cultivar names and to permit the adoption of *irvingii* as a new Latin bi-nome for a group of cultivars sharing the parentage *S. burserana* (formerly *S. burseriana*) × *S. lilacina*. The same has occurred in some other cases of old familiar terms, such as *S.* × *boydii*. But the system begins to bring order into the welter of hybrids and cultivars among the Porophyllum saxifrages that must eventually be accepted, I think, because it makes sense and is in conformity with codes of nomenclature being adopted by rhododendron fanciers and other horticulturists.

I fear that my own rather carefree breeding of saxifrages for a few years complicated Dr. Horny's problems. Starting in the late fifties, I purchased a few Kabschia saxifrages from the only source I knew at that time: Andre Michaux's Alpenglow Nursery in British Columbia, Canada. There were, as I remember now, such things as *SS. apiculata, irvingii,* × *elizabethae,* and *burseriana.*

For these precious small tufted plants, obviously pot grown, I constructed a small special bed with lumps of foamy slag from a nearby old iron foundry. They did flourish despite the fact that I put them into too shady and dank a corner. The first flowers were an enchantment. Then the plants grew leggy and less flowery; mosses and sagina crept into the loose tussocks.

Meanwhile I had begun experimenting with seed of saxifrages from the various seed exchanges. With beginner's luck I had fine success, and soon learned that most, and certainly the most winsome, are slow in developing beyond the first set of true leaves. It is best, I found, to leave them until the second year in the seed pan. Then each seedling goes into a small pot until it begins to push forth rosettes in all directions and fill the pot with roots.

Soon I was avid for more and more diversity. I sent orders to Lohbrunner in Canada and Suendermann in Germany. Some shipments survived, but I learned that the small, rooted cuttings of saxifrages, with sparse, tangled roots washed free of soil, as they must be for importation, are difficult to bring along.

Whatever survived and flowered was pampered, and if seed was set it was gathered and planted. To my surprise, from yellow-flowered *S.* x *elizabethae* and yellow 'Faldonside' I got some white-flowered seedlings. Bees and genetics were obviously at work.

Meanwhile I had made a sort of bastard alpine house out of an old saphouse and in it carried over in pots all the saxifrages I could lay hands on plus my own seedlings.

About this time I struck up a correspondence with Dr. Radvan Horny in Czechoslovakia, and also began to take cuttings from the best of my seedlings. I suppose I had tried cuttings before, but without a great deal of enthusiasm, because I had put myself down as a seed grower, not a cutting man. I just didn't seem to have a feel for when or how to take a bit of living stuff off a plant and make it into a self-supporting plant system. And the green fingers were never as green as I hoped.

As a spinoff from my correspondence with Dr. Horny there arrived one year, just before Christmas, by airmail from Czechoslovakia, a candy box stoutly wrapped in that foreign-looking paper and string. Inside the box were no exotic sweets. Instead in serried ranks were individual rosette cuttings of a sampler of saxifrages. Each cutting was nested in a tuft of moist sphagnum moss that had been precisely bundled about the base of the stem by a spiral of fine, strong thread enwrapping cutting, sphagnum, and a tiny red plastic label that bore a neatly printed name. The oblong of that candy box, when opened, displayed a work of art and nature eloquently combined into the perfect Christmas message across miles of space.

All of those cuttings, except two, rooted in sand under lights in my basement within two months. Most of them reside still in my alpine house and have given rise in turn to other cuttings shared hither and yon.

The arrival of those cuttings in the dead of winter and their success in rooting prompted a continuing program of cutting propagation in late fall and early winter. Most advice is that the ideal time to take cuttings is immediately after flowering. That is true. Saxifrage cuttings will root readily then, but there are disadvantages at that time of year. Spring is busier in the garden than winter. Cuttings root and need potting during the heat of summer and are still small when the following winter sets in. Saxifrages rooted in early winter may even be set outdoors in the fall of the same year.

The collection of new cultivars from Dr. Horny and my own increasing population of seedlings packed cheek by jowl in the smallest pots possible soon elbowed out almost all the former inhabitants of the alpine house. As they bloomed during the late winter and very early spring with new excitements each year, I kept on "pimping." With a small camel's hair watercolor brush I would transport pollen from one to another. One year it would be yellow on yellow or yellow onto pink. Another year pink on white or whatever was in bloom. Because each plant carried a number of blossoms and because each blossom stem was too frail to carry a separate tag, I kept few records of the crosses. When seed was set and collected I did record on the packet the name of the female parent at least.

One year I thought I should be more scientific and selected up to three open blossoms on a plant, plucked out the rest, and put onto the stigmas of those remaining pollen from a single plant. Into the pot went a label that bore a number and the full parentage; this information was recorded in a notebook.

Two years later I had a population of seedlings in small pots, each with a label bearing a number such as 69-021 *diapensoides lutea* × *lilacina*. These were lined up row on row on a flat wall around our parking area in light shade, near a source of water and close by for frequent inspection.

They were also at a convenient height for a grandson who came to visit. While the adults sat and chatted on the terrace out of sight, he amused himself by gathering the labels into neat bundles by color and size.

As a consequence of my own carefree pollen dabbing and this forgivable and doubtless inevitable thwarting of my one effort at orderliness, my saxifrage progeny have only a partial or putative parentage. I know this has been a vexation to Dr. Horny, who encouraged me to send samples of my cultivars.

He has been most patient about my partial and vague accounts of parentage and most generous in his praise of many of the individual plants. Like all breeders, I have certainly been biased in my admiration of the seedlings that came along from my

simple act of carrying pollen from the anthers of one saxifrage
to the stigmas of another. The best—and there have been too
many, I know, in my doting estimation—I have christened and
propagated and handed around. For names I have used constellations, mythological characters, figures from Shakespeare, and the
names of the members of my family and of horticultural friends.
A few have perished since their christening. Some have proved
so similar to cultivars already named that I have ceased to recognize them. Two have been distinctive enough to have been
elevated in Dr. Horny's pantheon to the status of his grex binomial Latin nomenclature: *S.* × *lincolni-fosteri* and *S.* × *wendelacina*.

I append a list of cultivar names I have been vain enough to
attach to seedlings of my own raising, with an indication of their
characteristics and what information I have about their parentage.
The list is doubtless longer than it should be. My only excuse for
including it is that most of these plants have been given to other
growers, and they may be curious about their history so far as
I can furnish it.

Some Millstream Saxifrages
'Aladdin': × *ferdinandi-coburgi,* yellow, flowers in heads of 6–8
'Ariel': *lilacina* × *? porophylla,* purple, handsome foliage,
    flowers intermediate
'Clarissa': ?, 'Faldonside', seedling white, large, crenate
    flowers
'Cleo': 'Faldonside' F2, white, compact spiny plant, large
    flowers on short stems
'Demeter': 'Petraschii' F2, white, tight bun
'Diana': *diapensoides* 'Lutea' × *burserana,* yellow, very
    compact, slow growing, type for Dr. Horny's *S.* ×
    lincolni-fosteri
'Dwight Ripley': *lilacina* × ?, deep rose, flat, hard rosettes

'Eliot Ford': *lilacina* × *burserana,* pale rose, tight cushion, early flowering

'Eliot Hodgkin': ?, yellow, cluster head, long pointed leaves

'Elizabeth Sinclair': 'Elizabethae' F2, yellow, large flowers, solitary

'Ellie B': *lilacina* × *porophylla,* purple, sister seedling of 'Ariel', larger rosettes

'Falstaff': 'Faldonside' F2, white, vigorous and floriferous

'Galahad': 'Bertolonii' F2, pale yellow, open growth, red flower stems

'G. M. Hopkins': ? white, hard cushion

'Icicle': 'Elizabethae' F2, white, blue-gray foliage

'Jason': 'Elizabethae' F2, bright yellow, solitary flowers

'Juliet': *lilacina* × *porophylla,* red–purple, sister seedling of 'Ariel'

'Klondike': *burserana* 'Sulphurea' F2, cream yellow, good round flowers

'Kath Dryden': *lilacina* × ?, deep rose, compact flat rosettes

'Lusanna': *lilacina* × *burserana,* white flushed with pink, sister seedling of 'Eliot Ford'

'Luna': 'Petrashii' × *ferdinandi-coburgi,* yellow, cluster head

'Midas': 'Elizabethae' F2, bright yellow, cone-shaped rosettes

'Moonbeam': *lilacina* × *yellow* ?, yellow suffused pink, very slow growing

'Millstream Cream': 'Elizabethae' F2, cream yellow, good compact grower

'Opalescent': ? apricot with pink suffusion, distinctive color and flower form

'Prince Hal': 'Faldonside' F2, white, good grower, sister seedling of 'Falstaff'

'Peach Blossom': 'Bertononii' F2, peach pink, sprawly growth, deep red sepals

'Sara Sinclair': *lilacina* × ?, rose, rapid grower, floriferous
'Stella': 'Petrashii' × ?, gold, neat and compact
'Sun Dance': *burserana* 'Sulphurea' F2, cream yellow with
   deep eye ring
'Timmy Foster': *lilacina* × *burserana,* deep pink, large flowers,
   very early, sister seedling of 'Eliot Ford'
'Valborg': 'Valerie Keevil' F2, rose, strong grower
'Valentine': 'Valerie Keevil' F2, rose, compact, late flowering
'Wendrush': *wendelboi* × *lilacina,* deep pink, tight mound
'Wendy': *wendelboi* × *lilacina,* strong pink, type for Dr.
   Horny's *S.* × *wendelacina*

H.L.F.

ON CULTIVATION OF SAXIFRAGES IN THE USA*

The huge variety of climate and the ecological diversity in the United States make it difficult to generalize about the problems and successes of growing Porophyllum saxifrages. A large proportion of rock gardeners are found along the east and west coasts of the country, but there is a growing interest in alpines in the wide and varied interior. Except in the southern states there are in all of these areas a few gardeners who strive to meet the challenges of growing porophylla.

An initial difficulty is finding a source for the plants. Garden centers and local nurseries depend on a rapid turnover of plants relatively easy to propagate and merchandise. There are a few mail-order and specialist nurseries, but most of these are devoted either to native American plants or dwarf conifers or special genera like the sempervivums. There is only one mail-order

*From Horny, Weber, Byam-Grounds, *Porophyllum Saxifrages,* Stamford, Lincolnshire, U.K., 1986.

nursery that lists some porophylla under Kabschia and Engleria saxifrages. The difficulty of importing these plants from abroad is discouraging. Those who wish to venture into the challenge of growing porophylla must usually rely on the generosity of those few fellow-members of the American Rock Garden Society who have pioneered and persisted in growing them.

Because these saxifrages have evolved in the loftier reaches of European and Asiatic mountain ranges, they do not readily adjust to the lowlands and latitudes where most rock gardeners dwell in the United States. Those who do succeed have resorted to various strategies, differing somewhat from region to region. Perhaps the most consistently satisfactory results have been gained by those who have grown their saxifrages in clay pots, plunged in sand on the benches of an alpine house. But even here there are problems with climate. In the Northeast, where most saxifrage enthusiasts are found, the extremes and rapid fluctuations of winter temperature require some source of supplementary heat and cooling fans. Winter temperatures may range from −20 Fahrenheit (−29 Celsius) at night to 50 Fahrenheit (10 Celsius) on a sunny day. During the summers, even with fans and some shading, the alpine house gets intolerably hot, and high nighttime temperatures persist out of doors in the 80s (27 Celsius) for prolonged spells in July and August. To the heat stress is added high air humidity and the danger of an invasion of the insidious red spider mite, difficult to detect and eradicate.

To grow porophylla outside the rock garden presents a variety of problems from region to region. To overcome them, all growers would agree on certain general principles. These saxifrages demand acid drainage around and under the cushion, but they must not be subjected to serious drought at the roots. One way to achieve these conditions is to grow the plants tucked between stones either on the upper surface or on the vertical face of raised beds. In these conditions the cushion rests on rock surface and sends its roots between and under the rocks into an open soil mix containing plenty of humus to retain moisture. Limestone or sandstone rocks are the most desirable, and some growers have found tufa satisfactory, but the latter will, during wet periods, tend to hold excessive moisture and encourage the proliferation of competitive mosses.

In order to ensure abundant bloom these saxifrages must receive plenty of light, but in most of the United States the sun is so intense that cushions fully exposed are likely to be scorched brown during the summer, and are particularly subject to fungus invasion during periods of high temperature and high humidity. Therefore the raised beds are ideally located where plants face either north or east and evade full sun during the hottest portion of the day. In regions such as the Southwest and some sections of the midland regions, where high summer humidity is replaced by very dry air and extended periods without rain, irrigation is essential.

In all regions the flowers of these saxifrages appear so early in the spring that out of doors they are frequently damaged by late snows and freezes. Moreover the early blooms are subject to severe damage by slugs, snails, and early flea beetles. There are, to be sure, many mountain areas in the United States where both winter and summer conditions are ideal for growing porophylla, but few gardeners live there.

H.L.F.

THE ELUSIVE SHORTIA

When Timmy and I heard, back in 1968 at the Winter Study Weekend East, that a large portion of the type site for Oconee bells *(Shortia galacifolia)* in Pickens and Oconee counties of South

Carolina was soon to be flooded by dams already under construction by the Duke Power Company, we determined to make an excursion there at blooming season. Frederick Case, a highly competent student and photographer of American wildflowers, who gave us the news of the power project, also kindly supplied us with the name of an employee of the power company who could guide us in our search for the plants: Charles Moore, in the Brevard, North Carolina, office of the Duke Power Co.

I wrote to Mr. Moore in January of the next year telling him of my interest in this beautiful plant and asking questions about its distribution, rarity, and possible color variations. In the letter I also included a hint that I hoped sometime to be able to visit Shortia Country at the flowering season. Mr. Moore was prompt in his reply and rose nicely to my thinly veiled bait, "Why don't you come down to North Carolina and let me give you a conducted tour? The middle of March is a sure time to see the display."

In his letter he also gave me references to a series of articles about *Shortia galacifolia* by Dr. P. A. Davies of the University of Louisville, which had appeared in botanical journals. Mr. Moore had provided much information and assistance to Dr. Davies, based on his many years of amateur plant hunting, collecting, and observation in the Blue Ridge and Smoky Mountains.

In preparation for our projected foray into the home country of Oconee bells, I followed up, in the library of the New York Botanical Garden, Mr. Moore's references, and others turned up in the course of my reading. I found a considerable, and to me fascinating, history of this single American species.

Shortia galacifolia was first collected by André Michaux, the French collector and botanist, who, during the latter part of the eighteenth century, had spent eleven years in the United States exploring for plants to grace the gardens of France. His time was the great era of botanical exploration in the new country.

Shortia galacifolia, however, was not dispatched by Michaux as living plant material, partly, perhaps, because Michaux did not himself see the plant in bloom to recognize its charm. As a sound botanist, however, he gathered the best material available of all plants for his herbarium. This material was carefully pressed and placed in Michaux's cabinets. Among a group labeled *Plantae Incognitae* was a sheet of a single shoot of the present plant with five mature leaves, three juvenile leaves, a portion of the rhizome with a few hair-roots, and two flowering stems without petals. These stems showed the five sepals and small leafy bracts beneath and a remaining pistil with elongated curved style. The label accompanying this specimen read: *"Hautes montagnes de Carolinie. Un pyrola spec. Un genus novum?"*

There is still some question as to just where and on which trip Michaux collected the particular specimens that became part of his herbarium. What we are sure of is that Asa Gray, on a trip to Europe in 1838–39, found the specimen in Michaux's herbarium in Paris. In 1838 Gray had been appointed to a chair in botany at the University of Michigan, but because the building to house the botany department was not ready in time for the opening of college, Gray was granted a year's leave. During the year 1838–39 he traveled in Europe primarily to study in the various noted herbaria there, with particular attention to American specimens. There in Paris he gave careful attention to the Michaux material collected in America.

His interest piqued, I suspect, by the suggestion on the sheet containing the unknown specimen that it might be a new genus, Asa Gray determined, after careful investigation and consultation, to christen the plant.

On April 8, 1839, Gray wrote to his friend and fellow American botanist John Torrey. In the letter he reported: "But I have something better than all this to tell you. I have discovered a new genus in Michaux's herbarium—at the end, among *plantae in-*

conitae. It is from the great unknown region, the high mountains of North Carolina. We have the fruit, with persistent calyx and style, but no flowers, and a guess that I have made about its affinities has been amply borne out on examination by Decaisne and myself. It is allied to Galax, but it is 'un tres distinct genus,' having axillary one-flowered scapes (the flower large and a style that of a Pyrola, long and declined). Indeed I hope it will settle the riddle about the family of *Galax* and prove Richard to be right when he says *Ordo Ericarum.* I claim the right of a discoverer to affix the name.

"So I say, as this is a good No. American genus and comes from near Kentucky, it shall be christened *Shortia,* to which we will stand as godfathers. So *Shortia galacifolia,* Torr. & Gr., it shall be. I beg you to inform Dr. Short, and to say that we will lay upon him no greater penalty than this necessary thing—that he makes a pilgrimage to the mountains of Carolina this coming summer and procure the flowers."

Dr. Charles Wilkins Short, of Kentucky, trained in medicine, but active as a botanist and college professor of science, was known to Asa Gray only as a correspondent. Though he collected widely in the southern states, it is doubtful that Short ever saw the plant which bore his name, as he died fourteen years before its rediscovery in the wild.

Despite his obvious excitement about the plant, as indicated by his letter from Paris, Asa Gray himself did not make the rediscovery. It was not for lack of hunting. Following the clue on the herbarium sheet—*"Hautes montagnes de Carolinie"*—and with the knowledge from Michaux's journal that the Frenchman had visited the high country, Gray made a journey in late June 1841 with two friends, John Cary and James Constable. They made their headquarters in Ashe County, North Carolina and visited most of the high country above 5,000 feet. Gray wrote a report of the trip in the form of a letter to Sir William J. Hooker, of England, which was published in the *American Journal of Science* and in the *London Journal of Botany.* This report includes the statement: "We were unsuccessful in our search for a remarkable undescribed plant with a habit of *Pyrola* and the foliage of *Galax,* which was obtained [originally] in the high mountains of Carolina. The only specimen extant is among the 'Plantae Incognitae' of the Michauxian herbarium, in fruit only: and we were anxious to obtain flowering specimens, that we might complete its history; as I have long wished to dedicate the plant to Professor Short of Kentucky. . . ."

A footnote to this passage contained the first published description of the new genus *Shortia,* assigning it to the family *Diapensiaceae* in 1842.

Again during the summer of 1843, for three months, in the company this time of another botanical friend, William S. Sullivant, Dr. Gray explored for plants in the mountains from Maryland to Georgia, always with an eye peeled for the elusive *Shortia.* Again the plant eluded him. In fact the very existence of the plant became the subject of skeptical doubts among Gray's botanical friends, and there may even have been a few with silent questions about the authenticity of the herbarium specimen back in the cabinet in Paris.

Before his two excursions to hunt for what he must himself have begun to think of as a rare chance discovery comparable to Bartram's *Franklinia* tree, never again to be found in the wild, Gray did consult Michaux's journal for further clues. Nevertheless, he passed over in the journal what has since, in the light of its eventual rediscovery, been interpreted as very clear directions for finding *Shortia.* On pages 45 and 46 of the French text published among the *Proceedings of the American Philosophical Society* in 1889 is this passage:

The roads became more difficult as we approached the headwaters of the Kiwi [now the Keowee] on the 8th of December, 1788. . . . There was in this place a little cabin inhabited by a family of Cherokee Indians. We stopped there to camp and I ran off to make some investigations. I gathered a new low woody plant with sawtoothed leaves creeping on the mountain at a short distance from the river. . . ." (Michaux camped there for three days. On the 11th he made a three mile foray into the hills.)

I came back to camp with my guide at the head of the Kiwi and gathered a large quantity of the low woody plants with the sawtoothed leaves that I found the day I arrived. I did not see it on any other mountain. The Indians of the place told me that the leaves had a good taste when chewed and the odor was agreeable when they were crushed, which I found to be the case.

For some time after the rediscovery of *Shortia* botanists considered this to be the passage in Michaux's journal that pointed to the type site. And, indeed, *Shortia* is abundant at the headwaters of the Keowee. However, it is likely that they were misled in thinking that this passage referred to the *Shortia,* as, indeed, Dr. Gray probably realized when he read it.

The key word here is: "I gathered a new low *woody* plant with sawtoothed leaves creeping on the mountain a short distance from the river." The fact is that *Shortia* is not a woody plant in the strict sense, even though its growth habit is quite similar to *Epigaea repens* and *Gaultheria procumbens,* both of which are classed as creeping shrubs. Michaux was a trained botanist, and if he gathered "a large quantity of the low woody plants with the sawtoothed leaves," he must have observed its woody nature. Even a large quantity of true *Shortia* would have provided him with nothing but herbaceous material. Moreover, Michaux could hardly have been deceived into thinking that *Shortia* leaves have a good taste when chewed and an agreeable odor when crushed. On the evidence of the passage it would appear that he was describing wintergreen, except that it seems surprising for him to refer to *Gaultheria procumbens* as a "new" plant. Or was it to him?

We can be almost certain, at any rate, that it was not on this December 1788 trip that Michaux found the small herbarium sample of *Shortia* that Asa Gray located later among the Frenchman's *Plantae Incognitae,* because by December every remnant of the flower parts have disappeared from *Shortia.* The persistent style on the herbarium specimen suggests that it must have been collected not later than June or possibly early July.

Michaux was in the same general area the preceding year, at the headwaters of the Keowee, arriving there on June 14. Since he was heading for the mountains to the west, he records, "We remained there more than two hours to rest our horses and to eat strawberries which were there in abundance." There is no mention in the journal of his collecting the plant which he later labeled *un pyrole spec? Un genus novum?* But it is entirely possible that it was on this occasion that he picked up the specimen, not immediately identifiable, and it became part of the general collection of various plants he made later in the mountains to the west; hence *Hautes montagnes de Carolinie.*

The first rediscovery of living *Shortia galacifolia* did not fall to the lot of any of the botanists engaged in its pursuit, but to seventeen-year-old George McQ. Hyams, of Statesville, North Carolina, in May of 1877. He was, however, unaware of the significance of his find. The occasion was later described by George's father, Mr. E. Hyams, in a letter to Dr. Gray. "We were passing along the road and my attention was called to an elevated hillside that I could not ascend as being at that time rather exhausted, being sixty years old, requested him to ascend and bring whatever was in flower. I have forgotten the locality, but he is fully known to it, as he lived within two miles of the place for several years."

The elder Hyams was a purchasing agent and collector of medicinal plants for a Baltimore drug company and managed the root and herb warehouse for the Wallace Brothers in Statesville. Though he was familiar with plants of the region from years of collecting herbs, this particular plant was quite new to him, despite its resemblance to the common *Galax*, which he frequently gathered. It was not until over a year later, however, that he dispatched a sample of the plant for identification to a friend in East Greenwich, Rhode Island, Joseph W. Congdon.

Mr. Congdon had his ear to the ground in the botanical world. With what must have been a stepfather feeling he wrote Dr. Gray announcing that he thought he had in his possession a flowering plant of *Shortia galacifolia.* The original godfather of the plant hastily replied, "Do send the plant."

Asa Gray, himself by this time the American botanical authority, leaves us in no doubt about how he felt when at last he had on his work table a flowering specimen of the plant that nearly forty years earlier had stirred him deeply in the Michaux herbarium in Paris. Immediately he wrote to William M. Canby, a close botanical friend who had occasionally taunted Gray with sly remarks about the mythical *Shortia:* "No other botanist has the news. If you will come here I can show you what will delight your eyes and cure you effectively of the skeptical spirit you used to have about *Shortia galacifolia.* It is here before me with corolla and all from North Carolina! Think of that! My long faith rewarded at last."

To emphasize the strength of his feelings, which might be missed despite the exclamation points, he confessed that the redis-

covery of Michaux's *Shortia* gave him a hundred times the satisfaction that his recent election to the Academie des Sciences of
the Institut de France had done, though this election was one of
the highest honors for a professional botanist.

Within the week Dr. Gray sent off a letter to the elder Hyams
warm in his praise of the discovery; and, reflecting the importance
he himself attached to it, lamenting with the father that he had
not sooner sent the specimen so that the immortality of his son
might have been assured by inclusion in the edition of Gray's
Flora, which had just recently gone to press. But he promised an
early recognition by way of an article in *Silliman's Journal.* He
concluded his letter by warning Mr. Hyams that he and his friend,
Mr. Canby, would descend on them the following May.

George Hyams's name appears as collector on the herbarium
sheet which Dr. Gray made of the first flowering specimen of
Shortia galacifolia, now resting in the Gray Herbarium of Harvard. A further measure of immortality is assured him in the
botanical literature in *Silliman's Journal,* which announced the
happy rediscovery of the plant. Young Hyams must have felt
considerable pride in the spring of 1879 when he guided an
illustrious group of botanists to the station of his find, though too
late in the season for blossom. Yet despite the early plant-collect-
ing trips with his father and the notoriety he received by way
of *Shortia galacifolia,* George Hyams did not pursue a botanical
career; instead he became proprietor of a general store and post-
master of Old Fort, North Carolina. There he resided until his
death in 1932.

In the group that descended on Statesville in June 1879, besides
Dr. Gray and his family, were the botanist William M. Canby
of Wilmington, Delaware; Dr. Charles S. Sargent, of Brookline,
Massachusetts; and J. H. Redfield of Philadelphia, Pennsylvania.
Both Gray and Redfield published accounts of the trip: Gray in

snowless winter and the heat and even occasional droughts of our New England summers, and it will self-sow in suitable sites. Why then, we wonder, has it not slowly self-sown northward out of its Blue Ridge refuge? One likely explanation may lie in the combination of its site preference and the brief viability of its seeds.

By experiment it has been fairly well established that only very fresh *Shortia* seed will germinate. Seed ripens in our area about the middle of June and if sown immediately will germinate within two weeks. Following germination the seedlings, of very tiny dimension and slow development, will not persist unless they are kept reasonably moist. A brief period of drought will annihilate them.

In the Blue Ridge, *Shortia* blooms early, the last part of March and the first part of April, and ripens its seed in May. The seed is very light and might easily be blown up out of the moist draws and stream sides where it grows under *Kalmia* and *Rhododendron maximum* or on the steep, eroded slopes along tributary creeks. Some of the thousands of seeds produced annually must reach locations where the substrate and moisture are suitable for germination, but following germination any minute seedlings that sprouted in the well-drained uplands above the moist, deeply shaded coves, which is *Shortia*'s accustomed habitat, would be at the mercy of the high temperatures and droughts likely to occur in midsummer. This is a possible explanation for the plant's present-day confinement.

Young plants, if they can be brought through the critical period of infancy, may have a tiny rosette of four leaves by fall, still only half an inch across. During the second year—if conditions are favorable, and by now it will have become more tolerant as the feeding roots strike more deeply—the plant will make appreciable growth of new foliage larger in the leaf blade and

longer in the petiole. By the third season it may even develop
in the center of the now husky rosette a flower bud. From then
on the plant will make offsets by extending underground stolons
until it forms a sizable carpet.

At the end of each runner is an overlapping arrangement of
leaves, a few long-petioled and up to three inches in the blade,
and at the center many smaller leaves. In autumn among these
smaller leaves are produced pointed buds from which arise the
flowers and new stolons. The flowers are very rapid to develop
in the first warm days of spring and though delicate in appearance
are remarkably resistant to frost or even a covering of late snow.
These blossoms, up to three from a bud, are carried singly on a
naked, reddish scape with two or three small, colored bracts just
below the five-parted calyx. The five sharply pointed sepals are
a glowing pink, a color strong enough to show through the
petals. The five petals, generally pure white, but occasionally pale
pink or, by report, pale blue, are slightly fringed at the flaring
tips and united below to form an open bell. The five golden
stamens, alternate to the petals and attached to the lower rim of
the corolla, surround the three-lobed stigma on an elongated
style, all forming a most elegant design of pink, white, and gold.

These handsome flowers are not as transient as their elegance
might suggest. Because there are few insects flying when *Shortia*
flaunts its inviting flowers, fertilization is frequently delayed for
many days. Though I can find no references to the actual agents
of fertilization, I suspect that the work is carried on by small flies
or in desperation by self-pollination. I do know that every flower
that opens sets seed. When the flower is fertilized, by whatever
means, the united corolla falls away, carrying with it the attached
stamens, to leave the still-beautiful cluster of pink sepals and
bracts around the swelling, pear-shaped capsule with long pistil
persistent. The greeny-white capsule rapidly enlarges and itself

takes on rich tones of reddish brown before, in June, it begins to split longitudinally into three segments exposing a myriad of small, yellow-brown granules adherent to the ovary. That is the moment to collect seeds and to sow them immediately. It is possible that their fertility might be prolonged if they were refrigerated.

For quick, easy propagation a clump of *Shortia* may be lifted after flowering and divided into as many parts as there are offsets at the ends of the runners. Each runner will have sent down many fine feeding roots as it advanced the previous season. For assured success it is wise to treat these separated runners as recently rooted cuttings. By all means pot them up and keep them moist and shaded, or coddle them until they are well established if they have been planted out in a permanent site. Large divisions with plenty of roots establish fairly readily in acid, leaf-moldy soil in shade.

Shortia will endure and flower in quite dense shade or will succeed in a fairly open site on a north slope, where in fall it will color more brilliantly than in deep shade. The coloring of the foliage does not, however, appear to be entirely related to amount of light. There may be a soil factor also or, on the other hand, coloring may be genetically controlled.

Because a considerable portion of the small natural homeland of *Shortia galacifolia* has now been cleared of vegetation and is within the impoundments of the Duke hydroelectric development, it is fortunate for gardeners that this rare plant has been introduced into horticulture and has proved amenable to cultivation. Special credit should be given to Mr. Charles Moore of Brevard, North Carolina, who has long been a student of the distribution of *Shortia* in the wild. When he, as an employee of the power company, learned of the plans to flood large segments of the plants' native home, he alerted gardeners and botanical

gardens and guided many aficionados into the remote area to
rescue the plants from inundation. Mr. Moore also established
large clumps in his own fascinating garden of wildflowers.

H.L.F.

Shortia (Schizocodon) soldanelloides

Another stunning Japanese mountain plant of the elite *Diapensiaceae* was for long known as *Schizocodon soldanelloides*. Then,
through the devious and mysterious workings of the taxonomic
wonderland, suddenly all botanists were proclaiming the new
christening: *Shortia soldanelloides*. Gardeners, reluctant and tradi-
tional souls that they are, God bless them, are beginning to fall
in here. Any mention of *Schizocodon* in the august pages of the
Alpine Garden Society publication will surely have an editor's
footnote setting matters up to date.

In our own household, where reference to the plant is fairly
frequent either to call attention to the exquisite occasion of the
flowering or change of foliage color or just to say "in that
Schizocodon patch," we stumble even over the pronunciation.
Should it be *Sky-zo-co-don* or *Shiz-ok-odon?* We teeter between
them and know where we are. Perhaps eventually we'll be content to shift into *Shortia*. But then we'll have to go to the species
designation for distinction, because other *Shortia*s give their name
to particular sites in the garden, and they grow side by side. This
is solely a private problem quite ignored, I'm sure, by the plants
themselves.

For purposes of this account we shall use *S.* for the genus. The
letter can, fortunately, represent either *Schizocodon* or *Shortia*.
No one so far as I know has chosen to monkey with the species
name: *soldanelloides*. There again we do have pronunciation differences. What the name means is "like the soldanella," and apt
that is. As for pronunciation of that suffix *oides,* of the Latin

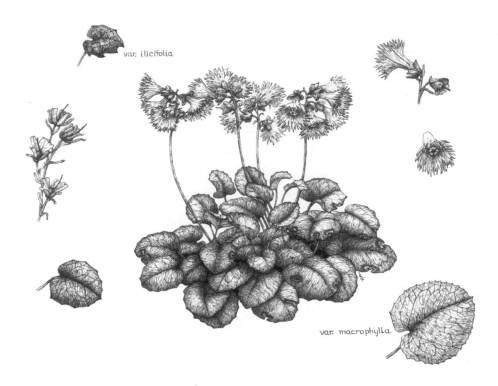

var. ilicifolia

var. macrophylla

Shortia (Schizocodon) soldanelloides   Gorgeous woodlanders from Japan.

meaning "like," there are at least three quite possible and accept-
able pronunciations: *oi-dees, o-eye-dees, o-ee-days.*

Despite wrestling with taxonomic uncertainties and stumbling
over syllables, you should strive by whatever means to have this
magnificent plant somewhere in your garden. The leathery evergreen foliage has very close similarity to the foliage of the more
familiar *Shortia,* with petioles somewhat shorter in proportion to
the leaf blade. In outline and in size the leaves vary considerably,
and at least three distinct varieties are described under the species.
All have leaves of a coriaceous texture, deep and glossy green
above, duller and paler beneath. In var. *ilicifolia,* as the name
suggests, the outline of the leaf is rather like that of the Christmas
holly, with wavy indentations between mucronate points. The
standard from which this variety and others depart is round,
slightly longer than broad, and with inconspicuous teeth around
the edge. In variety *macrophylla,* or *magnus,* the leaf is at least
twice as large, quite round, with heart-shaped base and with more
prominent toothing. There is an alpine form diminished in all its
aspects. In all varieties and forms the foliage takes on deep purple-
brown tones in the autumn.

The crowning glory and haunting beauty of all varieties are
the rose-pink fringed bells that hang on short pedicels, up to six
in a row at the summit of the four- to six-inch spike. Pale pink
at the deeply fringed edges, the bells deepen at the base and are
shot with reddish streaks and scintillations within. There is also
known a spectacular pure-white–flowered taxon, so far found
only in var. *ilicifolia.* These fringed flowers do echo the alpine
Soldanellas and carry in other respects their affinity with the
single-flowered *Shortias.* The flowering period is about a month
later than that of the *Shortias,* and seed does not ripen until quite
late in the fall.

Once the united corolla has fallen away, the persistent sepals and three-parted capsule with adherent pistil display the close relationship with *Shortia* proper. The lateness of the flowering and the delayed ripening of the seed are but further specializations to permit delayed germination of the seed after late dispersal and chilling over the winter. This adaptation is of advantage to the rock gardener who finds the seed listed in the exchanges. Its viability has not been lost, and it will germinate in the spring if given a proper medium and never permitted to dry out. Follow the methods perfected for growing seeds of rhododendron, and tiny seedlings will result. From there on, however, development is exceedingly slow, as in *Shortia* proper.

It may take up to five years to develop a flowering plant from seed, and in infancy and adolescence your seedlings demand shade, acid humus, rich soil, and good drainage but adequate moisture. In the absence of snow cover, it is wise to mulch all *S. soldanelloides* plants, young and old, with a light covering of pine needles or hard oak leaves. Or if you have but one, you may wish to play it absolutely safe by inverting a large glass jar over the plant for the winter, being sure that it is also partly shaded.

Though this is a plant with a woody base, it does not "runner-out" and root as readily as does *Shortia galacifolia.* It does increase the number of separate leaf clusters, among which develop in fall the pointed red buds of next year's flowers and growth, and it may in time reach ample compact proportions. If this clump is top dressed with a mixture of half peat and half sand you may encourage the new peripheral growth to root down so that it may be carefully excised and made into an independent plant. Even at best all divisions of *S. soldanelloides* should be carefully treated, more like barely rooted cuttings than independent plants.

Farrer, at the beginning of his rhapsodic description of *Schizocodon,* tells us that the Japanese name for the Nippon bells is *Iwakagami,* the mirror of the mountain.

H.L.F.

The Japanese Shortia

The Japanese relatives of the American *Shortia galacifolia* present us with exquisite beauty and taxonomic puzzles. Perhaps that is the appropriate posture for plants of Oriental beauty.

It is easy to accept the generic relationship of Japanese *Shortia uniflora,* the Nippon bells of northern Japanese highlands, to the American *Shortia galacifolia,* the Oconee bells of the Blue Ridge Mountains. The similarities between the two are so numerous that one is tempted to think that they are one species only, so recently separated that by mutation and selection they have diverged only slightly. The foliage of the two is almost identical. If the two species are grown side by side, and they do favor similar sites, I would defy anyone to distinguish between them except when they are in flower.

Then, indeed, and in my garden a full week earlier, *Shortia uniflora* does send up flowers of distinction. The color is an ineffable sunset pink, though seen in a sunset only as a suffusion upon a cloud bank. That is the effect as the blossoms, half-again larger than the flowers of the American species, spread the five petals of the united corolla. The expanded edges of these petals are most marvelously and irregularly fringed, fit garment for your favorite mythological goddess. The sequence of events after flowering is identical with that of the American species, and the precious brown granules of seed sit similarly as the three-parted capsule splits.

These similarities and differences give us no clues about the successful cultivation of Nippon bells. It is reported that for some reason good gardeners on the West Coast find the Japanese *Shortia* easier to grow than our own *Shortia galacifolia.* In England both have been grown in specialist gardens for many years. The form known there as *Shortia uniflora grandiflora* may be only a selection of the species for extra size of blossom, but because the color of the flower is white, as in typical *S. galacifolia,* I have a suspicion that this may be a hybrid between the two species, showing in its growth habit and flower size the typical "hybrid vigor." For now, this is a pure supposition that I hope to verify by controlled crossing of the two. By experiment I do know that seed from *S. uniflora* behaves just as does that from *S. galacifolia:* sowed fresh it germinates in two weeks, and the seedlings are exceedingly slow to move on. Given the gardener's patience and attention, however, they do come along. Now the next step is to preserve a bit of pollen of the earlier-flowering Japanese species to dot on the expectant stigmas of the American.

It will be a few years before we can know whether there has been a "take," an apomixis due to tickling the stigmas, or an undetected self-fertilization. But what fun, and perhaps, a glorious new constellation to be christened *Shortia* × 'Sam-Nipposan'.

Back down to earth: *Shortia uniflora* may be intolerant of extremely low temperatures and because of its Japanese alpine home also intolerant of high summer temperatures. The foliage, though I have said that it is indistinguishable from that of the American species, is actually of somewhat thinner texture. Hence it may be more sensitive to extremes of temperature and less able to endure periods of drought. Give it your best humusy acid soil in fairly constant but high shade. Give it the drainage provided by a sloping site, preferably north or west, and in periods of prolonged dryness, do water. The elegance of the plant is worth any effort, and once you have learned the secret of growing this gorgeous *Shortia* in your garden and you find its offset runners rooting down, which I can assure you they do, be bold enough to sever them at least at the tip to become a completely independent plant. Then once it has made its independence clear, dig it, pot it, plant it in a new section of your own garden or share it with that drooling friend.

Both the American and Japanese species are one-flowered.

Perhaps *Shortia uniflora* was given the name to distinguish it from its near relative on the Japanese mountains, *Schizocodon,* which carries a number of fringed bells on each stalk.

H.L.F.

SILENE CAROLINIANA

Silene caroliniana, with its two varieties, *pensylvanica* and *wherryi,* is a truly beautiful native of eastern North America. The showy pink flowers are displayed on compact, tufted plants for a fairly extended period in late May and early June, with new blooms opening in the dense cyme as the older ones begin to go to seed. Most commonly known as wild pink, it may also be referred to as catchfly or campion.

The name *Silene* was adopted by Linnaeus from earlier authors and is believed by some to have derived from mythological Silenus, the drunken foster-father of Bacchus. Silenus was depicted as covered with foam, just as many species of *Silene* are decked with viscid excretions, from which fact comes also the common name catchfly. This character is conspicuous on the swollen calyx at the time of seed gathering.

Among European botanists many of the *Silene*s, including our American species, are transferred to the genus *Melandrium,* a practice not now followed in America. Our plant will be found in some horticultural works under that designation, however.

In the seventh edition of *Gray's Manual of Botany,* on which many senior citizens cut their botanical teeth, the wild pink was listed as *S. Pennsylvanica* Michx., with the notation "(*S. caroliniana* Walt. ?)." The eighth edition of that bible has now given Walt. his recognition, and our plant is recognized as *S. caroliniana* Walt. with var. *pensylvanica* (Michx.) Fern. (giving Fernald, I assume, the credit for dropping one n from the variety name) and var. *wherryi* (Small) Fern. The differences are slight

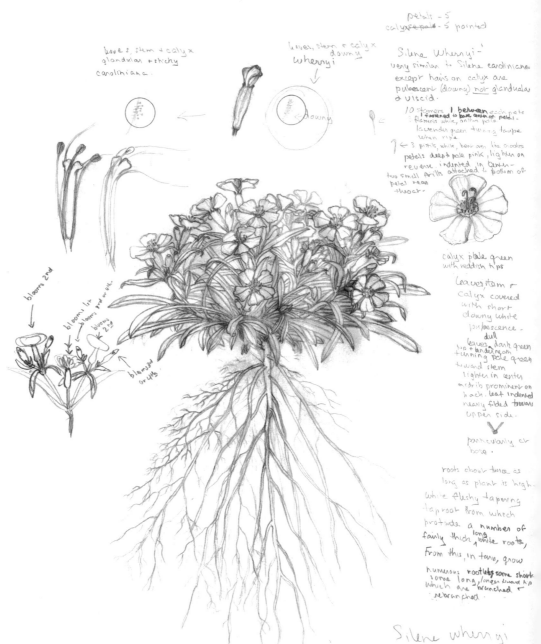

Silene caroliniana var. *Wherryi* Working sketch. Note the extraordinarily close observation recorded in this sketch, including the differences between glandular hairs and downy ones.

from a horticultural point of view, but there is some geographical separation among the three taxons.

All three varieties of *Silene caroliniana,* in their distribution from southern New Hampshire to South Carolina and into Missouri and Alabama, seem to prefer to grow in sandy or rocky soil, frequently well-drained banks and slopes in acid to medi-acid soils, in sun or light shade. This information from the botany books suggests that in the garden we should provide this charming wildling with similar conditions. Good drainage and gritty soil I have found essential, but I have had equal success in acid and limy soil as long as other conditions are favorable. I used to think this a short-lived plant, but I have found if conditions are ideal it persists for many years.

Indeed, this is an ideal rock garden plant. It flourishes among rocks in classic alpine garden conditions, bearing abundant, well-carried blossoms on a neat tuffet. In addition, this wild pink of the family *Caryophyllaceae* (pink family) is simple to propagate from seed, top cuttings, root cuttings and careful division.

The seed, which germinates readily from spring sowing, is a bit tricky to collect. The tubular calyx swells as the seeds ripen and remains open at the apex rather like an egg cup, so that the seed is readily spilled. The earliest flowers ripen their seeds and spill them as the later flowers fade. Since the whole process is swifter than one generally expects, start watching for ripe seeds by the end of June.

For rapid increase, good color forms may be propagated by careful division in early spring, by root cuttings in spring or early summer, and by green-wood cuttings in late summer of the ample husky clusters of basal rosettes that spring out from the heavy central caudex.

Good color forms do occur and may even reproduce from seed, but the general run of seedlings will range from a pale, chalky pink, almost white, to a deep, glowing carmine. I have never seen a pure white, but this is to be expected and might be a pleasant addition.

One plant with particularly brilliant flowers, brighter and of a deeper shade than any I had seen before, once turned up here at Millstream among a batch of seedlings. Seed collected from this plant has produced uniformly good color forms, and such seed has occasionally been contributed to the seed exchange as 'Millstream Select'. *Silene caroliniana* has been crossed with the fire pink, *S. virginica,* to produce intermediate hybrids, but these have not persisted with me in the garden for many years. The same cross has been recorded in nature from one county in Missouri.

Our easygoing native has been reported wild from many counties in our own state, and in the 1910 *Catalogue of the Flowering Plants and Ferns of Connecticut* was recorded as occasional in the southwestern part of the state.

There are many other very worthy *Silene*s for the rock garden, such as the temperamental but beautiful *S. hookeri* of the West; widespread and shy-flowering *S. acaulis;* Japanese *S. keiskei,* and the late-blooming *S. shafta.* There are here possibilities for hybridizing to enrich our rock gardens with showy and adaptable wild pinks for a long season of pleasure.

H.L.F.

TIARELLA

Tiarella cordifolia should find a welcome in every garden, as it combines handsome foliage, beautiful airy flowers, and ease of cultivation.

It takes a while to appreciate the fine qualities of this plant, innocuously called foamflower, as it occurs in the wild in the rich

Tiarella cordifolia   An easy and attractive woodland plant.

woodlands of the northeastern United States. It occupies that familiar range from New Brunswick to Michigan and south to the mountains of North Carolina and Tennessee, a range a bit more constricted than some of its forest companions. It is a shy member of that community. It is the Little Red Hen of our eastern natives, serviceable, somewhat retiring, always fittingly but not flamboyantly adorned. Given the right situation and a modicum of appreciation, she flourishes, gracing rather elegantly the pleasant, congenial combinations we bring together in our woodland gardens.

The foliage, not too large and not too small, is heart shaped at the base and shieldlike in outline, with points and indentations around the edges. Hairs scattered on the upper surface and thickly downy beneath add a touch of softness to the foliage. From plant to plant the firmness and depth of green color in these leaves varies considerably, so that one may choose to propagate, if he pleases, a heavy-textured plant that asserts a foliage dominance or a less assertive, thinner-textured, and lighter green clone if he wishes to pay less attention to leafage and more to flowers.

The flowers are arranged in a spike that rises from the leafy carpet from eight to ten inches. The flowery portion itself, closely set with spidery white to pink-tinged blossoms, makes up the upper three to six inches. Belonging as it does to the Saxifrage family, *T. cordifolia* has individual flowers with five petals, many conspicuous, graceful stamens, and two central styles. The shape of the pistil, which has a fancied resemblance to a small turban or crown, accounts for the genus's botanical name: the diminutive of the Latin *tiara*. The common name, foamflower, does suggest the total effect of a well-flowered clump of *Tiarella* as it blooms in late spring in rich woodlands. The plant sends out copious leafy runners throughout the growing season and soon makes large swatches. In the wild the blossom spikes may be rather sparsely scattered over the carpet. In rich garden soil, relieved from the incursions of invasive neighbors, even in considerable shade but especially in sunnier sites than it favors in nature, the blossom spikes become more numerous and larger. In fact this is one native wildling that responds splendidly to cultivation and fertility.

Moreover it is very readily propagated by the simple separation of rooted runners from the mother plant. In this manner one may rapidly provide for his own garden or for those of friends divisions of superior strains: those with especially handsome leaves (like one form I discovered by chance when I stopped to relieve myself along the Mass. Pike) or those with particularly full flower spikes or flowers of pinkish suffusions. The plant may be propagated also from the shiny black seeds, which are produced abundantly in boat-shaped capsules with an upper lid, or hatch, covering the boat for about half its length.

There is a closely related plant found in the southern portion of the range of *T. cordifolia,* from Virginia to Alabama and Mississippi. This was first named by Dr. Edgar T. Wherry as *T. cordifolia* var. *collina,* but is now generally recognized as a separate species quite fittingly called *T. wherryi.* In this species, by comparison with *T. cordifolia,* the leaves are more deeply and irregularly indented, overall much longer than broad, and frequently have a conspicuous long terminal segment. Moreover, this plant, unlike its close relative, does not send off stolons, increasing only by fattening its main rhizome. The flower spike tends to be more slender, is more commonly tinged with pink, and blooms later in the season. An additional character, not conspicuous, I'm sure, in herbarium specimens, is the autumn coloring of the foliage. As the deciduous leaves of *T. cordifolia* go into the winter, there may be a touch of red in some of the heavy-textured clones, particularly if grown in sun. With *T.*

wherryi all the leaves, even when grown in fairly dense shade, in late fall assume intense shades of reddish brown and purple.

T. cordifolia has long been admired in England and has been widely used in gardens there and on the Continent. There appeared, reportedly at Nancy, France, in 1917 a bigeneric hybrid between *T. cordifolia* and *Heuchera sanguinea,* coral bells. This sterile hybrid, known as × *Heucherella tiarelloides,* has carmine flowers and is somewhat stoloniferous. A similar cross with a white-flowered *Heuchera,* × *Heucherilla tiarelloides* var. *alba,* has pure white flowers on a tall scape and is completely nonstoloniferous. Both these handsome clones may be propagated by division.

In the mountain woodlands from Alaska to Oregon are two western species of *Tiarella,* there called coolworts: *T. trifoliata,* with leaves composed of three separate toothed leaflets; and *T. unifoliata,* with lobed, cordate leaves about four inches across. Both carry narrow panicles of white-petaled flowers with spidery stamens, similar in effect and usefulness to the eastern species. *T. polyphylla,* similar to the last species, is found in the Himalayas.

H.L.F.

TROLLIUS LAXUS

The American globeflower, *Trollius laxus,* is one of the rarest wildflowers of Connecticut. It has been found in only two or three wooded swamps underlain by limestone in the northwestern part of the state. Throughout its curious range, in fact, it is always a scarce plant in nature, found, in its eastern distribution, only occasionally, according to *Gray's Manual,* from western Connecticut to Michigan and south to Pennsylvania. A subspecies, *T. laxus albiflorus,* is found in the Rocky Mountains with a range from British Columbia to Colorado. And there is another species from Japan, *T. japonicus,* that is very similar to the American globeflower.

All three of these are like large-flowered, compact buttercups, blooming at an early season, worthy of cultivation in the rock garden. They grow most readily in a moist, rather heavy soil, in swampy seeps or along the banks of streams and ponds. Our eastern *T. laxus,* a member of the *Ranunculaceae,* or crowfoot family, begins to open its broad, saucerlike blossoms in early May, with a single flower on each short stem just above the expanding, palmately parted and cut leaves. As the season progresses the leaf stems and flower stems elongate so that at seed time the stems may be more than a foot tall and rather floppy, hence the specific name *laxus.* The genus name *Trollius* is a Latinized form of *troll* (a globe), from *Trolblume,* the Germanic vernacular for the European globeflower, *T. europeus.*

The name globeflower is appropriately applied to the European *Trollius,* which in Farrer's words is "a plant of the alpine meadows all the ranges over, often occurring in such abundance in damp places that you may see whole areas shining with the bland and moony citron of its unbroken mass of bloom." In this species the yellow, petal-like sepals do curve upward and inward to form a ball atop the stiff stems a foot or so high. Our species, on the other hand, opens wide its colored sepals to display the showy boss of sexual parts within.

The fully opened flower, up to two inches across, has an outer ring of five or six sepals, pale moonlight yellow in color enhanced by pale green veining. In the very center the numerous pistils rise into a green tentlike cone surrounded by multiple rings of golden stamens. Tucked beneath the outer edge of this showy crown are the true petals, small, fat, and rather inconspicuous though they are a glossy chrome yellow. After fertilization the flowering stems continue to grow, carrying aloft the five-parted seed capsule, each section of which is like a short, fat pea pod with slightly hooked styles attached. The capsule turns from green through tan to dark brown as it ripens and near the end of June opens at the apex to spill out the numerous shiny black seeds.

In nature these seeds are never permitted to dry out, as the lax stems spill the ripened seed onto the moist soil. If fresh seed is sown soon after collection it will germinate readily the following spring. If seeds are allowed to dry for an extended period, however, germination will be delayed up to three years and will be spotty.

The root system of *Trollius laxus* is rather extensive for the size of the plant and does not lend itself to simple division, nor does the plant make new crowns that are easily detached. It is possible, however, to make new plants by lifting the plant soon after flowering and prying or cutting away a portion of the crown with basal leaves and a few roots attached. Such divisions should be either treated as cuttings to encourage new roots or be carefully planted out and kept well watered to assure strong root growth before winter sets in. The deep root system of this swampland plant has doubtless been developed to prevent heaving and breakage so likely to occur in wet soils during the freezing and thawing of our winters. The nature of the root system also suggests that this plant is a good candidate for root cuttings, a method of reproduction worthy of more extended experiment.

There are, in addition to our American globeflower and its variants already noted, three excellent dwarf species, all with yellow cuplike flowers: *T. acaulis,* of the Himalayas; *T. pumilus,* of western China; and *T. ranunculinus,* of the Caucasus. These all bloom somewhat later than our native species, as does *T. europeus,* and will grow in sites somewhat dryer.

Sampson Clay, writing of *T. pumilus,* says: "In existence, but unfortunately not yet in cultivation, are forms in which the red staining sometimes seen on the reverse of the flowers has intensified to deep blood colour, and lapped over to paint the inside of the bloom a rich crimson." There is something to be coveted here, something perhaps worthy of mention by our secretary of state in his dealings with China.

H.L.F.

A DWARF CRANBERRY
Vaccinium

For those blessed with acid soil there is a most attractive, neat evergreen shrub fairly newly introduced by the Arnold Arboretum. It is a nonvining form of the American cranberry, named *Vaccinium macrocarpon* 'Hamilton', and is a real treasure. In sandy soil into which a generous dollop of peat has been mixed, it forms a slowly enlarging cushion about six inches tall, covered in spring with typical, pale, pinky-white, beaked cranberry flowers. Ours has never set the red berries (perhaps it needs a friend of another clone), but in some gardens it does fruit.

Though normally a bog plant, the American cranberry does perfectly well with normal rock garden moisture. Though not yet easily obtained in the trade, *V.m.* 'Hamilton' comes readily from cuttings, so if you have a friend lucky enough to have this enchanting little shrub, beg a snippet or two.

L.L.F.

VIOLA PEDATA

Among the vast, cosmopolitan genus *Viola,* which gives its name to the family *Violaceae,* there are species of great beauty, some rather bumptious and rampageous best left out of all but the wildest portions of the garden, others so difficult to tame that they challenge the skill of the best plantsmen. Our own *Viola pedata* and its var. *lineariloba* is acknowledged to be among the most beautiful and, though it is easily grown in many gardens, has frequently been perversely difficult, especially in England.

In the wild, *Viola pedata,* the bicolor variety, is found in sunny openings in clayey or sandy acid soils, from upland South Carolina to Louisiana northward to southern Connecticut and westward to Indiana, Illinois, and Missouri. The variety *V. p. lineariloba,* or *concolor,* has a far greater range, extending southward into Florida and Texas, northward to southern New Hampshire, and westward to Michigan, Wisconsin, and Minnesota.

It is in some ways, it seems to me, unfortunate that Linnaeus gave the specific name *pedata* (footlike) to the less widespread variety that has the two upper petals of velvety dark violet and the three lower ones paler in color. But that was the taxon he had when he named the species. The similarity of the leaves to a bird's foot, which prompted the Linnaean name, is found as clearly in the more widespread variety. It would be more convenient if this latter variety with uniformly colored petals and wide distribution were called *V. pedata* and the other taxon *bicolor* as a variety under it. Moreover, the varietal designation *lineariloba* does not distinguish the two nearly as well as the difference in flower color, because the leaves of the bicolor variety that I have seen tend to have more linear divisions than do those of the concolor. But we shall continue to respect the scientific classification as we pursue the problems of growing and propagating these showy birdfoot or pansy violets.

That they do prove difficult to grow in English rock gardens is attested to by some of the best plantsmen in the kingdom. Clarence Elliott, writing back in 1935, laments, "*V. pedata* is a North American species, an exquisitely lovely thing, whose temper in cultivation is revealed by the fact that it has for many years been imported annually and copiously, and yet the number to be found in gardens has never increased. There is a variety *V.p. bicolor* with flowers of deep-violet and lavender-blue. A superb plant, but who can grow it,—permanently?"

Farrer likewise complained: "*V. pedata* has always been a problem for the cultivator. Even in its own States of America, if brought into the garden from the fields or banksides where it abounds (as in the sandy levels of Long Island), the clump soon mimps away in exile. In England it has occasioned as much discussion and correspondence almost, as its beauty is worth. On the whole it seems likely that a sandy and perfectly drained woodland mixture, light and free, but specially rich and clammy and well watered from below in spring, will appease the plant's homesickness, if only it be enshrined in some place not too open to the furies of the sun."

Little change seems to have appeared, either in success or prescription, by the time Anna Griffith, in *Collins Guide to Alpines,* wrote in 1964: "*V. pedata.* Bird's-foot Violet. One of the most lovely species, but difficult to grow and keep. A shady position in leafy sandy soil offers the best hope of permanence."

There may be in these quotations some clues as to why our English friends fail so frequently with our birdfoot, or this plant may indeed be one of the most sensitive of our Eastern wildflowers, many of which do not flower and perform as well in England as they do in their homeland. (In the same way even many plants from our West or from New Zealand that we, in the eastern United States, find difficult to grow, do well in England.) Yet if we consider where these violets grow in nature, we may detect a partial explanation for the difficulties described. *Viola pedata* is primarily a child of the sun, and wherever found in woodlands in this country chooses a woodland that is generally very rocky or with only very meager, sandy soil, with only scattered and rather starved oaks providing light shade. Certainly the "furies of the sun" can nowhere in England begin to compare with the intensity of sunlight in which the birdfoot seems to flourish in its native haunts.

Whether the acid soils in which it thrives are primarily sand or stony clay, they are never "rich and clammy." In fact the plant is frequently found at its most bountiful in the raw and sterile subsoil of roadside cuts. Perhaps the English have been too indulgent in providing too rich a fare for a waif accustomed solely to poverty and lean rations, and their plants have succumbed to indigestion.

When we have, by some favor of the gods, succeeded in proudly displaying a thrifty colony of *Viola pedata* in variety and form, then we wish to learn how to propagate it so as to spread this grace to other areas of our own garden or, better, to share the progeny with fellow gardeners. There are some striking forms, especially in the variety *lineariloba* (how I want to say *concolor* or just plain *V. pedata*). There is var. *albiflora,* of purest white with a typical deep orange center composed of fat pollen-laden anthers. There are also large-flowered, shimmering, dusty blues, and there is forma *rosea,* and even a red hinted at in one text.

These forms must perforce be propagated by vegetative means to which, in a diversity of methods, the species does not seem to be averse. Despite Farrer's horror at the prospect: "There seems to us, little propagation except by division, and those clumped fleshy stocks are by far too precious to be harried . . . ," it is quite simple to lift a thriving clump after it flowers in May and boldly to slice with a sharp knife down through the crown and short vertical rootstock. Produce as many thin slices as you dare, with feeding roots attached to each slice, and insert them into a sand bed until, along about August, they declare their independence by beginning to produce new leaves at the crown. You will discover, if you are reminded, that at the site from which you dug your rootstock, especially if you cut close to the crown, there will be a whole new crop of small leaf crowns sprung from the feeding roots that you left in the soil. In fact, you might wish purposely to encourage this easy kind of root-cutting propagation by using a knife to cut closely around the rootstock when you lift it for splicing, and filling the hole with sand. The roots, despite the plant's reputation for the death wish, have a tremendous will to live. Portions of the roots may be used as root cuttings in the classic manner.

Seed, of course, may also be used for increase. As with all violets, the seed has an abbreviated viability. Capture it, if you can, just as the capsules begin to split at the tip and before they have flung the seeds by an abrupt flaring of the segments, which they do within a day or two. Fresh seed sown immediately will produce seedlings the following spring which in turn will flower the next spring.

Most violets have a propensity for indiscriminate hybridizing despite their reputation for infertility in the showy flowers and, in many species, their dependence on inbred, indulgent self-fertilization in the cleistogamic flowers. Not so, *V. pedata.* It displays its virtue in the perfect, demonstrative, fertile flowers, yet tends to breed relatively "true." A white-flowered plant in my garden has given rise to some white-flowered seedlings, or at least white-flowered progeny have appeared near a patch containing my original white form and some others of differing distinction. Who is to know what went on among which plants?

I cannot resist recommending some pages in that classic work by Lawrence D. Hills, *The Propagation of Alpines,* where on pages 391–392 (394–395 in the second edition) he discusses our *Viola pedata* and its propagation for the nursery trade. Hills is especially interesting on page 174, where he indulges himself in unwonted philosophical speculation occasioned by what he reports as the discovery of 1945 of cleistogamy in *V. pedata.*

Nor can I resist quoting from that amazing volume of 1,725 pages, *Flora of Missouri,* by Julian A. Steyermark. Among much learned scientific information about the rich flora of that border state, the author, a skilled botanist and horticulturist, has included those rare tidbits of plant lore that make us aware of the deep relationships among plants and people. Amidst his technical discussion of *Viola pedata* and its variants (most of which, by the way, reside cheek-by-jowl in many counties of Missouri) Steyermark reports: "In the Ozark region these violets are used in a game known as 'Hens and Roosters.' The 'roosters' are the bicolored type having the upper petals dark violet, while the 'hens' are the uniformly colored flowers. One child will hold the flower-stalk with attached 'hen' flower in one hand, another child the stalk with attached 'rooster' flower. The object of the game is to see who can pull away from its stalk the flower of the other person. This is effected by hooking the flower-stalks and attempting to pull the other flower off its stalk by strokes and thrusts of the opponents."

He follows this bit of homely information by a paragraph that is obviously the outcome of years of botanical and horticultural investigation: "This violet is a handsome gem for rock-gardens and succeeds in any sunny or semishaded, well drained, usually acid soils, where it thrives best on sand, sandstone, chert, granite, and similar acid rocks. It will also grow on limestone. Along highway cuts through cherty or sandstone substrata, one often sees thousands of these plants growing thickly in rocky or gravelly exposures."

This message is worth sending forth at home and abroad.

H.L.F.

III

ESSAYS

Reflections on the Gardening Art

SUMMER IS DYING

These are the last sweet days of summer
and the leaves
spin   float   drift   slip
through the sunspun air smelling of mushrooms
and woodsmoke
ripeapple   leafmold
spiced and laced with the sharp cold fragrance
of asters   and drying grass.

Plunge your hands in the fire of color.
Drink deep the smoky   spicy
bluehaze of summer's breath
for she is dying in glory
and there is a long grey time between.

These are the last days.
The air is blue with mist in the morning
and the hills are blue on the blue sky
And   in the evening
the mountains are crimson and gold,
the rivers streaks of scarlet.
Touch the scarlet   the crimson,
Bask in the flame hot reds
and the yellow
the bright   bright   yellow
while the birds

Trollius laxus   A rare native of the eastern United States.

and how soon a dwindle when set out in their assigned beds! Three plants in two different sites yet remain, one full, unflowered season unassailed. This fall they are rosettes a full foot across. The coarsely dentate leaves, large as mullein and as brave, are downed with the finest golden hair—does it sound silly to say?—as lovely as the down along the neck of a beautiful blonde girl.

If nothing happens after this, if the winter soddens their grace and the spring declares their demise, they have provided. The label says pink. If they bloom I may wish they were blue. But they have provided, no matter what comes now, an unimagined eminence. These are the rewards of the smaller patience, and I shall go on trying meconopsis year after year until I learn their secret.

There is also the bigger patience. With what sympathy I recollect reading a remark by the president of the American Rock Garden Society in which he casually commented that the dove tree was to bloom at long last this spring, and he would be away. How often we wait, sometimes for years, and then not infrequently the plant is an honest disappointment. But we strive to find excuses for its mere existence: "This is the only one in New England," or the like. With only slight regret do we, a few years hence, find it occupying space needed for new adventures, they in turn perhaps to be unseated. Or more happily, after a ten-year wait, a mixed brood of Dexter hybrid rhododendrons blooms, and one is a burst of pale pink fringed with red, a subtle combination which at a distance glows a cool sea-coral. This is the reward of the long patience.

Or in contrast there are those unexpected delights. Another draba, perhaps: in your winter enthusiasm you sent for the seed offered in the distribution of surplus from some seed exchange. Carelessly you sowed it too late, carelessly you tended that surplus frame, carelessly you filled in a space where some cherished oldster had perished. And behold, next spring, because, perhaps, you had not expected too much, or because you had hit happily on the right site and setting, there is a new jewel among the regulars. These are the unexpected rewards of not too attentive patience.

So we grow old, yet always younger with each season of answer to our promises, spurred to a new patience.

H.L.F.

RUMINATIONS ON THE ORIGINS OF HORTICULTURE

Horticulture is truly a most astounding occupation. It's one thing to grow purposely, in a manner and site convenient for harvest, those plants that feed our bellies, but quite another to deliberately expend energy in an attempt to grow plants that offer us only their beauty. When and where did this fundamentally frivolous endeavor have its start? We don't know; the beginnings of horticulture are shrouded by the mists of time.

We do know that flowers were gathered for ceremonial purposes very early; their crumbling remains have been found in a Neanderthal grave pit. But picking wildflowers is not gardening. Even the culture of food plants probably occurred no earlier than Neolithic times. The Lake Dwellers (c.8,000–6,000 B.C.) stored wheat, millet, and rye in sufficient quantities to make it unlikely that these were garnered solely from scattered plants in the wild. Primitive flint hoes and sickles have been found in the rubbish piles of the Natufian culture in the Middle East dating from about the same time, give or take a thousand years. But it is likely that these first attempts at cultivating wild grains consisted of saving some of the seed gleaned for food and sprinkling it on the rich alluvium of river banks following spring flooding, where it was allowed to grow without further attention (a method still used today in some areas), rather than by the actual preparation of the soil and cultivation of the crop. If in the same era a Mesolithic man or his mate transplanted a few wildflowers into holes poked into the earth at the mouth of their cave or scratched up the soil in some out-of-the-way corner and scattered it with the seed of flowering plants, there is no record of their having done so. Gardens are evanescent artifacts, and such early attempts at horticulture, if they occurred, have vanished without a trace.

It was not until mankind made rock carvings and paintings depicting horticultural activities, and incised on clay tablets bills of lading and lists of the numbers and kinds of exotic plants delivered as tribute by conquered peoples or as a result of trade, that we have any record of the creation of pleasure gardens, and this had to wait until about 4000 B.C. At about this time private gardens and public parks were created in ancient Egypt and in China and in many places between. Phalanxes of slaves carried tons of river muck in baskets to enrich the soil of these gardens and dug miles of ditches and brought jar after jar of water from wells and rivers in order to irrigate them. Caravans and triremes transported exotic plants from yon to hither to enhance the new gardens, and hordes of gardeners cultivated the beds of enriched earth, sowed the seed, transplanted and hoed and pulled weeds in order to maintain them.

Such gardens were created for the wealthy, powerful, and leisured, who lolled, played, made love, strolled, conversed, and contemplated what we hope were elevating thoughts in them. They did not themselves, as far as we can discover, actually dig and plant them, yet is it not possible that some slave became enchanted by the beauty of the blossoms under his care, filched a few seeds, and smuggled them home to plant them in a broken pot or a neglected corner near his quarters? Gardening, we know, is catching, and the virus, once it had struck, spread like the common cold throughout the ancient world.

We are told the gardens were at first areas in which mankind attempted to escape the chaos and dangers of the surrounding wilderness. Such areas were usually enclosed, partly as shelter from cold or searing winds, but, perhaps more importantly, to keep out wild or semidomesticated animals and even human neighbors who threatened not only the garden but the very lives and limbs of the gardeners themselves along with those of their tender wives and offspring. Gardens were places to sit outdoors among trees and flowering plants, protected from the outside world. In hot, dry climates water was frequently piped in to create pools and fountains both to supply a handy source for household use and filling watering pots and to cool and moisten the air for the pleasure of the occupants. In many countries gardens were, indeed, central to one's living space and were the scene of sundry household chores as well as places for contemplation and dallying. As such they tended to be formal and architectural in design, a tree or two and perhaps a trellised vine for shade and fruit; short-clipped grass or, in dry climates, bare, beaten earth sprinkled to keep down the dust or, in wealthier homes, covered with paving. Flowering shrubs and herbaceous plants were usually grown in pots or in small, frequently raised, geometrically shaped beds behind low fencing or ramparts of small rocks or crockery to prevent their being overrun by careless feet. True, in China and Japan gardens close to the house were occasionally deliberately created to resemble nature, but even these were carefully manipulated symbolic abstractions of nature rather than untamed nature itself.

On the whole, even today in our more informal, relaxed gardens, we tend to keep the wilderness at bay. Nature unbound, though perhaps no longer as perilous as formerly, tends to be both messy and uncomfortable. A snarl of untrimmed shrubs replete with broken branches, brambles, and poison ivy may appeal to the adventurous child, but not to the gardener's eye. A meadow of tall grasses and flowering herbs is lovely at a distance, but not very comfortable to sit on; it's likely to be damp and is certainly full of creepy, crawly things like ants and spiders and even—horrors!—snakes. Weedy plants, if not kept under control, will soon choke out those we desire. Thus we have learned that if we wish to have a garden, we cannot entirely let nature have its way or soon the wilderness will engulf us once more. And keeping the wilderness beyond the pale requires eternal vigilance and hard, usually dirty and uncomfortable work, as our forebears discovered. Those who perform this arduous labor are called gardeners, and strangely enough there are those who find joy in it, who actually derive great pleasure in working the soil themselves and nurturing the plants they grow.

The Chinese have a saying which advises you to plant a garden if you wish to be happy all your life. Why should this be so? "We are nearer God's heart in a garden than anywhere else on earth," sings the poet Dorothy Blomfield. Perhaps this explains it. According to Nan Fairbrother in her book *Men and Gardens,* Mohamet promised those of his followers who fought and died for Islam that a paradise awaited them—a paradise resembling a shaded garden filled with delicious fruits and fragrant flowers, the sound of singing birds and running water and, let's face it, beautiful and complaisant damsels (perhaps to do the gardening). Nonwarriors were apparently not welcome to this paradise, nor were virtuous ladies. Mohamet was, I'm afraid, a male chauvinist. More to our point, the followers of Zoroaster, according to Mrs. Fairbrother, "held the comfortable faith that gardeners went to heaven, and so, said the Buddhists, did their gardens." The Old Testament of the Christian Bible states that God made a garden eastward in Eden and filled it with every manner of tree and herb that was lovely to see or smell or was delicious to eat. In this garden he placed Adam "to dress it and keep it." Thus Adam,

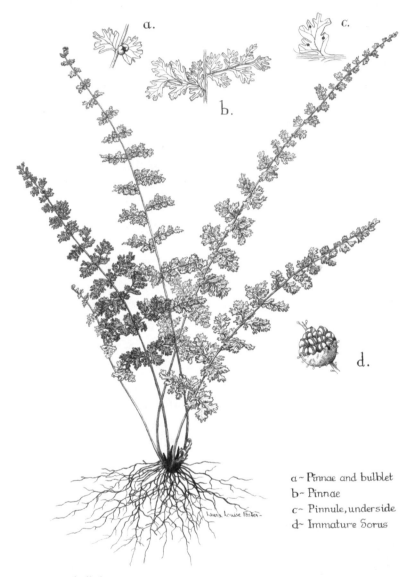

a. b. c.

a ~ Pinnae and bulblet
b ~ Pinnae
c ~ Pinnule, underside
d ~ Immature Sorus

Cystopteris bulbifera var. *crispa*   A graceful tufted fern that usually grows in large masses. This form was discovered by Linc Foster in 1952 near Falls Village, Connecticut.

before his fall, was the first gardener and, by extension, gardening is God's work.

Is this why we enjoy gardening? Is it an atavistic desire to return to our innocent beginnings? Or is it an effort to create, like gods, our own miniature gardens of Eden, where not only will the lamb and the lion lie side by side, but *Pyxidanthera barbulata* of the New Jersey Pine Barrens will spread its mats of starry blossoms beside the twiggy, flower-laden branches of *Rhododendron racemosum* of the Himalayas; where *Primula kisoana* from the woodlands of Japan will send its tuffets of soft, furry leaves and pink flowers among the glossy patterned foliage of *Cyclamen hederifolium* from southern Italy and the isles of Greece; where *Lewisia cotyledon* brought from the stony crests of the Siskiyous will spring from the same crevice as *Saxifraga longifolia* of the Pyrenees?

Is this what leads us to search the far corners of the world for new plants and persuades us that we can grow them together in the same garden? Is this what horticulture is all about? Or is it more simply the pleasure derived from working out of doors, far from the turmoil of the "wilderness" beyond our gates, among beautiful plants that are beholden to us for their well-being? God's work, indeed.

L.L.F

GREEN

As the northeastern quadrant of the United States slips inexorably toward the winter solstice, the green of our fields, swamps, and forested hills fades almost imperceptibly from day to day as though the rich color were being overlaid by a tarnish. Yet even as the green dims, a new light creeps across the stage and, as it strengthens, the landscape begins to brighten again, but now transformed, no longer green but glowing with hot color: lemon and gold, scarlet, purple, and crimson, which spreads and swells to an almost unbearable incandescence. The very air is suffused with its reflection. "Let fall no burning leaf," whispers the poet, and we hold our breath lest even the faint draft of our breathing shatter the beauty.

But it cannot last. The light thins and pales, and the curtain falls, and we, still bemused, sigh and rustle to our feet to return to the everyday, workaday world.

But would we, if we could, choose to live in this magic world forever? I think not. Soon our sensibilities would be exhausted by this flaming landscape; we would long for less vibrant colors on which to rest our eyes, just as a wanderer in the desert must long for the cool shade of a grove beside a spring. And just so we must remember, in our anxiety to have color in our gardens, that green, too, is a color and perhaps the most important color of all.

Green is the color of life. It is the green things in this world that nourish us and create the very air we breathe. It offers, too, the peace and rest we need. In the dog days of summer we seek the cool, ferny, green places to escape the hot, brilliant light. A jangle of colors may briefly excite us, but the eye soon becomes jaded with no place to rest. The loveliest blossom is lost in the kaleidoscopic tangle.

So when you plan your garden, first think of green. Green is the frame that gives shape to your landscape. Its subtle variations enhance the colors of the flowering plants. Deep blue-green gives a more vibrant glow to hot orange. Gray-green will tame the most vicious magenta. Pale yellow-green lends a richness to purple. Blue flowers acquire a jewel-like brilliance when set among silvery foliage.

We make white gardens and blue gardens, pink, lavender, and purple gardens, and gardens in hues of yellow, gold, and orange.

Why not a green garden? Blossoms are fleeting and soon gone, while you can have green in your garden throughout the year. Consider an evergreen garden to walk in or just to look at through the window to remind you during the cold, dead months of winter that there is still life in the earth and it will burgeon once more. Or plant a green garden for summer in which to enjoy the cool and shade on glaring hot days.

Green gardens are not as easy to create as one might think. Multicolored flowers can cover a multitude of mistakes in garden design by distracting the eye so that it overlooks clumsy proportions and awkward shapes. Shape and proportion must therefore be even more carefully considered than in a flowery garden in which the season of bloom and the combination, juxtaposition, and balance of the various flower colors are frequently the prime concerns.

In a green garden the shapes and textures of foliage are as important as the various shades of green. A planting of solid hemlocks, or large-leaved rhododendrons, or pines is monotonous and can even be depressing, but a combination of their contrasting foliage can delight the eye. On the other hand a helter-skelter mixture of plants with undistinguished leafage, such as that of average garden perennials or deciduous shrubbery, is equally dull and tends to be confusing and to appear merely weedy and messy. Bold contrasts in the shape, size, and texture of foliage placed in well-apportioned swatches are best suited to the primarily green garden.

For the shady garden consider the feathery fronds of *Dryopteris intermedia* and the lacy whorls of *Adiantum pedatum* combined with the broad planes of a few hosta and groups of the graceful ladderlike wands of Solomon's seal against the glossy foliage of mountain laurel or pieris; the intricate foliage of astilbe set off by the rugged polish of bergenia and the clustered lances of *Clintonia borealis* or *C. umbellata;* the neatly patterned leaves of

Hexastylis (Asarum) shuttleworthii or *Cyclamen purpurascens* in contrast to the tufted lacework of *Aruncus aethusifolius* and the soft, furry rosettes of *Primula kisoana;* the polished leather of *Shortia,* be it *S. galacifolia, S. uniflora,* or *S. soldanelloides,* with the delicate tracery of *Gymnocarpium dryopteris* rising from among the tangled skeins of *Mitchella repens* or *Linnaea borealis.* The permutations are endless.

For rock gardeners, whose plants tend to blossom in spring and early summer, the textures, shapes, and shades of green in foliage are of vital importance, and rock gardeners are fortunate in that so many of the plants they prefer have interesting leaves. In fact some, such as the huddled masses of sempervivums, are more attractive without their gawky upthrust of flowering stalks. Even the saxifrages, lovely as they are in bloom, present, perhaps, an even greater attraction when flowerless; there is an almost irresistibly touchable quality to the tight cushions of intricately patterned rosettes. Many rock garden plants also offer the advantage of having evergreen foliage, which with rocks to set it off can be as enchanting, if more subtle, out of season than in the full flush of bloom.

For a moist, well-shaded nook nothing could be much more appealing than a mossy limestone rock set beside a tiny pool of water and planted with a few lacy cowlicks of maidenhair spleenwort *(Asplenium trichomanes),* the rugose penwiper rosettes of *Ramonda myconi,* and the slender, creeping, pale green strands of fleshy leaves and stems of the shade-loving Eastern native *Sedum ternatum.* Or imagine a rocky pocket filled with leafy soil containing a clump of *Athyrium japonicum pictum* footed by the fairy foliage of *Thalictrum kiusianum* and the tripartite leaves of a few trilliums.

The variety of leafage in rock garden plants that like sun or light shade makes for an even wider possibility of striking combinations: buns, pads, mats, tuffets, and shrublets in every shade from almost black through emerald to sunny golden green, from "blue" to "silver" and sheened with bronze, striped, stippled, and splotched. There are leaves of all shapes and textures: hairy, felted and furry, crinkled and smooth, matte, succulent, and glossy; grasslike leaves and leaves dissected into hairlike segments; leaves that are toothed, lobed, and imbricate. There are leaves that invite the touch and leaves as prickery as a sea urchin, crisp leaves and feathery leaves and leaves as stiff as wrought metal.

As you clean up the garden this autumn, even though the foliage is past its best, pause to examine your plants. Note the delightful variety of their embroidery over the soil. Seek out plants whose leaves compliment each other in the contrast of their shape, texture, and color. Then you need not mourn if your *Aquilegia jonesii* refuses to bloom; enjoy its tuft of silver-blue filigree. Don't fret because guests arrive in midsummer to see your garden. Let them admire the rich brocade of the foliage undistracted by a clutter of bloom.

Inevitably some blossoms will mar your tapestry of green. These you can either consider a bonus or accept philosophically—after all they don't last very long. Or, of course, you can always cut them off.

L.L.F.

TEN BEST PLANTS

Have you ever contemplated—perhaps simply as an off-season amusement—choosing your ten favorite rock garden plants? As I contemplated this job, which I anticipated as a pleasant way to spend an evening in early spring while the wind roared through the tree tops and gusts of cold, sleety rain rattled against the clapboards of the house, I became more and more frustrated at the sheer enormity of such a task. How *does* one go about choosing ten favorites out of the hundreds and hundreds of species available? I cannot say I love them all equally—but only *ten?* Within ten minutes I could think of at least twenty-five I would not wish to do without, and in half an hour I could list a hundred or so.

I started by contemplating the early bulbs. I have never considered these among my very favorite plants, yet today, in these first cold, sodden weeks between winter and spring, a wide patch of *Eranthis hyemalis* had thrust their shining yellow cups through the inch or so of snow that overlay them, and they were spread in a profligate scattering of doubloons, as though flung across a white damask table cloth, each golden coin surrounded by a ruff of deep green leaves. Could I leave them out, these first cheerful harbingers of the tide of color to come? Or the crocuses clustered in the grass like clutches of painted Easter eggs, or for that matter, the blue, blue rivulets and pools of the scilla clan? And while I am on the subject of bulbous plants (these nonfavorites of mine), I would be loath to leave off my list the cool green and silver gray, nodding bells of *Ornithogalum nutans* or the buttered-egg blossoms of *Tulipa tarda* nestled in the center of their starfish of narrow green leaves, or the jostling, laughing crowd of daffodils. Yet, I had better leave them all out or my list will be hopelessly long.

How about the hepaticas, one of our first native plants to bloom, their frail blossoms of pink, white, and blue trembling above the sere leaves in the chill spring wind—shall I put them on my list? Surely their charm is in part their early appearance— or is it? It is hard, indeed, to ignore the rich blue of *Hepatica translyvanica* with its elegantly scissor-snipped leaves. But, perhaps these, too, I had better cross off my list or I shall never keep it down to ten.

Can I leave out the delicate, sweet-scented mayflower, the trailing arbutus, *Epigaea repens,* whose dainty pink and white flowers peep so shyly from beneath the mat of glossy evergreen leaves, or the fringed bells of *Shortia galacifolia* or *S. uniflora,* or the rosy campaniles of *Shortia soldanelloides,* with their burnished foliage still bronzed by winter's cold? How about *Trillium nivale,* the snow trillium, that raised its trilogy of unsullied white petals only an inch or two above the sodden ground in earliest spring, or those other, taller trilliums, *T. grandiflorum, T. vaseyi,* and that loveliest of all, *Trillium undulatum,* the painted trillium? No, this last one I can cross off my list; she is impossible to grow out of her native habitat and has shunned our most ardent efforts to please her in our garden. But what of the others?

And I suppose I should cross out *Caltha palustris* also. It is, perhaps, not a true rock garden plant, though it has sown itself in ribbons of pure sunshine in the rocky verges of the little artificial stream that runs through our garden. But can I leave out the dainty Dutchman's breeches and squirrel corn, *Dicentra cucullaria* and *D. canadensis,* which have seeded so profusely in our shady garden that their blossoming is like a fall of fresh snow? Can I exclude that other lovely native, *Sanguinaria canadensis,* which lights with its white candle flames the beds under our straggly grove of young pines near the house, or its lovely double form, *multiplex,* whose flowers float like miniature water lilies above the unfurling leaves?

At this rate I'll never manage to keep my list down to ten. But surely, I should include that exquisite exotic, *Jeffersonia dubia,* whose amethystine cups rise from among its still unfolded garnet leaves every spring. And can I leave out the pulsatillas: *P. vulgaris,* with its rich purple goblets brimming with golden stamens, whose clustered awns hover like balls of down over the alpine lawn in early summer; or *P. vernalis,* whose opalescent chalices are sheathed with spun-gold hairs against the cold; or our own

P. patens from the plains states, whose diaphanous, pearly-lavender blossoms are clad in silvery fur?

And I mustn't forget the elegant trout lilies, the erythroniums, each more beautiful than the last, whose revolute petals come in shades of rose pink, clear yellow, pristine white, and even smoky gray-blue, some with leaves as dappled as a fawn's coat. Nor have I yet mentioned the dainty soldanellas, though here I would leave out *Soldanella alpina,* which melts its way through alpine snows; it never opens its fringed bells of lavender-purple for us in the open garden unless we have a deep snow cover from November to March to protect its overwintering buds—too rare an occasion here. Instead I would choose the taller *Soldanella montana,* whose flowering stems, each hung with a shower of violet-blue flowers, rise without fail above their piles of penny-round leaves under our tall old pines no matter what the winter brings.

Already, I know, my list is well over the allotted ten, and I have yet to come to the rush of late spring and early summer, to say nothing of the beauties (though these are fewer in number) that bloom in midsummer and on into fall. Yet I haven't mentioned the ramondas with their felted, rugose, penwiper leaves of deepest green framing their sprays of blue-purple, pink and white African violet flowers that nestle so happily in the mossy crevices of our north-facing stone walls and ledges. And I should include at least one of the two blue-eyed Marys, so dissimilar despite their common name. I would dearly like to list them both, though perhaps I should skip *Collinsia verna* as a mere annual. Yet it comes up every spring in the same spot among the wild strawberries under one of our big maples from self-sown seed to gladden my heart with its shimmering cloud of blue and white butterfly flowers. *Omphalodes verna,* on the other hand, is solidly perennial. Its rosettes of heart-shaped leaves make over the years a mat of dark green by means of short strawberrylike stolons. This rug of leaves is covered in spring with clusters of large forget-me-not flowers, not washy blue, but of a strong, heart-stopping cobalt to rival that of any gentian.

Which, of course, brings to my mind the gentians. How about the glorious ultramarine trumpets of *Gentiana acaulis* and its ilk, their throats streaked and speckled with white and green? They would have to be on anyone's list of favorites. I shall reluctantly leave out *Gentiana verna* however, despite its more refined starry flowers of intense cerulean blue. It has proven too fussy a plant in the open garden, at least for us. But I would like to list the easygoing, summer-blooming *Gentiana septemfida,* which generously tips its procumbent leafy stems with clusters of azure blossoms. And I shall certainly include at least one of the stunning fall-blooming gentians from central China: *GG. farreri, ornata, veitchiorum,* et al., and their many lovely hybrids from whose pancakes of fine, grassy foliage spring swarms of upfacing trumpets of incredible blue from aquamarine to deep sapphire, feathered with bands of white and luminous green, proclaiming their glory to heaven until hard frost overtakes them. The only question is which one? I would not wish to leave any of them off my list of favorites, yet I must draw the line somewhere if I am to be allowed only ten choices; there are too many others to consider, and I have barely begun.

I have not yet come to the lewisias: *Lewisia cotyledon* in all its perfection of clustered blossoms of candy-striped pink, and perhaps even more lovely in the selected forms in shades of tangerine, apricot, gold, and vermilion; nor the huge, diaphanous flowers of *Lewisia tweedyi* shimmering in tints of opalescent apricot pink among its tongue-shaped, succulent leaves. Surely, these two should stand high on my list of ten favorites.

Nor can I leave out all the anemones. Two in particular are among my favorites. *Anemone nemorosa,* the wood anemone of

England, which scatters its white, pink, and blue stars so generously in our woods, and especially the double white form 'Vestal', with its central pompon surrounded by a ruff of petals must
be included. Also *Anemone sylvestris,* which despite its name is not
a woodlander for us, but lights a corner of our moist scree in sun
with its ample, unblemished white cups on stiff stems above the
crisp, dark green, intricately wrought leaves for weeks and weeks
from midsummer to early fall, to be followed by drumstick seed
heads that look like cotton grass as they ripen and shatter.

And what of the primroses—oh, the primroses! I think I could
almost fill my list with the genus. There are the little alpine
primroses of the Auricula Section, with smooth, fleshy leaves:
Primula allionii, P. hirsuta, et al., their large, clear pink flowers
nestled among the rosettes of leaves; *Primula clusiana,* its rich
rose-red blossoms with deeply cleft petals paling to white at the
center, and all the neat little bouquets of their hybrids, *P.* ×
pubescens. Then there is *Primula marginata,* whose dentate leaves
are delicately outlined with a silvery farina that also powders the
stems and calyces and the center of each lavender-blue flower.
And lovely indeed is *Primula auricula* itself—not the tricked-out
hybrids, whose flat faces are patterned with bizarre colors in bands
so precise as to appear painted on by a clever artificer—but the
wild species with clear yellow, fragrant flowers, white-centered
in var. *albocincta.*

Then there are the woodland primroses, of which *Primula
vulgaris,* the pale yellow primrose of English copses, with a
darker egg yolk center and rough, lettuce-green leaves, is, perhaps, my favorite. But there are also its multitudinous color
forms from white to shades of blue (milky-sky blue to the deep
blue of Gulf Stream water) or in tints of yellow and gold, orange,
pale pink, and rosy red, each blossom starred at its center with
deep yellow. In the 'Cowitchan Strain', the leaves are stained

with red, and the blossoms are a deep, rich, glowing ruby or garnet or else a velvety midnight blue. All these "acaulis" primroses have but a single flower on a stalk, but so bountiful is their blossoming that for every flower that fades two spring up to take its place, and for weeks the rosettes of leaves are as jammed with bloom as an old-fashioned nosegay.

And I must not leave out those dainty Japanese woodlanders, *Primula sieboldii* and *P. kisoana.* The former, perhaps the easiest of all primroses to grow, has loosely clustered heads of ruffled snowflake flowers of white or deep rose to shell pink (sometimes combined in the same flower) above the dentate, hairy, pale green leaves. This primrose, which forms mats by the slow increase of short, brittle, white rhizomes a few inches below the surface of the soil, thrives despite dense competition from other plants, and if in summer the weather becomes too dry to suit it, it simply retires underground and waits until spring moisture urges it to renew growth. *Primula kisoana,* on the other hand, disperses its riches widely in the fertile, leafy soil it prefers by means of long, threadlike underground stolons, which send up new rosettes of leaves, frequently at some distance from the mother plant. Its leaves are shaped like those of a geranium and are fuzzy with hairs, as are the pedicels, which carry to a height of six—occasionally ten—inches clusters of rosy red blossoms with notched petals, paler toward the center. There is a rare albino form with flowers of snowy white that is especially lovely.

Among the taller primroses, my list is short, as the glorious Himalayans: *PP. sikkimensis, florindae, viallii,* et al., do not do well for us. They dislike both our winters and our summers and, though for many years we tried to please them, after one summer of spectacular bloom they would dwindle away. I cannot in all conscience list among my favorites plants that demand endless cosseting when I must ignore so many beautiful and willing growers. *Primula denticulata* I shall also leave out, though it thrives in our garden wherever the soil is rich and reasonably moist and self-sows in swathes of cabbagy leaves from which rise in earliest spring the lavender-pink, white, and occasionally rose-red balls of bloom. It ages badly. The seed heads on their elongated stalks and the great trusses of cabbage leaves flop disconsolately in an unsightly limp tangle as soon as the heat of late spring and summer hits them despite the moist soil in which they grow and the shade of the trees that surround them. *Primula japonica,* with its tiers of crimson, rose-pink, and white blossoms, I shall include, along with the lavender-pink *P. beesiana* and the yellow-flowered *P. bulleyana* and their glorious hybrid offspring, *P.* × *bullesiana,* whose candelabras of blossom come in every delicious tint that can be created by their parents' genes. These species do well for us, though they require constantly damp feet along our brooklet or in a wet corner of the rich moraine where they self-sow quite happily. They are surely among my favorites.

It is indeed fortunate that I must leave out at least some of the primroses, as those on my list already add up to many more than ten, and I will have to skip over many favorites I am loath to exclude. But regardless of all strictures, I must list some of the phloxes, for what would our garden be without this genus? All through the month of May the alpine lawn foams with billows of *Phlox subulata,* the starry-flowered *Phlox bifida,* and their hybrids in white and delicate pastel shades of pink and lavender-blue. Under the warmth of the strong spring sun they fill the air with a fragrance like no other. Yes, I know, *Phlox subulata* is an easy, common, much maligned species, at least in the Northeast. But what plant is so willing to grow, so generous with its bloom? Even the great Reginald Farrer, who scoffed at most American natives, said of it, "There is no end to the kindliness and glory [of this phlox]. . . . The day that saw the introduction, more than a century since, of *Phlox subulata,* ought indeed be kept as a horticultural festival." Certainly it must stand high on my list of favorites.

P. subulata is but one among many in this genus that I favor; lovely as it is, however, I shall not list *Phlox divaricata.* Though goodness knows it is as easygoing and prodigal with its bloom as *Phlox subulata,* and when it blossoms our wooded areas shimmer with its lavender flowers—still, it does not have that special appeal. I am torn, however, by indecision as to whether to leave out or include that other woodlander, *Phlox stolonifera.* Its stay is comparatively brief, yet when it is in bloom the floor of our woods garden is tapestried with its delicate colors, pure white and every shade of lavender-blue and pink to wine and rich violet. And I cannot bear to leave out its beautiful relative: *Phlox adsurgens,* from the evergreen forests of the Siskiyous, whose every petal of pale coral is penciled with a central stripe of darker rose. Nor can I exclude all the lovely summer-blooming phloxes: *PP. pilosa, ovata, carolina, pulchra, buckleyi,* et al. With many-flowered heads of bloom in shades of delicious pink and rose on stems from twelve to eighteen inches tall, they froth in the openings in our woodlands when very little else is blossoming there.

Even if I left these out, how would it be possible to keep my list to only ten out of all the plethora of species that enthrall me? Would any list of favorites be complete that did not include the needle-leaved and silver-scaled muffins of the Kabschia saxifrages, whose hard domes enchant throughout the year and in earliest spring are transformed into heaped mounds of snow, strawberry ice cream, raspberry sherbet, and lemon ice? But which to choose of these delectable creations? And how about the sculptured rosettes of the encrusted saxifrages edged with dots of lime, which erupt with sprays of frothy white in June? Can they be excluded?

Can I compile a list of favorites that doesn't include even one species of the *Campanulaceae* that ring their blue and white bells all through the summer months, or the marble-leaved cyclamen that bridge the season with their startled, upturned petals, or that other inside-out flower, symbol of the American Rock Garden Society, the dodecatheon?

Surely I must add to my list the dainty Japanese woodlander *Thalictrum kiusianum,* which mists its two-inch-high mats of ferny foliage with puffs of lavender stamens for weeks and weeks in late summer. Nor have I yet mentioned the elegant *Arisaema sikokianum,* with its jaunty spathe striped in eggplant purple and pale green and lined with white porcelain to match its bell-clapper spadix. And who would leave out the aquilegias, their intricately folded flowers in every shade the rainbow offers, or *Daphne cneorum* and its low-growing sister species, whose clusters of blossom scent the whole garden, or the aethionemas that made a haze of palest pink over our alpine lawn in June? What list of favorites would be complete if it did not include *Dryas octopetala,* whose pristine cups overflow with golden stamens and float a few inches only above the neat mats of tiny, hard, oval, oaklike leaves and are later transformed by the bees into swirls of gray feathers?

Should not *Adonis vernalis,* with its golden suns framed in leaves of spun emerald, be on my list, and at least one of the clove-scented dianthus clan? Must I leave out all the iris, as lovely and evanescent as the daughter of the rainbow after whom they are named? And, if I may list one of the *Compositae,* I shall choose the Atlas daisy, *Anacyclus depressus,* that epitome of daisydom, its starfish pancakes of woolly gray, curled parsley leaves pressed tight to the ground and spangled with not-quite-meadow-sized, apparently stemless daisies, whose chalk-white rays close each night into pointed crimson buds and reopen petal by petal to disclose the yellow disks when the morning sun wakes them. I have a particular fondness for daily flowers; I shall not leave these out.

There are so many plants I love, mentioned and unmentioned, that each time I go over my list in an effort to cull it I think of still more that I should add. Making a list of ten favorite plants is an exercise in the impossible. Each is a favorite for its special grace. I cannot choose among them.

L.L.F.

VARIATION

Many, if not most, taxonomists would prefer to ignore variations.

Living organisms are not an undifferentiated continuum. They come as elephants, cats, ferns and pine trees, goldenrods and gentians. In order to classify them, taxonomists have therefore separated them into more and more refined categories according to their affinities. Thus the Plant Kingdom is differentiated from the Animal Kingdom by certain characteristics that belong only to organisms in one Kingdom but not to those in the other.

The Plant Kingdom is in turn divided into thirteen categories called Divisions, starting with the most primitive. The first twelve Divisions encompass such things as bacteria, algae, liverworts, fungi, mosses, and ferns and their allies, the latter being composed of plants that reproduce by spores and have vascular systems. The thirteenth Division is made up of flowering, seed-bearing plants. These Divisions are further divided into Subdivisions, of which there are two in Division XIII: the Gymnosperms, with ovules that are not enclosed in an embryo (conifers, yews, and the Ginkgo tree being examples), and the Angiosperms, whose ovules are enclosed.

These Subdivisions are once again divided into Classes, the

Angiosperms containing two: the Monocotyledons, whose embryos have but a single cotyledon or seed leaf, *i.e.,* grasses, lilies, and orchids; the Dicotyledons, whose embryos bear two seed leaves.

Classes are themselves separated into categories called Subclasses, of which there are two in the Dicotyledons. Subclasses are further divided into Orders, which are sometimes split into Suborders if they are very large. When trying to key out an unknown plant, one next arrives, thankfully, at the Family.

Though very few botanists and probably no amateurs can remember the names of all the Families of flowering plants, some are old friends: the *Compositae,* the *Ericaceae,* the *Primulaceae,* and the *Cruciferae.* Knowing at least the most common Families and their significant characteristics can be most helpful if one is trying to identify a plant; having a clue to which Family a plant belongs can cut out a great deal of aimless leafing through the pages of plant manuals. Very large Families are sometimes split up into Subfamilies and Tribes.

Unfortunately, in very intricately constructed or very minute flowers it is not always easy to see what is what. It is therefore quite possible for the amateur to assign a plant to the wrong Family if its flowers and/or seed capsules (the portions of the plant usually used to differentiate Families) are so small that their characteristics can only be discerned under strong magnification.

Such was the problem of misidentification of *Aruncus aethusifolius* (Rose Family) as an astilbe (Saxifrage Family). Because the two genera so closely resemble each other in leaf pattern and in the general texture and stance of the inflorescence, the average horticulturist, untrained in botany, might readily assume that the newly introduced aruncus was a small astilbe and fail to examine its individual flowers through a hand lens to make absolutely certain. There is also always the problem of having on hand the portion of the plant used in the keys for identification.

When one reaches the next level of classification, the Genus, things become even more complicated, as the differences between the Genera within the same Family, Subfamily, or Tribe become ever more subtle. Telling an *Aster* from an *Erigeron,* a cow parsnip *(Heracleum)* from an *Angelica,* or a hemlock parsley *(Conioselinum)* from poison hemlock *(Conium)* is not all that easy for the amateur, though it's not impossible. I am sometimes less than certain whether the plant I am admiring is a *Silene* or a *Saponaria* or even a *Lychnis.*

The next step is trying to identify the species of the plant in

Trillium parviflorum   A recently described species from Washington State closely related to *T. albidum.*

question. Separating the goldenrods—to pick a particularly con-
founding genus to classify—is a job for an expert, and trying to
key out one of the species of Microphlox from another can add
a number of white hairs to even the most knowledgeable head.
Hybrids among species, and variations within species, don't help
simplify matters.

Humankind seems to have a passionate need to name that
which it sees, as though putting a name to something gave it an
existence it did not otherwise have. Names are certainly essential
if one is to speak of something to someone else: "That little white
flower about two inches tall that you see in the woods in the
spring," simply does not suffice. And it helps, if one wishes to
communicate with a person who speaks another language, to have
a name common to all languages. Try talking to a French, Italian,
or Japanese gardener about "columbine" and see how far you get.
In order to name something one must be able to describe it in
unmistakable terms.

One can readily see from the above preamble on classification
why taxonomists seek to classify living organisms by tucking
them into a series of increasingly small containers that fit inside
each other like pigeonholes within cabinets within rooms, each
container having within it a group of plants or animals with
fundamental qualities, or "essences," that separate one group from
another. Variation plays hob with such a system. How can one
correctly assign organisms into specific pigeonholes—or into
generic cabinets or family rooms, for that matter—if variations,
as they frequently do, refuse to fit neatly into a clearly defined
container, but, rather, tend to slop over into adjacent containers?
Should one give them another pigeonhole of their own and, if
so, into which cabinet should it be put?

For example, a so-called species with a wide geographic distribution is likely to have somewhat different characteristics at the limits of its range. These characteristics frequently intergrade between the extremes as the species adjusts itself to somewhat different external circumstances. Should such varying "species" be separated into two or more species? If so, at what point or points should the dividing lines be drawn? In addition, a wide-spread "species" may have within it disjunct colonies that live in a variety of habitats and have developed certain characteristics not shared with the rest of the population in order to cope with their special ecological niches. How much variation from the "essential" norm must a colony have in order to be considered a new species?

In their efforts to answer such questions taxonomists have developed different methods of classification. The so-called "splitters" are more than likely to assign separate pigeonholes to each local, somewhat variant population, thus establishing a plethora of species, each rather narrowly defined. This multiplicity of species, based on what are frequently rather minute differences, is considered nit-picking by many critics.

The other taxonomic school, called "lumpers," broadens the criteria for each species and stuffs into a single pigeonhole all variations that fall within these criteria. This frequently enrages those of us who enjoy finding obscure species—the more the better—as is true of those birdwatchers whose life-lists were shortened by a number of species in a recent ornithological lumping. We plantsmen can sympathize. We have lost species in the taxonomic revision of our own ARGS emblem, *Dodecatheon,* and not too long ago lost a whole genus when our American *Douglasia* was swallowed up by *Androsace.*

But we must remember, even as we gnash our teeth over the lumping or splitting of our old familiar species and genera, that classification is a matter of opinion rather than a set of absolute

Dodecatheon   The emblem of the
American Rock Garden Society.

laws. At the moment, lumping is perhaps more fashionable in
taxonomic circles than is splitting. This may change. The inclusion of the genus *Douglasia* in the genus *Androsace* is, after all,
the work of a single Scandinavian author, Dr. P. Wendelbo,
writing in 1961, and although this classification has been followed
by Dr. A. Dress of the Munich Botanic Garden among others,
it has not, by any means, gained wide acceptance among informed
experts. Taxonomy is, indeed, a question vexed.

As any really careful student of wildflowers knows, even
within a field of daisies—all, probably, closely related—one can
find innumerable variation in individual plants among such visu-
ally obvious characteristics as size of the disk, and width, length,
shape, and number of the rays on the flowers. Consider, therefore,
the unseen variation among these daisies: differences in season of
bloom, cold-hardiness, ability to withstand drought and heat,
susceptibility to disease. Horticulturists are well aware that *Cornus florida* varies not only in the color and size of the bloom, but
in winter-hardiness as well. A flowering dogwood from Florida

or Georgia will frequently lose its flower buds and even succumb
to winter temperatures when brought north and planted in Connecticut. Yet individuals of this species planted in the same site,
but native to the northern portion of its range, come through the
same winter unscathed.

Some species, such as *Trillium ovatum* and *Trillium grandiflorum,* are notorious for variation. *Lewisia cotyledon* varies
enough in growth habit, flower color, and leaf shape to have once
been divided into a number of separate species: *howellii, finchii,
heckneri,* et al., and some taxonomists still consider this classification valid. Some species seem to have greater genetic flexibility
than others and almost, it would appear, make a game of experimenting with variations of all kinds.

Although such variations may be a headache to taxonomists,
they can be a joy to horticulturists and hybridists who are always
seeking a sweeter pea, a hardier, more prolific wheat, a wilt-
resistant squash, or—unfortunately—a less squashable tomato.
Rock gardeners, not satisfied with those plants which are naturally short, creeping, or bun-shaped, are forever searching for
more compact, dwarfed variations of plants that are normally tall
in stature, wide spreading in growth habit, or simply too vigorous to suit the somewhat precious limits of the ideal rock garden
plant.

Some variations that are beneficial to a plant may maintain
themselves by permitting such plants to outbreed their cohorts.
Other variations may be detrimental and usually vanish, as individuals bearing genes for such a variation are likely to lose the
battle for existence before they can produce progeny. In a few
cases, however, such a gene, a tendency for dwarfness, for example, which would prevent a plant from getting enough light to
exist among its taller companions, might prove beneficial to a
plant—one, say, whose seed landed on a mountaintop where

high, desiccating winds would cut down its normal, tall siblings. Such a plant could in time be the progenitor of a whole new species suited to that particular habitat. But under normal conditions a deleterious gene is swamped out either by the death of its bearer before it can reach breeding age or as a result of interbreeding with its healthier, better-adjusted kind. Just as human beings have developed social taboos to prevent intermarriage of close relatives—thus preventing the pooling of deleterious genes that might prove fatal or at least debilitating to the group—so plants have developed barriers to prevent or at least make difficult a plant's fertilization of itself.

Species within a genus can also usually interbreed. Although frequently prevented from doing so in the wild because of geographic separation or a difference in blooming period, such species frequently miscegenate quite happily if brought together in a garden. Even in the wild, species can mix, for example when a late flower of one species is still sexually active at the same time an early flower of another, related, species appears. Could such a cross give rise to a new species?

In theory, genera are not interfertile, and this is considered one of the characteristics that differentiate genera from species. Yet bigeneric crosses are possible, as witness the × *Phylliopsis,* the × *Heucherella,* and the × *Solidaster.* And some species within a genus will not hybridize, even when encouraged to do so by dint of human interference. Lepidote (scaly) rhododendrons and elepidote (scaleless) rhododendrons will not cross with each other nor with azaleas (usually), nor with the species in the Camtschaticum Series. Yet all are now considered by taxonomists to belong to the genus *Rhododendron.* Should this genus therefore be split into four separate genera?

It becomes increasingly evident as one discusses the problems faced by taxonomists that the classification of plants or animals is an artifact, a rigid structure that we attempt to impose on endlessly flexible organisms which by their very nature cannot be categorized. An inflexible organism is almost inevitably headed for extinction. Variation enables organisms to immunize themselves against disease. It is variation that enables plants to adjust to changes in their environment (and environments, as we know, change rather rapidly). Variation permits plants to colonize new ecosystems. Variation is the raw material of evolution. It is what has given us the rich flora that clothes nearly every ecological niche on earth, from the deserts to the lush rain forests, from sea level to mountain tundras, from the tropics to the poles. Variation may be a nuisance to those who wish to classify living matter into immutable, nameable groups, but it is also a fundamental reality of nature. It is primary. Variation is life itself.

Indeed, without variation, where would *we* be?

L.L.F.

PLANT NAMES

One of the problems with which I am faced as editor of the ARGS *Bulletin* is the swarm of plant names, botanical and colloquial, with which I am faced upon the arrival of every manuscript. Each name presents me with a number of decisions.

First, I must decide the orthographic form in which the name should appear. If it is a scientific name, I must be sure that the generic name starts with a capital letter and the specific name does not and that both are underlined so that the compositor will set them in italics. If there are more than two Latinized words in a botanical name I must discover if these denote a botanical form or variant, in which case they too must be italicized, as in *Aquilegia flabellata nana alba*. If, however, the additional name or

gled for years to reach agreement and at last, perhaps to avoid prolonging the battle over species and even genera, had to agree before they all died and were forced to pass on their lifetime notations to a new group of disputants. Their decision in most cases is to lump.

We, however, possess only the first three volumes of *Flora Europaea,* and though each volume contains an alphabetical index to the plants in that volume, including (in italics) their former names with a reference to page and section where they are described under their latest epithet, there is no general index for all three volumes, which is understandable. One must therefore know in advance in which volume to search, as these are arranged, in the best botanical tradition, by order and family. Unfortunately, neither your editor nor her able assistant, to whom such matters as nomenclature are usually left, have had courses in systematic botany; we learned our plants and their names one by one as we met them and never inquired into their family backgrounds. Consequently a search for a particular name through the pages of our three volumes of *Flora Europaea* is, for us, a tortuous and prolonged one. And *Flora Europaea,* as its name implies, covers only the plants of Europe. What of the flora of the Americas, Asia, the Middle East, Africa, Australia, and New Zealand? Our book shelves do not house the books that would give us information on the plants of the world, not even of the temperate regions, and the nearest botanical library is at least an hour and three quarters away.

What to do? Should we engage a team of taxonomic experts to check each article? This seems a little extreme and certainly time-consuming even if we could find the experts who would be willing to serve.

It is, indeed, a quandary of plant names.

L.L.F.

SOME PROBLEMS AND PLEASURES OF DRAWING
PLANTS

Anne Ophelia Dowden, who is, I think, one of the greatest botanical artists of this or any generation, has told me that she would love to be a gardener but has found that drawing and growing plants is an impossible combination of activities. I must agree.

Though it is a great convenience to have your models available at your doorstep, growing them there presents a number of problems to the gardening artist. Not the least of these is a psychological block. It is, of course, quite possible with some plants to cut off one or two flowering stems and, using these as models, draw a reasonable facsimile of a complete plant. But you cannot do this with an androsace or Kabschia saxifrage. Must you then dig up and pot that rare and precious plant you have nurtured from seed through parlous adolescence to healthy maturity so you can examine it closely and draw it with comparative ease? Or do you leave it growing where it is, deep in a bed of surrounding plants, and crouch beside it for hours on end trying the while not to crush its neighbors, your muscles cramping, the cold spring breeze congealing your fingers to stiff sticks or, in summer, the sun baking your brain and searing your eyeballs? And if you dare dig, can you also shake the soil from its roots and perhaps even wash them so you can see their structure? Unless you draw only weeds or those excess plants you should pull out anyway, such a traumatic decision is preliminary to almost every drawing. And even if you draw only those more common subjects, you are faced with yet another quandary. When you should be sketching, you should also be weeding or planting, and it is impossible to do both at the same time. Therefore your gardener

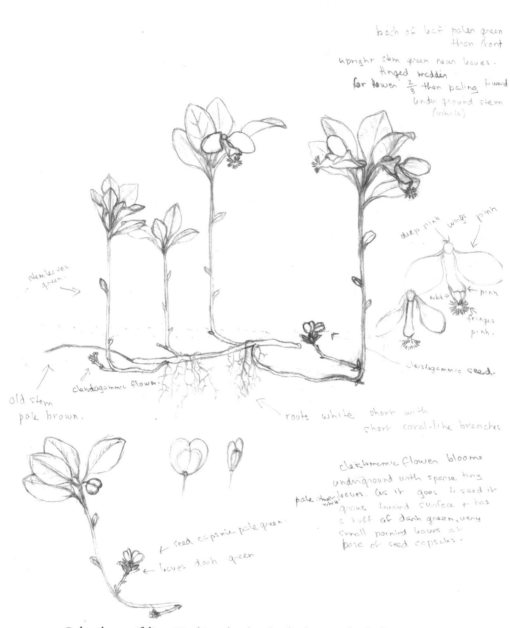

Polygala paucifolia   Working sketch. The final pen-and-ink illustration appears on page 280.

cum artist spends most of the spring, summer, and fall in a schizoid frame of mind, and in winter, when there is plenty of time to draw—well, that problem is obvious, for this botanical artist, at least, who finds it next to impossible to draw from anything but living material.

Even the nongardening botanical artist faces certain dilemmas. Though the evanescent character of flowers is an intrinsic part of their charm, it can also be most frustrating. How do you explain to an editor, who in July wants a picture of an hepatica, that it will be ten months before you can produce it? And, in spring and early summer, what are you to do when every day, indeed it seems almost every hour, another and yet another plant rushes into bloom? While you draw the bud its petals unfurl, and the flowers on other plants you intend to draw are fading. It is then that you wonder why you did not take up photography.

And why not? Why not catch on film each blossom at its moment of perfection and then, in the long months of winter when there is no press of growing things to distract you, leisurely, sitting in a warm room on a comfortable chair, translate these photographs into drawings and paintings? Alas, it doesn't work, at least not for me. I am forever trying to turn the photograph over to see how the petals are fastened at the back, or peering at the picture through a magnifying glass in a vain attempt to check the stance of the stamens. Is the tube of the flower glabrous or pubescent? Are there hairs on the leaves? If so, where? Are they long or short, soft or bristly? Few photographs offer this detailed information. Indeed, in most cases the foliage is as indistinguishable as a plateful of cooked spinach.

A good botanical text will usually supply the answers to some of these questions. The description of a plant will include such items as the shape of its leaves: whether they are flabellate, cuneate, cordate, ovate, obovate, lanceolate, lingulate, or spatulate and whether they are entire, pinnulate, or bipinnate with edges that are dentate, undulate, crenate, or serrate. Some botany books even provide a glossary so the lay reader can translate such terms. But even so you get very little notion of the precise leaf shape or the set of the foliage: whether it arches from the stem or thrusts out stiffly, whether it is limp or firm, how it twists to the light; all of which are important factors if a drawing is to give the feeling of a growing plant.

Although it is no substitute for a living model, a good descriptive botany is a valuable tool for the artist. Even with plant in hand it is wise to refer to a botanical text so as not to miss important clues to identification. In some cases these are quite subtle: the position of veins in a leaf, the proportion of one part of a flower to another, the type and placement of hairs on a stem. Such characteristics are easily overlooked but should be included and sometimes even slightly exaggerated in a botanical drawing.

There is no satisfactory stand-in for a living plant, but it is possible sometimes, by referring to several really clear photographs, a botanical text, and dried herbarium material, to reconstitute a plant's main features and delineate a reasonable likeness of its growing self. This is a tricky and uncertain business, and I always have a lingering uneasiness about a drawing thus made. Heaven knows it's hard enough to draw a decently accurate and lifelike picture of a plant when you can examine the living, breathing article, but if you have as a model only an assemblage of bits and pieces of information cobbled together with threads of memory and uncertain imagination, it is all too easy to go astray.

Thus it is with my drawing of *Dicentra cucullaria*. It was drawn in late winter to meet a publication deadline. Several photographs, two botanical texts, and some potted tubers had to serve in lieu of the plant. Come spring and Dutchman's breeches, I hastened to dig a plant and check the drawing for accuracy.

The picture was recognizable, but it was botanically incorrect. In fact, each mature cluster of tubers bears a single flowering stalk and *two* leaves. (Some of the flowering plants in the drawing had but a single leaf.) In reality, each leaf stem springs from the tip of a tuber, but the flowering stalk arises from *between* these leaf-bearing tubers. (In my drawing the flower stalk as well as the leaves rose from the tips of tubers.)

In digging a clump of plants, I also discovered that in addition to innumerable seedlings—each with an immature leaf attached to the single tuber and a number of small bundles of tubers each bearing a single large leaf—most of the mature flowering masses of bulblets have one or more smaller aggregations of tubers loosely attached, with a leaf springing from the tip of the highest tuber in each of these clusters. I also found that in every group of naked white bulblets there are several dark, flaccid bodies that appear to be the empty husks of spent tubers. Though some of the unattached single tubers have no accompanying husk, all those with a leaf have a dark skin fastened to the base.

These observations raise a number of questions. Does a seed produce only an underground tuber the first year? Does a tuber, having once produced a leaf, shrivel up so that its function, bearing the foliage needed for photosynthesis, must be taken over annually by another tuber in the cluster? Does a mature clump of bulblets break up after growing a flowering stalk, or does the same cluster flower year after year?

Of course, while such questions may be of interest to a gardener, they are probably not of vital consequence to an artist, who can certainly draw a leaf, root, or blossom without needing to know how it works. But for me such ramifications add immensely to the fascination I find in botanical drawing.

In addition, the mere act of examining a plant intently enough to delineate it accurately has the effect of opening my eyes in a most extraordinary way. It is as though a veil, which had previ-

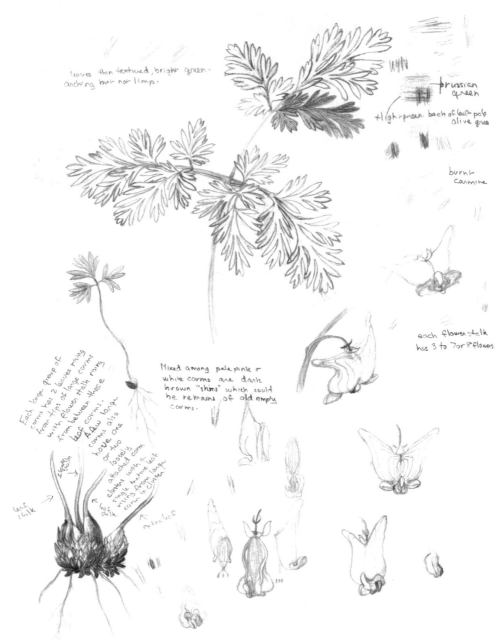

leaves thin textured, bright green. arching but not limp.

prussian green

light green, back of leaf pale olive green

burnt carmine

each flower stalk has 3 to 7 or 8 flowers.

Mixed among pale pink or white corms are dark brown "skins" which could be remains of old empty corms.

Each large group of corms has 2 leaves rising from tips of large corms with flower stalk rising from between those leaf corms. A few large corms also have one or two loosely attached corm clusters with a single texture large rising from large corm in cluster.

leaf stalk

leaf stalk

extra leaf

Dicentra Cucullaria   Working sketches executed in the field. This drawing shows the measures Laura Louise Foster took to record every detail of a plant and its blossoms.

ously dimmed my vision, is whisked away, and I can suddenly see with exquisite clarity, as if for the first time, the texture of petal and leaf, the style and stance of the plant itself, and the intricate beauty of blossom, fruit, and root system. And I think perhaps, at least in part, that it is this excitement engendered by the renewed ability to really see that makes botanical drawing such a pleasure to me even as I curse in frustration at my inability to transfer this vision onto paper accurately.

L.L.F.

SEED COLLECTING AND SEED CLEANING

As the seed exchanges of the various plant societies grow in importance and favor, the amateur contributors are annually faced with the rather fussy job of collecting and cleaning. The quality and fertility of the seeds in the offerings depend in large measure on the care with which these two steps are carried out; it does not seem amiss, therefore, to offer a few suggestions about procedures. These may also help some gardeners with a job that seems so mysterious and difficult that it dissuades them from making contributions.

It is, of course, necessary to keep an eye on ripening seeds so as to collect them as close to maturity as possible, but before they have scattered and vanished. Not all ripen at the same rate, and frequently not all seeds on a plant mature simultaneously. I have found, however, that it is not essential to gather every day. Once a week on a regular schedule is generally adequate, though some early-blooming plants do ripen their seeds very quickly and must be watched more closely. Dicentras will suddenly open their seed pods when they are still quite green on the outside. The same is true of bloodroot, violets, and geraniums. Although hepatica seeds begin to fall from the cluster while still quite green, most seeds change color when mature, and most seed capsules darken before opening.

I have found that it is quite possible to gather most seeds before they are completely ripe if one gathers the whole stem with the capsules adhering and puts them into a paper sack to mature. With campanulas, for instance, the last flowers will be opening when the seeds of the earlier flowers are fully ripe. If one cuts the whole flowering stem at this time and encloses it in a paper sack, the ripe seeds will fall out, and the rest will mature in the capsules. Seed in a pulpy fruit will also go on ripening if gathered on the branch. The same is true for the *Compositae,* many of which will be carried quickly away by the wind if left to ripen completely. It is wise to test by pulling gently a few seeds from the disk when the awns begin to change color. If they separate easily and the seed part is beginning to turn from green or white to brown, it is safe to gather. Seeds with awns or feathery stigmas can usually be pulled away from the disk when ripe and, without further cleaning, put into seed packets with appendages attached.

With some plants, such as poppies, shortias, trollius, many bulbous plants, and primulas, which open their capsules at the top, it is possible to wait until the pod opens and merely shake the ripe seeds into a coin envelope by bending over the stems.

Seed pod of *Trillium albidum.*

Seed pod of *Trillium ovatum.*

It is a good plan to have on hand a supply of paper sacks of various sizes for your collecting forays. These can be purchased reasonably from your grocer or hardware man, who generally has an assortment of sizes. As you gather your seeds, be sure to carry a pencil and write on the bag the full name of the plant from which you have collected the seed. Don't trust to memory.

Plunge flowering stems collected for post-ripening head-down into a paper sack of sufficient size to allow air around the heads to prevent mildew. Store them in an airy, dry room until ready for cleaning. There is no reason why most of them should not be kept thus until near the end of the collecting season so that all cleaning operations can be done at the same time.

Cleaning is, to be sure, an intricate and wearisome chore. If all seeds were of the same size and all loosened themselves from their moorings in the same fashion, the process would be simpler. The seeds of some plants, it is true, can be shaken from the ripe capsules or pulled loose quite easily, but most will not be parted from their holdings so simply. Because there are many gradations of size and shape, you do need a variety of equipment for this operation. Fortunately, except for the final packets into which you shuffle the cleaned seed, most of these implements are at hand in the kitchen or attic.

Upon a large table, preferably in a place where chaff and "flug" may freely scatter, congregate sieves and strainers of all sorts available, a smooth-sided colander, and a number of shallow cardboard boxes such as those used for handkerchiefs, socks, candy, soap bars, etc. Such boxes and their lids are most useful if they have a smooth finish on the inside surfaces. You should also have on hand a good magnifying glass.

Place the colander in a wide but shallow cardboard box and shake into it the dried seed heads from one of the sacks, making sure to search out stray seed caught among the bottom folds. Plunge your hand into the mass of dried heads in the colander and gently shift them back and forth, watching meanwhile to see if something resembling seeds falls through into the box. Without crumpling the seed heads, shift the colander to another empty box and study the contents of your first box through the magnifying glass. If you detect brown or black uniformly shaped objects, these are probably seeds. But not all seeds are of those colors. Common sense, however, and a perceptive eye aided by the magnifying glass will usually distinguish seed from chaff.

If most of your catch is seed, lift the box and its contents to mouth level with both hands. First tilt the box away from you until all the seed and chaff are at the distant end, then tip the box toward you on a slight angle and gently shake it from side to side while at the same time you gently blow across the tumbling slide. The heavier seed should roll downhill and congregate against the lower rim of the box; the chaff will be blown toward the top or off into space beyond the farther edge. Next, carefully, so as not to mix the separated piles of chaff and seed, tip the box sideways over two other boxes placed side by side so that the seeds falls into one and the chaff into the other. It is now quite simple to spill the seed into an envelope and the chaff into a nearby waste bin.

Frequently, unfortunately, the operation is not so simple. Often, upon examination of the first fall-through, you will find there is not enough obvious seed to justify the separation by blowing. You must then replace your catch in the colander, which still contains the material that did not sift through before, and manipulate the flower heads more forcefully to release the seed (if any). Again, study the fall-out through the magnifying glass. Now there will probably be a greater proportion of crushed leaves and other chaffy stuff, but there may be also a few seeds. At this point you may prefer, instead of blowing, to separate the chaff from the seed by sifting through one of your sieves. You can work it either direction. Either use a screen size to hold back the seed and by rubbing work through the broken "flug," or by shaking in a wider-mesh sieve let through the seed and hold back all but the finest blowable chaff. Sometimes it takes a number of successive operations with colander, sieves, blowing, and even finger pushing to separate the seed from the chaff. The process has its own fascination and is subject to refinements according to the ingenuity of each experimenter.

A few types of seed call for special treatment either in gathering, storage, or cleaning.

Seed contained in pulpy fruit is difficult to extract. If the ripened fruit is soaked in water until it has fermented, most of the pulp will disintegrate and you'll be able to rinse it off by putting the rotting fruit in a sieve under running water. The seed can then be spread out on a paper towel or newspaper to dry, and any remaining pulp will separate quite readily from the seed.

Some seeds, like those of dicentras and bloodroot, have a soft, fleshy appendage at the point of attachment. If this becomes dry, germination is greatly retarded, or the seed may even be destroyed. Clean such seeds as soon as they are ripe, and enclose them in a glass jar.

Seeds with thin coatings, like those of lewisias and dianthus, are easily crushed and damaged. Avoid using pressure when sieving; and when shipping protect the seeds from crushing during transit.

Rhododendron and some other *Ericaceae* have fine seeds enclosed in very hard capsules. In time they split and spill their contents, but this may be in very late fall or during the winter. The capsules may be gathered before they open but after they have changed from green to brown. If they are stored in a warm, dry place, they may split of their own accord or they may have to be forced open. This latter process is hard on the fingers but can be done by using pliers or a Mouli grater.

For storing and sending very fine seed like that of saxifrages, calceolarias, and ramondas, it is safest to put them in a small glassine envelope or fold them securely into a piece of waxed paper before placing them in the paper envelope on which the name of the seed is printed, carefully and clearly. And be sure, always, to be as accurate as possible in naming and spelling.

By following these directions or working out your own refinements of the process, you may be enriching the gardens of your fellow rock gardeners and deriving a real sense of satisfaction. You will also cheer the heart of the hard-working seed-exchange directors if you send in packets of carefully cleaned and labeled seeds.

H.L.F.

SEED SOWING

Growing plants from seeds can be both the most rewarding and the most frustrating of occupations.

The rewards are obvious. How else is one to acquire a population of some of the more exotic rock garden plants? And, just as the children of human parents vary in appearance, physical sturdiness, and personality, so too can seedlings from the same pod vary in growth habit, color of blossom, and tolerance to climates other than that of their natural habitat.

As you may know, both British and Czech rock gardeners grow superb *Lewisia cotyledon,* many of which are spoken of as hybrids: sturdy, cabbagy plants with large flowers in a rainbow selection of sunset colors. These are not hybrids but rather selections grown in gardens for many years from what was originally wild-collected seed. By attrition (the less amenable plants died young) and careful selection of seed from only the best of these garden-grown lewisias, a hardy race of glorious garden plants has emerged. Yet Roy Elliott has reported that even good British gardeners find it difficult to keep plants grown from seed collected in the wild. These plants need to become domesticated to the garden. We may eventually be able to grow and flower in our gardens even such impossible plants as *Eritrichium nanum* and *Diapensia lapponica,* especially if we grow them from seed collected originally from wild plants growing at the lower elevations in the most southerly extension of their range. A forlorn hope, perhaps, but has it been tried?

The frustrations of growing plants from seed are familiar to most of those who have tried it. Perhaps the most common complaint is of seed that does not come up as what it was purported to be.

This is forgivable if the seed has been gathered in the wild, particularly so if the collecting was done in unfamiliar territory. Professional collectors are either very familiar with the locality and with its plants or else try to scout the area in advance so as to identify and mark the plants while they are in bloom, returning later in the season in the hope that they will find again those same marked plants with ripe seed still attached. A chancy business.

Unfortunately, most of us visiting a strange or distant locale see the plants either in bloom or in seed, not both, and even quite knowledgeable botanists find it difficult to give a specific name to a plant seen only in seed. This accounts for the designation *sp.,* meaning species unknown, after a generic name in seed listings.

But misnaming garden-collected seed is less excusable. True, labels get lost and memories are fallible, and, unfortunately, plants acquired from nurseries, plant sales, and seed lists, even those of botanical gardens where students usually collect and clean the seed, are all too frequently misidentified. But after all, one has a garden-raised plant at hand and can study it in all seasons, so it should be possible to check its identification against the descriptions in texts when it is in bloom to make sure it really is what its name suggests. Surely it is better to spend a few minutes confirming the identification of a plant new to you than to continue the deception, even though unintentionally, by sending out seeds or plants under the wrong name. And surely it is not too much to ask, once the plant has been found true to name, to print that name clearly on the seed envelope, correctly spelled. The volunteers who man the seed exchanges are not, after all, cryptographers.

But misnamed seedlings are not the only frustration faced by the seed-sowing gardener.

When someone plants seeds for the first time he tends to hover over the garden plot or seed pan, examining it almost daily for signs of life, and he must frequently feel that the old adage, "A watched pot never boils," could be recast to, "A watched seed never germinates." But usually after a period of several weeks, if the directions on the seed packet have been followed and the soil has been faithfully kept moist but not waterlogged, he will be rewarded with the sight of tiny scraps of green thrusting up through the dirt. Not always, though, and many a neophyte gardener gives up and loses interest, and after a few months the pot goes unwatched and unwatered, and that is that. It may, indeed, be the last time he tries to grow plants from seed.

But even if this first seed sowing leads to success and consequent enthusiasm and assurance, when the gardener branches out into sowing seeds more exotic than the brightly packaged (and tested) vegetable and annual seeds from the local hardware store, he will learn to his chagrin that he may not always reap all he sows. Not all seeds come in neat packets with explicit directions for successful germination, and many an inexperienced gardener, having waited patiently a year for germination (for he has learned

some seeds require a winter to pass between sowing and germination) will throw out the potful if there are no signs of life that
first spring.

There may be many reasons why. In a few cases there simply
was no seed in the packet. This is not a case of deliberate hoax
on the part of the seed gatherer, but rather a case of misidentification. Many seeds are dustlike in size if not in shape, and without
a hand lens it is not always easy to tell if there is, indeed, any
seed mixed with the debris that results from the breaking up of
seed capsules and receptacles. Sometimes the seed itself has been
devoured by insects and those blackish specks, mistakenly identified as seed, are, in truth, the droppings of the departed diners.
Sometimes the seed was not fertilized, and there are only shriveled seed coatings as empty of life as a scarecrow's jacket. Or the
seed may have been gathered before it was sufficiently mature; or
conversely, the seed may have already dispersed, and all that is
left to put in the seed packet is "flug."

But even when the seed is present and viable it may not
germinate, because the requirements needed to break its dormancy may not have been met.

It is surprising how many people, even those who have gardened for several years, are appalled to learn that it may take
more than one spring to persuade some seeds to sprout. "Wait
two years for germination," they exclaim in horrified tones, and
you can see them make the instant mental decision to write off
any possibility of their growing *that* plant from seed. They have
yet to learn that without patience no one can truly call himself
a gardener.

Sometimes it takes more than patience to make a seed germinate. The phenomenon of seed dormancy and seed germination
is a complicated one still not completely understood; in many
cases we have yet to learn just what is needed to make the tiny

spark of life enclosed within a seed spring into action. We know some seeds need several alternating periods of heat and cold (sometimes of rather precise duration) to urge them into growth. Others need light to germinate. The seeds of some desert plants may wait years until a sufficient number of inches of rain soak them before they will sprout; some, indeed, require the scouring and abrading of floodwaters to summon them to life. The seed of some pines will germinate only if the cone in which it is enclosed is opened by the heat of a forest fire, which incidentally assures an open seed bed with no competition for the young pine seedlings.

Seeds may be prevented from germinating by something either present or lacking in the soil on which they fall. Some plants (black walnut is a notorious example) give off a chemical inhibitor that discourages the germination of many seeds that fall within its influence, particularly those of their own species. The seeds of others, such as *Jeffersonia* and *Adonis vernalis,* seem almost to require the benign influence of a parent and can hardly be persuaded to germinate except under their mother's skirts, where they sprout like cress. Some seed, such as that of *Dentaria,* refuses to be born into captivity and will not germinate in a pot, but will come to life quite readily if sown in the open.

Some seed is encased in an inhibiting covering and will not sprout until this coating has been stripped away, either by the crops and digestive juices of birds and animals or by the bacteria of decay.

Some seeds need specific soil temperatures to germinate. Grass seed needs a soil temperature above 50° Fahrenheit, and rhododendrons germinate best at temperatures above 70, while the seeds of many alpines seem to prefer a cool soil and will frequently sprout when it is still cold enough for the surface of the soil to freeze at night. Light intensity, too, and even day length appear to play a part in the germination of the seed of some plants. Year after year such seeds will send up their cotyledons simultaneously on a certain date no matter when they were planted.

Some seeds will sprout within a few weeks if planted immediately when they are ripe but will go into a stubborn dormancy if allowed to rest before planting. Others lose viability completely if not planted as soon as they are mature, while still others require an after-ripening period before they will germinate.

In most cases seed dormancy and the means by which it is broken make great good sense. It may be one of the many means whereby seed is scattered to start new colonies, or it may delay germination until a propitious time for the survival of the seedling, but in some instances the combination of mechanisms needed to break seed dormancy seems unduly complicated and difficult to achieve.

Field studies in West Cornwall, Connecticut, have brought to light a case in point. While conducting a study of the seed germination of pioneering species in a small plot within Gold's Pines, an ancient stand of *Pinus strobus,* Peter Del Tredici of the Arnold Arboretum of Harvard University was interested to note great numbers of seedlings of the sweet fern, *Comptonia peregrina,* among the annuals, biennials, and perennials sprouting in the area, which had been clear-cut and scraped by a bulldozer the previous fall to encourage white pine regeneration. Because the plot was completely surrounded by mature pines and hemlocks and there was no *Comptonia* in the vicinity, his curiosity was aroused.

Sweet fern, which is not a fern but a shrub closely related to bayberry, *Myrica pensylvanica,* and by some botanists put in the same genus, grows about three feet tall and spreads by deep underground suckers to form colonies in dry, sandy soil. It is not uncommon from Nova Scotia to Saskatchewan and south to Minnesota, the coast of North Carolina, and the uplands of

Georgia, and it has long been considered a pioneer species in sandy wastelands. The alternate, rather leathery leaves are long, slender, and deeply lobed. It is this leaf shape and their delicious spicy fragrance that gives *Comptonia* its colloquial name.

The seed of sweet fern is a hard nutlet contained in a burlike fruit formed by the eight bristly bracts that enclose it. When ripe, in July, these seeds fall to the ground under the parent plants at the slightest disturbance. As they are too heavy to be distributed by either wind or rain and are not particularly palatable to birds, insects, or beasts, they are likely to remain where they fall and, in time, to be covered by the litter of leaves and blowing dust and sand that collects around the parent plants. Yet a search for seedlings around a colony of mature plants is fruitless. Nor, as Mr. Del Tredici discovered, can the seed be germinated by means of any standard seed treatments under artificial conditions.

It has long been noted that the most likely place to find *Comptonia peregrina* seedlings is in disturbed, sandy soils. Henry Thoreau, that keen observer of all things natural, noted in his journal on October 22, 1860, that sweet fern was one of the first plants to come into railway cuts through the woods. Obviously the seeds germinate best on bare mineral soil in full light. Why then would they not sprout when sown under such conditions?

Mr. Del Tredici discovered that a powerful and long-lasting chemical inhibitor in the seed coat that surrounds the embryo prevents germination. As further insurance against premature germination the seed is enclosed in the hardened ovary wall. Not until these were removed would the naked embryo sprout, though Mr. Del Tredici found that soaking the seed in a solution of gibberellic acid neutralized the inhibiting chemical thus permitting the seed to germinate.

As gibberellic acid is not a usual component of soils, Mr. Del Tredici reached the conclusion that other soil chemicals could, over a sufficient period of time, also break down the inhibitor so that the seed could germinate as soon as it was brought to the surface, which in this case had taken place when the clear-cut area had been bulldozed.

How long a burial is needed to break the dormancy of sweet fern seed? Mr. Del Tredici does not say in his monograph, but in the case of the seed in Gold's Pines, West Cornwall, it was a very long time indeed; the trees that had shaded out the original colony of *Comptonia peregrina* ranged in age from 96 to 124 years when they were felled.

So, seed sowers, don't throw out that seed pan of ungerminated seed. Leave it in your will to your grandchildren and perhaps they will reap what you have sown.

L.L.F.

SEED-SOWING MEDIA

Everyone has his pet soil mixture for seed sowing, but very few media are ideal for all the different seeds we wish to grow. A mixture lean enough to discourage damping off may be difficult to keep from drying out too much, and no seeds will germinate without moisture.

After trying various sterile media, such as sifted ashes, baked soil, and mica, I finally discovered a seeding substance easy to work and maintain, free from damping off, practically weed free, and apparently congenial to many types of seed. This is ground-up sphagnum moss, not the commercial peat moss, but the green, growing moss of swamps and bogs.

This can be used as a two- to three-inch layer on top of a soil mixture, or it can be used for the whole content of pot, pan, or flat. The seeds are merely scattered directly on the surface. A shade glass over the container is beneficial until germination takes place. Practically no watering is necessary, as the sphagnum is like a sponge and holds a quantity of moisture without being soggy.

The surface must not be permitted to dry out, however, as it tends to form, when dried, an impervious crust.

Seedlings can be grown much closer together in this medium because there is no danger of damping off. The seedlings may be left in the sphagnum for a long time without damage, not making much growth unless chemically fed, but surviving nonetheless.

Transplanting is easy because a good root system is encouraged, and the sphagnum is so light that it comes away without much breakage of the fine rootlets.

Sphagnum is an ideal substance in which to grow members of the *Ericaceae,* most of which have fine seeds and like the acidity of the moss. However, plants which are normally lime lovers do not seem to resent the sphagnum. In fact, I have a pan of *Saxifraga aizoon* seedlings that have been growing in sphagnum for six months, and though they have made little growth are perfectly happy. Some already transplanted from this crowded pan made rapid growth immediately after being set out.

Sphagnum may not be the final answer to seed-sowing problems, but it does, for many types of seed, take away some of the headaches. For tree and shrub seeds it is especially recommended.

H.L.F.

LIGHT BOXES

This is partly a form of winter therapy for the impatient rock gardener, but it seems to be also a slick way to get a big jump on "hard-to" propagations.

It began a little over a year ago by coincidence when I received as a thrilling Christmas present a candy box full of immaculately wrapped and touchingly labeled Kabschia saxifrage cuttings, sixty different named sorts for which I had been angling.

In my basement I have a light box that I have used for some

years for starting rhododendron seeds. Normally I don't begin until about February 1 because, otherwise, the seedlings get too crowded before they can be moved on into outdoor situations when the weather is favorable. (That's a separate story.) This box is like a coffin with one side open, set upside-down on a platform. (My platform happens to be an old ping-pong table on saw-horses.) To the inside of the roof of this box is fastened a four-tube, four-foot-long fluorescent light fixture. The inside of the box is painted white for reflection. The front (open side) has a curtain of plastic attached at the top. A one-by-two fastened along the bottom of this plastic flap holds it flush to the table top when closed and perches on top of the box when the flap needs to be raised for working and watering.

The lights go on and off automatically by a timer. The consumption of electricity is minimal, and the results to date are fabulous, plus the added pleasure of frequent visits to the basement to pore over the rows of cuttings, to smell the damp growing atmosphere and to catch a very faint sun tan glow.

Last year I had almost 100 percent success with the new saxifrage cuttings, and many of them are about to bloom in the alpine house just a little over a year after their long overseas voyage. Because I was impatient to propagate some of my own new saxifrage hybrids, this year I began a new cycle between Christmas and New Year.

I snipped off a few cuttings from the various cultivars of saxifrage, some well-known named forms like *S*. 'Faldonside', 'Iris Prichard', 'Cranbourne', et al., for passing along to meet the growing interest, and some promising-looking seedlings: 6714, 6838, 6920, 7001. Each set of cuttings (only about twenty takes at a time) was put in a plastic bag with label listing name or number.

Then came the fascinating work of preparing and inserting the cuttings. Some Baggies contained up to ten usable cuttings, others only a single rosette daringly clipped off at the base of a tiny plant of last year's rooting or a two-year-old seedling.

Some sorts have a fairly long, bare base to the rosette and are easily stripped of any dead leaves, ready for insertion. Others are very tiny and may spare only two or three green leaves, pinched off by a sharp fingernail to expose a bit of base stem for insertion. (But rest assured, the smaller the cutting the more vigorous the rooting.)

In preparation for each batch of cuttings I filled a small standard plastic tray with drainage holes in the bottom. First a bit of peat to cover the bottom, then a standard soil mix one inch deep, then a layer of sharp sand, all pressed down firmly and watered by soaking from below. Each cutting after basal preparation was dipped in a rooting-hormone powder (this I don't think is necessary, but it permitted seeing the base of the cutting more clearly when inserting). Using a finishing nail of firm proportions, I stuck a hole in the sand deep enough to take the base of the cutting. Then the cutting, with excess powder shaken off, was pressed into the hole with the left hand (and when a cutting was really small, this meant pressing on top of a tiny rosette with the index finger) while sand was packed close around the base with the blunt top of the finishing nail.

Cuttings were lined up very close together with a label at the head of each row. Some rows had as many as three different labels. Into a flat of eight by five inches, three inches deep, one can get nine rows with up to six cuttings in each row. That makes an impressive fifty-four possible saxifrage plants. And you had better think about that a little in advance.

I ended up with 174 different cultivars in 14 flats, and there was still plenty of room in the light box. For the first week the lights were on for twelve hours daily. Then I increased this to fourteen hours. Rooting was very rapid, and all were ready for transplanting within six weeks. When transplanted, they, of course, are more widely spaced in similar flats, hence more room was needed. A second light box of similar construction was brought into service, because in the meantime the free space in the first had been filled with other things.

Among these were, for instance, seed of *Dionysias* from the Gray-Wilson 1971 expedition sowed in early December and given some freezing exposure in a cold frame before they were put under the light during the first week in January. Germination occurred in ten days, at least for three of the species. There is always a question of whether there is any seed at all among the packets of chaff and flug that are swept from *Dionysia* cushions, apparently the accepted method of collecting seed from these plants.

The big advantage of the light box, at least for the saxifrage cuttings, is that you can give them a long day and at a time when, after dormancy, they are full of vigor. Also you can control the moisture, can work on them in comfort, can give them proper attention during an otherwise slack time in the gardening year, and can get them growing on well before the trying summer months.

Another year I'll try this method on such things as *Androsaces* and those difficult to root *Acantholimons*.

H.L.F.

BOG HOPPING

Although the plants which make their homes in the quaking bogs may be ruled out of the rock garden of the purist, for the less precise there are charming herbs and shrubs of small stature which can be transported to the drier conditions of the rock garden with a good chance of success and certainly much delight.

It is in the coolness of the bog, uncrowded by the coarser vegetation and competition of meadow and forest, that we find many plants of boreal association and relatives of true alpines. In fact, as we wander around one of the extensive quaking bogs where, because of the actual starvation, all the plant life is dwarfed, there is a feeling of separation from the ordinary and crowded and gross, a feeling of intimacy with trees and shrubs that rise no higher than our knees, a feeling of space and proportion. Except for the wet, yielding carpet of sphagnum moss, we might be wading through the *krummholz* near the timberline of some high peak.

Here in the quaking bog are the open areas of vari-tinted sphagnum moss, spattered in season with the brilliant blooms of *Calopogon* and rose pogonia, the bright yellow of the grape-scented *Utricularia,* tiny spangled leaves of the sundew amid the fat, gaudy traps of the pitcher plant. The dazzling white of the tall white fringed habenaria is a startlingly beautiful sight against the late-summer green of stunted larch or bog spruce. Few of these herbaceous plants, especially the orchids, will lend themselves to the ordinary conditions of the alpine garden. They require a special site which, when carefully placed and well constructed, need not clash with the general setting of the rock garden.

In what is a natural small valley amid some higher rises of the rockwork, or beside a stream or pool if the garden is fortunate to have such a feature, a miniature bog is simple enough to make. An old wash tub or a hogshead sawed in half may be sunk in the ground with no part of it rising above the surface to reveal its presence. This can be filled with commercial peat and a carpet of growing sphagnum laid on top to give the final natural setting for these plants which require a constant supply of underground

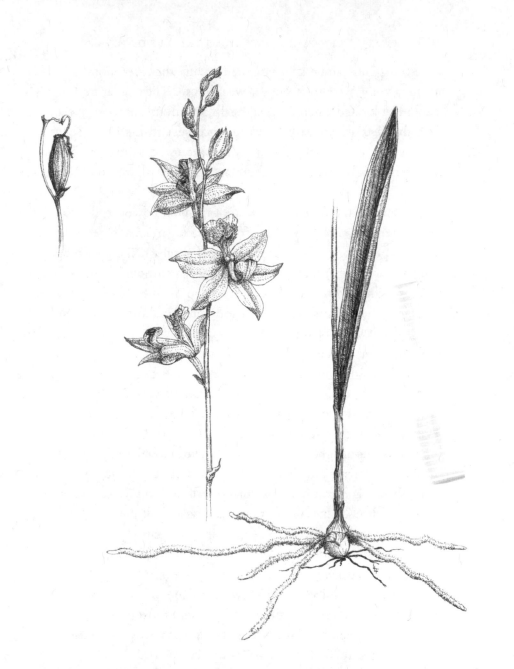

Calopogon tuberosus This orchid is native to acid bogs, swamps, and wet places in the northeastern United States.

moisture. This can be kept saturated during the drier months by turning the hose into it once a week or so. The miniature bog should be located where it receives almost full sun, as most of the bog dwellers are accustomed to full exposure to the light. Such a structure in the rock garden will prove to be a further boon as a remarkably happy spot for many difficult alpines that like an acid soil.

It is among the shrubby material of the bog, however, that we find the most satisfactory plants for the rock garden. There in the bog, in great tangled masses, the dwarf shrubs make charming patterns of color and texture. The leather leaf, though not spectacular with its coriaceous rusty leaves and small early-blooming bells, is a desirable shrub for various sites in the rock garden, especially if some of the denser, more dwarf strains are searched out and selected. Here is a field for some enthusiast to pursue. The plant is so common and so varied in most bogs that a good strain should be located, one which would be best suited to the rock garden. It grows perfectly well in full sun or part shade, even in fairly dry sites, as long as it has an acid soil.

Among its neighbors is the tiny-leaved bog laurel, *Kalmia polifolia,* the first of the laurels to bloom, with a delicate, beautifully shaped and colored blossom—a rich pink on darker, long, slender pedicels. This laurel, if cut back when collected from the bog, where it is likely to get leggy in competition with other shrubs, will remain quite compact and low in the drier condition of the rock garden.

Perhaps the choicest of the dwarf woody plants is the bog rosemary, which creates in the wild masses of a smoky green, a blue-green as though bathed in fog. Hung with early-blossoming pink lanterns, the bog rosemary is a thing of real delight.

Others, too, the labrador tea and sheep laurel, should be carefully selected for stature and more especially for color. These may all find a welcome in the rock garden if carefully placed and given acid soil, not too rich in order to keep their stature low.

H.L.F.

CONSERVATION

As gardeners, most of us are tempted time and time again to move into our personal landscapes the lovely wildlings of forest, swamp, and mountain, no matter how rare, and most of us succumb at least occasionally to the temptation. The more choice, rare, and difficult the plant, the greater the challenge to try to grow it, and all too frequently we dig up or buy from so-called "wildflower nurseries" plants which should better be left *in situ*.

Most rare and difficult plants are rare in the wild and difficult to tame because they have over aeons developed genetic characteristics that make it possible for them to grow in particular sites. In so doing, they have frequently cut off their options so they can grow only under these very specific conditions, conditions which may be limited both in number and extent in the wild and almost impossible to replicate in the average garden. Temperature of both soil and air, light factors, day length at various seasons, moisture, both in the atmosphere and in the soil during certain periods of growth and dormancy, soil composition and chemistry, fungal and bacterial components, and other subtle influences may, singly or in combination, play a part in the well-being, even the existence, of such plants.

It is, of course, true that certain plants are endangered not so much by their collection as by the increasing destruction of their special habitats. Lumbering and agriculture, draining, filling, and the construction of highways, factories, airports, marinas, shopping plazas, and homes all play a part. But one has only to read some of the articles in conservation journals to realize that collecting also plays a role in the disappearance of some of our flora. The wanton, wholesale digging for the trade of rare cacti in our American deserts and the present vogue for growing plants, among them some of the smaller and uncommon insectivorous species, in closed glass containers have resulted in the drastic depletion of some species in the wild. And these are but two examples of the detrimental effect of commercial collecting for the gardening trade. What is particularly sad is that most of these plants are badly dug and carelessly stored and shipped, and that they will, to a great extent, be bought by people who have no knowledge of their value or how to grow them, people who will treat them as a passing fancy soon to be discarded on the rubbish heap.

But even some of our more dedicated gardeners are no better: the plant is beautiful and rare in gardens, and they covet it for their own. How well I remember one such gardener. She had asked us if we would take her into one of our local sphagnum bogs—we have very few in our area, and they are not easily accessible. We agreed, and one summer day, after a tortuous drive over twisting dirt roads, we plunged down the thickly forested slope that enclosed the bog. As we reached the bottom of the embankment, we saw growing in the deep, cool leaf mold under a thicket of laurel, a single plant of *Habenaria orbiculata,* the tall, slender spike of long-spurred, long-lipped flowers rising from between the two basal leaves, round and large as butter plates, pressed flat to the ground. We pointed it out to our gardening acquaintance, telling her it was an excessively rare orchid in Connecticut, that it grew, as far as we knew, only in this one small area and nowhere else in the state. As we looked at the orchid, the breeze ruffled the tree branches above our heads and a vagrant sunbeam shone for an instant on the plant, lighting the delicate greenish white flowers so they gleamed like phosphorus against their dark background.

"Oh, how beautiful," she exclaimed, "how I would love to have it." She fell on her knees beside the habenaria and, noting the greedy shine in her eyes, we hastened to explain that it should not be dug, not only because of its rarity, but because it would not survive transplanting. "I'm sure I could make it grow," stated this gardener, but she reluctantly got up and followed us down into the bog.

After several hours of squelching and bouncing through the floating mat of sphagnum, admiring the *Calopogon,* bog rosemary, bog and sheep laurel, wild calla, buckbean, round- and spatulate-leaved sundews and pitcher plants, we returned to the shore and changed into dry shoes before starting up the slope. Our companion was already heavily laden with trophies, but as we came to the habenaria she couldn't resist.

"I just know I can make it grow," she exclaimed, and before we could stop her, she had plunged her hands into the leaf mold on either side of the plant and ripped it up. Our return to the car was pregnant with gloomy silence on our part and bubbling enthusiasm on hers. Needless to say, we never took her on another field trip, and the orchid and all her other collections died, as we knew they must. We knew her garden: on an exposed rocky hillside with a small, evanescent trickle of a brook, dry except in spring, under a few thin poplars at the foot of the rocky outcrops.

The miracle is that so many plants from varied climes *will* do in our gardens; that plants from the deserts of southwestern North America, the sun-baked hills of the Mediterranean basin, the cool forests of the Appalachians, and the peaks of the Alps, the Himalayas, and the Sierras will grow, practically cheek by jowl in our gardens, with others from the islands of Japan, the Aleutian Peninsula, and the sandy coastal plains of mid-Atlantic United States. But not all plants will do in all gardens, and it behooves us as responsible gardeners to discriminate among those available and decide which are likely to live in our particular situation. To persist in trying to grow plants that will not survive in our climate and terrain is foolish, and if the plants are rare it is almost akin to murder—a type of herbicide, if you will.

Certainly there are occasions when rare plants should be rescued from the advancing blades of bulldozers or logging equipment, but one must be very careful not to rationalize such rescues. One must beware the little devil of temptation who whispers, "It is growing very near the road and will surely be destroyed if I do not dig it up and take it home"; or, "If I don't take it, someone else, less capable of growing it than I, certainly will"; or, like the avid gardener who dug the habenaria, "If I leave it here, no one will ever see it to enjoy it. I'm sure I can make it grow in my garden, where I and my friends can see it." Perhaps, if the plant is truly growing in a site doomed to imminent destruction, it might be better to move it, but not necessarily into our garden. Transfer it rather to another suitable and safer place in the wild, perhaps on protected land, and there nurture it until it becomes established.

In any case, unless a specimen is one of a particularly good form in a widespread population, it is better to collect the seeds of a wild plant, or to take layers or cutting material for propagation, or dig one or two young plants rather than take a mature plant at a time when it is in full growth (probably in flower); a time usually unsuitable for transplanting. And by all means propagate it and pass it around rather than succumbing to the temptation of being able to boast that you have the only specimen.

Many plants now fairly common in cultivation have, for one reason or another, become rare or even extinct in the wild: *Shortia galacifolia, Franklinia alatamaha,* and *Ginkgo biloba* come to mind. And many superb forms, such as the double-flowered *Sanguinaria canadensis multiplex* and 'Cole's Prostrate' hemlock, would have lived and died without producing progeny except that they were rescued *and disseminated* by knowledgeable, dedicated gardeners willing to take the pains to grow and propagate their finds.

So think carefully and responsibly before digging up or purchasing wild plants for your garden. The role of a good gardener is to nurture plants. Let us not be counted among their destroyers.

L.L.F.

MUS MUSCULUS

The mouse, in his place, is a bewitching fellow, in Disney films or on Christmas cards, but not in the garden or alpine house. Unless I harden myself to undertake a steady campaign of traps, beginning in early fall, mice move into the relative comfort and the sybaritic banquets of the alpine house. They know a good thing when they see it or smell it. If you whap off the early invasion, another will swarm in to the empty niche with the next warm spell. And so on through the winter. You dare not relax, and as the winter lengthens the mice grow hungrier and hungrier for a bit of vitamin-rich greenery.

They do enjoy a well-balanced diet and will, between courses of salad, dig down into the soil of pots for buried seeds or worms. This kind of appetite does outweigh caution. I have found that snap-traps baited with a fat sunflower seed wedged into the trigger are irresistible even in the midst of plenty. I have tried other baits such as peanut butter, raisins, and the usual cheese, but all these seem to lose their attraction with age. Not so the tempting sunflower seed.

I am convinced, however, that there is one sort of food for which a mouse will shun even a sunflower seed, and that is a phlox seed. For a number of years when I was experimenting with crosses among the various phlox species, I found that even amidst traps temptingly baited mice would slither their way under any protective covering and head for those pots that had "Phlox" on the label, choosing them from among a mixed assortment of seed plantings. There would be miniature craters in the soil, surrounded with the boatlike husks of the phlox seed.

Occasionally I foiled them and germinated some of those hybrid seeds. I remember one year how I glowed with anticipation when there were two flourishing seedlings of a cross I had made between short-styled *Phlox triovulata* that went on flowering well in the alpine house and finally overlapped the flowers of short-styled *Phlox nivalis* blossoming outdoors to supply the pollen. Those two seedlings were to be the beginning of a whole new revolution in the phlox world. In the fall I moved into the alpine house those two stalwart seedlings well spaced in a four-inch plastic pot. Was it a mistake and an invitation to leave plunged beside them that label marked *P. triovulata* × *nivalis* 'Avalon'?

Mice surely cannot read, especially my handwriting. Nevertheless from whatever motive, at a certain hour during the night of November 20, or perhaps the 19th, in 1966 (or was it 1967?) a mouse or mice of unknown identity did consume, devour, munch the aforesaid seedlings down to stumps. No vestige of green or life was left. From the decapitated stubs of those two plants, though they were carefully nurtured and watered through the winter and spring, no visible evidence of life ever again displayed itself.

And meantime, though *P. nivalis* continues to thrive, the parent plant of *P. triovulata* has, alas, departed this world. Someday I may be able to try that cross again.

That magnificent form of our native New Mexican, *P. triovulata,* which in some remote past found its way to the cherish-

ing hands of English rock gardeners and hence once into mine,
is probably the most beautiful dwarf phlox of all the tribe. But
like so many real beauties, human or floral, it has a genetic or
temperamental fragility. To have married it with a lovely but
more plebeian member of the tribe seemed a worthy enterprise.

But I was defeated by mouse or mice unknown. Do you
wonder I trap them?*

H.L.F.

THE CHANGING YEAR

Here in the Northern Hemisphere the sun has been steadily
slipping south as the summer advances, and now its rays are less
direct, temperatures are gradually sinking, and the days draw in.
To this cooling and shortening of daylight hours the inhabitants
of the plant world respond according to their kind.

Annual plants, having bloomed and set and scattered the seed
of future generations, will shrivel to dry husks with the first hard
frosts, their brief life span over, but perennial plants, in order to
survive the cold months, are preparing for winter dormancy.

Many reduce transpiration by discarding the lush green leaves
they produced in spring to take advantage of the long, warm,
sunny days of summer for essential photosynthesis. Here in New
England, deciduous trees and shrubs flame briefly in mid-October
with the phoenix fire of autumn. The conflagration spreads from
the cooler lowland swamps until the hills, too, catch fire and burn
scarlet, crimson, and gold before the leaves fall like spent embers

---

*In the authoritative work, *The Mammals of the Eastern United States,* by W. J. Hamilton, Jr.,
I find on page 321 these comments about the red-backed mouse: "Merriam remarks on the tender
and well flavored flesh of this mouse. I have sampled the meat but I found the picking too lean
to pass judgment on its merit." It gives me an idea.

to the ground below. Herbaceous perennials lose not only their leaves but also their soft top growth, though not as spectacularly. In some it dies away completely, leaving only a resting bud at or beneath soil level; in others the leaves and stems retreat to a winter rosette close to the ground where it is out of the wind and can receive some remnant warmth from the earth and, in most seasons, protection of winter snow.

Though evergreens do not reduce the surface from which transpiration takes place, some change the color of their leaves in winter. These may turn darker or redden with anthocyanin, which permits them to absorb more readily the warmth of the sun's weak rays.

Both evergreen plants and those that reduce their above-ground tissues must make additional adjustments in order to survive the icy blasts of winter, however. They "harden off," a complicated process entailing physical and chemical changes within the cells. The protoplasm—the essential substance of the cell—develops low structural viscosity to better withstand the deformation of freezing, and the cell walls themselves become more permeable to permit the rapid resorption of water from melting intercellular ice crystals. The free water content of the tissues decreases, and there is an increase in the soluble proteins and sugars, which act as an antifreeze, in the sap. There are, in addition, small increases in osmotic pressures within the cells, which may enable them to more readily absorb moisture from frozen soil. All these techniques increase the plant's ability to withstand desiccation as well as frost. It is essential that plant tissue stay moist if the plant is to remain viable. This is one reason a snow cover is so helpful to wintering plants.

But in addition to these ploys that help the plants withstand the winter months, other more long-range preparations are going forward. Growth buds, wrapped in protective layers of scales, sometimes waxed, varnished, or woolly to retain moisture in the vital tissues, are being formed in readiness for the next growing season, and food is being stored in roots and overwintering stems and leaves in preparation for the resurgence of spring.

And just so the gardener, too, must look ahead. In addition to cleaning and putting away his tools, battening down the storm windows, renewing the woodpile, and getting the winter woollies out of moth balls, he should prepare for the next season of growth. While the garden is dormant and, with luck, muffled in snow, he should not settle into indolent waiting. Winter is the time to store his mind with information about new plants to try.

In the waning days of autumn the gardener should start collecting beside his easy chair: paper and well-sharpened pencils for taking notes, books for reference, and plant lists and catalogues. He should try to track down those books he wants in his library for permanent reference: those in print, from his bookstore or directly from the publishers; those no longer in print, from secondhand bookstores or book finders. He should borrow from his friends, his lending library, or the ARGS-PHS (Pennsylvania Horticultural Society) Library Service those books he wishes to examine for possible purchase, and those he wants to check through but not necessarily to own. In addition to collecting books, he should send to the advertisers in our *Bulletin* for their catalogues, which frequently make for informative and exciting reading during the nongardening months, and he should send in orders for those new plants he wishes to try. He should buy Bernard Harkness's *Seed List Handbook* and check in it those seeds he wants so he'll be ready to send in his order as soon as the lists arrive from the seed exchanges. Those fortunate enough to have a file of back copies of the ARGS *Bulletin,* should get them down from the attic and dust them off. They make wonderful winter and bedside reading and are full of useful firsthand information.

And he should always keep that pencil and paper handy for taking notes.

Now that Autumn is here—prepare for Spring.

L.L.F.

AND SO TO BED

Here it is the last week of November, and the garden has assumed, slowly, a new face. It has been a fine, gradual autumn. Rains have come, well spaced and gentle. There have been gray days and blue, blue days.

The fall foliage was as splendid as ever I remember it. (Was it ever any less, any year?) Now the last loose leaf is down; only a few reluctant shreds hang brown on apple and an oak and on scattered shrubs. There is still color in persistent leaves of azaleas and geraniums. The greens of conifers and broadleaved ever-greens are now the accent amidst the lichen-molded gray of rock and the russet carpet of down leaves out on the fringes of the garden where the forest fingers down from the mountain.

No leaves now carpet the open rock garden; only the maple keys (which chipmunks by day and, I surmise, mice by night are vacuum cleaning) are left from the fall drop on the rock garden proper. Beds under the pines, where needles form a bolstering mulch, are permitted to retain their catch of leaves. Here are mostly the plants that in their native homes receive a cover of leaves from tree and shrub. Most other leaves have been gathered up and tossed into the billowy heaps of the two compost piles.

There is a different radiance to the rock garden at this somber season when the lushness of summer is spent. Now each fretted blade of the saxifrage rosette is firm and precious. The silver fur on the *Oenothera caespitosa* seedlings is like premature hoarfrost. The new silvered whorl of needles on the fans of the two young *Anacyclus* are elegant in design.

As the structure in the shorn tree stands starkly beautiful, each separate plant now has a new identity undiminished by a burst of bloom. Even the laggard species which deny their flowering, *Primula clusiana* and *Gentiana acaulis,* have their stance and promise.

The late gentians are done. *G. scabra,* a week ago, was a wheel of magnificent blue amidst the brown of fallen leaves. *Gentiana farreri* and *G. ornata,* lush of leaf, refused to flower this year.

Others, forward in a flowerless season, too eager to bloom, flaunt a fall blossom. Here amidst a bed of youthful vigorous *Primula acaulis* are precocious individuals, one with a flamboyant head of deep, deep blue and another of spotless white flowers. Or here, an out-of-season gift of phlox blossom, or a single blue star of *Houstonia.* One longs to still their eagerness but loves them for their daring. *Iberis saxatilis,* and a hybrid of it, will yearly yield a spate of fall bloom.

Now more than ever the firm ruggedness of rock, unadorned, makes clear its rightness or its wrongness. Now is the time to take the measure, not of bloom, but of structure. Now the bare bones of the garden, like the inner frame of a handsome woman, take the eye.

At this time of year one moves through the garden full of remembrance and anticipation. It is not very difficult to recall those days of early May when here was almost too riotous a blanket of blossom, and the senses jangled under the demand. Only in certain nooks is there subtlety then. Now in late November every sweep is gentle with the variety of quiet texture and subtle shape. But most of all there is the promise.

Along this path are the new seedlings which have never before bloomed here, new townsendias, each a cup of buds ready to be touched by the first spring warmth, new little tuffets of various sorts: erigerons, anemones, dianthus, aethionemas, campanulas, penstemons, and others, all in youthful health.

Along the other path is a whole new aspect, created last summer, of two raised beds on low, planted walls, one of acid rock backed with acid soil, the other, satisfactorily harmonious, of weathered limestone. This is one of those additions, either a revision of past mistakes or an entirely new extension (for whichever purpose, always an annual demand), built not only to satisfy the everlasting discontent of the rock gardener but to provide at last that perfect site for the new seedlings and special cuttings which beguiled so much attention. From the February sowing of the seed till their final domestication in August, they won a deal of fretful attention. Now, with only a daily benediction, even if every one shrivels beneath the blasts of an unprecedented winter, or if mice move in in hungry hordes beneath a shelter of snow, they make November a wonderful month.

Who could ask for more of remembering and anticipation than two new beds crammed with such precious jewels as these from cuttings or this year's seedlings:

Saxifraga oppositifolia, sancta, valdensis, schleicheri, hostii, biasolettii, longifolia, elizabethae, boeckleri, rocheliana, lingulata, chochlearis minor, grisebachii, 'Riverslea', and 'Cranbourne'; *Draba polytricha, mollissima, athoa, oligosperma, dedeana, rigida, borealis, rupestris,* and *incerta; Dianthus callizonus, neglectus, glacialis,* and *alpinus; Campanula elatines glabra, cenisia, planiflora alba,* and *aucheri; Primula pubescens, minima, hirsuta, cottia, clusiana, marginata, pedemontana, wulfeniana, glaucescens,* and *villosa commutata.*

And there are many others in this new raised limy bed, young and full of life at this point; *Penstemon pinifolius, Soldanella alpina, Myosotis rupicola, Globularia nana, Aethionema* 'Warleyensis', *Silene acaulis, Asperula pontica, Anemone vernalis, Geum reptans, Saponaria ocymoides* 'Rubra Compacta' and *Androsace sempervivoides.*

Many of these same species and others, such as gentians and the dwarfest of *Ericaceae,* are being tried in the companion wall bed of acid rock and soil.

Will spring ever come?

H.L.F.

WINTER

"Now is the winter of our discontent. . . ." Thus quoth Will Shakespeare, and though the Bard of Avon may have left the actual weeding to Anne Hathaway (he had, after all, plenty of other things to do, what with writing all those plays and sonnets and dancing attendance on Good Queen Bess), he was surely a gardener at heart. He certainly knew his plants, both wild and cultivated, and though he waxed lyrical on the joys of spring and summer, for the damp and cold blustery winds of winter he had very little good to say.

Yet winter has its compensations even for the most dedicated gardener. It gives one time to catch up on nongardening activities, to cease the frenetic pace of weeding, watering, pruning, mowing, transplanting, repotting, and dividing; it gives one time to plan.

If we lived in one of those salubrious climates where—according to the advertisements—it is spring year 'round, we would never catch up. Dust would felt the furniture and curl in windrows from beneath the beds; window panes would become impenetrably opaque, unanswered letters would topple in sliding piles from desk to tabletop; the floor of the barn would probably collapse under the weight of oddments accumulated against the day when there will be time to tidy up. If it were not for winter our family would probably disown us and our friends—those few who do not share our addiction—would undoubtedly desert us permanently, for during the growing season we are so in-

The cemetery near Millstream House.

volved in our near-monomania that we socialize hardly at all and tend, moreover, to be rather dull as dinner partners. Soil mixtures, watering schedules, and fungus diseases are not exactly sparkling topics for general conversation.

Fortunate, therefore, are gardeners who make their home where weather closes down the gardening season for several months of the year. Consider, if you please, a garden in which weeds never cease to spring, where trees, shrubs, and vines grow exuberantly and insects proliferate unchecked from year's end to year's end. And consider the gardener in such a garden.

Thank Heaven for winter, when we can sit quietly and ease our aching knees and backs, with time to peruse seed lists, read, visit friends, write letters, and dream of yet more perfect gardens.

L.L.F.

GLOSSARY

ACID SOIL *See* pH.

ACUTE Terminating in a sharp point; as of a leaf, bud, or other portion of a plant.

ALKALINE SOIL *See* pH.

ALPINE Above treeline in mountainous areas.

ALPINE-HOUSE A well-ventilated, cool greenhouse where winter temperatures may go as low as 20°F.

ALPINE LAWN An area planted to resemble a flowery mountain meadow.

ALPINE PLANTS Plants native to mountainous areas, usually above treeline.

ALTERNATE LEAVES Leaves placed at regular intervals along a stem with none springing from the same point (1).

ANTHER The pollen-bearing portion of the stamen (2).

AWL-SHAPED Tapering rather abruptly to a sharp point (3).

AXIL, AXILLARY The angle between a stem and a leaf or another stem (4).

BASAL LEAVES Leaves growing directly from the crown of a plant or from the lowest section of the stem (5).

BATTER The slight backward slope of a wall.

BEDDING-PLANE The angle of the layers (strata) in sedimentary rock.

BIPINNATE Characterizing a leaf deeply cut into segments or leaflets, which are in turn cut into subleaflets (6).

BLUESTONE A hard bluish-gray stone frequently crushed to surface driveways.

BONSAI An artificially dwarfed and shaped tree or shrub grown in a pot; originally an oriental art.

BORAGE-LIKE Resembling plants of the Borage Family; hairy-leaved herbs with 5-petaled flowers like forget-me-nots.

BOULDER FIELD An area formed primarily of loose rocks of all sizes, whether broken and angular or weatherworn and smooth, among which fine particles of decayed vegetable, animal, and mineral matter have been deposited.

BRACT A leafy structure, usually green but sometimes brightly colored and petal-like, closely connected with the flowering part of a plant, occasionally large enough nearly to conceal the flower (7).

BULB, BULBOUS A swollen underground leaf bud made up of fleshy scales which remains dormant until favorable conditions urge it to spring into growth (8).

BULBLET A small bulblike structure usually borne in leaf axils on the stem.

CALCICOLE Found growing only in limestone soils.

CALYX (PL. CALYCES) The outer section of a flower, made up of sepals that are usually green and frequently joined together at the base to form a lobed tube (9).

CAMPANULATE Bell-shaped or cup-shaped.

CARTILAGINOUS Hard and tough but flexible.

CILIATE Fringed with hairs along the margin (10).

CLASPING LEAF A leaf whose base partially surrounds the plant stem (11).

CLONE A group of plants all of which have been derived by vegetative propagation from a single individual.

COMPOSITE, COMPOSITAE A plant belonging to the Compositae Family, the flowers of which are densely packed into a head resembling a single flower. For example, aster, daisy, dandelion, goldenrod.

COMPOUND LEAF A leaf divided into several separate leaflets (12).

CONIFER A cone-bearing tree, such as pine.

CORDATE Heart-shaped (13).

CORIACEOUS Leathery in texture.

CORM A solid fleshy enlargement formed underground at the base of the stem (14).

COTTONSEED MEAL A fertilizer made of cottonseed pulp from which the oil has been extracted; particularly good for conifers and acid-loving plants.

COURSE In wall construction, a continuous band of stones or blocks laid side-by-side.

CRENATE With rounded teeth along the margin (15).

CRENULATE Finely crenate.

CROSIER A shape like a bishop's staff or shepherd's crook (16).

CROWN The thickened junction of stem and root (17).

CRUCIFER A plant belonging to the Mustard Family, the flowers bearing four petals and four sepals in the form of a cross (18).

CUNEATE Wedge-shaped, with the narrow angle at the stem end (19).

CUTTING A part taken from a plant for propagation purposes.

CUTTING-FRAME An enclosed container into which light may penetrate, filled with a special soil-mix in which cuttings are inserted for propagation.

CYLINDRICAL Shaped like a cylinder (20).

CYME A broad, more or less flat-topped flower cluster in which the central flowers open first (21).

DAMPING-OFF Collapse and death of seedlings due to parasitic fungi encouraged by wet conditions and overcrowding.

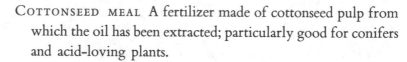

DECIDUOUS Losing its leaves for a portion of the year; opposite of evergreen.

DECUMBENT Reclining but with the tip ascending.

DEFLEXED Bent downward.

DENTATE Sharp-pointed teeth, as along the margin of a leaf, usually pointing outward (22).

DIE-BACK The death of young shoots due to disease or other adverse conditions.

DISK An enlargement of the receptacle of a flower which surrounds the ovary. In composite flowers, the central part of the flower head (23).

DIVISION Separating a plant to form two or more plants, each complete in itself.

DRY WALL A wall in which the stones are fitted together without the use of mortar.

DRY WELL An excavation filled with loose rock into which water is drained and from which it then seeps into the soil.

DUFF The layer of partly decayed vegetable matter found on the floor of a forest.

EDGING The removal of weeds and grasses that grow into the edge of a flowerbed by slicing down through the top growth and roots with an implement such as a sharp spade and entirely digging out all weed growth within this cut edge.

ELLIPTICAL Oval in shape, rounded about equally at both ends (24).

ENCRUSTED Coated with a hard, limy crust on the edges.

ENDEMIC Native to a particular region.

EQUISETUM-LIKE Resembling *Equisetum*-horsetail (25).

ERICACEOUS Belonging to the Heath Family (usually requiring acid soil), as do blueberry, heather, laurel, rhododendron.

FARINA, FARINOSE A meal-like powder; thus a farinose stem is powdered.

FASTIGIATE Of an erect plant whose branches are upright and close together, producing a narrow column (26).

FIBROUS-ROOTED Characterized by coarse threadlike roots growing directly from the crown.

FIDDLEHEAD An unfurling fern frond, shaped like the head of a fiddle. *See* Crosier.

FLOWERS OF SULPHUR Finely powdered pure sulphur used to control mildews and red spider mites.

FLOWER STALK The stalk that carries the flower above the leaves (27).

FORM As used in horticulture, a term loosely synonymous with "variety" but more properly applied to the original plant of a clone.

FRACTURE LINE The angle at which rock cracks naturally under stress.

FROND The expanded leaf of a fern. Fertile fronds bear spores, usually on the back; sterile fronds bear no spores.

FRUITING-STALK A stalk bearing the sporing bodies of certain ferns, different from the leafy frond (28).

GARDEN HYBRID A hybrid plant produced under garden conditions.

GENUS (PL. GENERA) A category of classification for a group of closely related species. Groups of closely related genera form a family. The generic name of a plant is the first part of the Latin binomial, thus: *Allium* (genus) *flavum* (species) belongs to the Liliaceae (or Lily Family).

GLABROUS Not hairy and hence smooth.

GLANDULAR Bearing glands, usually on the tips of hairs (29).

GLAUCOUS Covered with a whitish bloom, giving a grayish or bluish color to the leaf or stem.

GLOBULAR Round and solid (30).

GRAVEL Small fragments of rock either rounded as in pebbles or with sharp angles as in crushed or broken rock.

GRIT A very fine gravel or very coarse sand.

GROUND-PINE-LIKE Resembling ground pine. *See* Lycopodium-like.

GROW-ON To place young plants in a controlled environment following propagation and prior to setting in permanent sites.

HALF-BLOCK A term used in this book to describe the dimensions of half a 16-inch cement block, 8 × 8 × 8 inches.

HALF-RIPENED WOOD A shoot of this year's growth which is no longer soft but is beginning to become firm and mature.

HAND POLLINATION A process used in hybridizing plants in which the pollen taken from the anthers of one plant is placed on the stigma of another plant, usually by means of a small watercolor brush.

HARDEN-OFF To introduce more light and a drier atmosphere by gradual degrees to plants that have been grown under moist and shaded conditions.

HARDPAN A compacted, sometimes almost cemented lower layer in certain soils virtually impervious to plant roots and water.

HEATH A site of acid sandy-peaty soil suitable for growing ericaceous plants.

HERBACEOUS Characterizing a plant that dies down to the ground at the end of the growing season.

HORSETAIL-LIKE *See* Equisetum-like.

HUMUS A dark brown organic material formed of partially decayed vegetable and animal matter.

HYBRID A plant having parents of different species, occasionally of different genera.

INFLORESCENCE A complete flower head.

INVOLUCRE, INVOLUCRATE A collection of bracts or leafy —31 structures surrounding a flower cluster or single flower (31).

KIDNEY-SHAPED Shaped like a kidney (32).

KILL-BACK Death of a portion or the whole upper part of a plant, the roots remaining alive and sending up new growth.

32

LABIATE Lipped; having one portion lip shaped (33).

LANCEOLATE Shaped like a lance head; much longer than broad, with a narrow pointed tip, broadest toward the base but somewhat tapering toward the stem (34).

33

LAYER A branch or shoot that develops roots where it contacts the soil. Also used as a verb to describe the process of making a branch develop roots in this manner.

LEAF AXIL *See* Axil.

LEAF-CUTTING A leaf that is induced to send out roots and a growing point so that it becomes a complete plant.

34

LEAFLET A single division of a compound leaf, usually having its own stem (35).

35— LEAF MOLD Partially decayed leaves.

LEAF NODE *See* Node.

LEAFY-BRACTED Bearing leafy bracts at intervals throughout the length of a flower stalk.

LIME-PITTED Having deposits of lime on a leaf, usually along the edge. *See* Encrusted.

36

LINEAR Long and narrow, with almost parallel edges (36).

LINEAR-OBLONG A narrow oval with almost parallel edges (37).

37

LOAM The upper layer of soil; a mixture of mineral particles and decayed organic material.

LOBED Partially divided into segments; deeply indented but not completely separated (38).

38

39

LYCOPODIUM-LIKE Resembling *Lycopodium* (ground pine), finely branched and densely clothed with scale-like leaves (39).

MEDIUM-ACID Somewhat acid (referring to soil). A pH of about 6.

MONOCARPIC Flowering only once and then dying.

MORAINE A site where a deep layer of rock particles has been deposited by moving water and through which water still flows, with a small amount of partially decayed vegetable matter washed between the rocks.

MOUND LAYERING A method of propagation in which soil is piled over the base of a plant in an attempt to make the partially buried shoots develop roots.

MUGGS A colloquial term to describe both weather conditions of high temperature and high humidity and also the resulting damage, especially to cushion plants.

40

MULCH Any substance such as straw, leaves, gravel, ground bark, etc., spread upon the surface of the ground as insulation, for moisture retention, or to prevent mud-splash.

NATURAL HYBRID A hybrid plant produced by natural causes in the native habitat of its parents.

41

NEUTRAL SOIL *See* pH.

NODE The point on a stem from which leaves or other stems rise, usually somewhat thickened (40).

OFFSET A short lateral rosette or leafy shoot, primarily propagative, which arises near the base of a plant (41).

42

OPPOSITE Springing from the same point on a stem but on opposite sides; describing leaves or branches (42).

ORBICULAR Circular (43).

43

OUTCROP A section of underlying rock stratum that is exposed on the surface of the ground.

Ovate Egg-shaped, broadest at the stem end (44).

Ovoid A solid with an ovate outline (45).

Palmate Radially lobed or divided (46).

Panicle A loosely branched flower cluster, longer than wide, the basal flowers opening first (47).

Pappus (pl. pappae) The hairs or bristles attached to the dry, hard, one-seeded fruit of many of the composite plants, replacing the calyx (48).

Peastone Gravel, either rounded or broken, with a diameter of about ⅜ inch.

Peat Semicarbonized vegetable matter that has partially decomposed in water. Michigan peat is a name generally applied to sedge peat, which is almost black and is formed of rather thoroughly decomposed grasses and sedges. It is less acid than peat from sphagnum moss, which is light brown and more fibrous because it is not as thoroughly decomposed.

Peat block Peat originally removed from a bog in blocks that when dried are hard and tough. These are then processed to make the crumbly material used horticulturally.

Pedicel The stalk of a single flower in a cluster of flowers (49).

Peduncle The primary flower stalk, springing from a leafy stem, which bears either a cluster or a solitary flower (50).

Perfoliate leaf A leaf having a stem that appears to pass through it (51).

Petal A single segment of the corolla which surrounds the sexual parts of the flower; usually brightly colored and conspicuous (52).

Petiole The stem of a leaf (53).

pH A symbol indicating the degree of alkalinity or acidity. Acid soil has a pH below 6; neutral soil has a pH of 7; alkaline soil has a pH of 7 and above.

PINE BARREN A site where an acid sandy soil is kept moist from below by a high water table, located almost exclusively on the East Coast of North America, inhabited by stunted pines and containing certain endemic plants.

PINNATE Composed of leaflets arranged on either side of a central stalk and referring to a compound leaf (54).

54

PISTIL, PISTILLATE The female organ of a flower; when complete consisting of ovary, style, and stigma. The adjective usually applies to flowers having no stamens.

PIT HOUSE A greenhouse; the top is translucent, the walls are underground.

PLANTED WALL An uncemented wall of stone or cement block containing soil so plants will grow in its sides and top.

PLANTING POCKET A hole filled with soil, usually among rocks, deep enough and sufficiently well drained to accommodate comfortably one or more plants.

PLUNGE To insert a flowerpot to its rim in water or in a quick-draining but moisture-retaining substance such as sand, which had been placed in a bed in a greenhouse or in a sheltered position out-of-doors.

POUCH A swollen, hollow, sack-shaped petal (55). 55—

PROCUMBENT Prostrate or trailing but not naturally rooting at the nodes.

PUBESCENT Covered with hairs, especially if soft, short, and downy.

RACEME An unbranched, long, slender flower head (56).

RAISED BED A freestanding flowerbed, enclosed and raised off the ground by built-up walls of stone or similar material on all four sides. The walls as well as the top may be planted.

56

RAY FLOWERS The conspicuous flowers with a single strap-like petal around the margin of some composite flower heads, such as daisies (57).

57

RHIZOME, RHIZOMATOUS A swollen, prostrate, usually subterranean and horizontal stem producing roots on its lower side and leaf-shoots on its upper side. A plant having stems of this nature is called rhizomatous (58).

RHOMBIC Having a diamond shape (59).

ROCKERY Rocks placed in a close-set group and planted with material generally unsuitable to such a site.

ROGUE To weed out inferior individual plants, leaving only those with desirable qualities.

ROOT-CUTTING A section of root which is to be used to produce a complete plant.

ROOTING MEDIUM A material into which cuttings are inserted in an effort to make them grow into a complete plant.

ROOTLETS The fine roots that branch out from the main root or rootstock (60).

ROOTSTOCK An upright rhizome from which roots and rootlets spring (61).

ROSETTE A cluster of leaves arranged in a circular form, frequently arising directly from the crown of a plant at ground level (62).

RUE-LIKE Resembling rue, usually referring to the shape of the leaf, which is broadly triangular and bipinnate, the leaflets deeply cut into many spatulate or wedge-shaped lobes; almost feathery in general effect (63).

RUGOSE Wrinkled.

SAGITTATE Shaped like an arrowhead, as of a leaf, with basal lobes toward the stem.

SAND FRAME An area, usually enclosed by sides and preferably shaded, filled with sand or a very sandy soil mixture.

SAXATILE Growing among rocks.

SCAPE A flower stem bearing one or more flowers, growing
directly from the crown of a plant, either leafless or with bracts
only (64).

64 ——

SCREE A site consisting mostly of rock particles of various sizes,
usually broken from and accumulated at the base of large rock
masses. A small amount of decayed vegetable matter is admixed with the broken rock.

SEDIMENTARY ROCK Rock originally formed by the
deposition of sediment in water. For example, sandstone, shale,
limestone.

SEPAL A single segment of the calyx (the outer section of a
flower) usually green but occasionally brightly colored and
petal-like.

SERRATE Having sharp teeth that point forward (65).

SESSILE Without a stalk of any kind.

SHARP SAND Sand with grains that are angular rather than
rounded.

SHOOT-WOOD A newly grown stem with its leaves.

SPADIX A fleshy spike bearing flowers (66).

SPATHE A single large bract enclosing a flower head (67).

SPATULATE Spoon- or paddle-shaped (68).

SPECIES A closely related group of individuals with similar
characteristics which may interbreed. A group of related species form a genus. The specific name is the second part of the
Latin binomial, thus: *Allium* (genus) *flavum* (species).

SPHAGNUM A particular genus of moss which grows in very
moist sites. It is porous, will absorb great quantities of moisture, and is almost surgically sterile. When partially decayed
it forms an acid peat.

SPHAGNUM SOUP Pulverized sphagnum moss kept saturated
with water, used for germinating some types of seed.

SPIKE An elongated flower head of stalkless or nearly stalkless
individual flowers (69).

SPIRAL An arrangement of branches, leaves, or flowers in a coil around the stem (70).

SPORE The one-celled, sexless reproductive germ of ferns and their relatives which grows into an organism containing both male and female functions.

SPRING-CUTTING A cutting, usually a soft stem-cutting, removed from the parent plant during the period of active growth.

STAMEN, STAMINATE A male pollen-bearing organ of flowering plants, consisting of the anther and a supporting filament (71). The adjective is usually applied to a flower bearing no pistils.

STELLATE Star-shaped; usually applied to branching hairs (72).

STEM-CUTTING A section of the stem of a plant which is induced to grow roots and become a complete plant.

STEM-LEAVES Leaves that grow from the stem of a plant (73).

STEMLESS Characterizing flower and leafstalks that spring directly from the crown (74).

STEMMED Characterizing flower and leafstalks that branch out from a stem ascending from the crown (75).

STERILE FROND *See* Frond.

STIGMA The part of the female organ (pistil) which receives the pollen; normally sticky when ripe and situated at the top of the pistil (76, see next page).

STOLON A runner or basal shoot that develops roots. Stoloniferous plants are those commonly producing stolons (77). Root-stolons run out underground from the crown of a plant and send leafy stems to the surface, sometimes at considerable distance from the parent plant.

STONE CHIPS Gravel; small particles of rock ranging from about ⅜ inch to 2 inches in diameter, either rounded or angular.

STRAPLIKE Shaped like a strap; long and wide, with nearly parallel sides.

STRATA The layers in sedimentary rock, sometimes differing from each other in texture and composition. Stratified rock is that which is formed in layers.

STRIKE A horticultural term to describe the forming of new roots on a cutting.

STRIP To remove unwanted leaves from the basal part of a stem-cutting.

STYLE The usually thin portion of the pistil which holds the stigma above the ovary (78). This will occasionally persist in some plants after the seed matures and will develop into an organ for disseminating the seed (79).

SUCCULENT A fleshy and juicy plant.

SUMMER-CUTTING A cutting, usually a stem-cutting (which may be termed summer-wood), removed from the parent plant shortly after the period of most active growth.

TALUS SLOPE An unstable area of broken rock sloping away from the base of a cliff.

TAPROOT A long, descending main root (80).

TAXONOMY The technical classification of plants and animals into groups.

TENDER PERENNIAL A plant that would live several years in a warm climate but is unable to survive frost; but because it blooms the first year from seed it may be grown as an annual in colder climates.

THONG-ROOT One of several thick roots descending from the crown.

TIP-CUTTING The tip of a stem with its terminal growth-bud which is induced to develop roots and become a complete plant.

TOMENTOSE Densely covered with matted woolly hair.

TONGUE-SHAPED Long and broad, widest near the tip and ending in a rounded point (81).

TOOTHED With a jagged margin.

TOPDRESSING A very thin layer of such ingredients as soil, gravel, humus, and fertilizer spread over and around plants most commonly as nutriment.

TOP-SPIT The top layer of soil in which decayed organic matter is mixed with the mineral soil; usually about a spade depth.

TUBER A short thickened subterranean stem or root serving for food storage and having buds (82).

TUBULAR Shaped like a tube; long, slender, and entire, with very little or no spread at the top (83).

TYPE SPECIES The specimen or group of nearly identical specimens from which the original description of the species was made.

UMBEL, UMBELLATE A flower head in which all the individual pedicels spring from the same level (84).

UNSTRATIFIED ROCK Rock that has no distinct layers.

URN-SHAPED Shaped like a bell with a narrowed mouth (85).

VARIETY (ABBREVIATED VAR.) A group of plants within a species with one or more characteristics different from those of the type, such as size, growth habit, an obvious flower color variation, or marked difference in shape or color of leaf. Variety may be indicated by a third Latin adjective following the plant's binomial name, thus: *Juniperus* (genus) *squamata* (species) *prostrata* (variety).

VIABLE A seed capable of sprouting and growing.

VISCID, VISCOUS Sticky.

INDEX OF PLANT NAMES

*Boldface numbers indicate illustrations.
This is a Latin binomial index, but since
the Fosters often referred to plants by
common names many common names are
cross-referenced. The index is not,
however, intended to be a complete listing
of all common names used in the text; in
particular, common names that include the
genus are not referenced.*

Acantholimons, 405
Acer palmatum, 87; *platanoides,* 50;
   rubrum, 50; *saccharinum,* 50;
   saccharum, 50
Aconite, winter, see *Eranthis hyemalis*
Actaea, 131; *pachypoda,* 38; *rubra,* 38
Adiantum pedatum, 59, 359; as
   maidenhair fern, 87
Adlumia fungosa, 106
Adonis, 131–137; *aestivalis,* 137; *aleppica,*
   137; *amurensis,* 132–136, **133**; *annua,*
   137; *flammea,* 137; *vernalis,* 132–136,
   135, 370; *vernalis,* seeds of, 398
Aesculus carnea, 51; *discolor,* 52;
   hippocastanum, 51, 52; *octandra,* 52;
   parviflora, 30, 52; *pavia,* 52
Ajuga reptans, 57; as blue bugle, 69
Alberta Spruce, see *Picea alberta conica*
Alchemilla alpina, 96
Allegheny vine, see *Adlumia fungosa*
Allium schoenoprasum, 41
Alpenrosen, see *Rhododendron hirsutum*
Alyssum saxatile, 69, 85; *saxatile* var.
   citrinum, 85
Amaryllis, hardy, see
   Lycoris squamigera
Amelanchier canadensis, 30
Anacyclus, 418; *depressus,* 91, 370
Anagallis arvensis, 95
Anchusa myosotidiflora, 104

Andromeda, Japanese, see *Pieris
japonica;* mountain, see *Pieris
floribunda*
Androsace, 405; *sempervivoides,* 386
Anemone canadensis, 57; *caroliniana,* 127;
   deltoides, 127; *nemorosa,* 67, 366–367;
   as English wood anemone, 105;
   nemorosa 'Vestal', 366; *oregana,* 127;
   quinquefolia, 127; *ranunculoides,* 88;
   sylvestris, 366
Anemonella thalictroides, 88, 127,
   138–141; *thalictroides* forma *favilliana,*
   138, 139; *thalictroides rosea flore-pleno,*
   thalictroides 'Schoaf's Double Pink',
   139–141
Apothecary's rose, see *Rosa gallica*
Aquilegia canadensis, 38, 62; *flabellata
nana alba,* 84; *jonesii,* 361;
   scopulorum, **44**
Arabis albida flore-pleno, 35
Arbutis, trailing, see *Epigaea repens*
Arisaema, 141–156, *atrorubens,* 148,
   155–156; as Indian turnip, 43;
   candidissimum, 141, **142**, 146, 148,
   152–153; *consanguineum,* **147**,
   148–149, 152; *dracontium,* 149–150;
   flavum, 150, **151**; *ringens,* 150–151,
   154; *robustum,* 152–153; *sikokianum,*
   141, 145–146, 153, 370; *stewardsonii,*
   153, 155; *thunbergii* var. *urashima,*
   155; *triphyllum,* 155–156;
Arrowhead, see *Sagittaria*
Aruncus aethusifolius, 360, 372
Asarum, 156–164; *canadense,* 61, 120,
   157–159, 163; *canadense* var.
   acuminatum, 159; *canadense* var.
   ambiguum, 159; *canadense* var.
   reflexum, 159; *caudatum,* 120, 157,
   159; *caudigerum,* 163; *causasicum,* 163;
   europaeum, 163; *hartwegii,* 120, 157,

Asarum (continued)
159; *macranthum,* 163; *shuttleworthii,*
see *Hexastylis shuttleworthii;*
virginicum, see *Hexastylis virginica*
Asperula odorata, 87
Asplenium platyneuron, 61; *trichomanes,*
61, 360
Aster linariifolius, 164–166
Aster, golden, see *Chrysogonum
virginianum;* New England, 164, 258;
New York, 164, 258
Astilbe × *arendsii,* 57; *chinensis,* 57;
chinensis var. *pumila,* 93; *crispa,* 93;
glaberrima var. *saxatilis,* 93; *koreana,*
57
Athyrium japonicum pictum, 360
Atlas daisy, see *Anacyclus depressus*
Azalea, royal, see *Rhododendron
schlippenbachii;* torch, see
Rhododendron kaempferi; azalea, Foster
hybrids, 8, 9, 13, 24–29 *passim*

Baltic ivy, see *Hedera helix baltica*
Baneberry, see *Actaea pachypoda* and *A.
rubra*
Basket-of-gold, see *Alyssum saxatile*
Bayberry, see *Myrica pensylvanica*
Beargrass, see *Xerophyllum tenax*
Beech tree, 50–51
Beetleweed, see *Galax aphylla*
Bellwort, large flowered, see *Uvularia
grandiflora*
Bethlehem sage, see *Pulmonaria
saccharata*
Bird-on the-wing, see *Polygala
paucifolia*
Bird's-foot violet, see *Viola pedata*
Bishop's cap, see *Mitella diphylla*
Bloodroot, see *Sanguinaria canadensis;*
double, see *Sanguinaria canadensis*
var. *multiplex*
Bluebell, Virginia, see *Mertensia
virginica*
Blue bugle, see *Ajuga reptans*
Blue-eyed Mary, see *Collinsia verna* and
Omphalodes verna
Bluets, see *Houstonia caerulea;*
thyme-leaved, see *Houstonia
serpyllifolia*

Bog laurel, see *Kalmia polifolia*
Bog orchids, 15, 406, 410, 411
Bog rosemary, 408, 411
Bog stars, see *Parnassia glauca*
Box, Korean, see *Buxus koreana*
Boxberry, see *Gaultheria procumbens*
Boxleaf holly, see *Ilex crenata convexa*
Bruckenthalia spiculifolia, 55
Buckbean, see *Menyanthes trifoliata*
Buffalo rose, see *Callirhoe involucrata*
Bugbane, Japanese, see *Cimicifuga
simplex*
Bunchberry, see *Cornus canadensis*
Buxus koreana, 33–34

Calla palustris, 15
Callirhoe alcaeoides, 169; *digitata,* 169;
involucrata, 166–169, 167; *papaver,*
169; *triangulata,* 169
Calluna vulgaris, 71
Calopogon tuberous, 407
Caltha palustris, 90, 363
Campanula, seed of, 390; *cochleariifolia,*
92; *grandis,* 172, 173; *latiloba,* 172;
nitida, 170–172; *parryi,* 171–173;
persicifolia, 170, 172–174; *persicifolia*
forma *planiflora,* 173–174; *planiflora,*
170–174; *pyramidalis,* 172;
rotundifolia, 94–95; *versicolor,* 171
Candytuft, see *Iberis sempervirens*
Cardamine, see *Dentaria*
Carex fraseri, 128
Castanea dentata, 52–53; *mollissima,* 53
Catmint, see *Nepeta* × *faasseni* and *N.
mussinii*
Caulophyllum thalicroides, 130
Chaenomeles japonica alpina, 36
Chamaecyparis obtusa compacta, 34
Chamaelirium luteum, 130
Chamaepericlymenum canadensis, see
Cornus canadensis
Checkerberry, see *Gaultheria procumbens*
Chestnut, American, see *Castanea
dentata;* Chinese, see *Castanea
mollissima;* horse, see *Aesculus
hippocastanum* and *A. parviflora*
Chickweed, star, see *Stellaria silvatica*
Chimaphila maculata, 119; *menziesii,*
119; *umbellata,* 119

Chiogenes, see *Gaultheria*

Chives, see *Allium schoenoprasum*

Christmasberries, see *Photinia villosa*

Chrysogonum virginianum, 131, 174–177; *virginianum* var. *australe*, **175**

Cimicifuga simplex, 59

Claytonia caroliniana, 37, 125, 178–180; *lanceolata*, 125; *megarrhiza*, 180; *montana*, 180; *virginica*, 37, 125, 178–180

Clematis verticillaris, 35, 130 *virginiana*, 35

Climbing hydrangea, see *Hydrangea petiolaris*

Clintonia borealis, 129, 359; *umbellata*, 129, 359; *uniflora*, 129

Clove pinks, see *Dianthus plumarius*

Collinsia verna, 180–183, **181**, 364

Columbine, Japanese, see *Aquilegia flabellata nana alba*

Compositae, seeds of, 390

Comptonia peregrina, seeds of, 399–401

Convallaria majalis, 57

Coolwort, see *Mitella diphylla, Tiarella trifoliata*, and *T. unifoliata*

Coral bells, see *Heuchera sanguinea*

Cornus canadensis, 121–122, 183–187, **186**; *canadensis* forma *purpurescens*, 185; *florida*, 185, 376–377; *florida* forma *rubra*, 185; *kousa*, 185; *nuttallii*, 185; *suecica*, 185–188

Cotoneaster adpressa, 32

Cowslips, see *Primula veris*

Cranberry, dwarf, see *Vaccinium macrocarpon*

Creeping dalibarda, see *Dalibarda repens*

Creeping snowberry, see *Gaultheria hispidula*

Cyclamen hederifolium, 357; *purpurascens*, 360

Cymophyllus fraseri, see *Carex fraseri*

Cypripedium acaule, 188–194, **191**; colloquial names for, 188–189; *acaule* forma *albiflorum*, 189; *calceolus*, 188; *calceolus* var. *pubescens*, 67, 106; *reginae*, 15

Cystopteris bulbifera crispa, **356**; *fragilis*, 61

Daboecia cantabrica, **99**

Dalibarda repens, 120–121, 194–198, **195**

Daphne cneorum, 33–34, 370

Dentaria, seeds of, 398; *laciniata*, 126; *gemmata*, 126; *tenella*, 126

Dew drop, see *Dalibarda repens*

Dianthus plumarius, 41, 84

Diapensia, 288; *himalaica*, 202; *lapponica*, 198–202, **199**, 395; *purpurea*, 202; *wardii*, 202

Dicentra, seed of, 389, 393, 398; *canadensis*, 37, 126, 203–207, 212; *cucullaria*, 37, 61, 88, 126, 203–212, 386, **388**; *cucullaria*, colloquial names for, 207; *cucullaria* var. *occidentalis*, 204, 212; *cucullaria* forma *purpuritincta*, 212; *eximia*, 126, 206–207, 212; *formosa*, 126, 210; *nevadensis*, 126; *oregana* 126; *peregrina*, 126, 206, 208, 210; *uniflora*, 126, 207

Dionysias, seed of, 405

Diphylleia cymosa, 130

Dodecatheon, 370, 375, **376**; *amethystinum*, 2; *meadia*, 87

Dog tooth violet, see *Erythronium americanum*

Dogwood, see *Cornus*

Doll's eyes, see *Actaea pachypoda*

Douglasia vitaliana, 91–92

Dryas drummondii, 214–217; *octopetala*, 212–217, 370; *octopetala* var. *integrifolia*, 215; *octopetala* var. *lanata*, 215; *octopetala* var. *minor*, 215; *octopetala* var. *tenella*, 215; × *suendermannii*, 217; *tomentosa*, 214

Dryopteris intermedia, 359; *marginalis*, 60

Dutchman's breeches, see *Dicentra cucullaria*

Epigaea asiatica, 217; *repens*, 122, 217–220, 312, 363; as trailing arbutus, 289

Equisetum arvense, 85

Eranthis hyemalis, 59, 87, 362

Eritrichium nanum, 395

Erythronium, 105, *albidum*, 129, 222; *albidum* var. *mesochoreum*, 222; *americanum*, 129, 221–223; *grandiflorum*, 129; *mesochoreum*, 129

Fagus grandifolia, 50; *sylvatica,* 50
False hellebore, see *Veratrum viride*
False violet, see *Dalibarda repens*
Fawn lily, see *Erythronium*
Fern, Christmas, see *Polystichum
  acrostichoides;* fragile, see *Cystopteris
  fragilis;* interrupted, see *Osmunda
  claytonia;* maidenhair, see *Adiantum
  pedatum;* marsh, see *Thelypteris
  palustris;* sweet, see *Comptonia
  peregrina*
Fetter-bush, see *Pieris floribunda*
Flagellarisaema urashima, see *Arisaema
  thunbergii* var. *urashima*
Foamflower, see *Tiarella*
Forget-me-not, see *Myosotis scorpioides*
  and *Myosotis sylvatica;* creeping, see
  Omphaloides verna
Franklinia alatamaha, 412

Galax, 287, 314, 316; *aphylla,* 123–124,
  223–226, **224**
Garland flower, see *Daphne cneorum*
Gaultheria hispidula, 121, 227–231
  passim; hispidula, colloquial names
  for, 230; *humifusa,* 121, 231;
  miqueliana, 231; *ovatifolia,* 121, 231;
  procumbens, 121, 227–231, 312;
  procumbens, colloquial names for,
  228; *trichophylla,* 231
Gay wings, see *Polygala paucifolia*
Gentiana acaulis, 365, 419; *farreri,*
  348–349, 365, 419; *ornata,* 365, 419;
  scabra, 419; *septemfida,* 365; *verna,*
  365; *veitchiorum,* 365
Geranium, seeds of, 389; *macrorrhizum,*
  69; *maculatum,* 60, 62, 87; *robertianum,* 31
Ginkgo biloba, 412
Globeflower, American, see *Trollius
  laxus;* European, see *Trollius
  europaeus*
Grass of Parnassus, see *Parnassia glauca*
Green-and-gold, see *Chrysogonum
  virginianum*
Green dragon, see *Arisaema dracontium*
Gymnocarpium dryopteris, 360

Habenaria orbiculata, 410–411, white
  fringed, 406

Hardy amaryllis, see *Lycoris squamigera*
Harebell, see *Campanula rotundifolia*
Hedera helix baltica, 56
Hellebore, false, see *Veratrum viride*
Hemlock, Canada, see *Tsuga canadensis;*
Hepatica, 88; seeds of, 389–390;
  acutiloba, 37, 124, 232–236 *passim;*
  acutiloba 'Millstream Pink', 124, 236;
  americana, 232–236 *passim;* ×
  ballardii, 234; *nobilis (H. triloba),* 124;
  translyvanica (angulosa), 234, 362;
  triloba, 37, 234; *triloba* var. *americana,*
  124; × *media* 'Ballard's var.', 234
Heuchera sanguinea, 336
× *Heucherella,* 378; *tiarelloides,* 336;
  tiarelloides var. *alba,* 336
Hexastylis, 120, 158–161; *arifolia,* 159,
  161; *heterophylla,* 161; *lewisii,*
  161–163; *maniflora,* 161; *minus,* 161;
  shuttleworthii, 161, 360; *virginica,* 161,
  148, 162, as *Asarum virginicum,* 316
Holly, boxleaf, see *Ilex crenata convexa*
Horsetail, see *Equisetum arvense*
Houstonia caerulea, 236–240; *caerulea
  forma albiflora,* 239; *caerulea*
  'Millard's Variety', 238; *caerulea* var.
  faxonorum, 239; *serpyllifolia,* 237, 239
Hutchinsia alpina, 92
Hydrangea petiolaris, 56

Iberis saxatilis, 419; *sempervirens,* 69
Ilex crenata convexa, 33
Indian turnip, see *Arisaema atrorubens*
Iris bracteata, 129; *chrysophilla,* 124;
  cristata, 61, 64, 128, 240–242;
  innominata, 129; *sibirica,* 87; *tenax,*
  129; *tenuis,* 129; *verna,* 129, 240–242,
  241
Isopyrum biternatum, 118; *stipitatum,*
  118
Ivy, Baltic, see *Hedera helix baltica*

Jack-in-the-pulpit, see *Arisaema*
Jacob's ladder, see *Polemonium caeruleum*
Jeffersonia, seeds of, 398; *diphylla,* 105,
  125, 243–245; *dubia,* 105, 125,
  243–245, 363
Juniperus horizontalis, 32; *procumbens
  nana,* 34; *squamata prostrata,* 34

Kaempferi azalea, see *Rhododendron kaempferi*
Kalmia latifolia, 245; *polifolia*, 408; as bog laurel, 411
Kalmiopsis leachiana, 245–247

Ladies' mantle, see *Alchemilla alpina*
Ladies' tresses, see *Spiranthes cernua*
Lady's slipper (orchid), pink, see *Cypripedium acaule;* showy, see *Cypripedium reginae;* yellow, see *Cypripedium calceolus* var. *pubescens*
Laurel, bog, see *Kalmia polifolia*
Lavandula spica, 41; *spica* 'Hidcote', 41
Lewisia cotyledon, 357, 365, 377, 394–395; *finchii*, 377; *heckneri*, 377; *howellii*, 377; *tweedyi*, 365
Lilium candensis, 129, 221; *grayi*, 129; *philadelphicum*, 129; *superbum*, 221
Lily, fawn, see *Erythronium;* naked, see *Lycoris squamigera;* trout, see *Erythronium*
Lily-of-the-valley, see *Convallaria majalis*
Lily-of-the-valley, wild, see *Maianthemum canadense*
Lily-of-the-valley shrub, see *Pieris floribunda*
Lily-turf, see *Liriope spicata*
Linnaea borealis, 105, 118, 247–249, 360; *borealis* var. *americana*, 247–248
Liriope spicata, 59
Lithospermum canescens, 291
Lobelia cardinalis, 130
Loiseleuria procumbens, 201
Love-in-the-mist, see *Nigella damascena*
Lungwort, see *Pulmonaria angustifolia*
Lungwort, red, see *Pulmonaria montana rubra*
Lycoris squamigera, 106–107

Maianthemum bifolium, 118; *canadense*, 118
Malva neglecta, 168
Maple, Japanese, see *Acer palmatum;* Norway, see *Acer platanoides;* red, see *Acer rubrum;* silver, see *Acer saccharinum;* sugar, see *Acer saccharum;* swamp, see *Acer rubrum;* tree, 49–50
Marsh marigold, see *Caltha palustris*

Mayflower, see *Epigaea repens*
Meconopsis, 349–351; *cambrica*, 106
Melandrium, see *Silene*
Menyanthes trifoliata, 15
Mertensia virginica, 67, 104
Michaelmas daisies, 164
Mitchella repens, 121, 250–253, 316, 360; *repens*, colloquial names for, 250; *repens* forma *leucocarpa*, 121, 253; *undulata*, 253
Mitella diphylla, 37–38; as miterwort, 58
Miterwort, see *Mitella diphylla*
Moneses uniflora, 120
Moss pinks, see *Phlox subulata*
Mountain andromeda, see *Pieris floribunda*
Mountain avens, see *Dryas octopetala*
Mugho pine, 32
Myosotis scorpioides, 88–89; *sylvatica*, 88
Myrica pensylvanica, 399
Myrtle, see *Vinca minor*

Nailworts, see *Paronychia*
Naked lily, see *Lycoris squamigera*
Navel-seed, see *Omphalodes verna*
Navelwort, see *Omphalodes verna*
Nepeta × *faasseni*, 41; *mussinii*, 41
Nigella damascena, 137
Nippon bells, see *Shortia uniflora*

Oaks, see *Quercus*
Oconee bells, see *Shortia galacifolia*
Oenothera caespitosa, 418
Omphalodes luciliae, 253; *verna*, 104, 253–255, 364; *verna* 'Alba', 254; *verna* 'Anthea Bloom', 254; *verna*, colloquial names for, 254
Orchids, bog, 15, 406, 410, 411
Ornithogalum nutans, 362
Orphanidesia, 217
Osmunda claytonia, 58
Oxalis acetocella, 119; *montana*, 119; *oregana*, 119

Pachysandra, 41; *procumbens*, 128; *terminalis*, 128
Parnassia, 255–259; *californica*, 258; *fimbriata*, 258; *glauca*, 94, 255, **256**, 258–259; *grandiflora*, 258; *nubicola*,

Parnassia (continued)
255; *palustris,* 255, 259; *wightiana,*
257
Paronychia, 259–262; *argentea,* 260;
argyrocoma, 260–261; *canadensis,* 260,
262; *nivea,* 260; *pulvinata,* 262;
serpyllifolia, 260
Partridgeberry, see *Mitchella repens*
Petasites frigidus, 131
Pheasant's eye, see *Adonis aestivalis* and
A. annua
Phlox, 33, 41, 110, 263–278, 413–414;
adsurgens, 118, 272–273, 278, 369;
adsurgens 'Wagon Wheels', 273;
alyssifolia, 271; *amoena,* 269, 278;
andicola, 271; *bifida,* 265, **266,**
273–278 *passim,* 368; *buckleyi,* 268,
369; *caespitosa,* 270–271; *carolina,*
269, 369; 'Chattahoochee', 268;
diffusa, 271; *divaricata,* 62, 64, 267,
369; *divaricata* 'Fuller's White', 268;
douglasii, 277; 'Douglasii hybrids',
277; *hoodii,* 271; *hoodii muscoides,*
270; *kelseyi,* 270; 'Laura', 273;
longifolia, 271; *Microphlox* subsection,
263, 269; 'Millstream Coraleye',
273–274; 'Millstream Jupiter', 273,
278; *missoulensis,* 270; *multiflora,* 270;
nana, 271; *nivalis,* 275, 414; *ovata,*
268–269, 369; *ovata pulchra,* 269;
ozarkiana, 269; *paniculata,* 268;
pilosa, 268, 369; × *procumbens,* 278;
× *procumbens* 'Millstream', 274, 278;
pulchra, 369; *salina,* 270; *sibirica,* 263;
speciosa, 271; 'Star Bright', 273;
Stoloniferae subsection, 272; *stolonifera,*
118, 267–274 *passim,* 369; *stolonifera*
'Ariane', 267; *stolonifera* 'Blue
Ridge', 267; *stolonifera* 'Pink Ridge',
267; *stolonifera* 'Sherwood Purple',
267; *subulata,* 25, 40, 84, 264–265,
269, 273–278, 368–369; *subulata*
australis, 277; *subulata brittonii,* 277;
subulata 'Daphne', 274; *subulata*
'Scarlet Flame', 276; *triovulata,* 271,
414; *triovulata* × *nivalis* 'Avalon',
414; 'Unique', 274; *variabilis,* 270;
viscida, 270; 'White Star', 273
Photinia villosa, 42

× *Phylliopsis,* 378
Picea abies, 49; *alberta,* as Alberta
Spruce, 81, *alberta conica,* 32;
mariana, 61; *pungens,* 48
Pieris floribunda, 32; *japonica,* 32
Pine, Scots, see *Pinus sylvestris;* white,
see *Pinus strobus*
Pink, clove, see *Dianthus plumarius*
Pink, wild, see *Silene caroliniana var.*
pensylvanica
Pink moccasin, see *Cypripedium acaule*
Pinus strobus, 49; *sylvestris,* 49
Pitcher plant, see *Sarracenia purpurea*
Plagiorhegma dubia, see *Jeffersonia dubia*
Podophyllum, 131
Polemonium caeruleum, 60, 87
Polygala paucifolia, 121, 279–281, **280,**
384; *paucifolia* forma *alba,* 281
Polygonatum biflorum, 62; as Solomon's
seal, 329; *canaliculatum,* 59
Polystichum acrostichoides, 60; as
Christmas fern, 87
Poppies, seeds of, 390
Poppies, Welsh, see *Meconopsis cambrica*
Poppy mallow, see *Callirhoe involucrata*
Primrose, 39, 64, 67, 92, 100–104
passim, 110, 262, 283, 366–368; see
also *Primula*
Primula, 252, 390; *acaulis,* 419; *allionii,*
366; *aurantiaca,* 101; *auricula,* 284–285,
366; *auricula* var. *albocincta,* 366;
beesiana, 101, 368; × *bullesiana,* 101,
368; *bulleyana,* 368; *carniolica,* 282–
286; *clusiana,* 366, 419; *cockburniana,*
101; × 'Cowitchan Strain', 366;
denticulata, 284, 368; *florindae,* 367;
frondosa, 89; *hirsuta,* 366; *japonica,*
56–57, 101, 386; as Japanese
primrose, 91; *juliae,* 92–93; *juliani,*
63; *kisoana,* 357, 360, 367; *marginata,*
284, 366; *polyanthus,* 104; ×
pubescens, 285, 366; *pulverulenta,* 101;
sieboldii, 63, 88, 367; *sikkimensis,* 367;
× *venusta,* 285–286; *veris,* 62, 104;
viallii, 367; *vulgaris,* 62, 103, 366
Puccoon, see *Lithospermum canescens;*
red, see *Sanguinaria canadensis*
Pulmonaria angustifolia, 60, 87, 104;
montana rubra, 105; *saccharata,* 60

Pulsatillas patens, 364; *vernalis*, 363–364; *vulgaris*, 363
Pyrola picta, 119
Pyxidanthera, 200; *barbulata*, **286**, 286–290, 357; *barbulata* var. *brevifolia*, 290; *brevifolia*, 290
Pyxie moss, see *Pyxidanthera barbulata*

Quaker ladies, see *Houstonia caerulea*
Quercus, 51
Quince, dwarf flowering, see *Chaenomeles japonica alpina*

Ramonda, 366; *myconi*, 360
Rhododendron, seeds of, 393, 398; *amoenum*, 32; *arnoldianum*, 31; *caroliniana*, 81; Dexter hybrids, 351; elepidote type, 378; Foster hybrids, 8, 9, 13, 24–29 *passim*, 54, 65, 110–111; *hirsutum*, 36, 81; *kaempferi*, 31–32; as kaempferi azalea, 103, 205; *lapponicum*, 201; *leacheanum*, see *Kalmiopsis leachiana;* lepidote type, 378; *maximum*, 320; *minus*, 81–82; *myrtifolium*, 81–82; *obtusum*, 40; *racemosum*, 64, 81, 101, 357; *schlippenbachii*, 64
Robert, see *Geranium robertianum*
Rock cress, see *Arabis albida flore-pleno*
Rosa gallica, 40
Rose, apothecary's, see *Rosa gallica*
Royal azalea, see *Rhododendron schlippenbachii*
Rue anemone, see *Anemonella thalictroides;* rue anemone, double pink, see *Anemonella thalictroides* 'Schoaf's Double Pink'

Sage, Bethlehem, see *Pulmonaria saccharata*
Sagittaria, 15
Sang-dragon, see *Sanguinaria canadensis*
Sanguinaria canadensis, 60, 124–125, 290–296, 363; as bloodroot, 67, 87, 104, 243; seeds of, 291, 389, 393; *canadensis* forma *Colbyorum*, 291; *canadensis forma rosea*, 125; *canadensis* var. *multiplex*, 104, 125, 138, 293–296, 363, 412–413; *canadensis* var. *plena*, 293; *canadensis* var. *rotundifolia*, 291; *major flore pleno* (archaic), 293

Sarracenia, as pitcher plant, 406; *purpurea*, 15
Saxifraga, 110, 296–307, 360; cuttings of, 402–405, 418; *aizoon*, 402; *apiculata*, 299; × *boydii*, 299; *burserana*, 299; *caespitosa*, 91; 'Cranbourne', 403; *decipiens*, 91; × *elizabethae*, 299–300; encrusted type, 92, 296–297; 'Faldonside', 300, 403; 'Iris Prichard', 403; Kabschia section, 297, 306, 402; × *lilacina*, 299; × *lincolni-fosteri*, 303; *longifolia*, 357; Millstream hybrids, 303–304; mossy type, 91, 296–297; Porophyllum section, 305–307; 'Walter Irving', 299; × *wendelacina*, 303
Scarlet pimpernel, see *Anagallis arvensis*
Schizocodon, see *Shortia soldanelloides*
Scilla sibirica, 87, 103
Scouring rush, 38
Sedum glaucophyllum (nevii), 119; *spurium*, 35; *ternatum*, 119, 360
Shadblow, see *Amelanchier canadensis*
Shooting-star, Eastern, see *Dodecatheon meadia*
Shortia, 200, 289, 307–329; seeds of, 246, 390; *galacifolia*, 122–123, 307–323, 326, 328, 360, 363, 412; *soldanelloides*, 319, 323–326, **324**, 360, 363; *soldanelloides* var. *ilicifolia*, 319, 325; *soldanelloides* var. *macrophylla (magnus)*, 319, 325; *uniflora*, 123, 319, 327–329, 360, 363; *uniflora grandiflora*, 327
Silene acaulis, 332; *caroliniana*, 127, 329–332; *caroliniana* var. *pensylvanica*, 329; *caroliniana* var. *wherryi*, 127, 329, **330**; *hookeri*, 127; *hookeri* var. *bolanderi*, 128; *keiskei*, 332; 'Millstream Select', 332; *shafta*, 332; *virginica*, 127, 332
Silverling, see *Paronychia argyrocoma*
Smilacina racemosa, 62; *stellata*, 62
Snow trillium, see *Trillium nivale*
Snowberry, creeping, see *Gaultheria hispidula*
Soldanella alpina, 364; *montana*, 364
× *Solidaster*, 378
Solomon's plume, see *Smilacina racemosa*

Solomon's seal, see *Polygonatum biflorum;* great, see *Polygonatum canaliculatum*

Spiranthes cernua, 93

Spleenwort, ebony, see *Asplenium platyneuron;* maidenhair, see *Asplenium trichomanes*

Spotted dog, see *Pulmonaria saccharata*

Spring beauty, see *Claytonia caroliniana* and *Claytonia virginica*

Spruce, Alberta, see *Picea alberta conica;* black, see *Picea mariana;* Colorado blue, see *Picea pungens*

Squirrel corn, see *Dicentra canadensis*

Starwort, see *Stellaria silvatica*

Starry Solomon's seal, see *Smilacina stellata*

Steer's head, see *Dicentra uniflora*

Stellaria pubera, 88; *silvatica,* 88

Streptopus amplexifolius, 62; *rosea,* 130

Sweet fern, see *Comptonia peregrina*

Sweet woodruff, see *Asperula odorata*

Synthyris missurica, 119; *reniformis,* 119

Taxus cuspidata, 22

Thalictrum kiusianum, 360, 370

Thelypteris palustris, 59

Thymus serpyllum, 84

Tiarella cordifolia, 37, 60, 127, 332–336, 333; *cordifolia* var. *collina,* 335–336; *polyphylla,* 336; *trifoliata,* 336; *unifoliata,* 336; *wherryi,* 127, 335–336

Toothworts, see *Dentaria*

Torch azalea, see *Rhododendron kaempferi*

Trailing arbutus, see *Epigaea repens*

Trillium albidum, seed pod, 390; *erectum,* 38, 62, 88; *grandiflorum,* 88, 105, 363, 377; *nivale,* 363; *ovatum,* 377; *ovatum,* seed pod, 390; *parviflorum,* 373; *undulatum,* 363; *vaseyi,* 363

Trollius, seeds of, 390; *acaulis,* 338; *europaeus,* 94, 337–338; *japonicus,* 337; *laxus,* 89, 130, 336–339; *laxus albiflorus,* 336; *pumilus,* 338–339; *ranunculinus,* 338

Tsuga canadensis, 48; Cole's prostrate (used without genus), 413

Tulipa tarda, 362

Turkey grass, see *Xerophyllum asphodeloides*

Twinflower, see *Linnaea borealis*

Twinleaf, see *Jeffersonia diphylla*

Twisted stalk, see *Streptopus amplexifolius*

Uvularia grandiflora, 59

Vaccinium macrocarpon, 339

Vancouveria hexandra, 131

Venus shoe, see *Cypripedium acaule* and *Cypripedium calceolus*

Veratrum viride, 58

Veronica latifolia 'Crater Lake Blue', 41

Vinca minor, 41

Viola canadensis, 61, 104; *papilionacea,* 31; *pedata,* 128, 339–344; *pedata bicolor,* 340–341; *pedata lineariloba (concolor),* 340–341; *pedata lineariloba* forma *rosea,* 342; *pedata lineariloba* var. *albiflora,* 342; *priceana,* 31; *pubescens,* 61; *rotundifolia,* 61, 128

Violet, seeds of, 389; bird's-foot, see *Viola pedata;* Canadian, see *Viola canadensis;* Confederate, see *Viola priceana;* dog tooth, see *Erythronium americanum;* false, see *Dalibarda repens*

Virginia bluebell, see *Mertensia virginica*

Virgin's bower, see *Clematis virginiana*

Wandflower, see *Galax aphylla*

Welsh poppies, see *Meconopsis cambrica*

Whitlow-worth, see *Paronychia*

Wild calla, see *Calla palustris*

Wildflowers, requirements of, 102

Wild geranium, see *Geranium maculatum*

Wild ginger, see *Asarum* and *Hexastylis*

Wild lily-of-the valley, see *Maianthemum canadense*

Wild pink, see *Silene caroliniana* var. *pensylvanica*

Windflower, Canadian, see *Anemone canadensis*

Wine cups, see *Callirhoe involucrata*

Winter aconite, see *Eranthis hyemalis*

Wintergreen, see *Gaultheria procumbens*

Woodruff, sweet, see *Asperula odorata*

Woodsia obtusa, 61

Xerophyllum asphodeloides, 130; *tenax,* 130